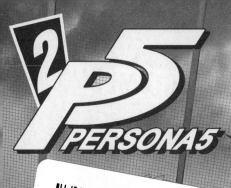

Original Concept by **ATLUS**
Art and Story by **HISATO MURASAKI**

P5 PERSONA5 — VOLUME 2

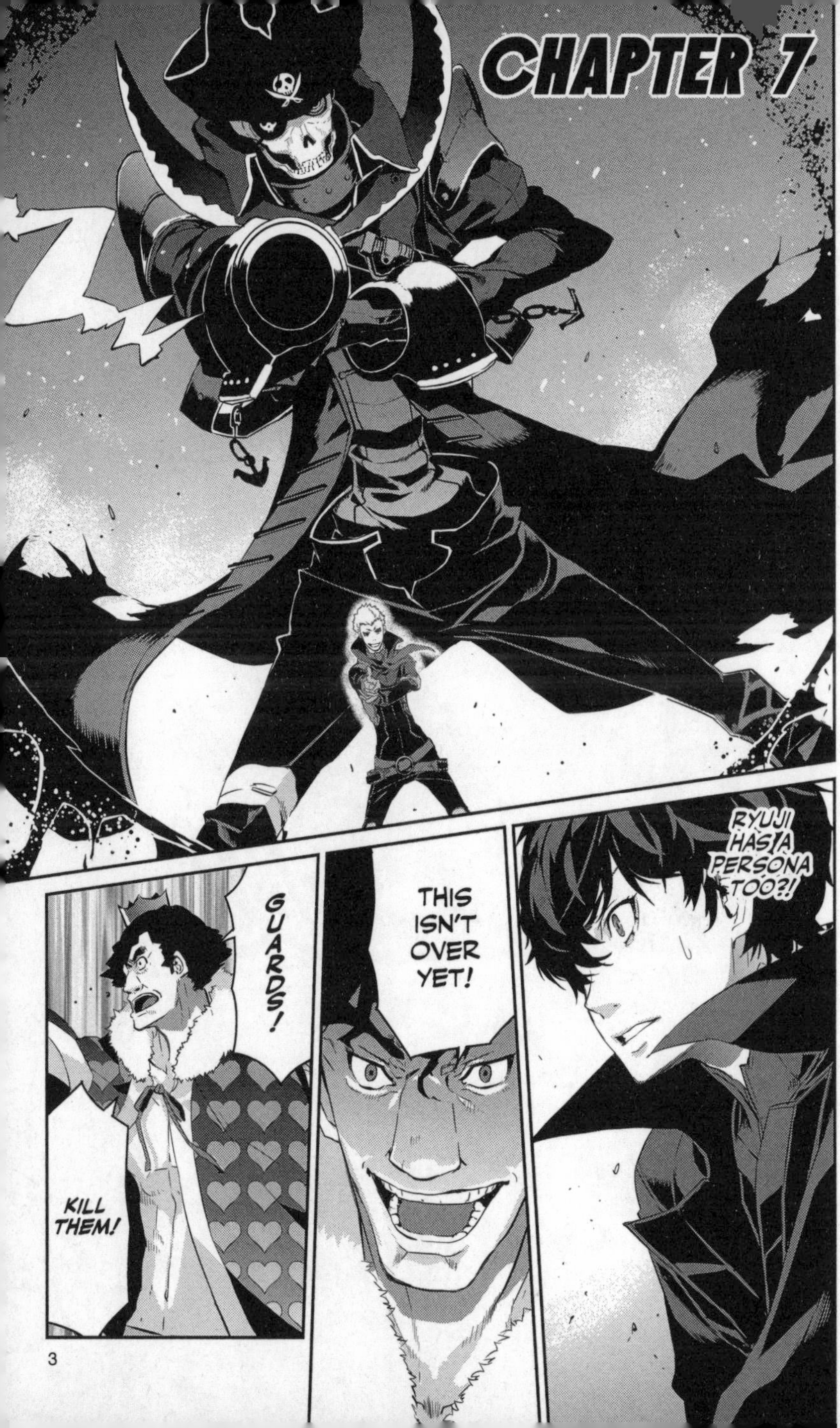
CHAPTER 7
RYUJI HAS A PERSONA TOO?!
THIS ISN'T OVER YET!
GUARDS!
KILL THEM!

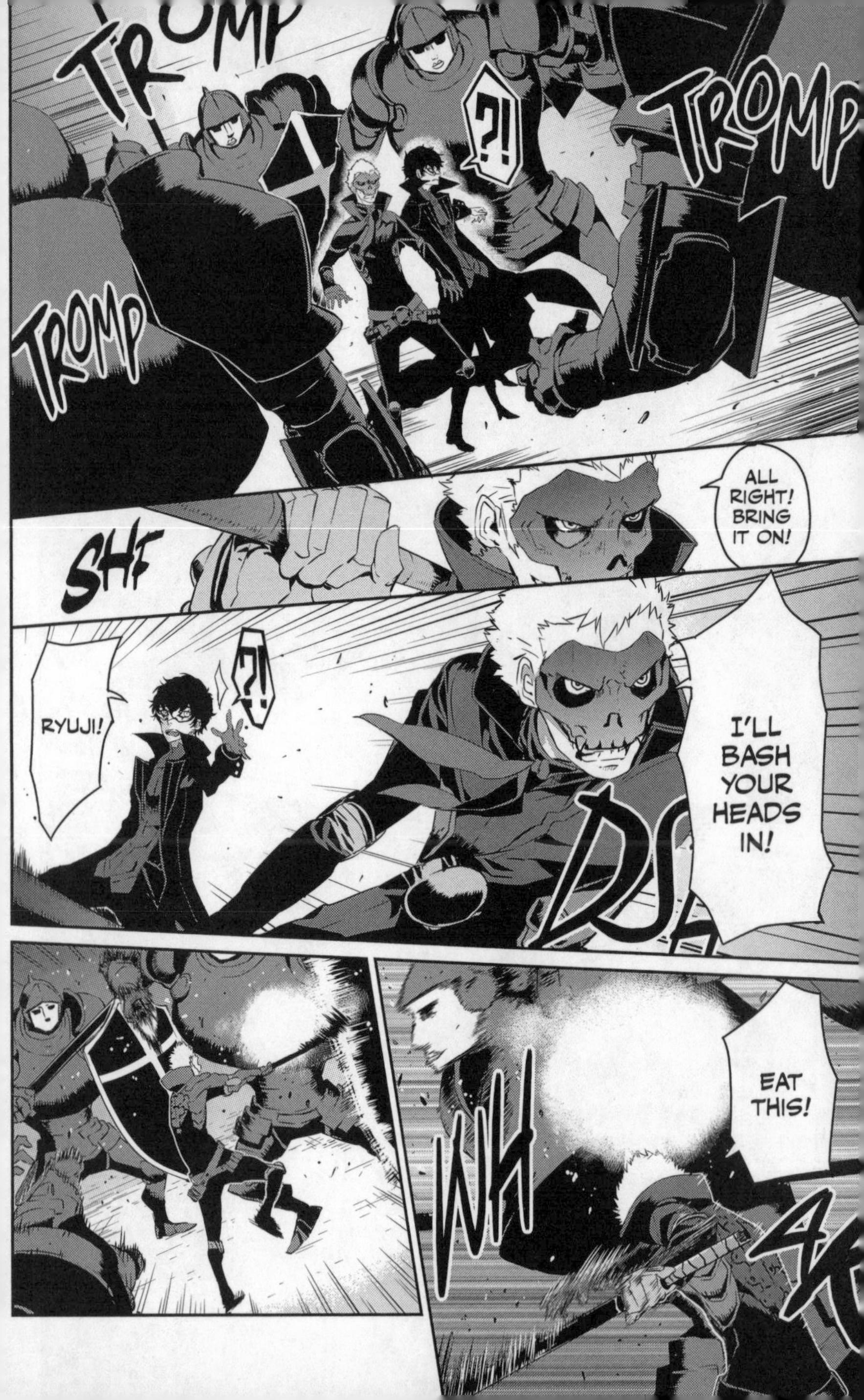
TROMP
?!
TROMP
TROMP
ALL RIGHT! BRING IT ON!
SHF
I'LL BASH YOUR HEADS IN!
DS
?!
RYUJI!
EAT THIS!
WH

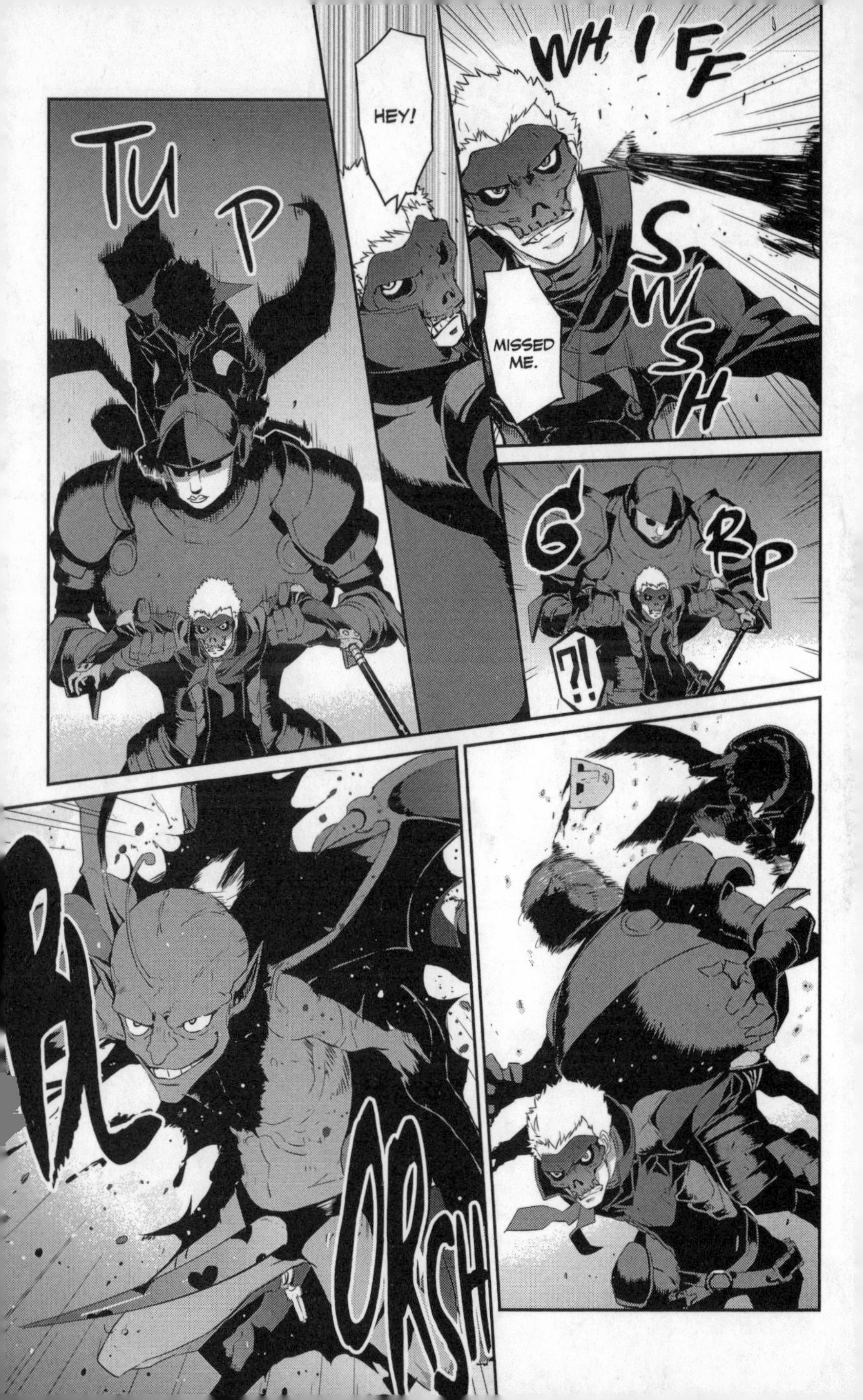
WHIFF
SWSH
MISSED ME.
HEY!
TUP
GRP
?!
ORSH

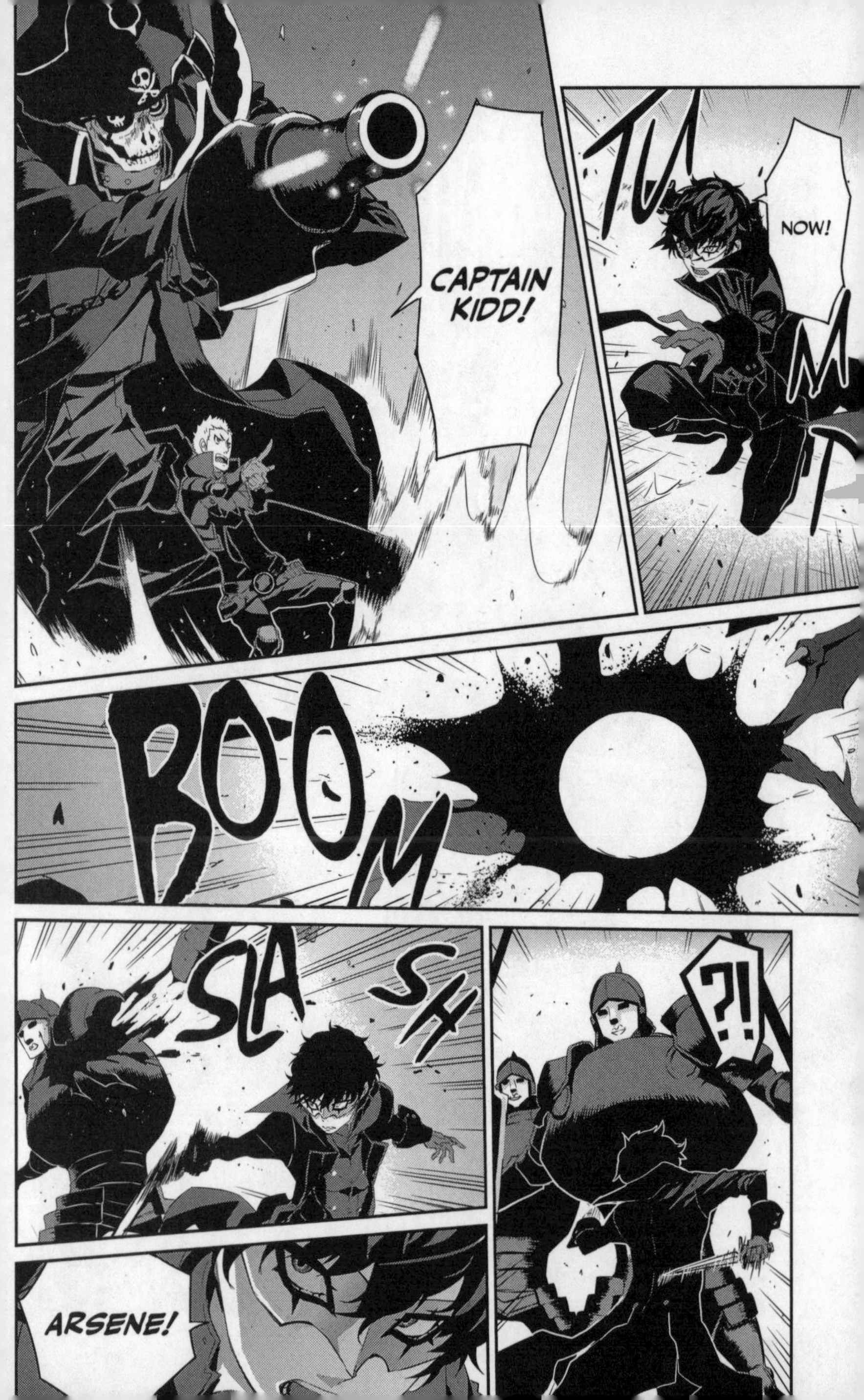
NOW!
CAPTAIN KIDD!
BOOM
?!
SLASH
ARSENE!

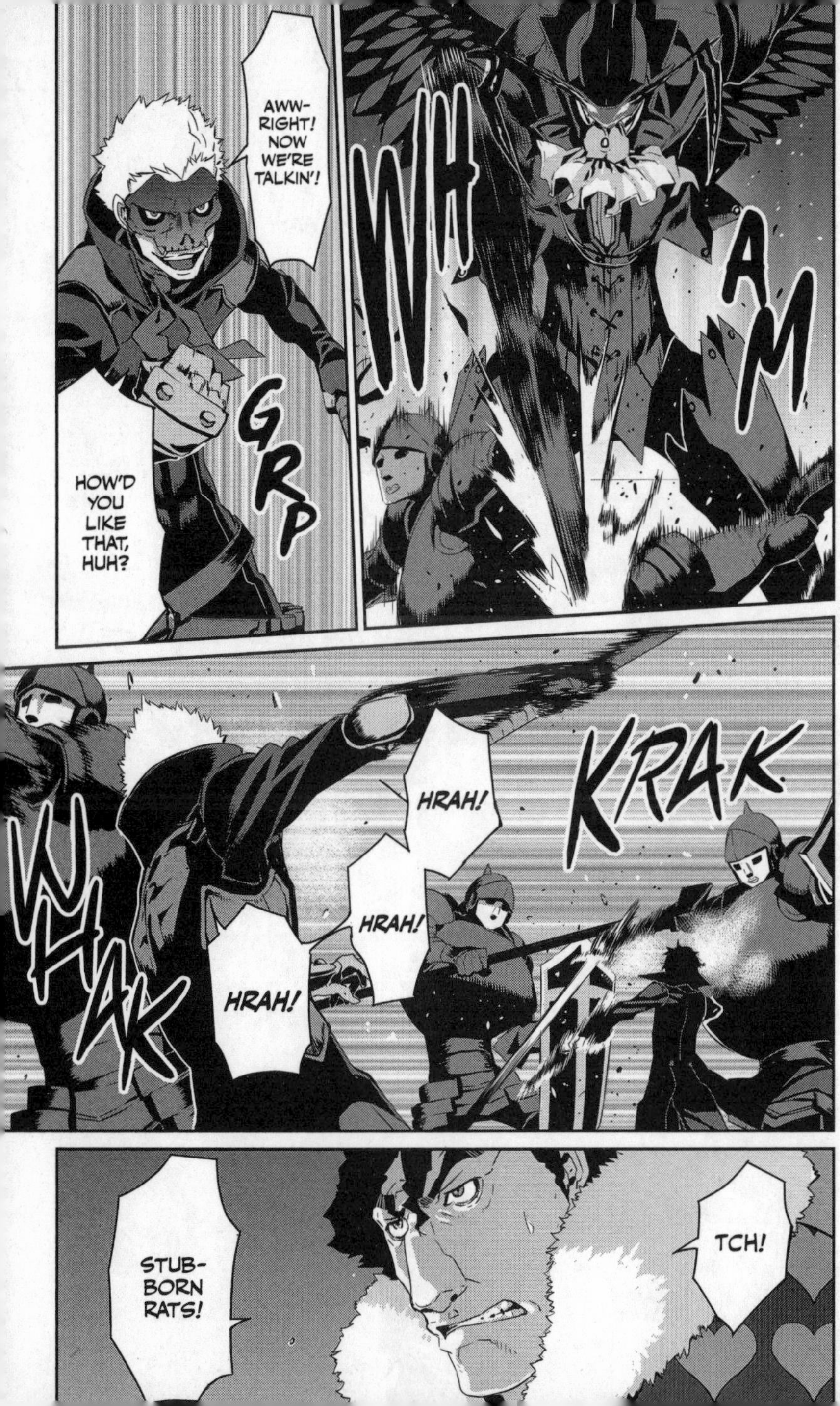
WHAM
AWW-RIGHT! NOW WE'RE TALKIN'!
GRP
HOW'D YOU LIKE THAT, HUH?
KRAK
HRAH!
HRAH!
HRAH!
WHAK
TCH!
STUB-BORN RATS!

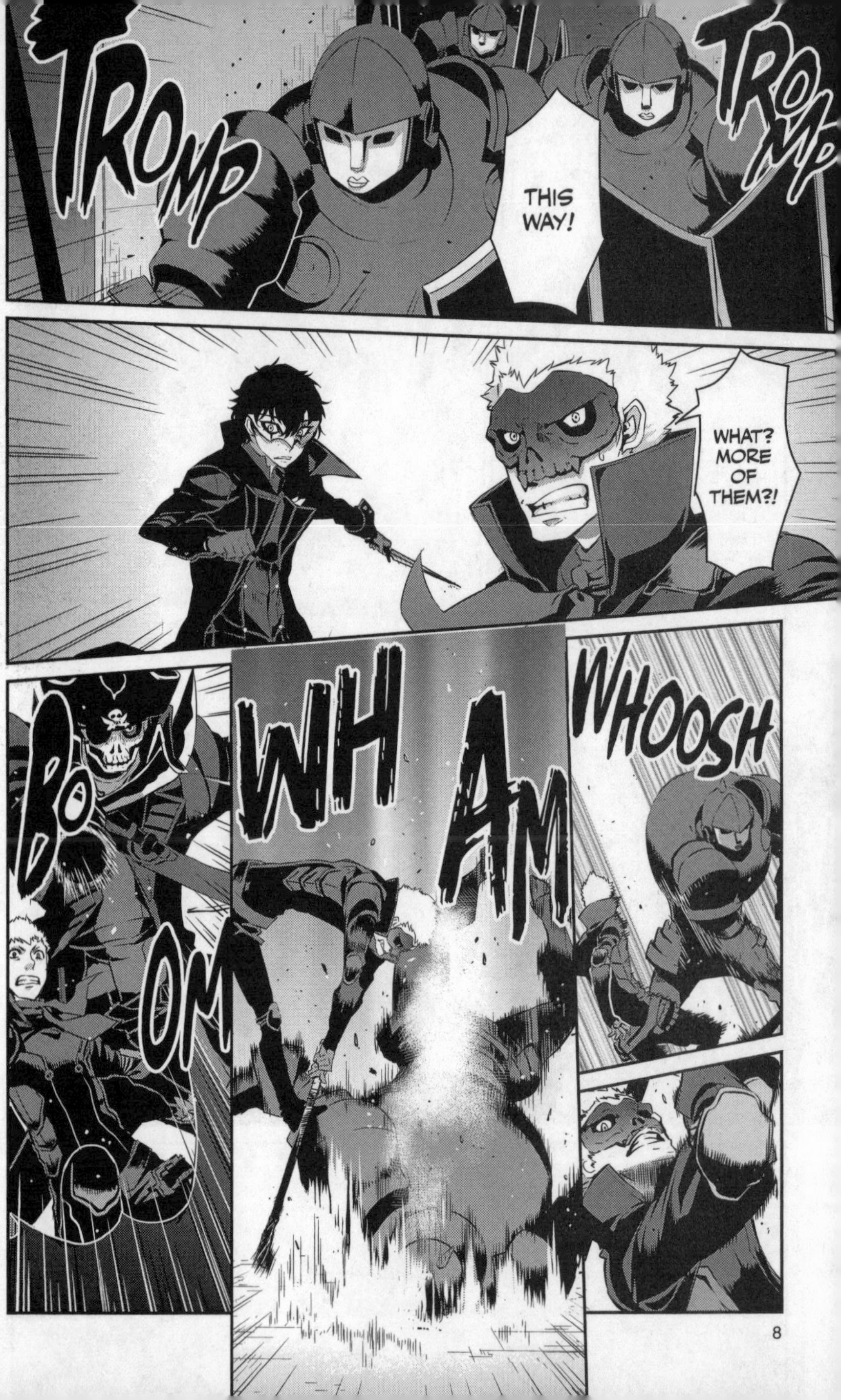
TROMP
TROMP
THIS WAY!
WHAT? MORE OF THEM?!
WHOOSH
WHAM
BOOM

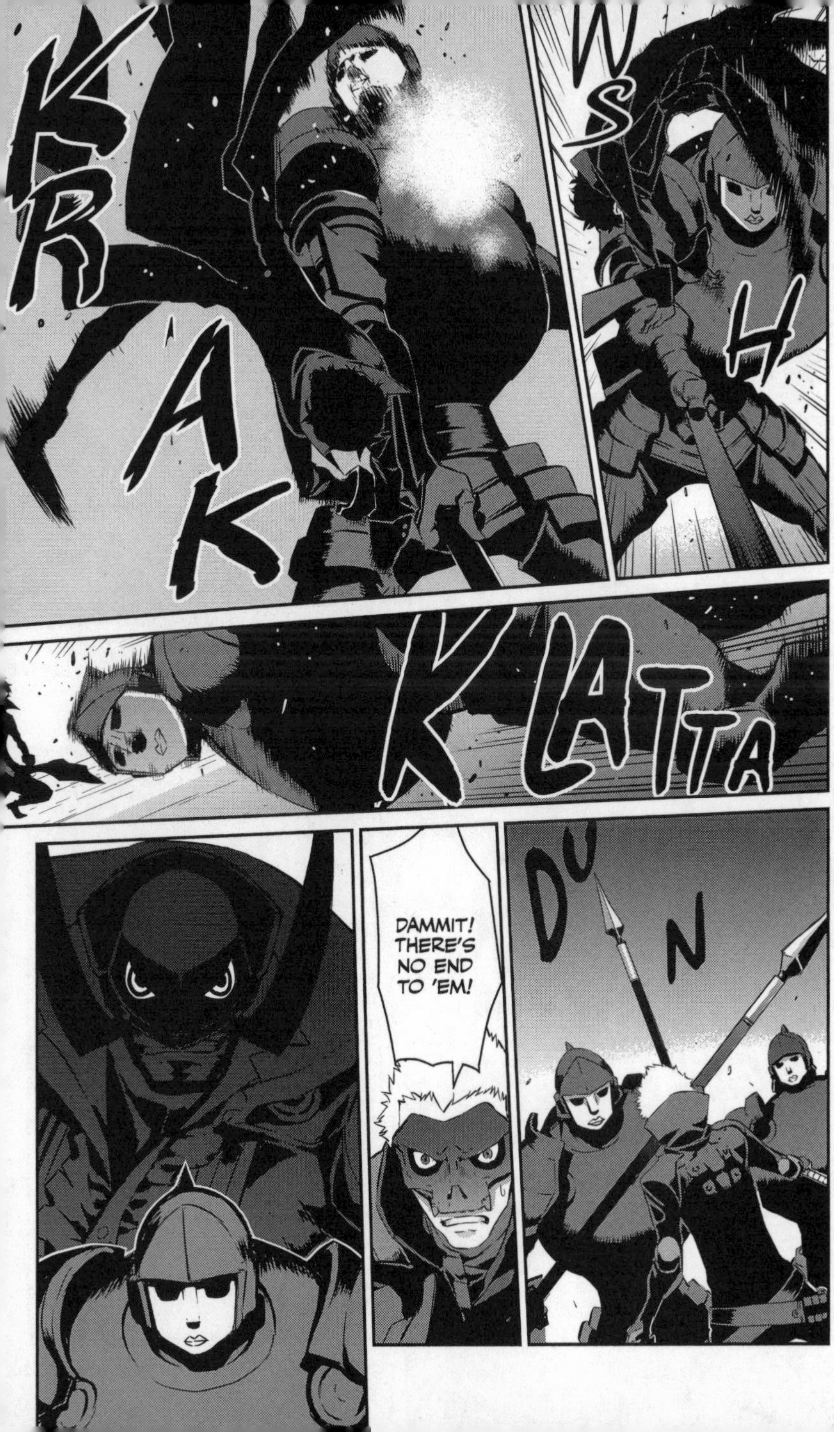
WSH
KRAK
KLATTA
DUN
DAMMIT! THERE'S NO END TO 'EM!

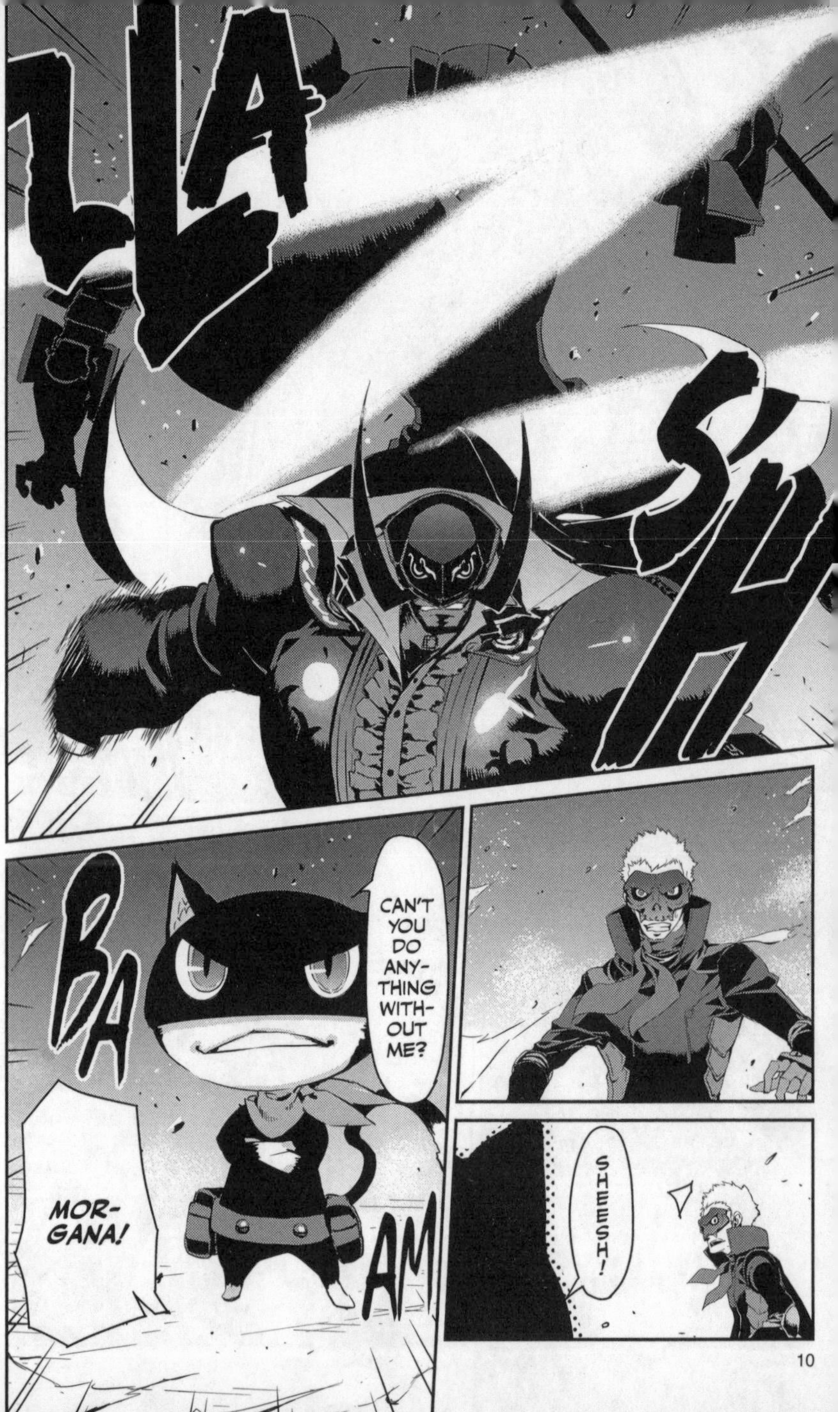

SH
LA
SHEESH!
CAN'T YOU DO ANY-THING WITH-OUT ME?
BA
AM
MOR-GANA!

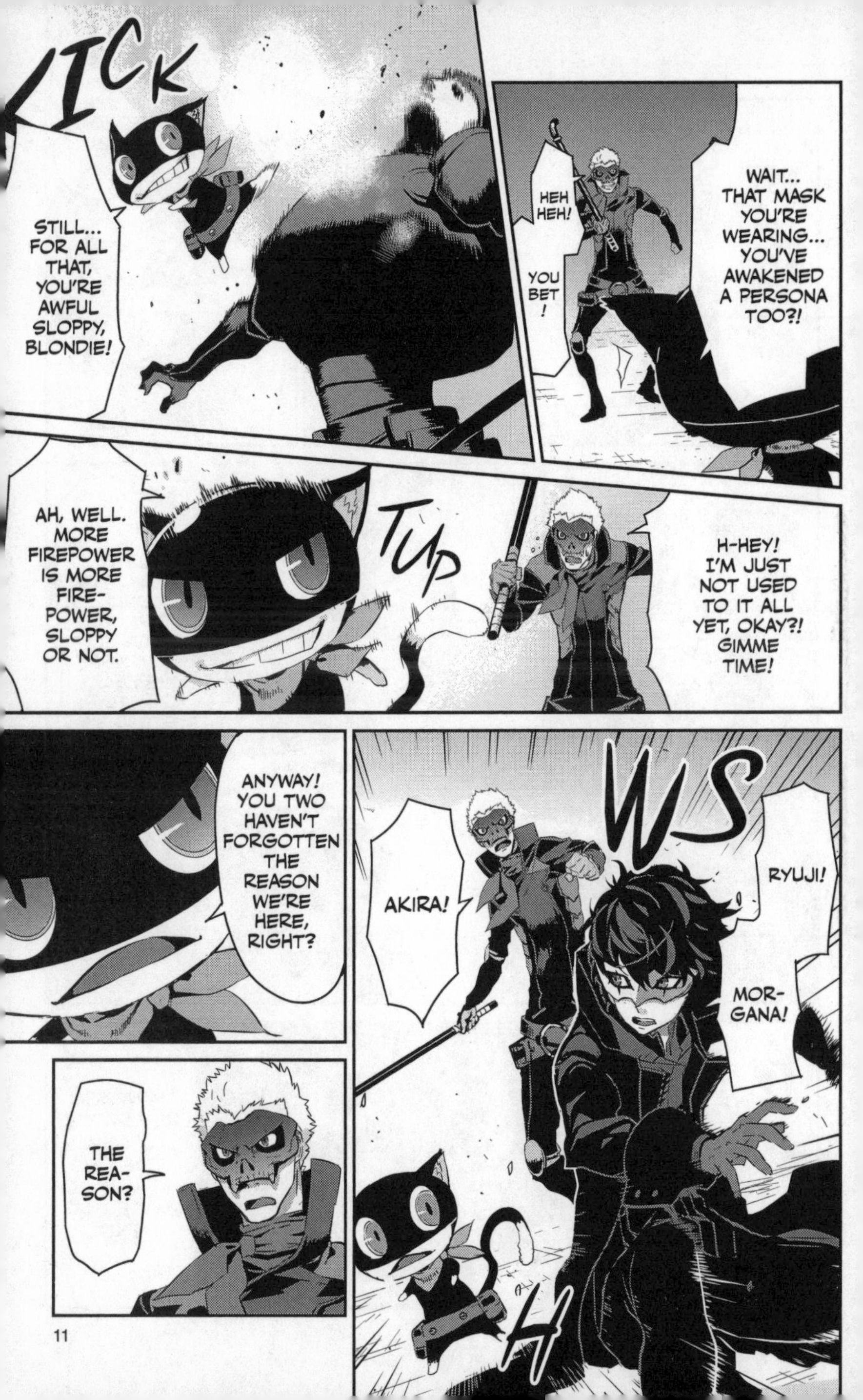
WAIT... THAT MASK YOU'RE WEARING... YOU'VE AWAKENED A PERSONA TOO?!
HEH HEH!
YOU BET!
KICK
STILL... FOR ALL THAT, YOU'RE AWFUL SLOPPY, BLONDIE!
AH, WELL. MORE FIREPOWER IS MORE FIRE-POWER, SLOPPY OR NOT.
TUP
H-HEY! I'M JUST NOT USED TO IT ALL YET, OKAY?! GIMME TIME!
WS
RYUJI!
MORGANA!
AKIRA!
H
ANYWAY! YOU TWO HAVEN'T FORGOTTEN THE REASON WE'RE HERE, RIGHT?
THE REA-SON?

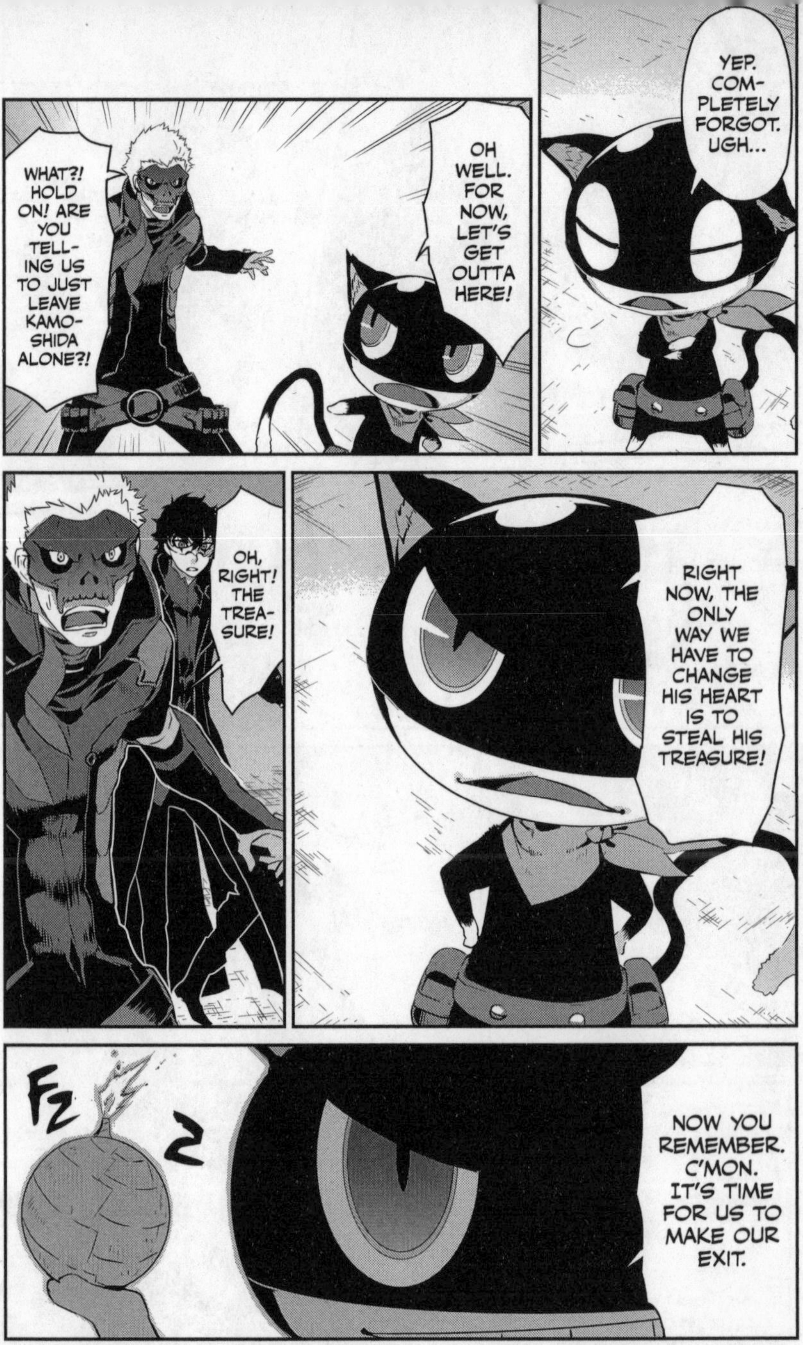
YEP. COMPLETELY FORGOT. UGH...
OH WELL. FOR NOW, LET'S GET OUTTA HERE!
WHAT?! HOLD ON! ARE YOU TELLING US TO JUST LEAVE KAMOSHIDA ALONE?!
RIGHT NOW, THE ONLY WAY WE HAVE TO CHANGE HIS HEART IS TO STEAL HIS TREASURE!
OH, RIGHT! THE TREASURE!
NOW YOU REMEMBER. C'MON. IT'S TIME FOR US TO MAKE OUR EXIT.
FZZ

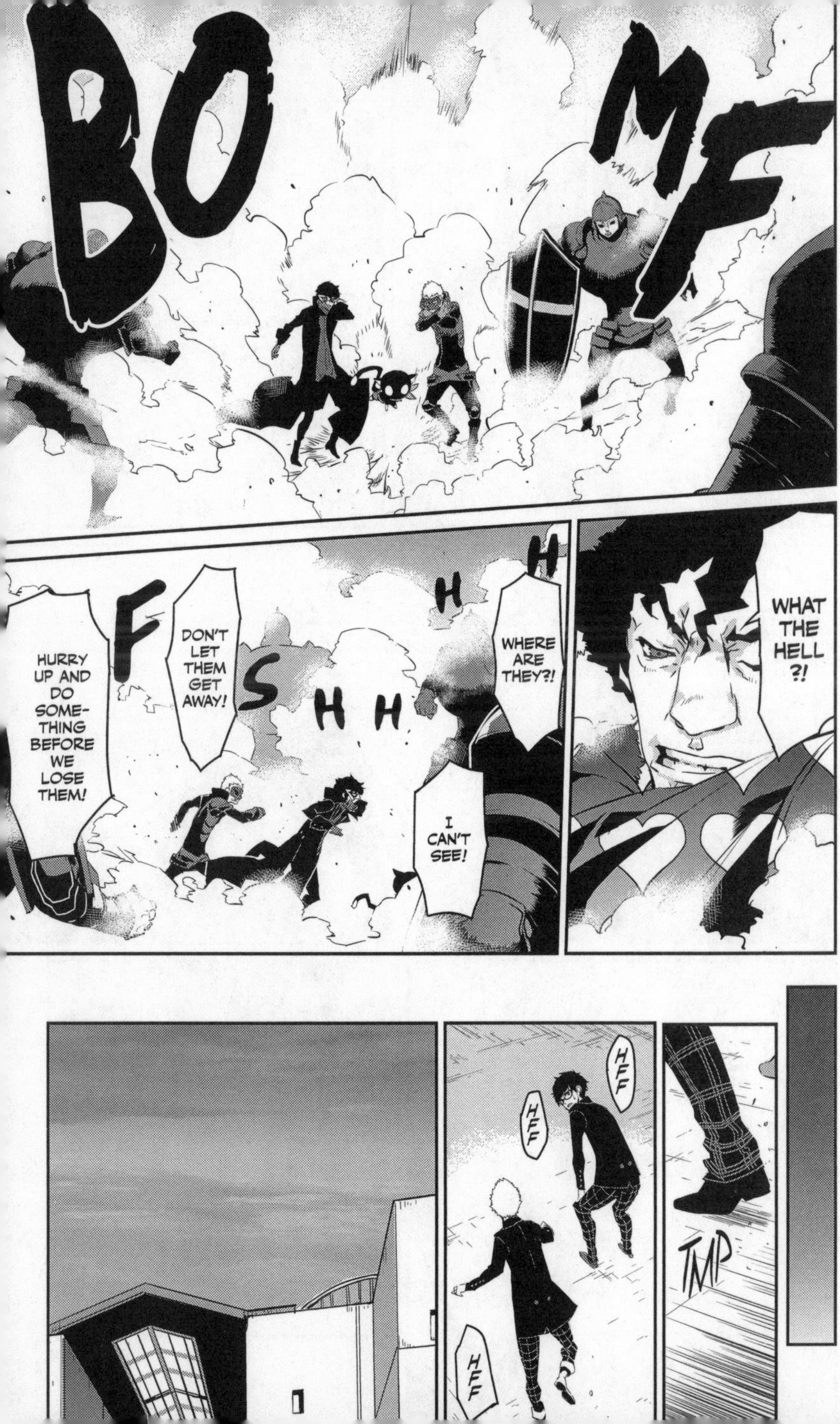
BOMF
WHAT THE HELL?!
FSHHHH
WHERE ARE THEY?!
I CAN'T SEE!
DON'T LET THEM GET AWAY!
HURRY UP AND DO SOME-THING BEFORE WE LOSE THEM!
TMP
HFF
HFF
HFF

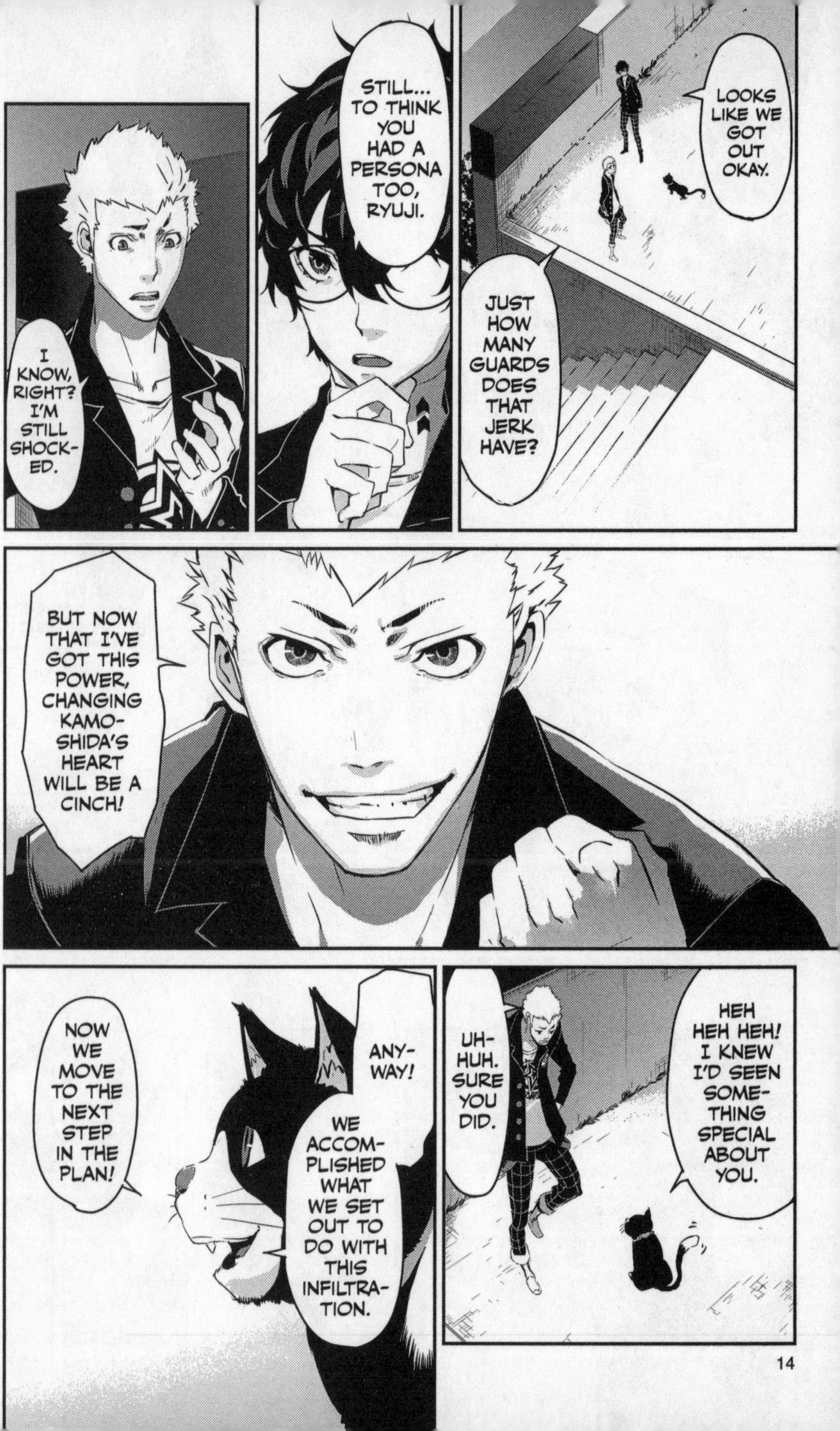
LOOKS LIKE WE GOT OUT OKAY.
JUST HOW MANY GUARDS DOES THAT JERK HAVE?
STILL... TO THINK YOU HAD A PERSONA TOO, RYUJI.
I KNOW, RIGHT? I'M STILL SHOCK-ED.
BUT NOW THAT I'VE GOT THIS POWER, CHANGING KAMO-SHIDA'S HEART WILL BE A CINCH!
HEH HEH HEH! I KNEW I'D SEEN SOME-THING SPECIAL ABOUT YOU.
UH-HUH. SURE YOU DID.
ANY-WAY!
WE ACCOM-PLISHED WHAT WE SET OUT TO DO WITH THIS INFILTRA-TION.
NOW WE MOVE TO THE NEXT STEP IN THE PLAN!

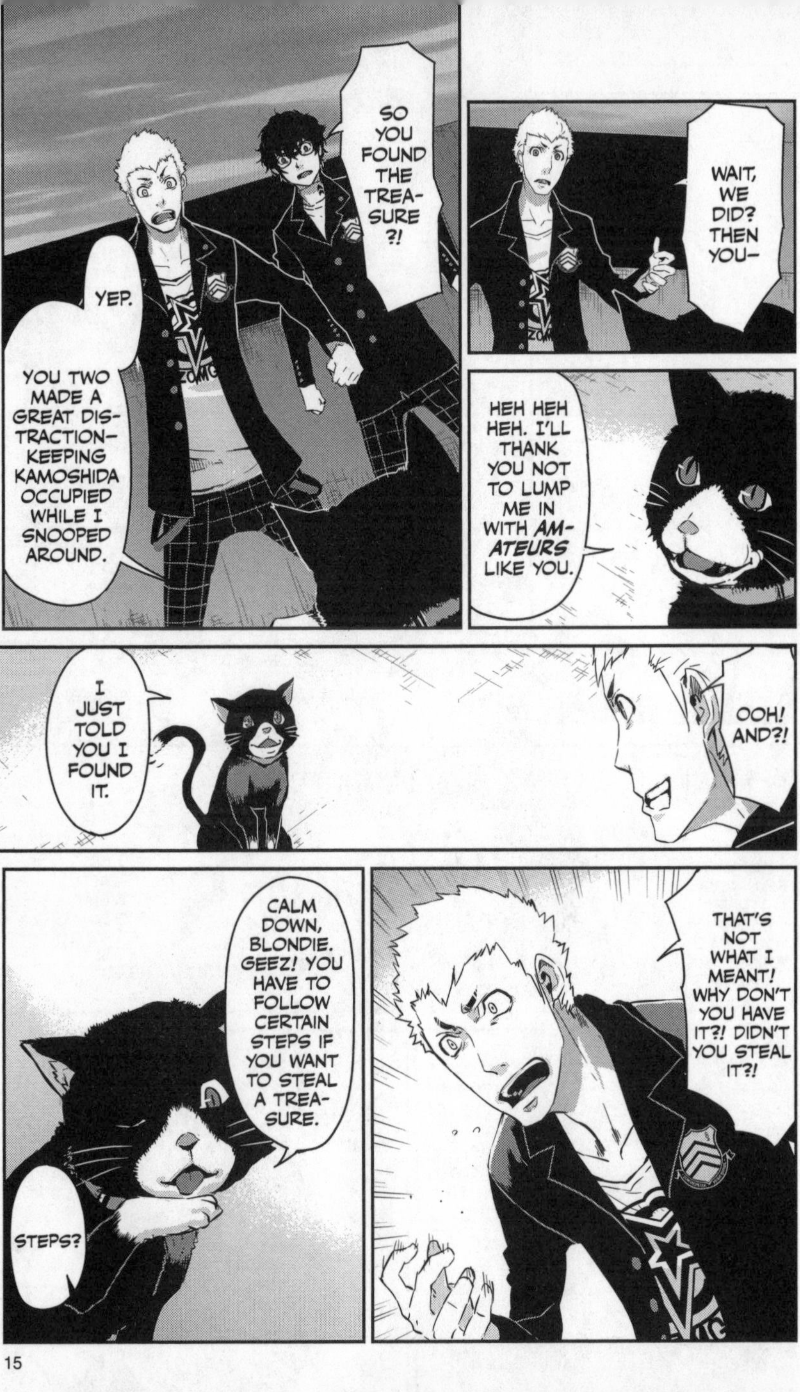
WAIT, WE DID? THEN YOU—
HEH HEH HEH. I'LL THANK YOU NOT TO LUMP ME IN WITH *AMATEURS* LIKE YOU.
SO YOU FOUND THE TREASURE?!
YEP.
YOU TWO MADE A GREAT DISTRACTION—KEEPING KAMOSHIDA OCCUPIED WHILE I SNOOPED AROUND.
OOH! AND?!
I JUST TOLD YOU I FOUND IT.
THAT'S NOT WHAT I MEANT! WHY DON'T YOU HAVE IT?! DIDN'T YOU STEAL IT?!
CALM DOWN, BLONDIE. GEEZ! YOU HAVE TO FOLLOW CERTAIN STEPS IF YOU WANT TO STEAL A TREASURE.
STEPS?

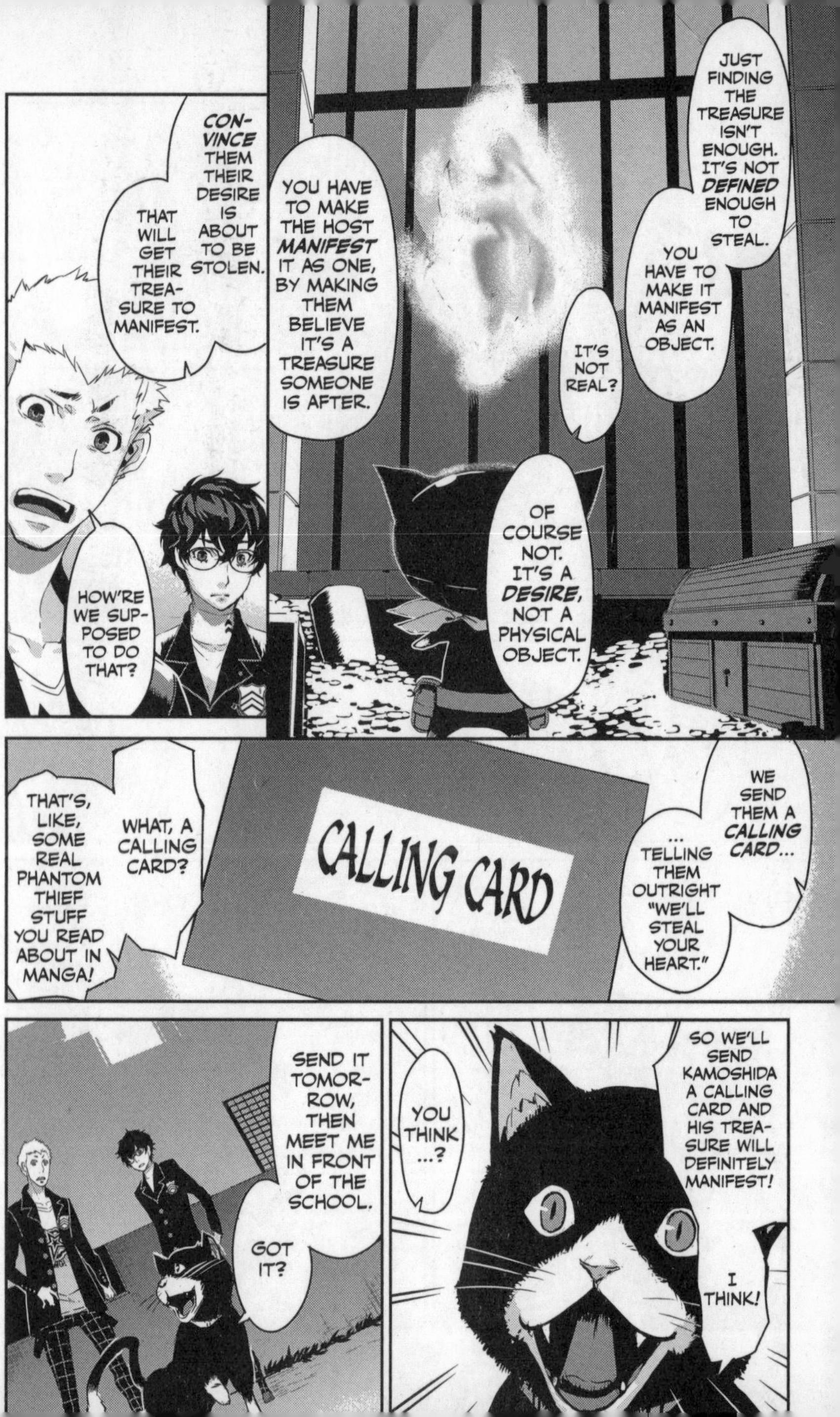
JUST FINDING THE TREASURE ISN'T ENOUGH. IT'S NOT *DEFINED* ENOUGH TO STEAL.
YOU HAVE TO MAKE IT MANIFEST AS AN OBJECT.
IT'S NOT REAL?
OF COURSE NOT. IT'S A *DESIRE,* NOT A PHYSICAL OBJECT.
YOU HAVE TO MAKE THE HOST *MANIFEST* IT AS ONE, BY MAKING THEM BELIEVE IT'S A TREASURE SOMEONE IS AFTER.
CON-VINCE THEM THEIR DESIRE IS ABOUT TO BE STOLEN.
THAT WILL GET THEIR TREA-SURE TO MANIFEST.
HOW'RE WE SUP-POSED TO DO THAT?
WE SEND THEM A *CALLING CARD*...
...TELLING THEM OUTRIGHT "WE'LL STEAL YOUR HEART."
CALLING CARD
WHAT, A CALLING CARD?
THAT'S, LIKE, SOME REAL PHANTOM THIEF STUFF YOU READ ABOUT IN MANGA!
SO WE'LL SEND KAMOSHIDA A CALLING CARD AND HIS TREA-SURE WILL DEFINITELY MANIFEST!
YOU THINK...?
I THINK!
SEND IT TOMOR-ROW, THEN MEET ME IN FRONT OF THE SCHOOL.
GOT IT?

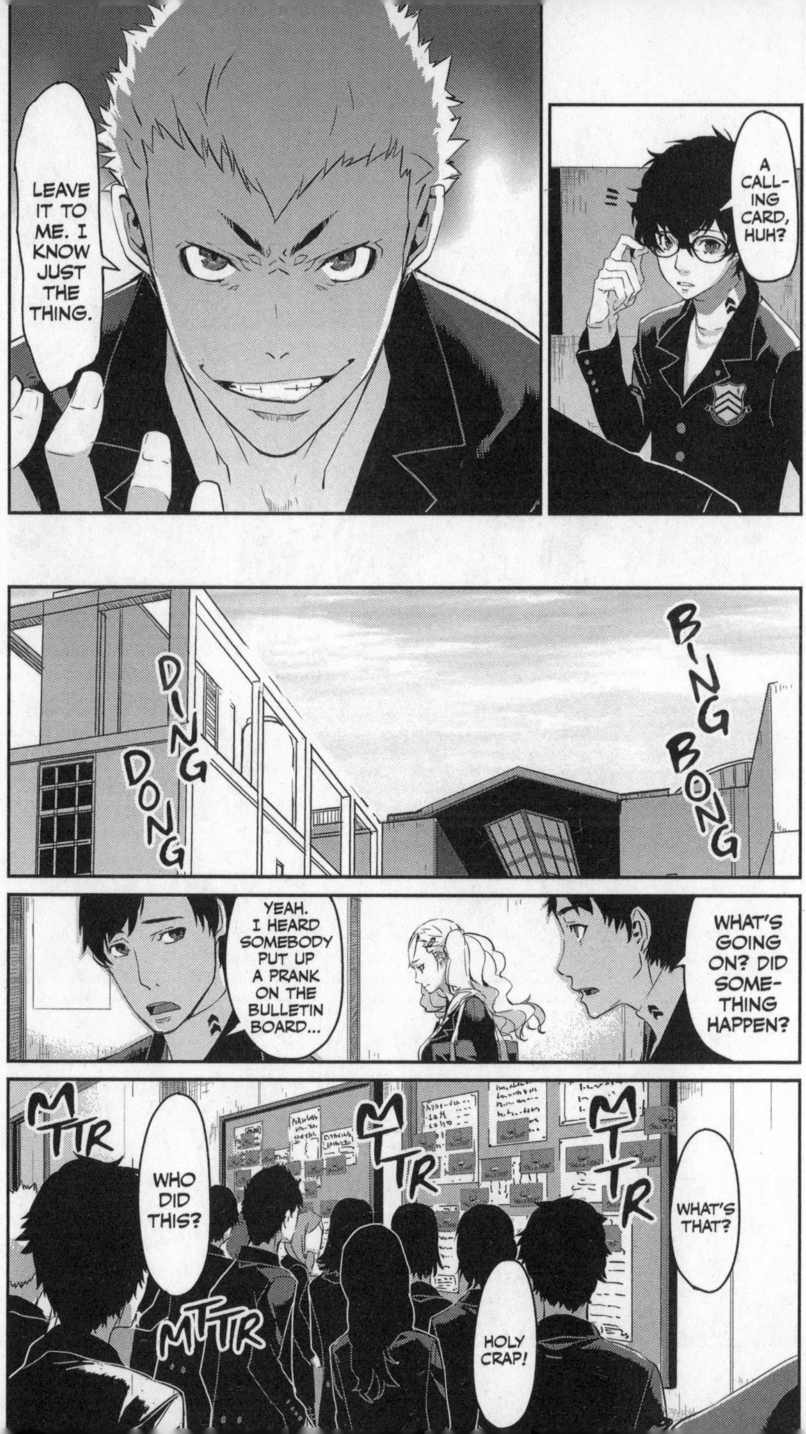

A CALLING CARD, HUH?
LEAVE IT TO ME. I KNOW JUST THE THING.
BING BONG
DING DONG
WHAT'S GOING ON? DID SOMETHING HAPPEN?
YEAH. I HEARD SOMEBODY PUT UP A PRANK ON THE BULLETIN BOARD...
MTTR
WHAT'S THAT?
MTTR
WHO DID THIS?
MTTR
HOLY CRAP!
MTTR

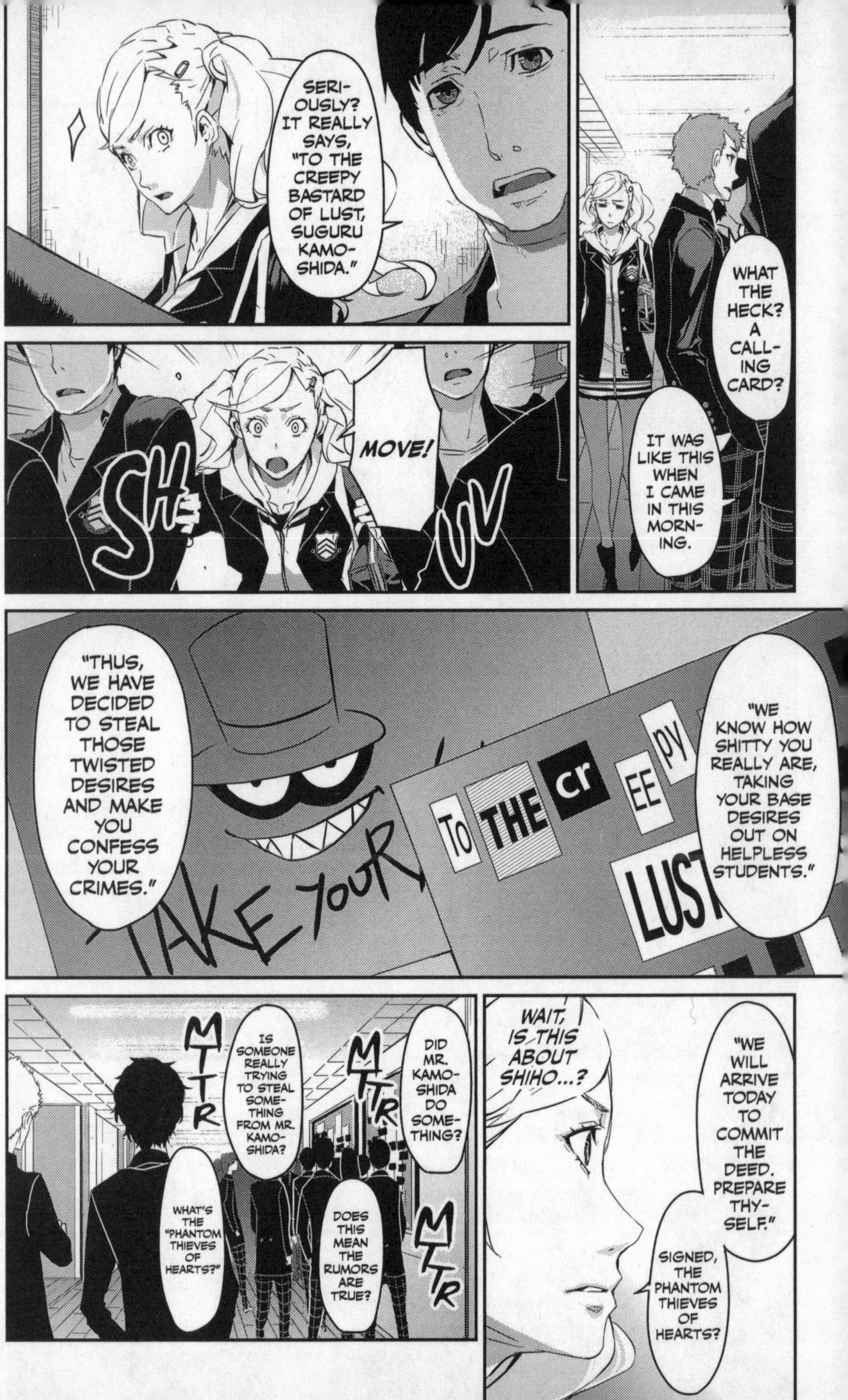
WHAT THE HECK? A CALLING CARD?
IT WAS LIKE THIS WHEN I CAME IN THIS MORNING.
SERIOUSLY? IT REALLY SAYS, "TO THE CREEPY BASTARD OF LUST, SUGURU KAMOSHIDA."
SHUV
MOVE!
SH
"WE KNOW HOW SHITTY YOU REALLY ARE, TAKING YOUR BASE DESIRES OUT ON HELPLESS STUDENTS."
LUST
To THE cr EE py
TAKE YOUR
"THUS, WE HAVE DECIDED TO STEAL THOSE TWISTED DESIRES AND MAKE YOU CONFESS YOUR CRIMES."
"WE WILL ARRIVE TODAY TO COMMIT THE DEED. PREPARE THYSELF."
WAIT, IS THIS ABOUT SHIHO...?
SIGNED, THE PHANTOM THIEVES OF HEARTS?
DID MR. KAMOSHIDA DO SOMETHING?
MTTR
IS SOMEONE REALLY TRYING TO STEAL SOMETHING FROM MR. KAMOSHIDA?
MTTR
MTTR
DOES THIS MEAN THE RUMORS ARE TRUE?
WHAT'S THE "PHANTOM THIEVES OF HEARTS?"

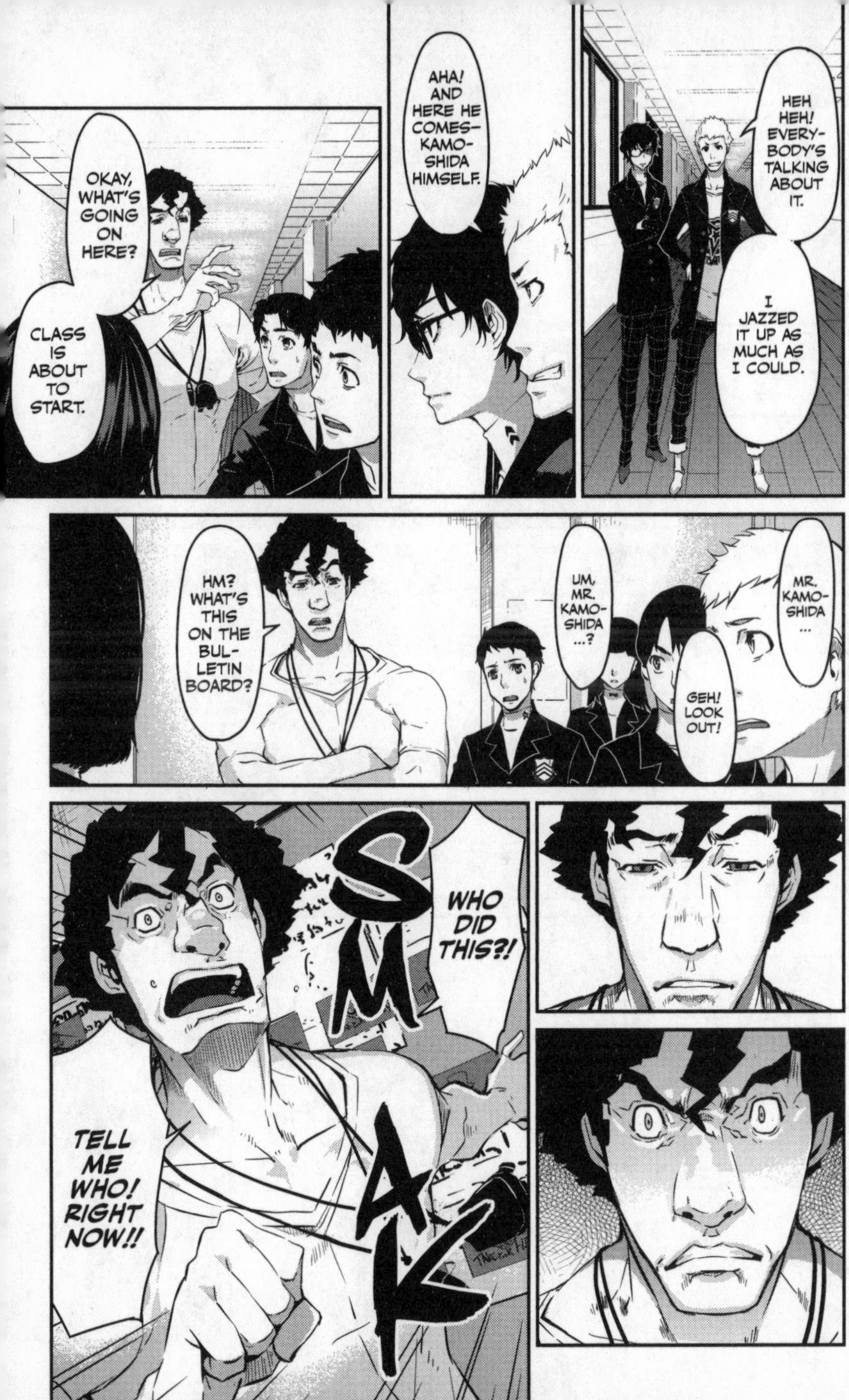
HEH HEH! EVERYBODY'S TALKING ABOUT IT.
I JAZZED IT UP AS MUCH AS I COULD.
AHA! AND HERE HE COMES- KAMOSHIDA HIMSELF.
OKAY, WHAT'S GOING ON HERE?
CLASS IS ABOUT TO START.
MR. KAMOSHIDA ...
UM, MR. KAMOSHIDA ...?
GEH! LOOK OUT!
HM? WHAT'S THIS ON THE BULLETIN BOARD?
WHO DID THIS?!
TELL ME WHO! RIGHT NOW!!

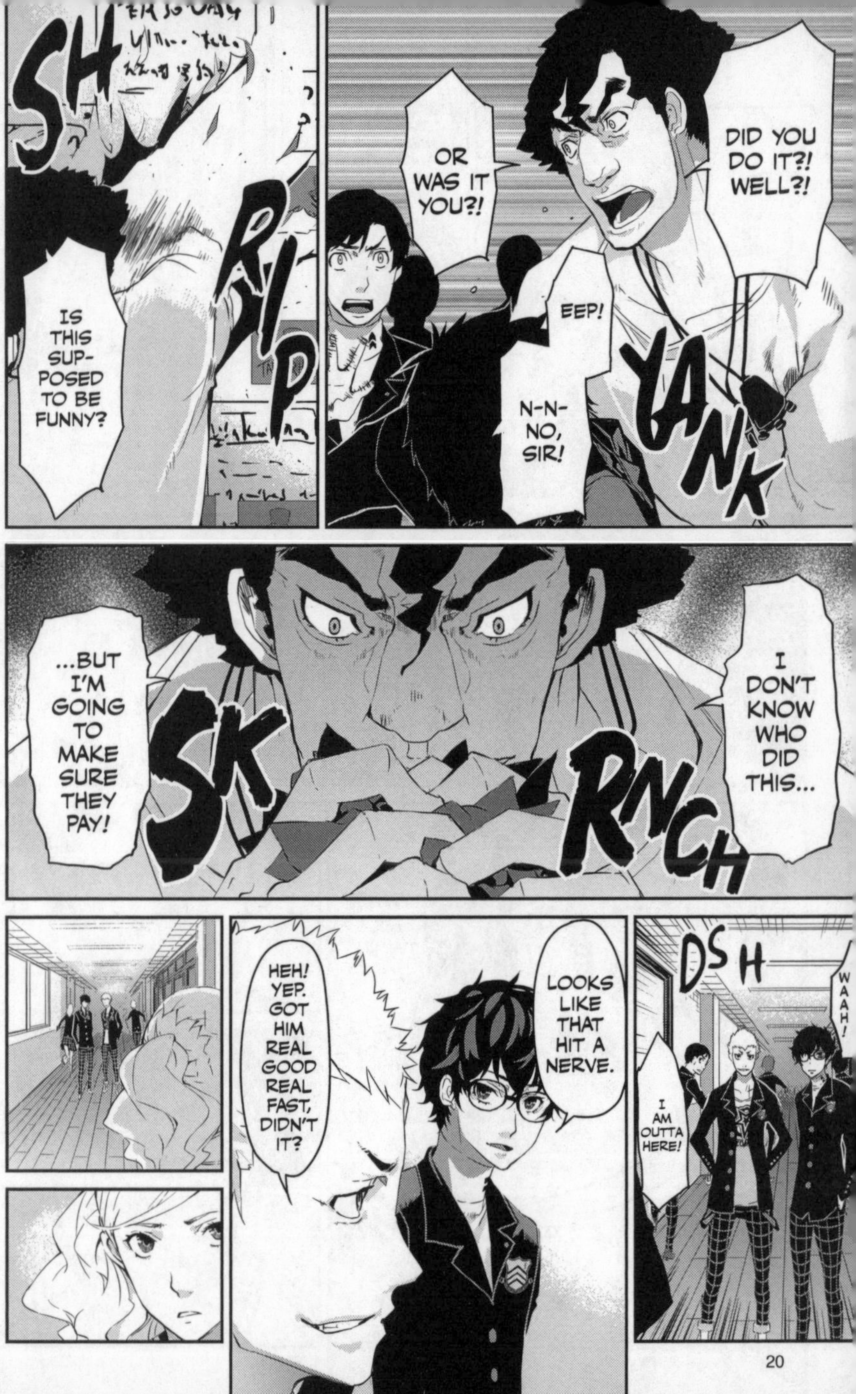
DID YOU DO IT?! WELL?!
OR WAS IT YOU?!
EEP!
YANK
N-N-NO, SIR!
SH
RIP
IS THIS SUP-POSED TO BE FUNNY?
I DON'T KNOW WHO DID THIS...
RNCH
SK
...BUT I'M GOING TO MAKE SURE THEY PAY!
DSH
WAAH!
I AM OUTTA HERE!
LOOKS LIKE THAT HIT A NERVE.
HEH! YEP. GOT HIM REAL GOOD REAL FAST, DIDN'T IT?

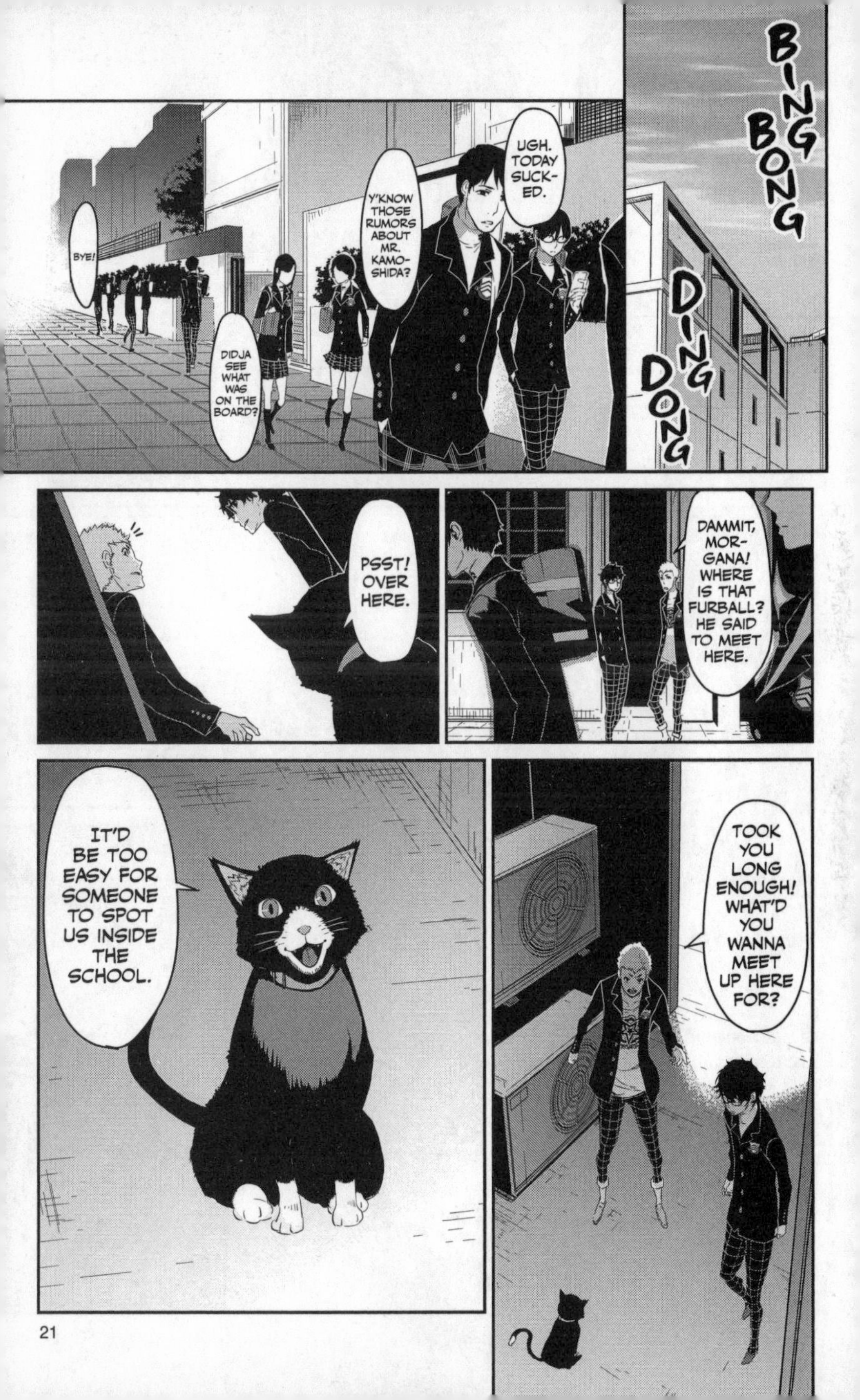
BING BONG
DING DONG
UGH. TODAY SUCK-ED.
Y'KNOW THOSE RUMORS ABOUT MR. KAMO-SHIDA?
DIDJA SEE WHAT WAS ON THE BOARD?
BYE!
DAMMIT, MOR-GANA! WHERE IS THAT FURBALL? HE SAID TO MEET HERE.
PSST! OVER HERE.
TOOK YOU LONG ENOUGH! WHAT'D YOU WANNA MEET UP HERE FOR?
IT'D BE TOO EASY FOR SOMEONE TO SPOT US INSIDE THE SCHOOL.

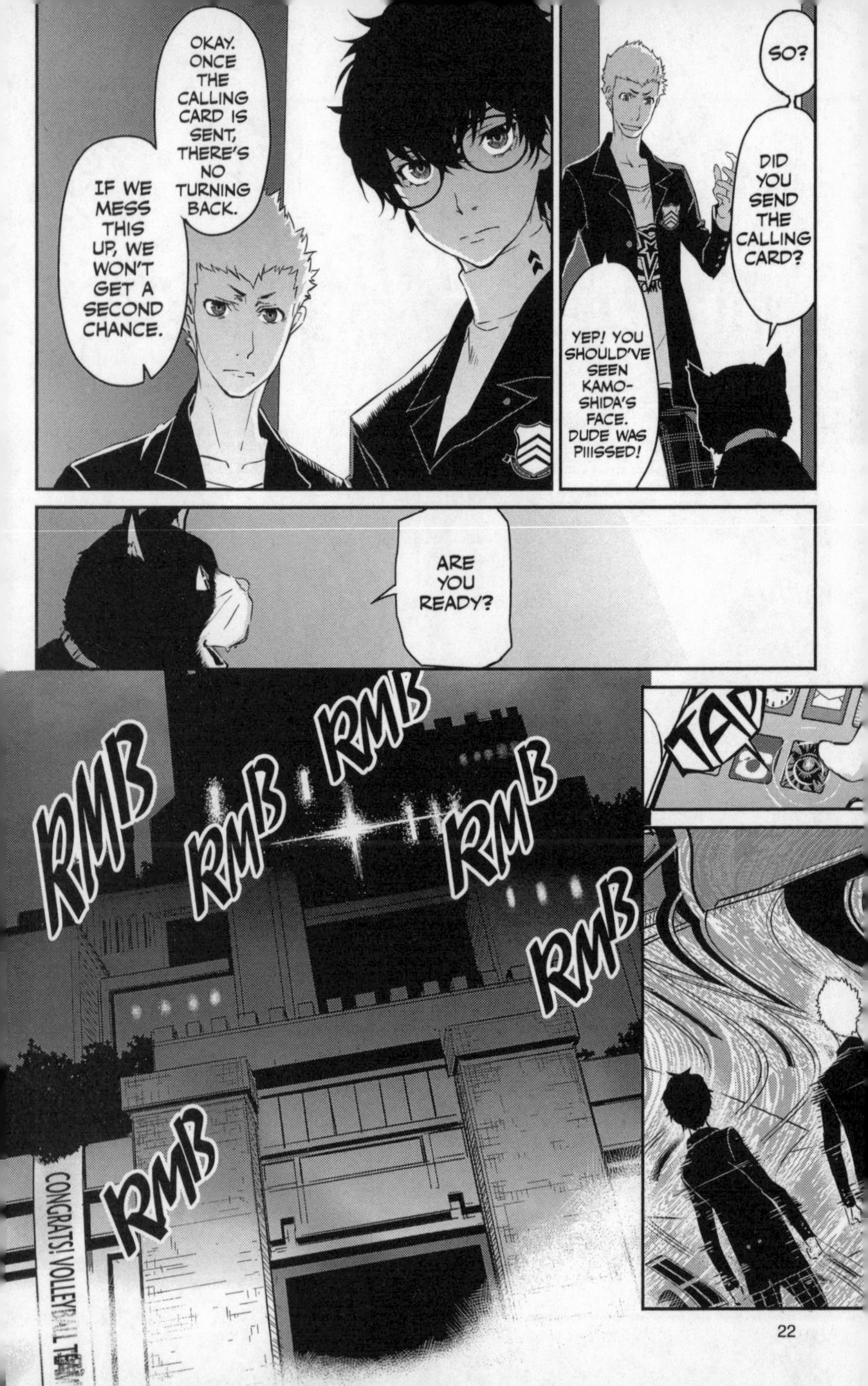
SO?
DID YOU SEND THE CALLING CARD?
YEP! YOU SHOULD'VE SEEN KAMOSHIDA'S FACE. DUDE WAS PIIISSED!
OKAY. ONCE THE CALLING CARD IS SENT, THERE'S NO TURNING BACK.
IF WE MESS THIS UP, WE WON'T GET A SECOND CHANCE.
ARE YOU READY?
RMB
RMB
RMB
RMB
RMB
RMB
RMB
CONGRATS! VOLLEYBALL TEAM

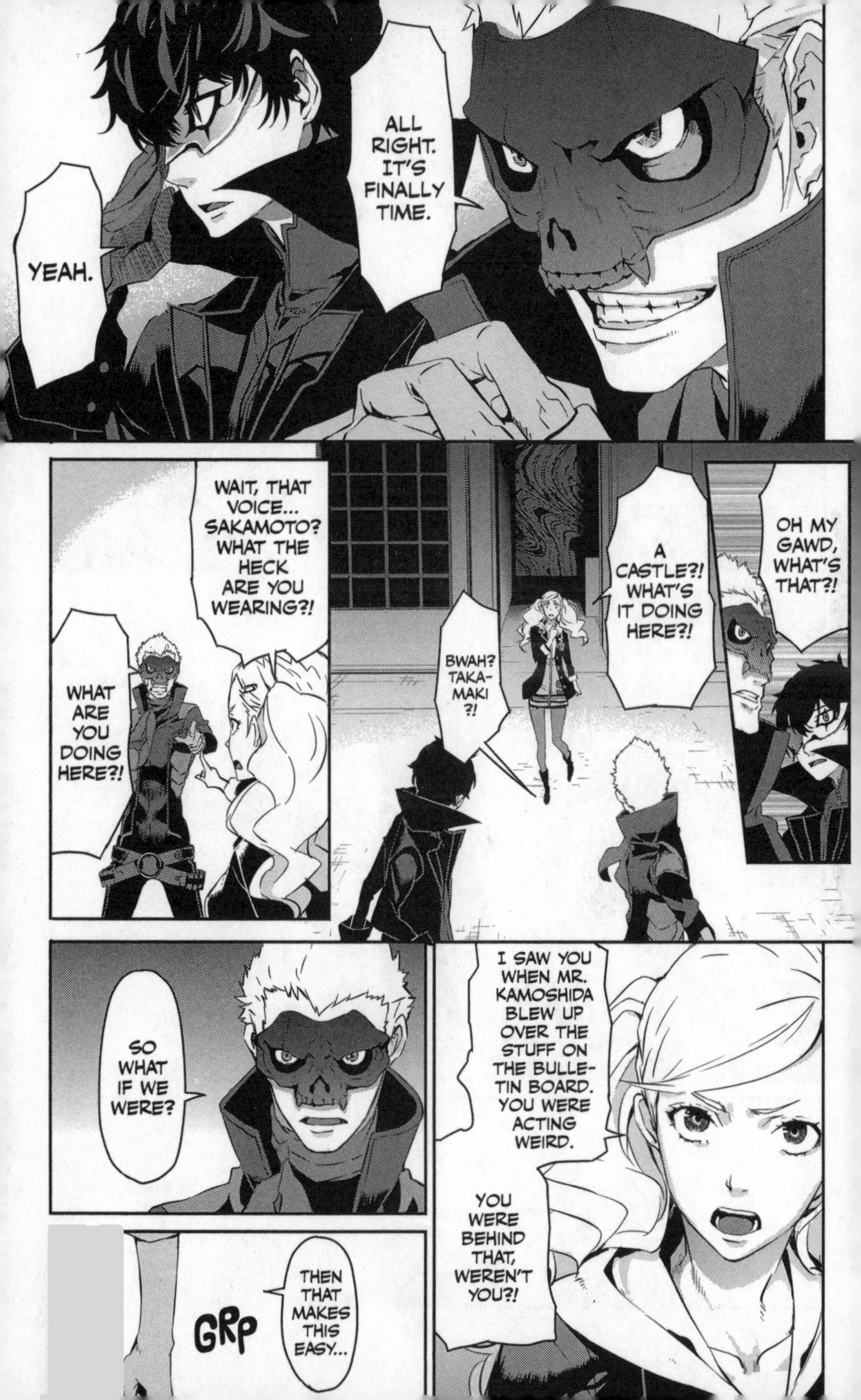
ALL RIGHT. IT'S FINALLY TIME.
YEAH.
OH MY GAWD, WHAT'S THAT?!
A CASTLE?! WHAT'S IT DOING HERE?!
BWAH? TAKAMAKI?!
WAIT, THAT VOICE... SAKAMOTO? WHAT THE HECK ARE YOU WEARING?!
WHAT ARE YOU DOING HERE?!
I SAW YOU WHEN MR. KAMOSHIDA BLEW UP OVER THE STUFF ON THE BULLETIN BOARD. YOU WERE ACTING WEIRD.
YOU WERE BEHIND THAT, WEREN'T YOU?!
SO WHAT IF WE WERE?
THEN THAT MAKES THIS EASY...
GRP

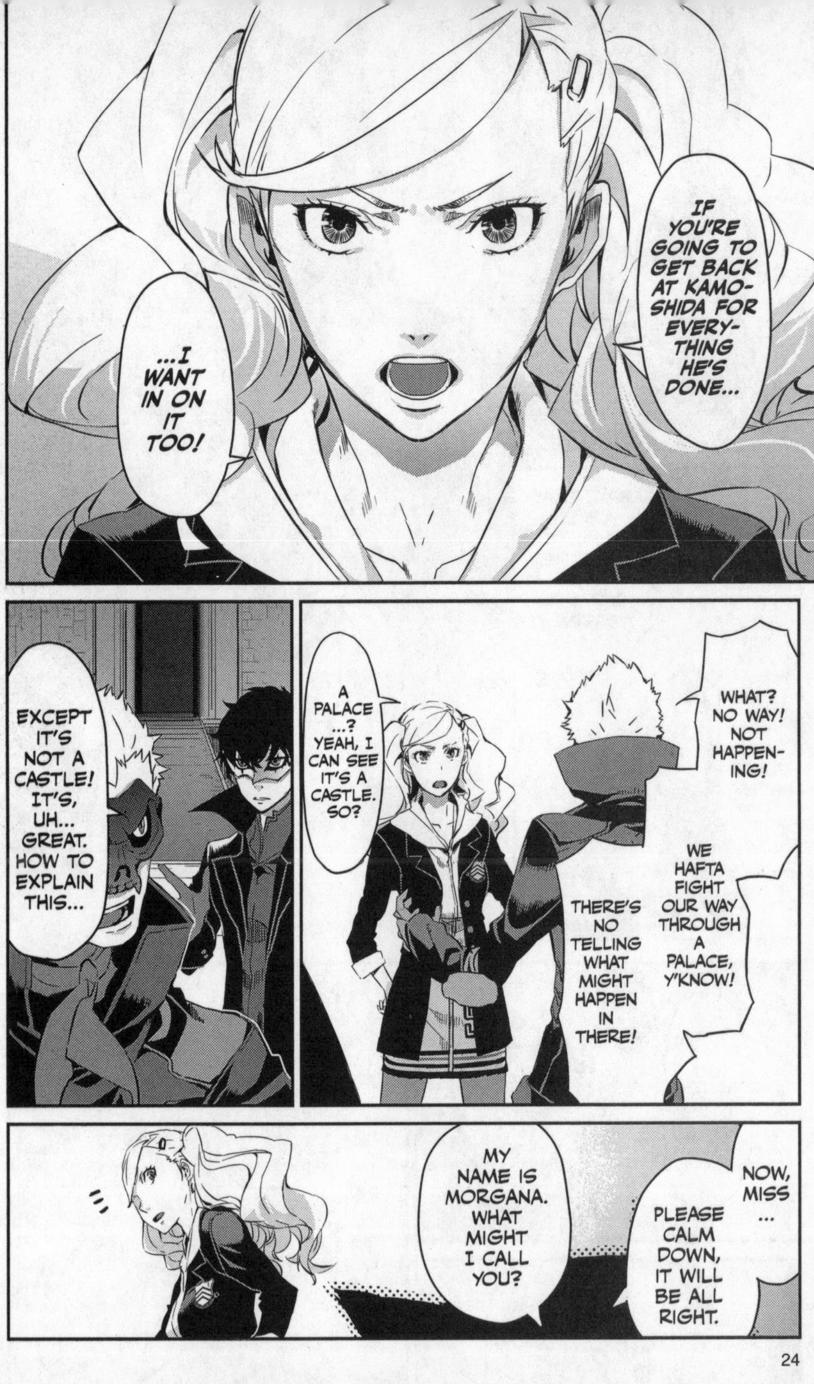
IF YOU'RE GOING TO GET BACK AT KAMOSHIDA FOR EVERYTHING HE'S DONE...
...I WANT IN ON IT TOO!
WHAT? NO WAY! NOT HAPPENING!
WE HAFTA FIGHT OUR WAY THROUGH A PALACE, Y'KNOW!
THERE'S NO TELLING WHAT MIGHT HAPPEN IN THERE!
A PALACE ...? YEAH, I CAN SEE IT'S A CASTLE. SO?
EXCEPT IT'S NOT A CASTLE! IT'S, UH... GREAT. HOW TO EXPLAIN THIS...
NOW, MISS ...
PLEASE CALM DOWN, IT WILL BE ALL RIGHT.
MY NAME IS MORGANA. WHAT MIGHT I CALL YOU?

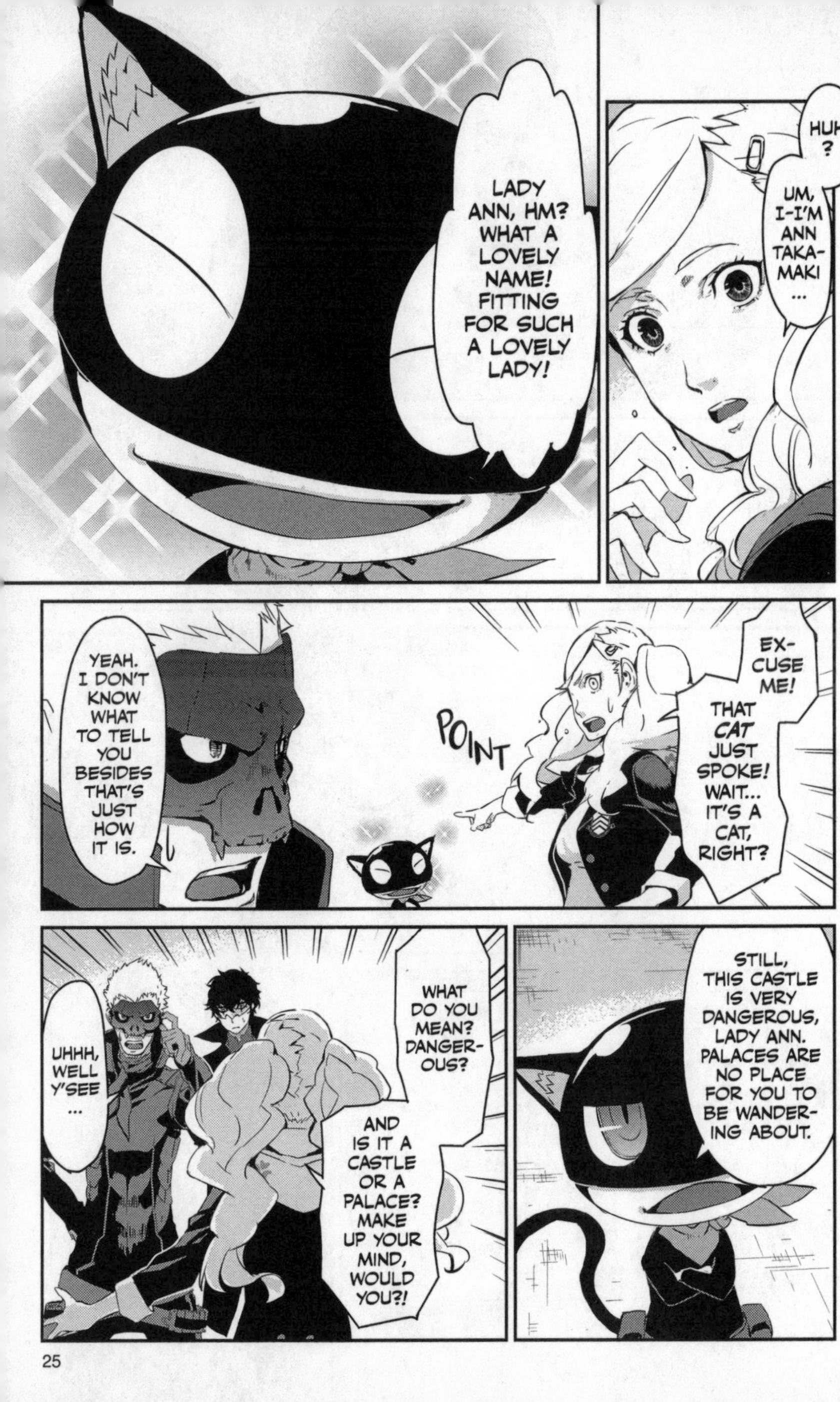
HUH?
UM, I-I'M ANN TAKAMAKI...
LADY ANN, HM? WHAT A LOVELY NAME! FITTING FOR SUCH A LOVELY LADY!
EXCUSE ME!
THAT *CAT* JUST SPOKE! WAIT... IT'S A CAT, RIGHT?
POINT
YEAH. I DON'T KNOW WHAT TO TELL YOU BESIDES THAT'S JUST HOW IT IS.
STILL, THIS CASTLE IS VERY DANGEROUS, LADY ANN. PALACES ARE NO PLACE FOR YOU TO BE WANDERING ABOUT.
WHAT DO YOU MEAN? DANGEROUS?
AND IS IT A CASTLE OR A PALACE? MAKE UP YOUR MIND, WOULD YOU?!
UHHH, WELL Y'SEE...

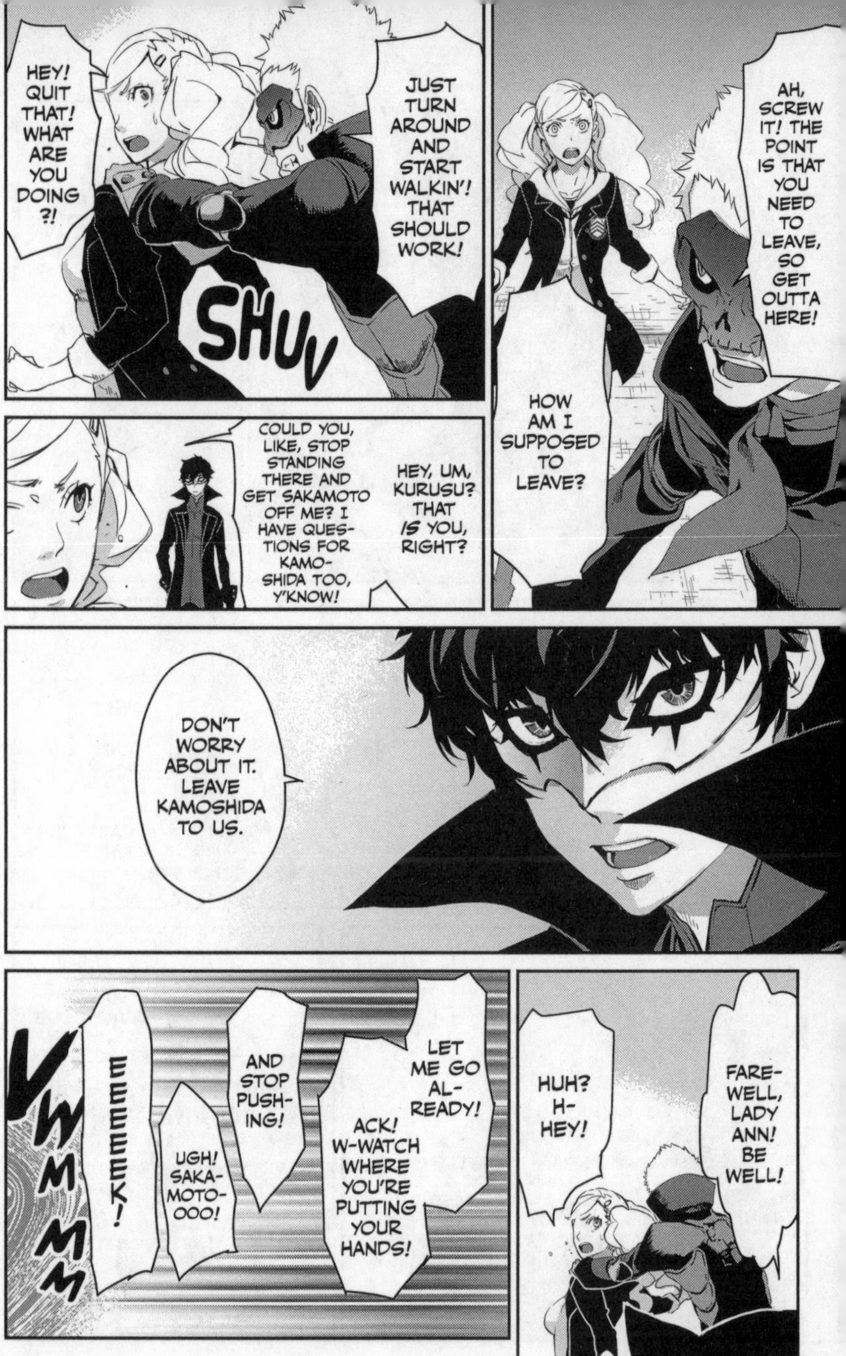

AH, SCREW IT! THE POINT IS THAT YOU NEED TO LEAVE, SO GET OUTTA HERE!
HOW AM I SUPPOSED TO LEAVE?
JUST TURN AROUND AND START WALKIN'! THAT SHOULD WORK!
HEY! QUIT THAT! WHAT ARE YOU DOING?!
SHUV
HEY, UM, KURUSU? THAT *IS* YOU, RIGHT?
COULD YOU, LIKE, STOP STANDING THERE AND GET SAKAMOTO OFF ME? I HAVE QUESTIONS FOR KAMOSHIDA TOO, Y'KNOW!
DON'T WORRY ABOUT IT. LEAVE KAMOSHIDA TO US.
FAREWELL, LADY ANN! BE WELL!
HUH? H-HEY!
LET ME GO ALREADY!
ACK! W-WATCH WHERE YOU'RE PUTTING YOUR HANDS!
AND STOP PUSHING!
UGH! SAKAMOTO-OOO!
EEEEEEK!
VWMMM

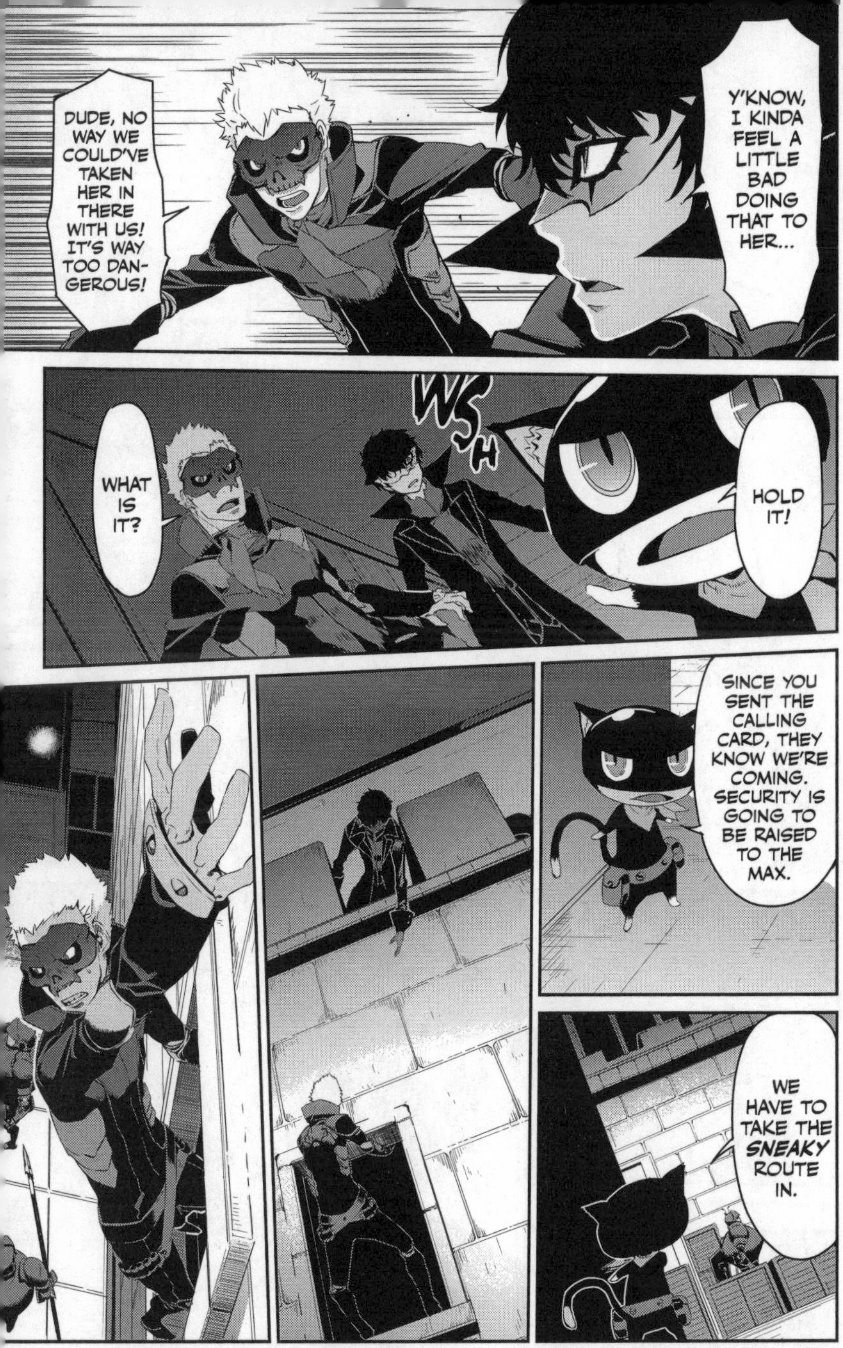
Y'KNOW, I KINDA FEEL A LITTLE BAD DOING THAT TO HER...
DUDE, NO WAY WE COULD'VE TAKEN HER IN THERE WITH US! IT'S WAY TOO DAN-GEROUS!
WSH
HOLD IT!
WHAT IS IT?
SINCE YOU SENT THE CALLING CARD, THEY KNOW WE'RE COMING. SECURITY IS GOING TO BE RAISED TO THE MAX.
WE HAVE TO TAKE THE *SNEAKY* ROUTE IN.

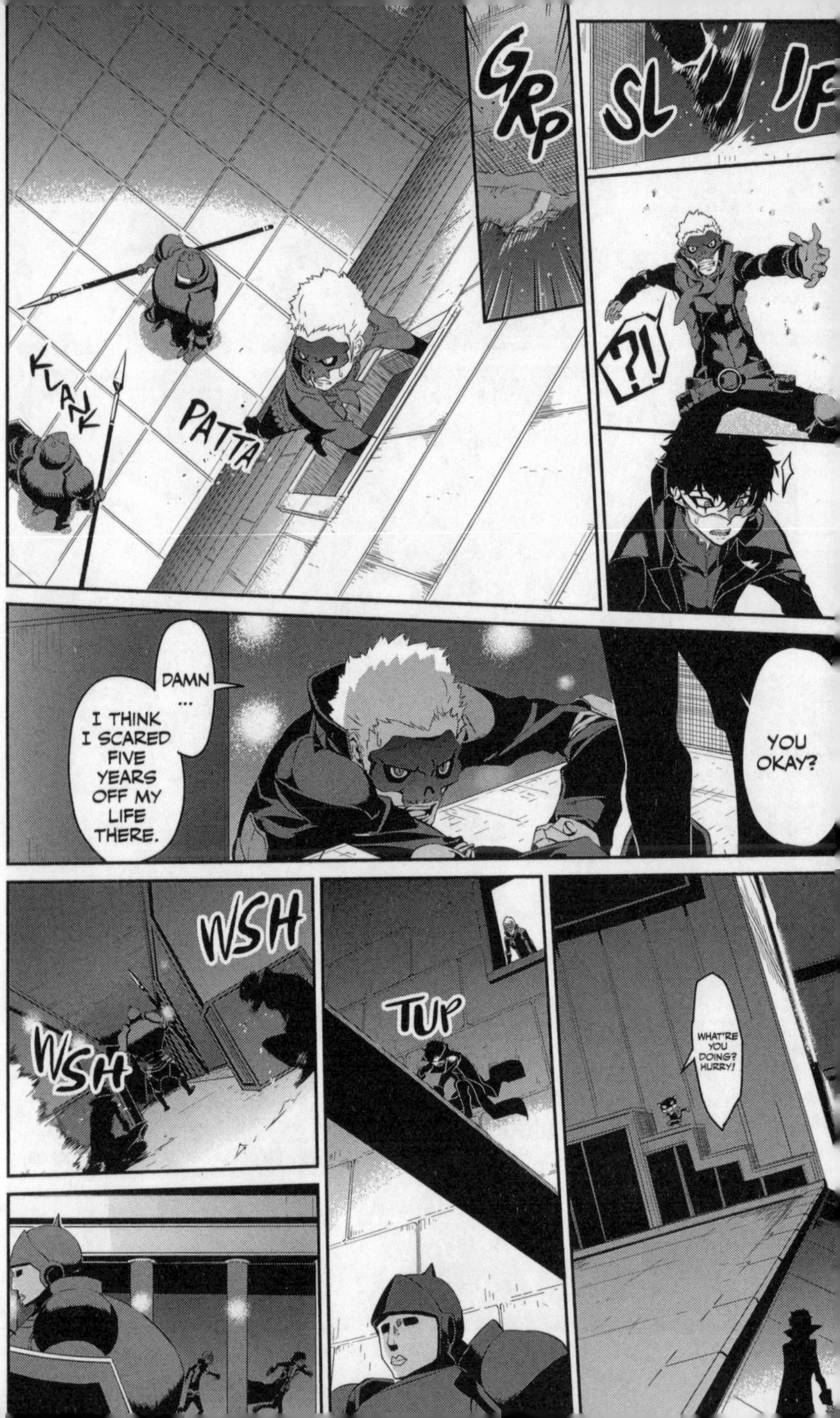
SLIP
?!
GRP
KLANK
PATTA
YOU OKAY?
DAMN... I THINK I SCARED FIVE YEARS OFF MY LIFE THERE.
WHAT'RE YOU DOING? HURRY!
TUP
WSH
WSH

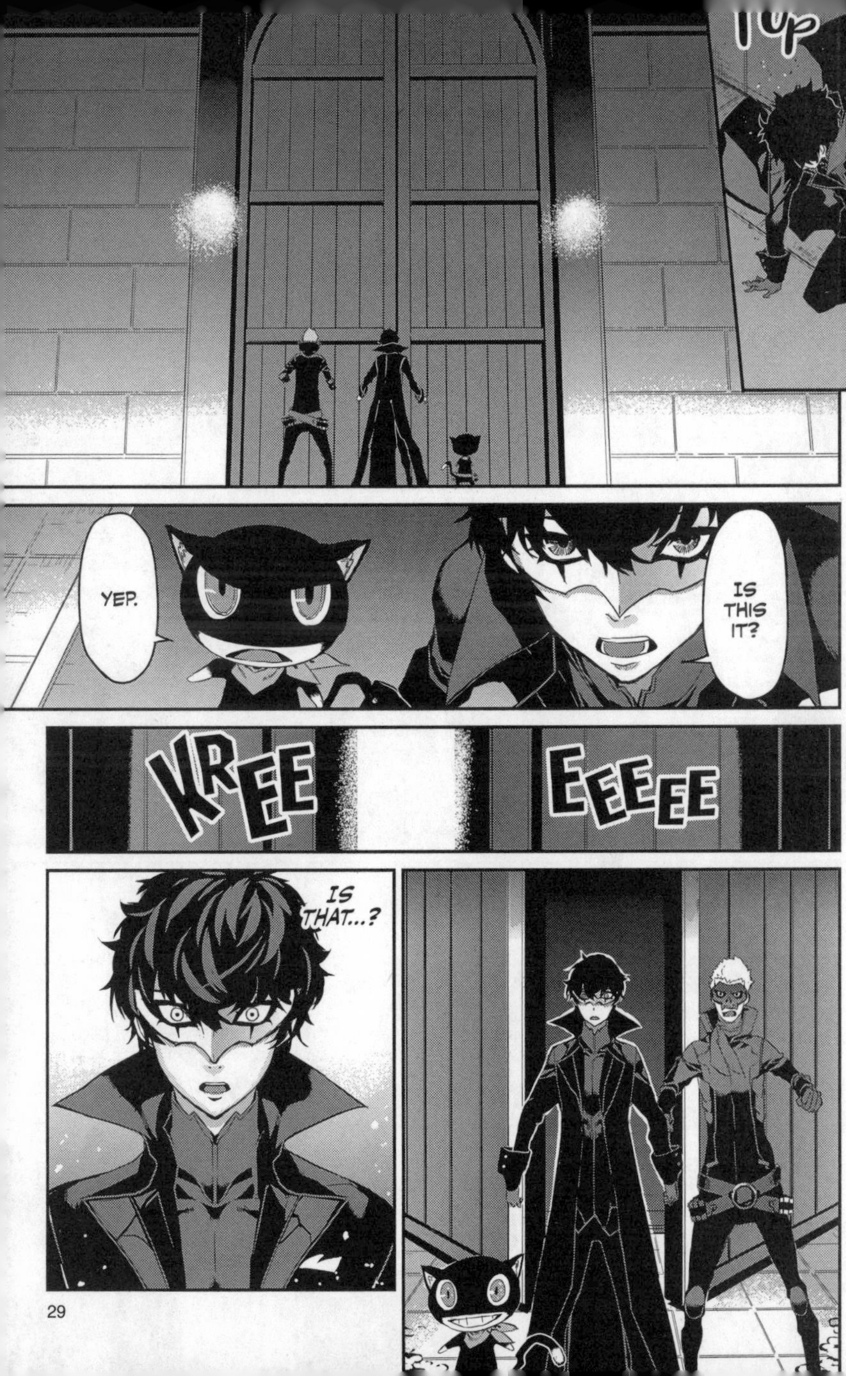
Tup
IS THIS IT?
YEP.
KREE
EEEEE
IS THAT...?

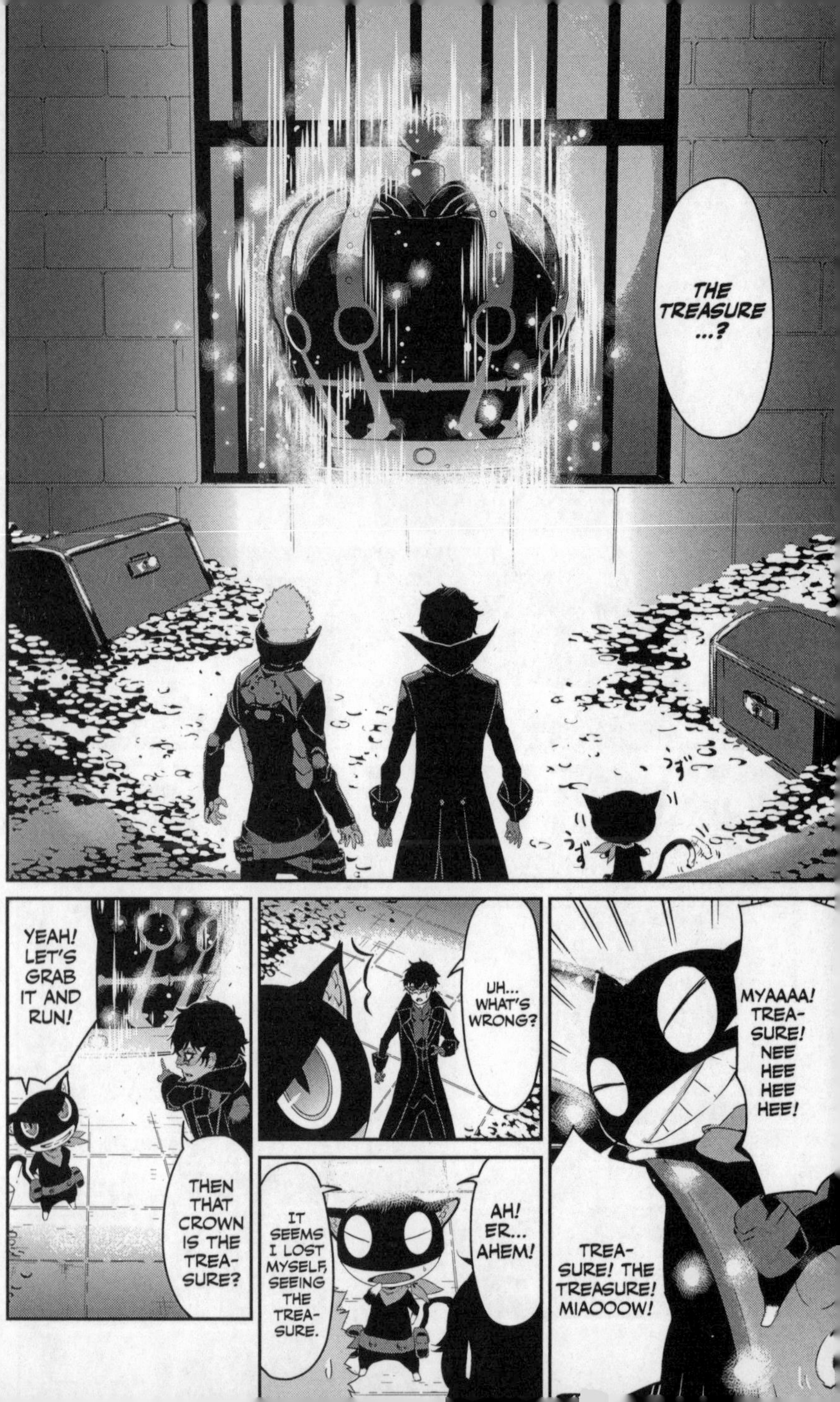
THE TREASURE ...?
MYAAAA! TREASURE! NEE HEE HEE HEE!
TREASURE! THE TREASURE! MIAOOOW!
UH... WHAT'S WRONG?
AH! ER... AHEM!
IT SEEMS I LOST MYSELF, SEEING THE TREASURE.
THEN THAT CROWN IS THE TREASURE?
YEAH! LET'S GRAB IT AND RUN!

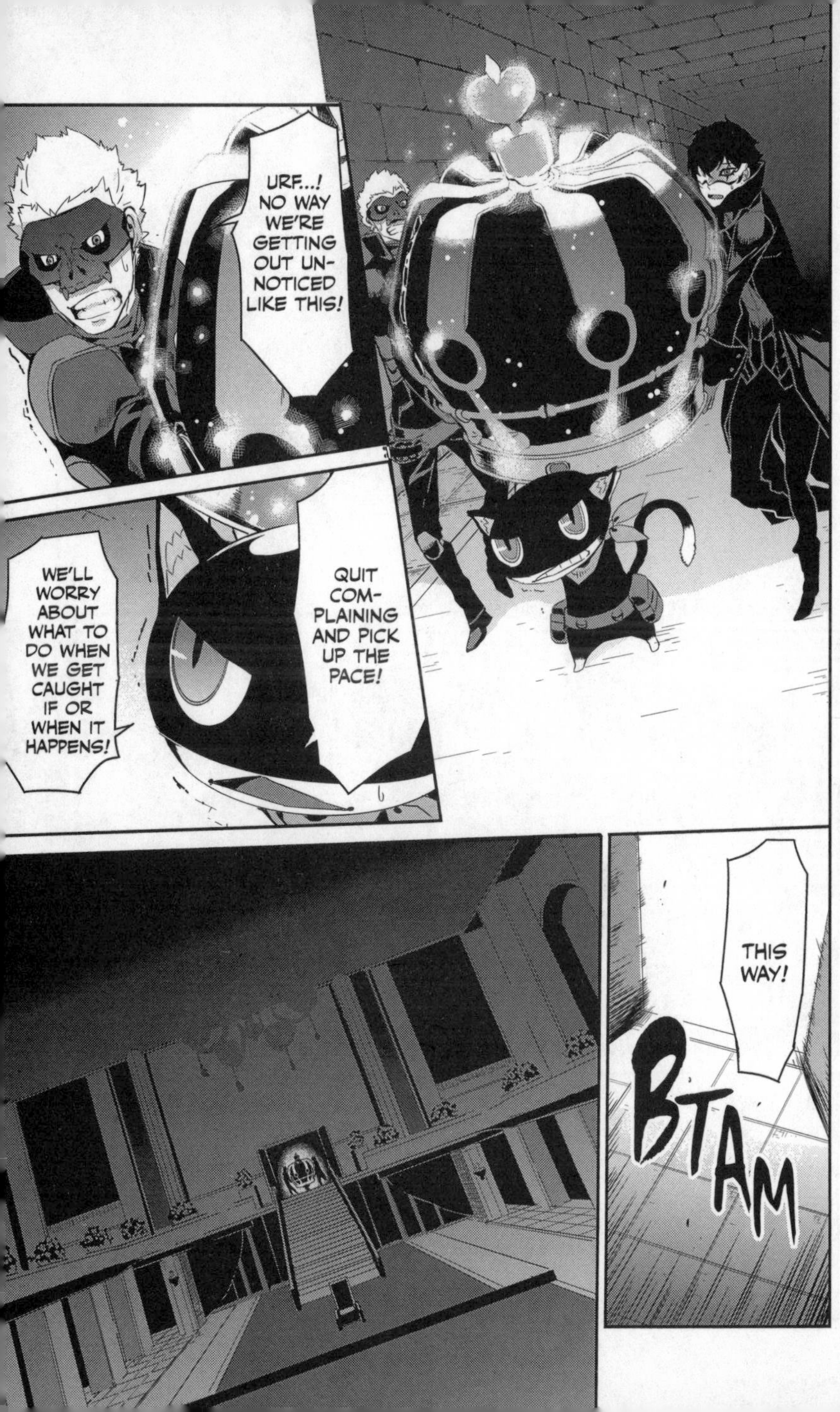
URF...! NO WAY WE'RE GETTING OUT UN-NOTICED LIKE THIS!
QUIT COM-PLAINING AND PICK UP THE PACE!
WE'LL WORRY ABOUT WHAT TO DO WHEN WE GET CAUGHT IF OR WHEN IT HAPPENS!
THIS WAY!
BTAM

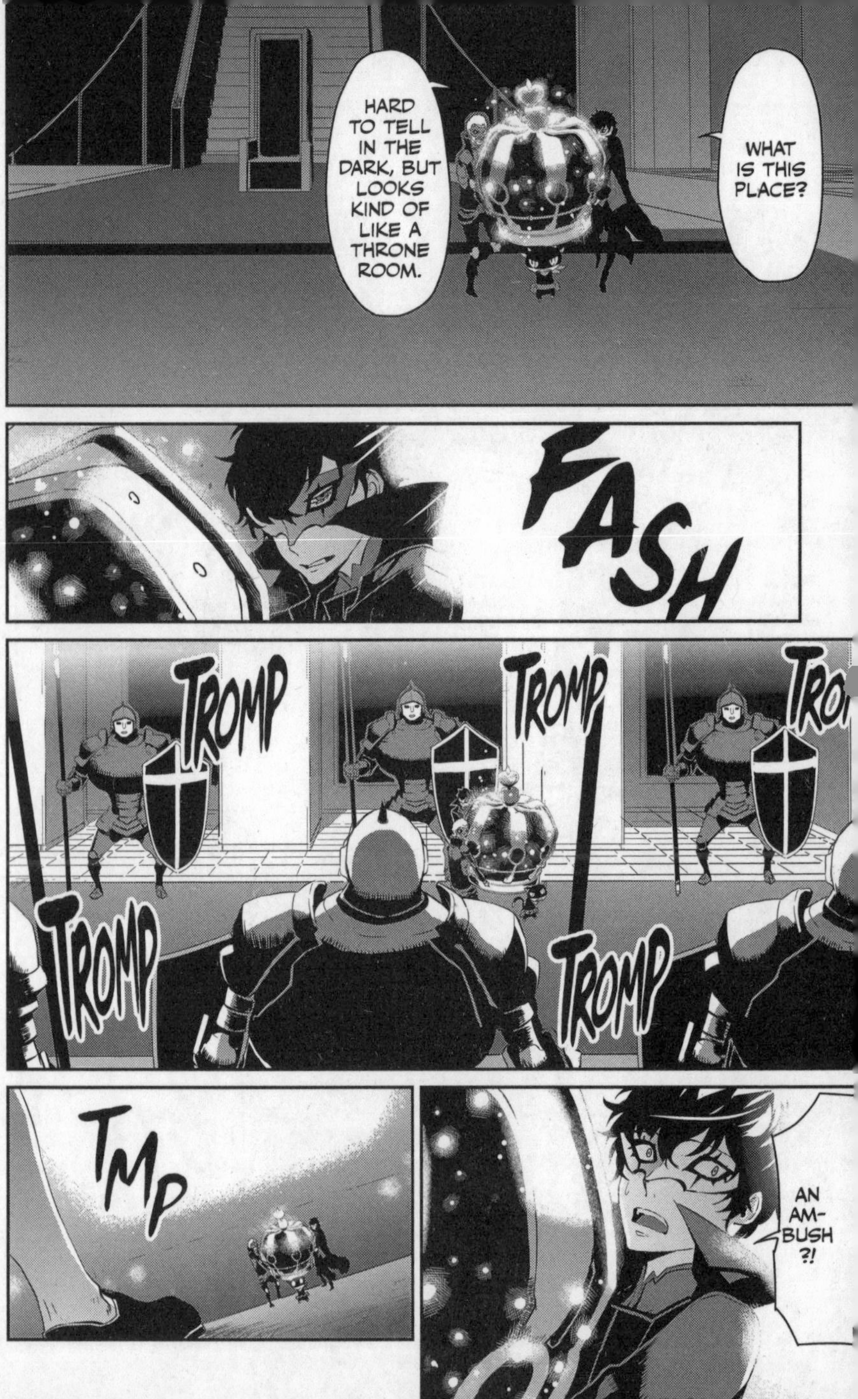
WHAT IS THIS PLACE?
HARD TO TELL IN THE DARK, BUT LOOKS KIND OF LIKE A THRONE ROOM.
FASH
TROMP
TROMP
TROMP
TROMP
AN AM-BUSH?!
TMP

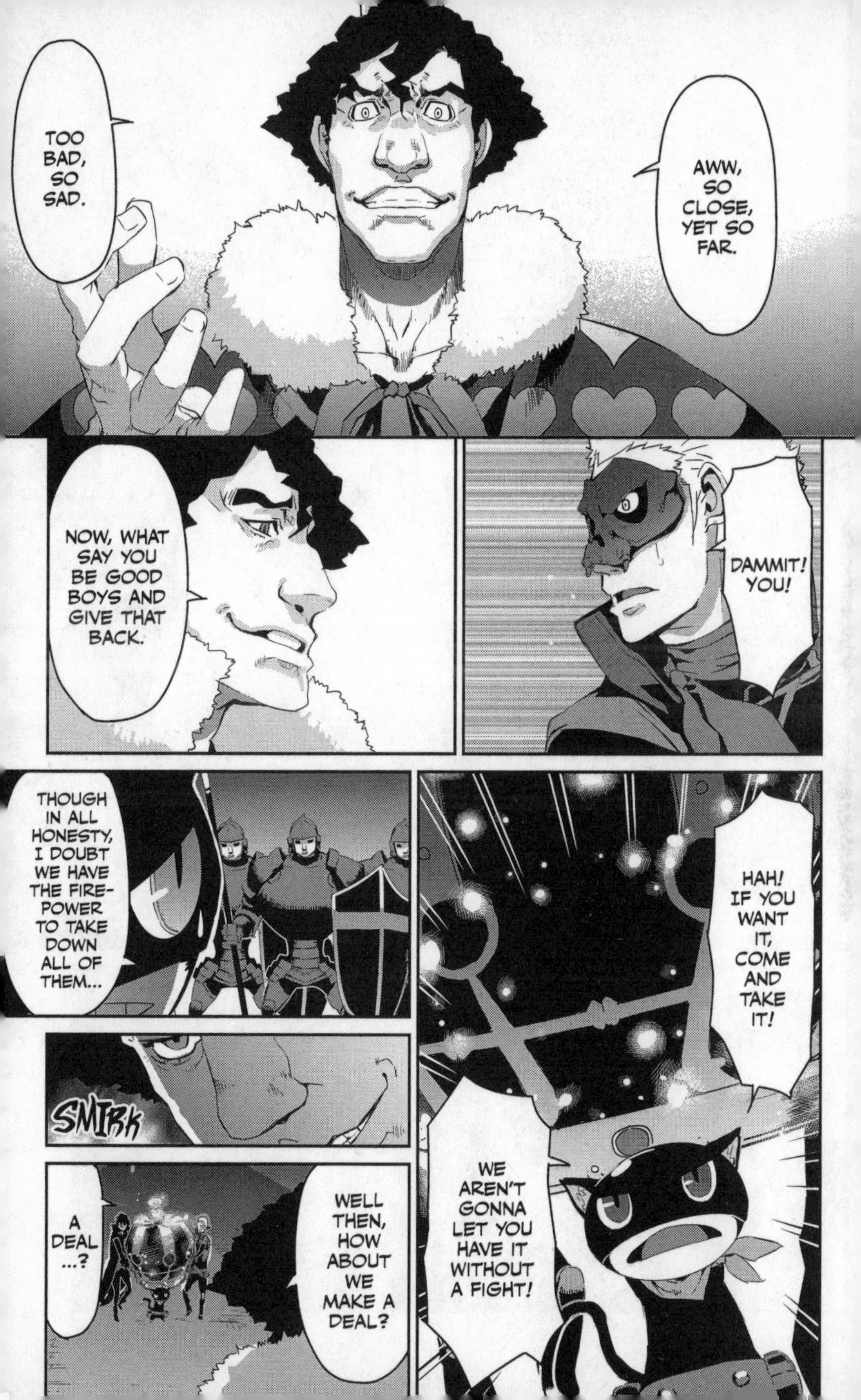
AWW, SO CLOSE, YET SO FAR.
TOO BAD, SO SAD.
DAMMIT! YOU!
NOW, WHAT SAY YOU BE GOOD BOYS AND GIVE THAT BACK.
HAH! IF YOU WANT IT, COME AND TAKE IT!
WE AREN'T GONNA LET YOU HAVE IT WITHOUT A FIGHT!
THOUGH IN ALL HONESTY, I DOUBT WE HAVE THE FIRE-POWER TO TAKE DOWN ALL OF THEM...
SMIRK
WELL THEN, HOW ABOUT WE MAKE A DEAL?
A DEAL ...?

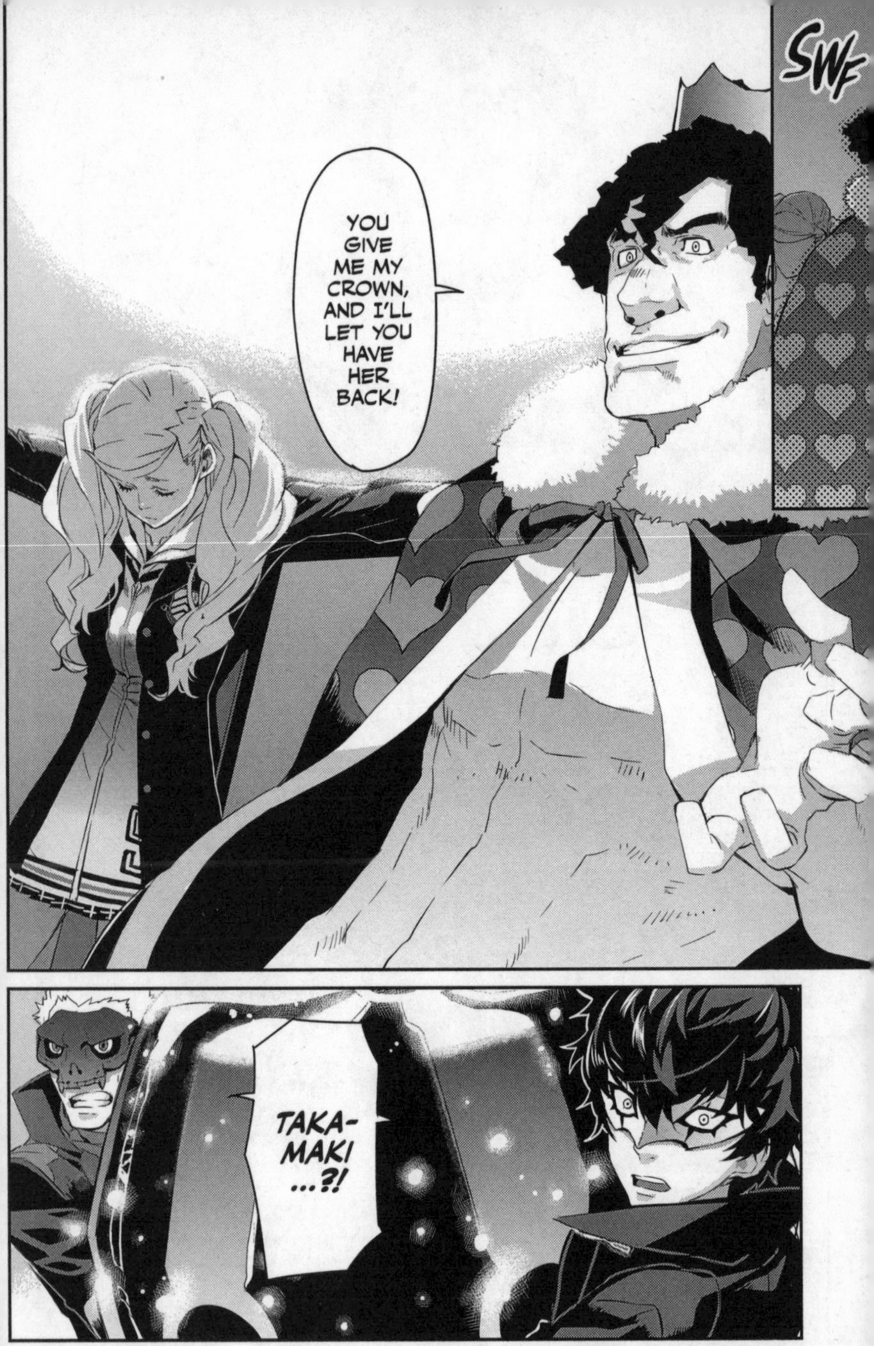
SWF
YOU GIVE ME MY CROWN, AND I'LL LET YOU HAVE HER BACK!
TAKAMAKI ...?!

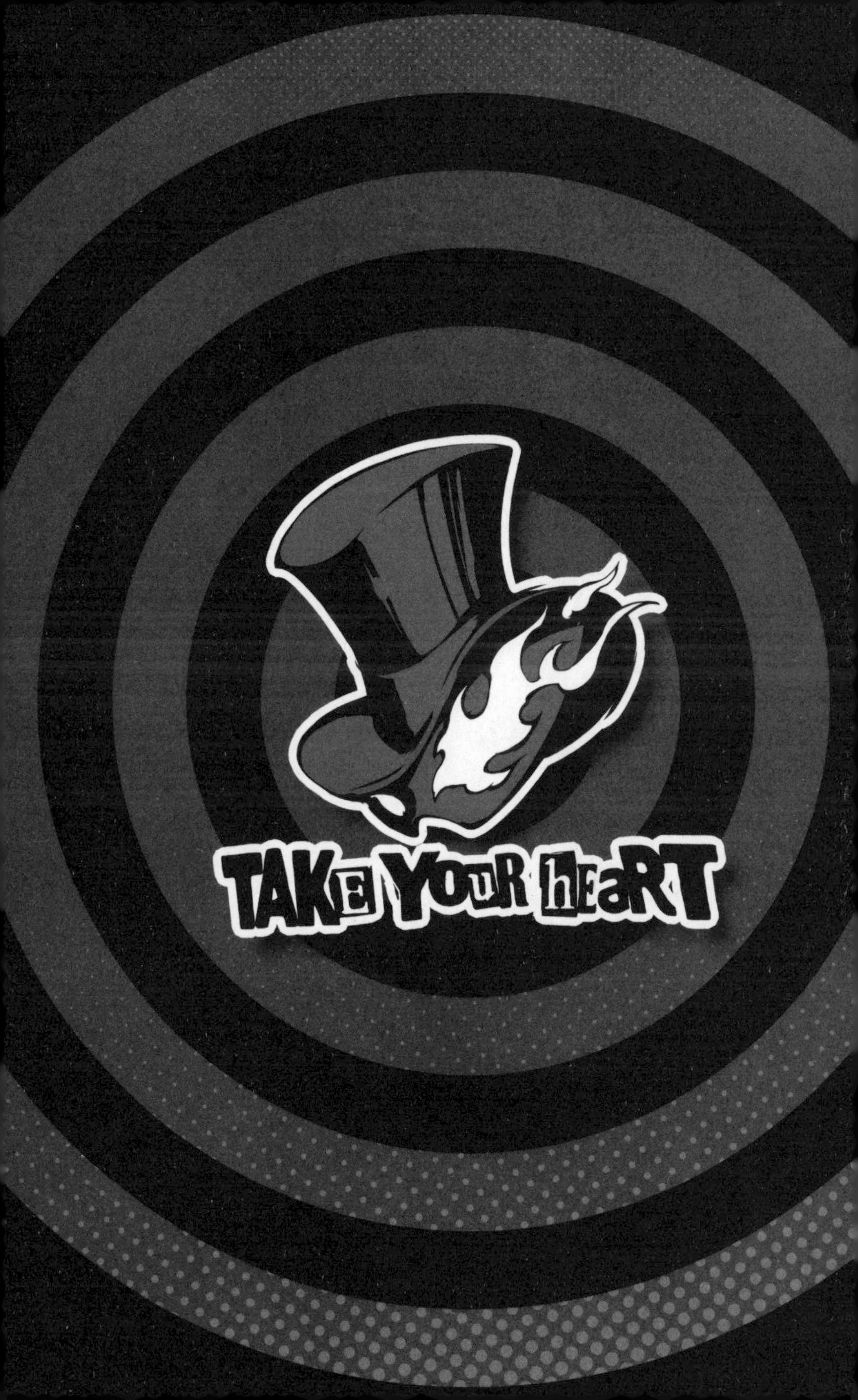
TAKE YOUR HEART

P5
PERSONA5

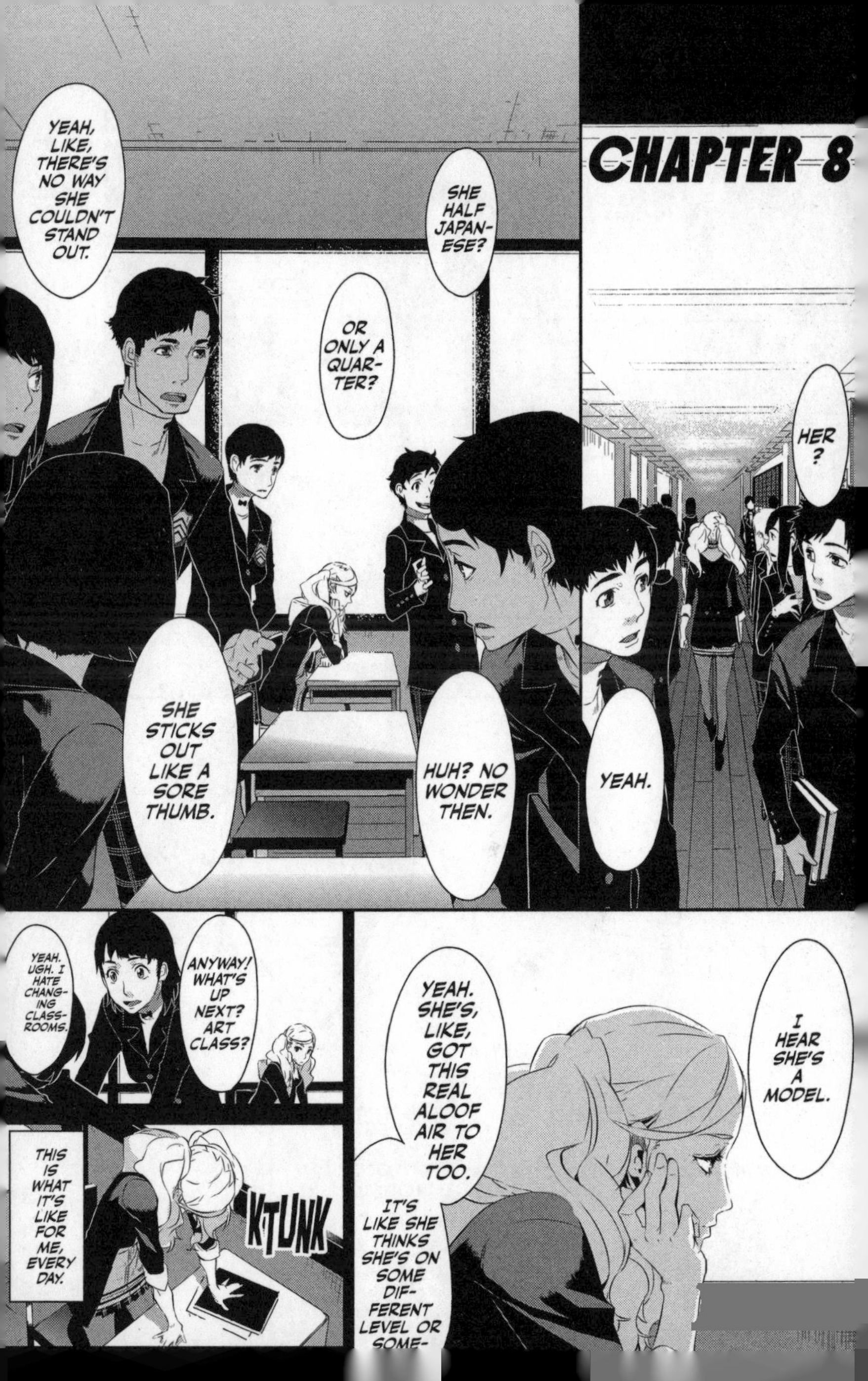
CHAPTER 8
HER?
YEAH.
SHE HALF JAPANESE?
OR ONLY A QUARTER?
YEAH, LIKE, THERE'S NO WAY SHE COULDN'T STAND OUT.
HUH? NO WONDER THEN.
SHE STICKS OUT LIKE A SORE THUMB.
I HEAR SHE'S A MODEL.
YEAH. SHE'S, LIKE, GOT THIS REAL ALOOF AIR TO HER TOO.
IT'S LIKE SHE THINKS SHE'S ON SOME DIFFERENT LEVEL OR SOME-
ANYWAY! WHAT'S UP NEXT? ART CLASS?
YEAH. UGH. I HATE CHANGING CLASSROOMS.
K-TUNK
THIS IS WHAT IT'S LIKE FOR ME, EVERY DAY.

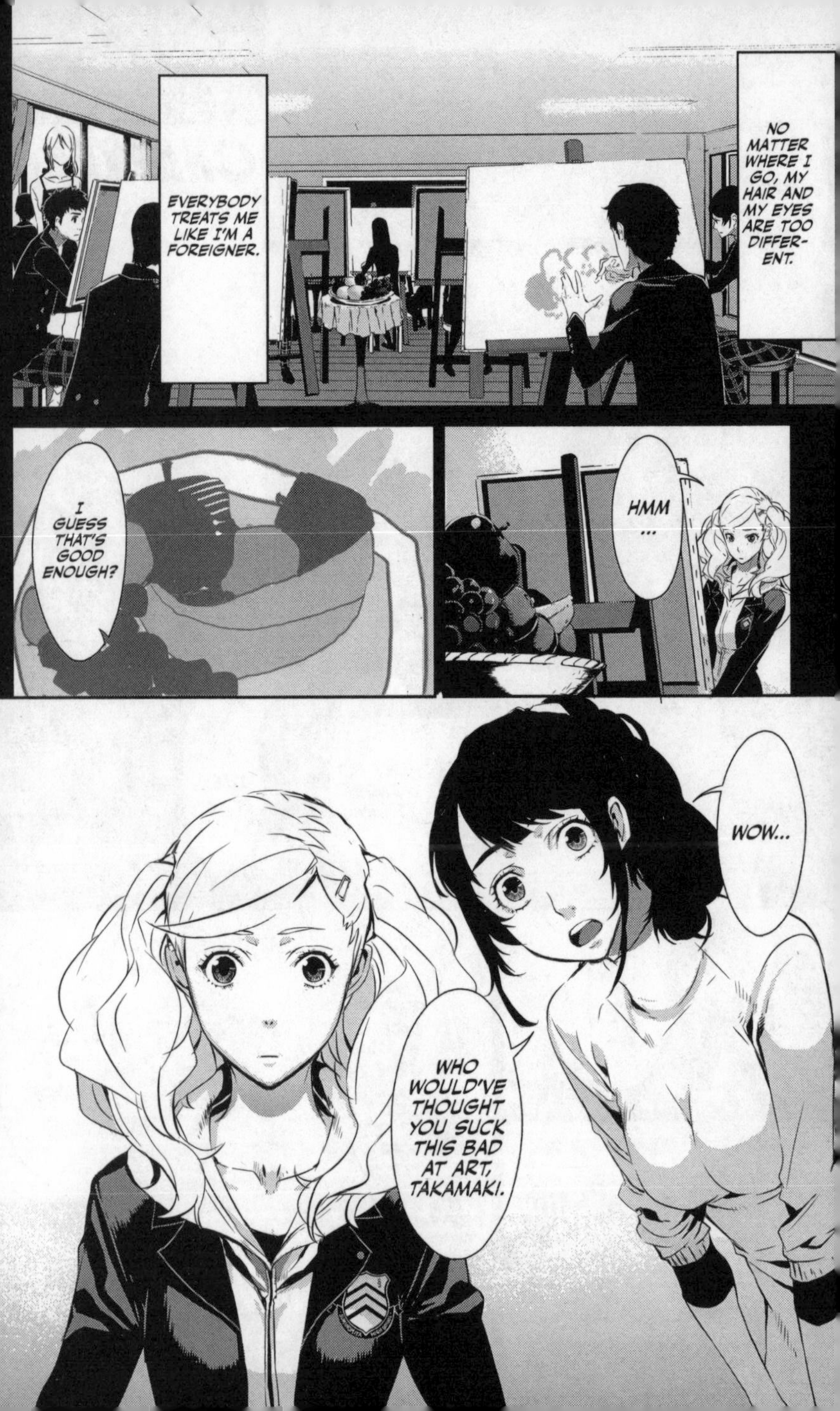
NO MATTER WHERE I GO, MY HAIR AND MY EYES ARE TOO DIFFERENT.
EVERYBODY TREATS ME LIKE I'M A FOREIGNER.
HMM...
I GUESS THAT'S GOOD ENOUGH?
WOW...
WHO WOULD'VE THOUGHT YOU SUCK THIS BAD AT ART, TAKAMAKI.

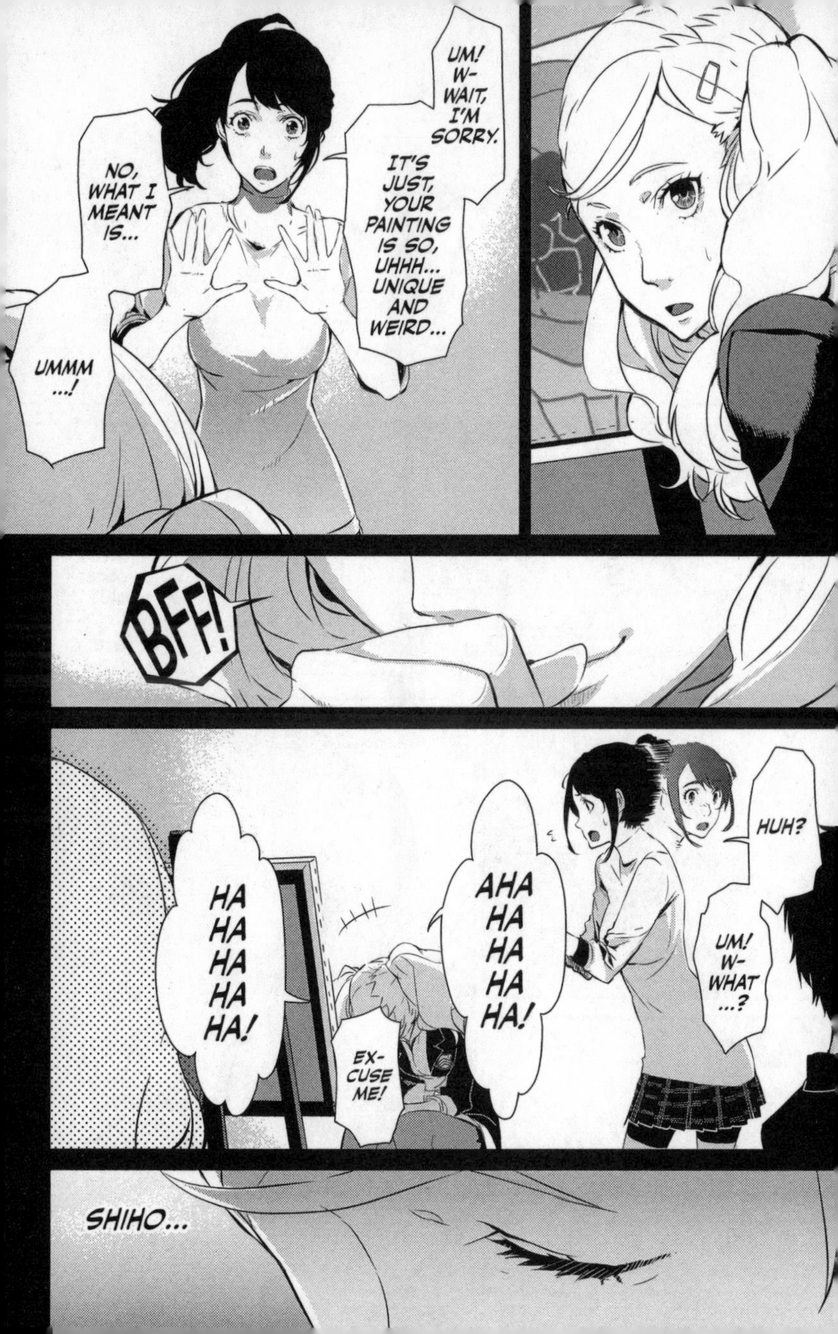
UM! W-WAIT, I'M SORRY.
IT'S JUST, YOUR PAINTING IS SO, UHHH... UNIQUE AND WEIRD...
NO, WHAT I MEANT IS...
UMMM ...!
BFF!
HUH?
UM! W-WHAT ...?
AHA HA HA HA HA!
EX-CUSE ME!
HA HA HA HA HA!
SHIHO...

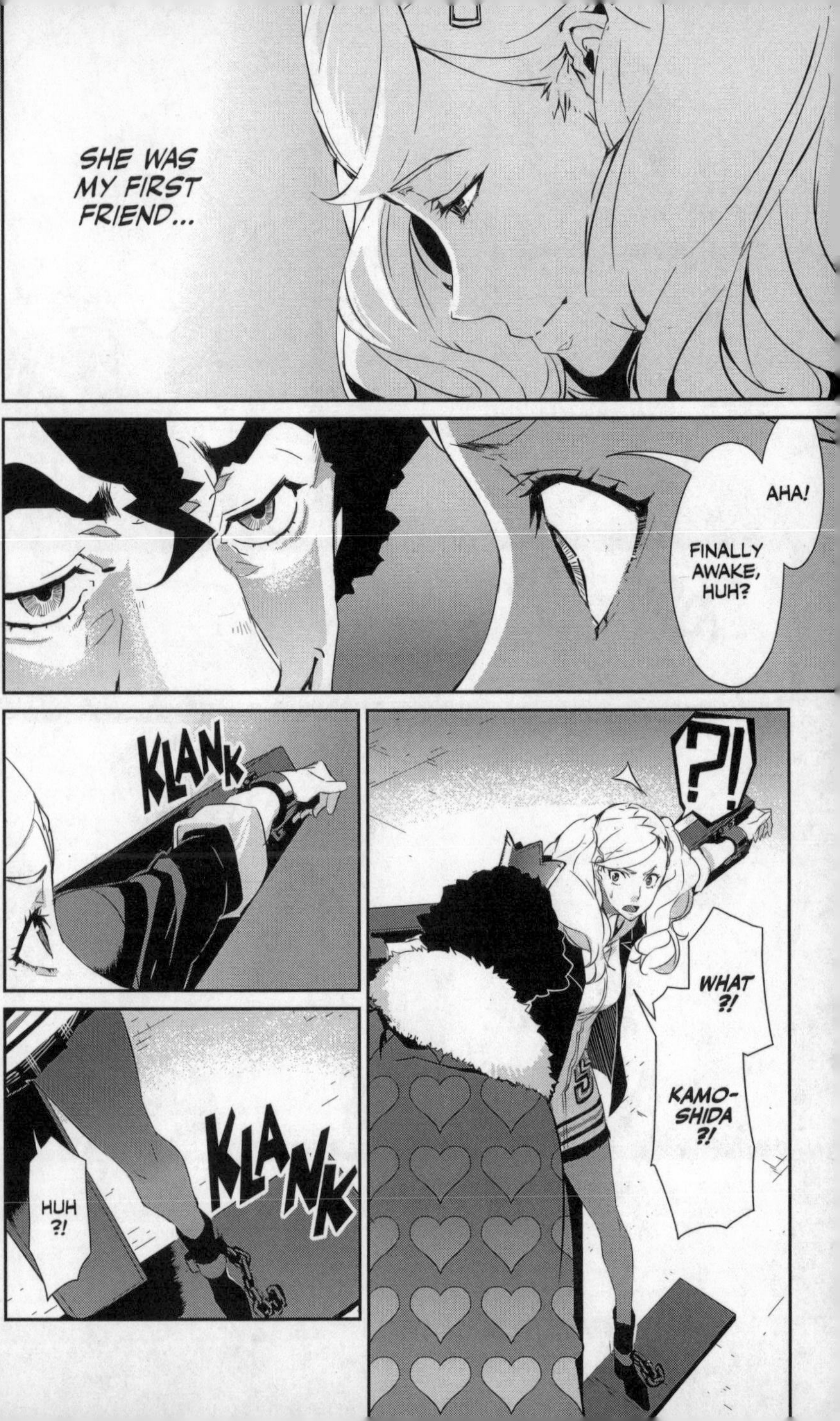
SHE WAS MY FIRST FRIEND...
AHA!
FINALLY AWAKE, HUH?
?!
WHAT?!
KAMO-SHIDA?!
KLANK
KLANK
HUH?!

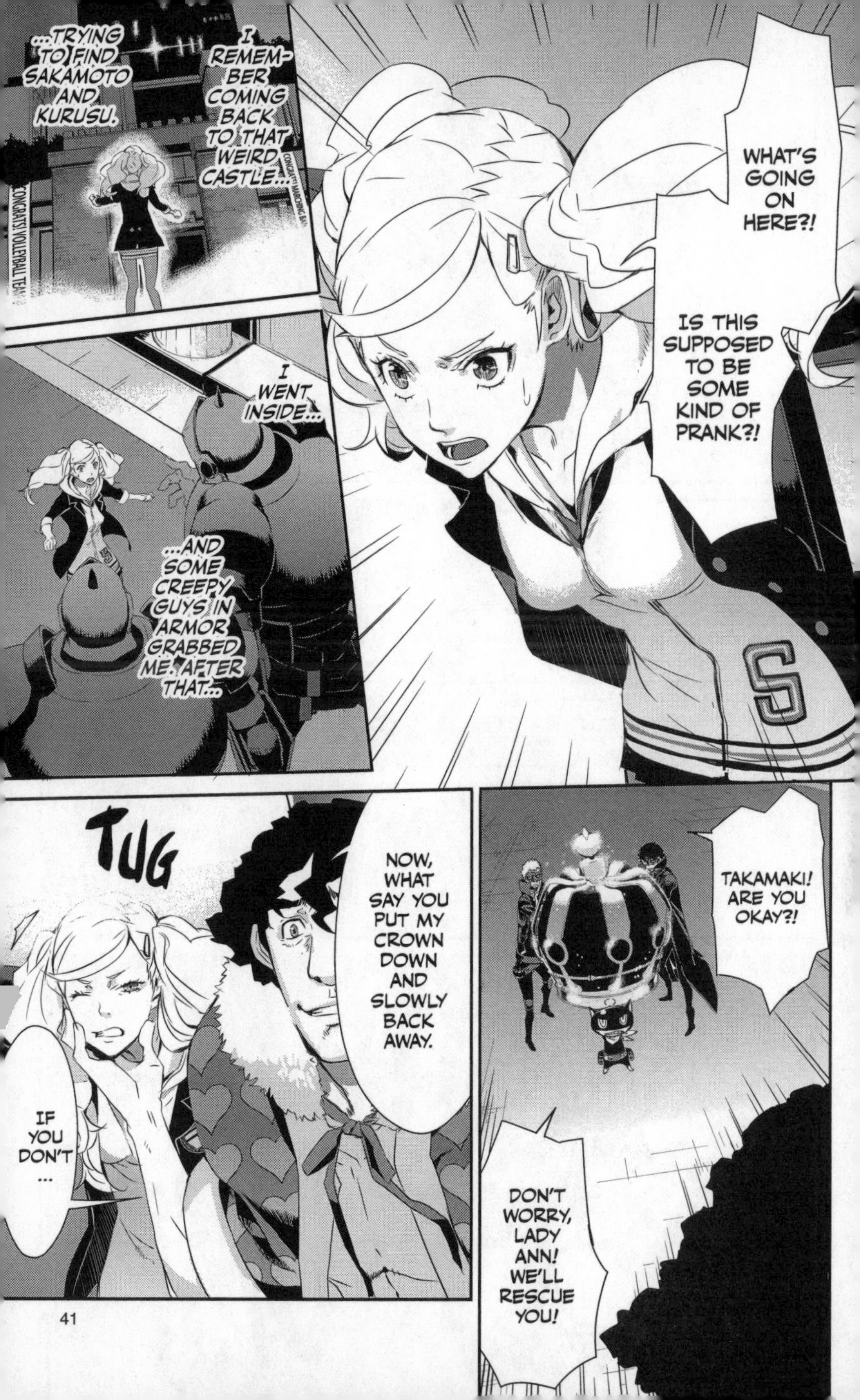
WHAT'S GOING ON HERE?!
IS THIS SUPPOSED TO BE SOME KIND OF PRANK?!
I REMEMBER COMING BACK TO THAT WEIRD CASTLE...
...TRYING TO FIND SAKAMOTO AND KURUSU.
CONGRATS! VOLLEYBALL TEAM
I WENT INSIDE...
...AND SOME CREEPY GUYS IN ARMOR GRABBED ME. AFTER THAT...
TAKAMAKI! ARE YOU OKAY?!
DON'T WORRY, LADY ANN! WE'LL RESCUE YOU!
NOW, WHAT SAY YOU PUT MY CROWN DOWN AND SLOWLY BACK AWAY.
TUG
IF YOU DON'T...

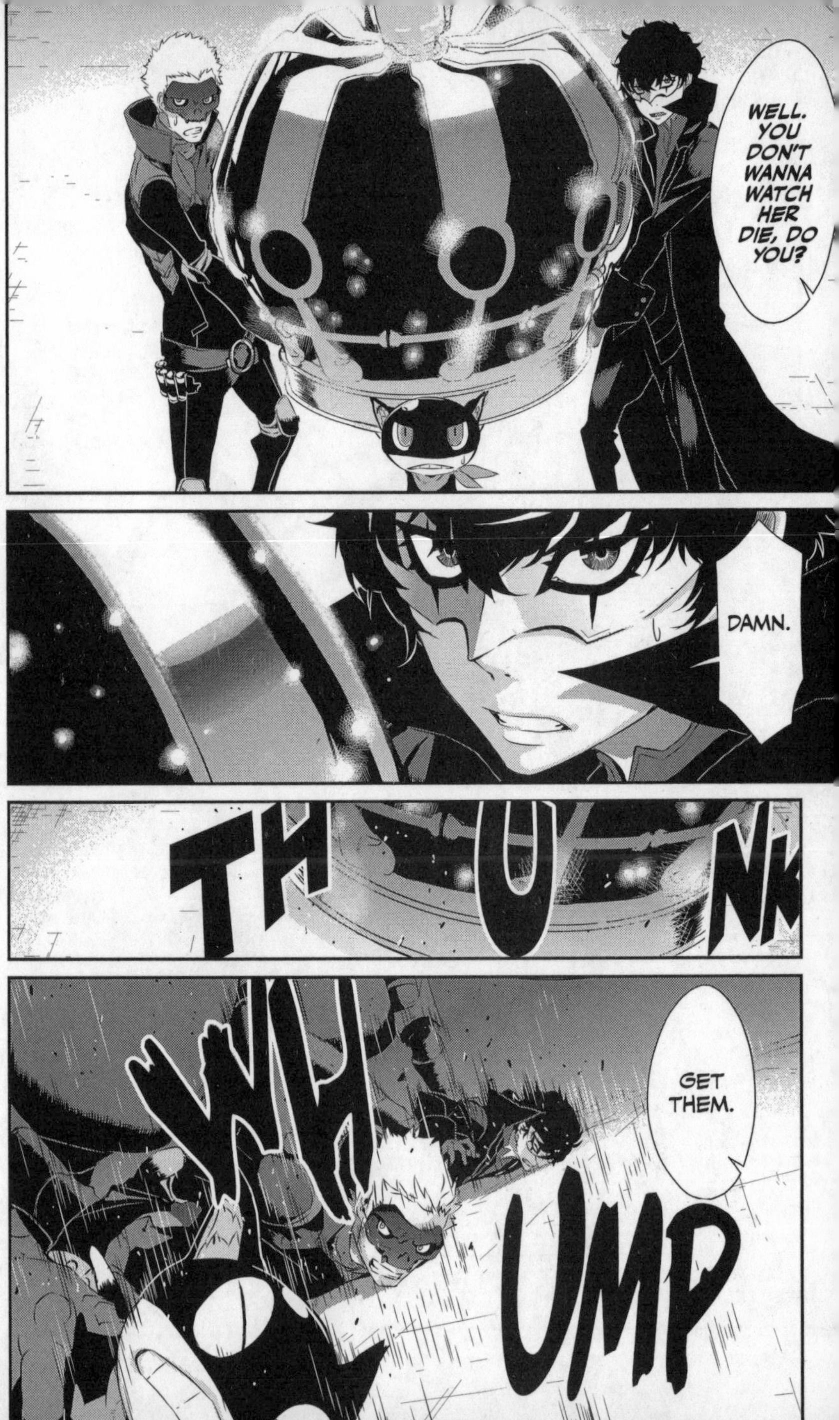
WELL. YOU DON'T WANNA WATCH HER DIE, DO YOU?
DAMN.
THUNK
GET THEM.
WHUMP

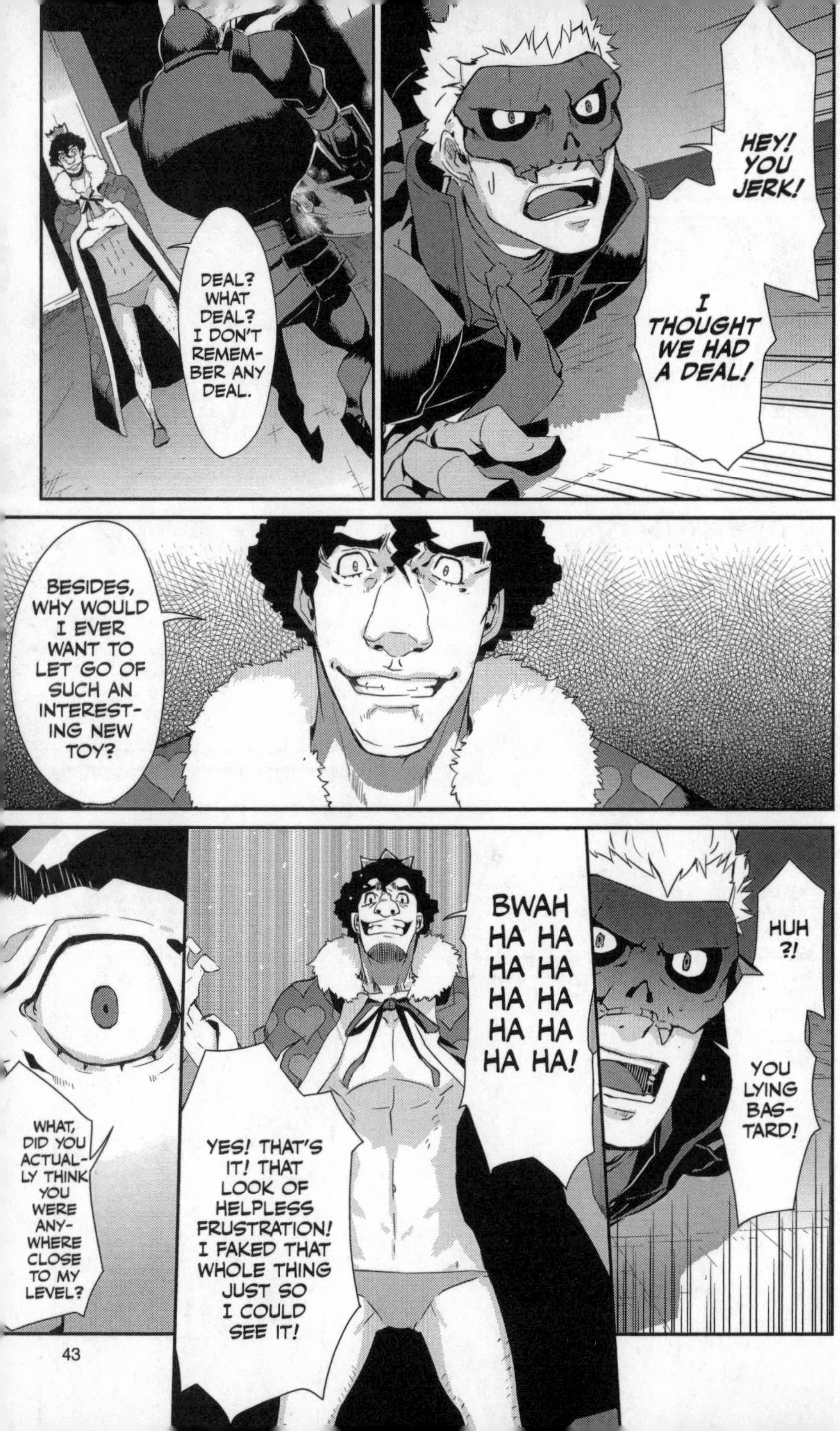
HEY! YOU JERK!
I THOUGHT WE HAD A DEAL!
DEAL? WHAT DEAL? I DON'T REMEMBER ANY DEAL.
BESIDES, WHY WOULD I EVER WANT TO LET GO OF SUCH AN INTERESTING NEW TOY?
HUH?!
YOU LYING BASTARD!
BWAH HA HA HA HA HA HA HA HA HA HA!
YES! THAT'S IT! THAT LOOK OF HELPLESS FRUSTRATION! I FAKED THAT WHOLE THING JUST SO I COULD SEE IT!
WHAT, DID YOU ACTUALLY THINK YOU WERE ANYWHERE CLOSE TO MY LEVEL?

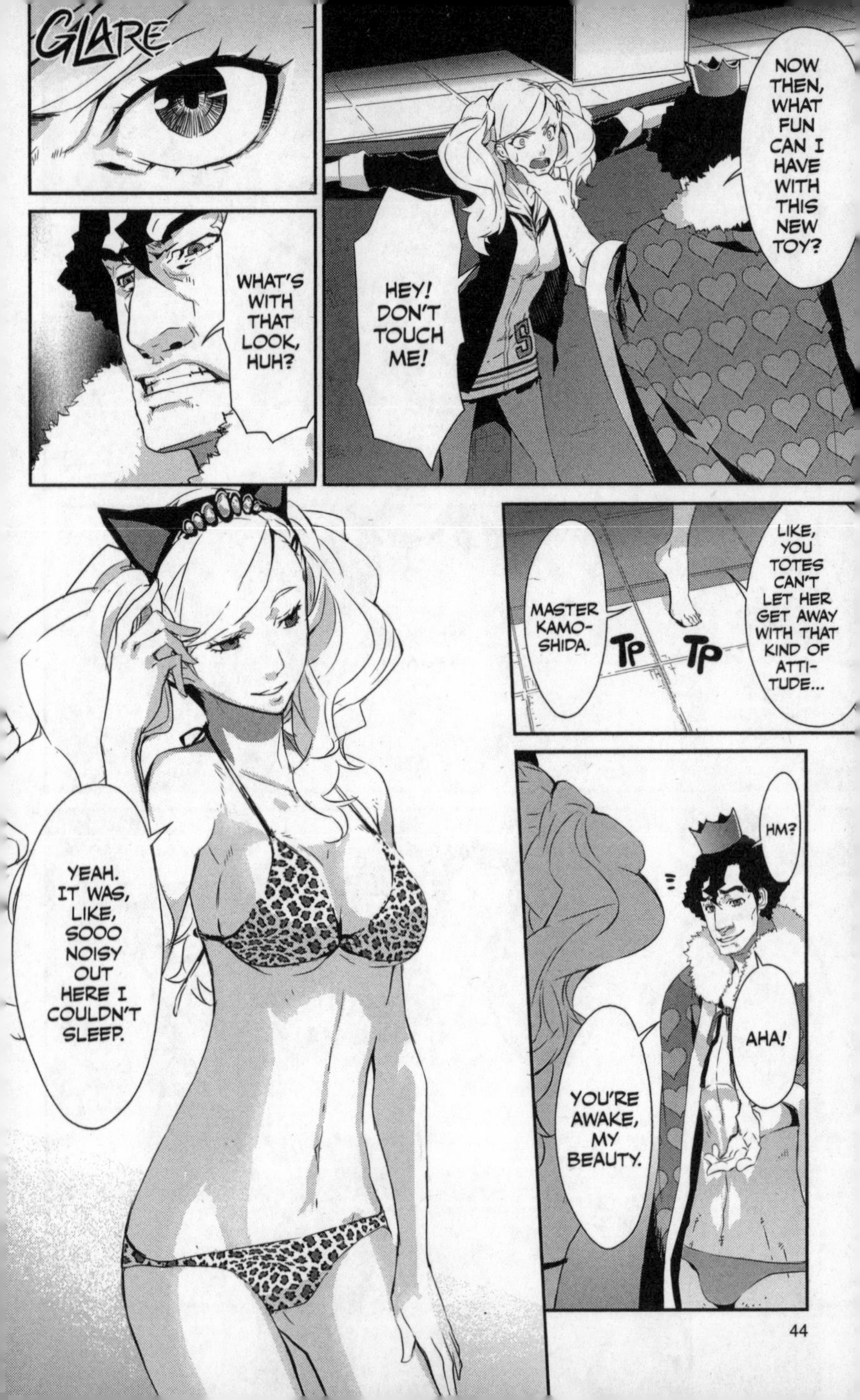
NOW THEN, WHAT FUN CAN I HAVE WITH THIS NEW TOY?
HEY! DON'T TOUCH ME!
GLARE
WHAT'S WITH THAT LOOK, HUH?
LIKE, YOU TOTES CAN'T LET HER GET AWAY WITH THAT KIND OF ATTITUDE...
MASTER KAMOSHIDA.
TP TP
HM?
AHA!
YOU'RE AWAKE, MY BEAUTY.
YEAH. IT WAS, LIKE, SOOO NOISY OUT HERE I COULDN'T SLEEP.

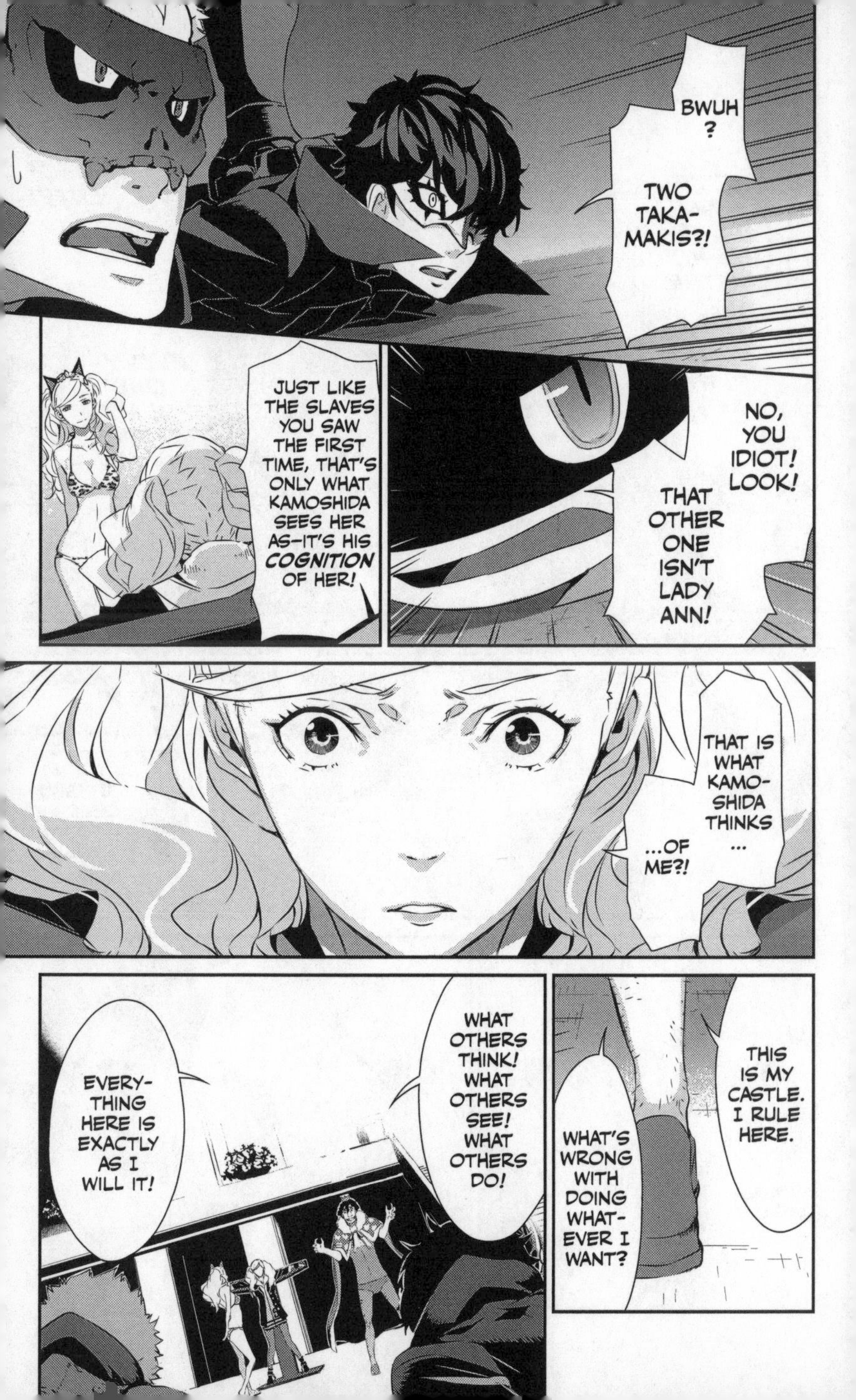
BWUH?
TWO TAKAMAKIS?!
NO, YOU IDIOT! LOOK!
THAT OTHER ONE ISN'T LADY ANN!
JUST LIKE THE SLAVES YOU SAW THE FIRST TIME, THAT'S ONLY WHAT KAMOSHIDA SEES HER AS—IT'S HIS *COGNITION* OF HER!
THAT IS WHAT KAMOSHIDA THINKS ...
...OF ME?!
THIS IS MY CASTLE. I RULE HERE.
WHAT'S WRONG WITH DOING WHATEVER I WANT?
WHAT OTHERS THINK! WHAT OTHERS SEE! WHAT OTHERS DO!
EVERYTHING HERE IS EXACTLY AS I WILL IT!

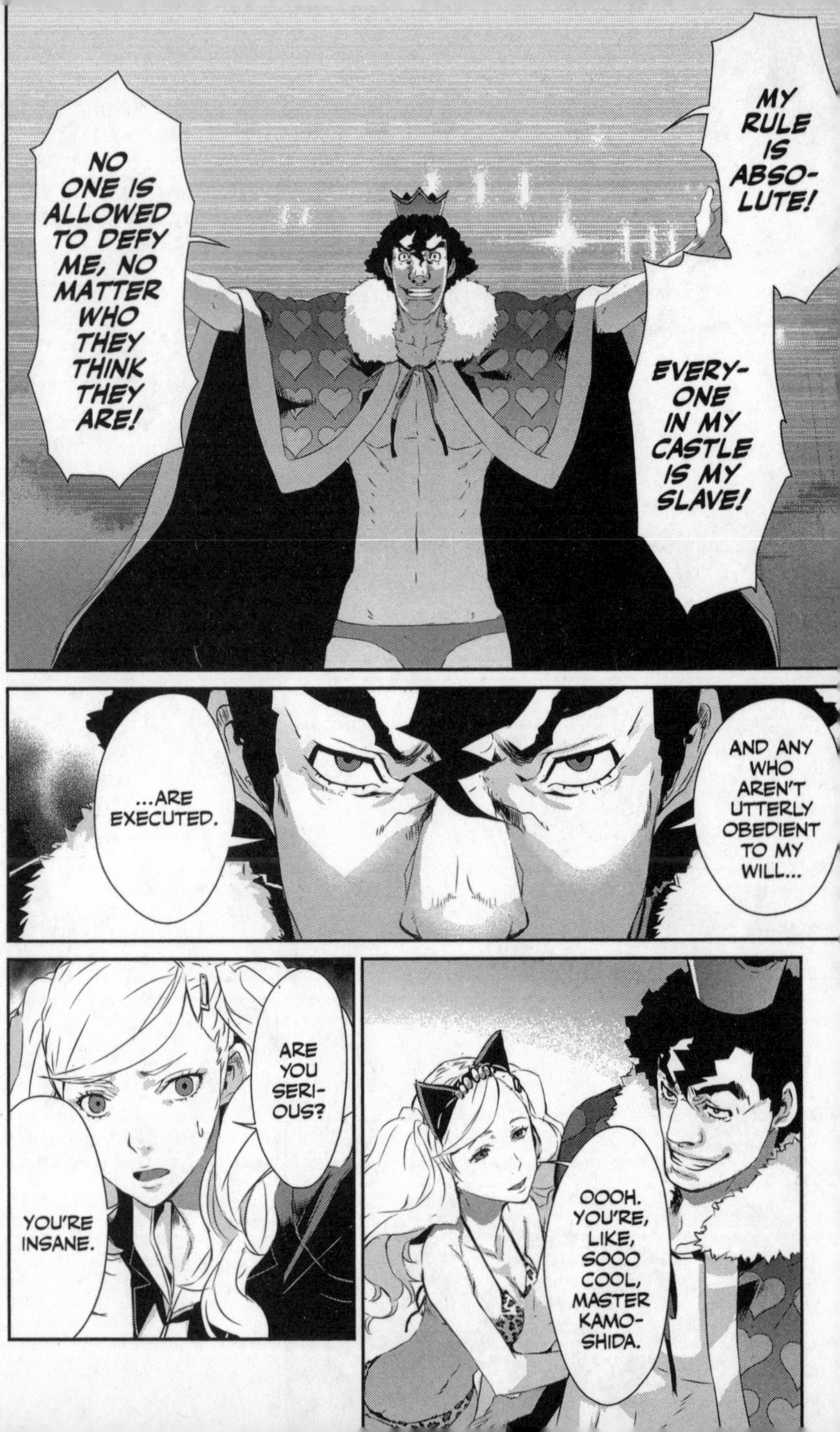
MY RULE IS ABSOLUTE!
EVERYONE IN MY CASTLE IS MY SLAVE!
NO ONE IS ALLOWED TO DEFY ME, NO MATTER WHO THEY THINK THEY ARE!
AND ANY WHO AREN'T UTTERLY OBEDIENT TO MY WILL...
...ARE EXECUTED.
OOOH. YOU'RE, LIKE, SOOO COOL, MASTER KAMOSHIDA.
ARE YOU SERIOUS?
YOU'RE INSANE.

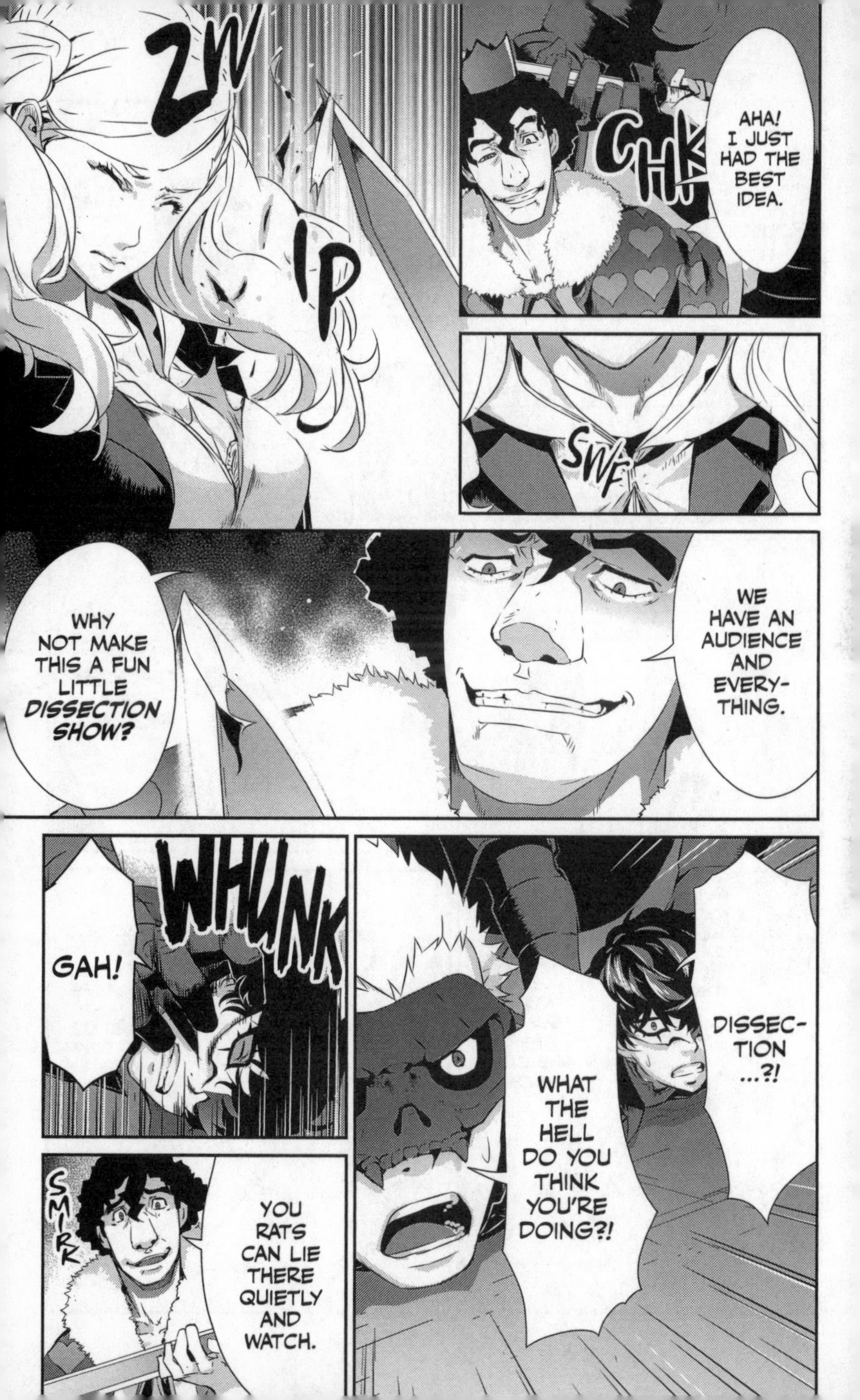
AHA! I JUST HAD THE BEST IDEA.
CHK
SWF
ZW
IP
WE HAVE AN AUDIENCE AND EVERY-THING.
WHY NOT MAKE THIS A FUN LITTLE *DISSECTION* SHOW?
DISSEC-TION ...?!
WHAT THE HELL DO YOU THINK YOU'RE DOING?!
WHUNK
GAH!
SMIRK
YOU RATS CAN LIE THERE QUIETLY AND WATCH.

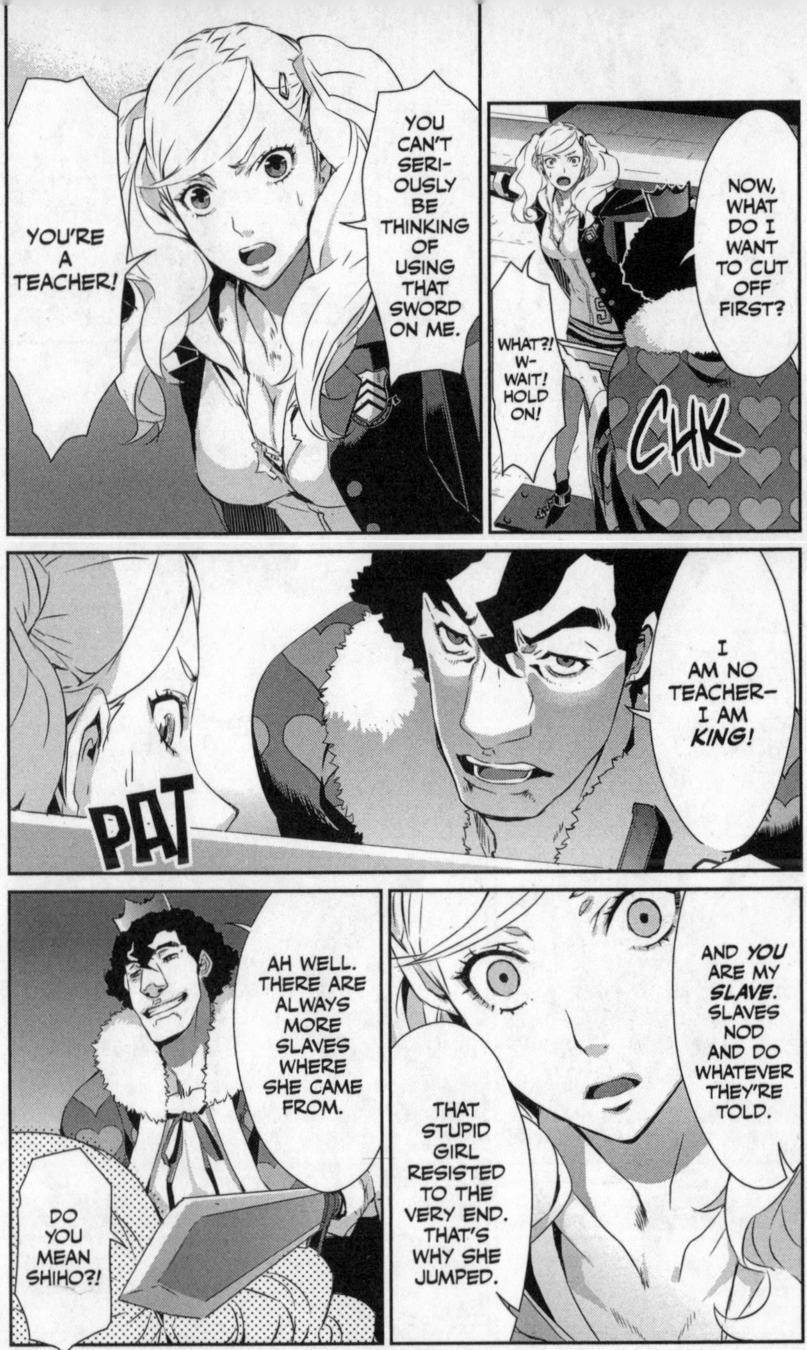
NOW, WHAT DO I WANT TO CUT OFF FIRST?
CHK
WHAT?! W-WAIT! HOLD ON!
YOU CAN'T SERIOUSLY BE THINKING OF USING THAT SWORD ON ME.
YOU'RE A TEACHER!
I AM NO TEACHER— I AM *KING*!
PAT
AND *YOU* ARE MY *SLAVE*. SLAVES NOD AND DO WHATEVER THEY'RE TOLD.
THAT STUPID GIRL RESISTED TO THE VERY END. THAT'S WHY SHE JUMPED.
AH WELL. THERE ARE ALWAYS MORE SLAVES WHERE SHE CAME FROM.
DO YOU MEAN SHIHO?!

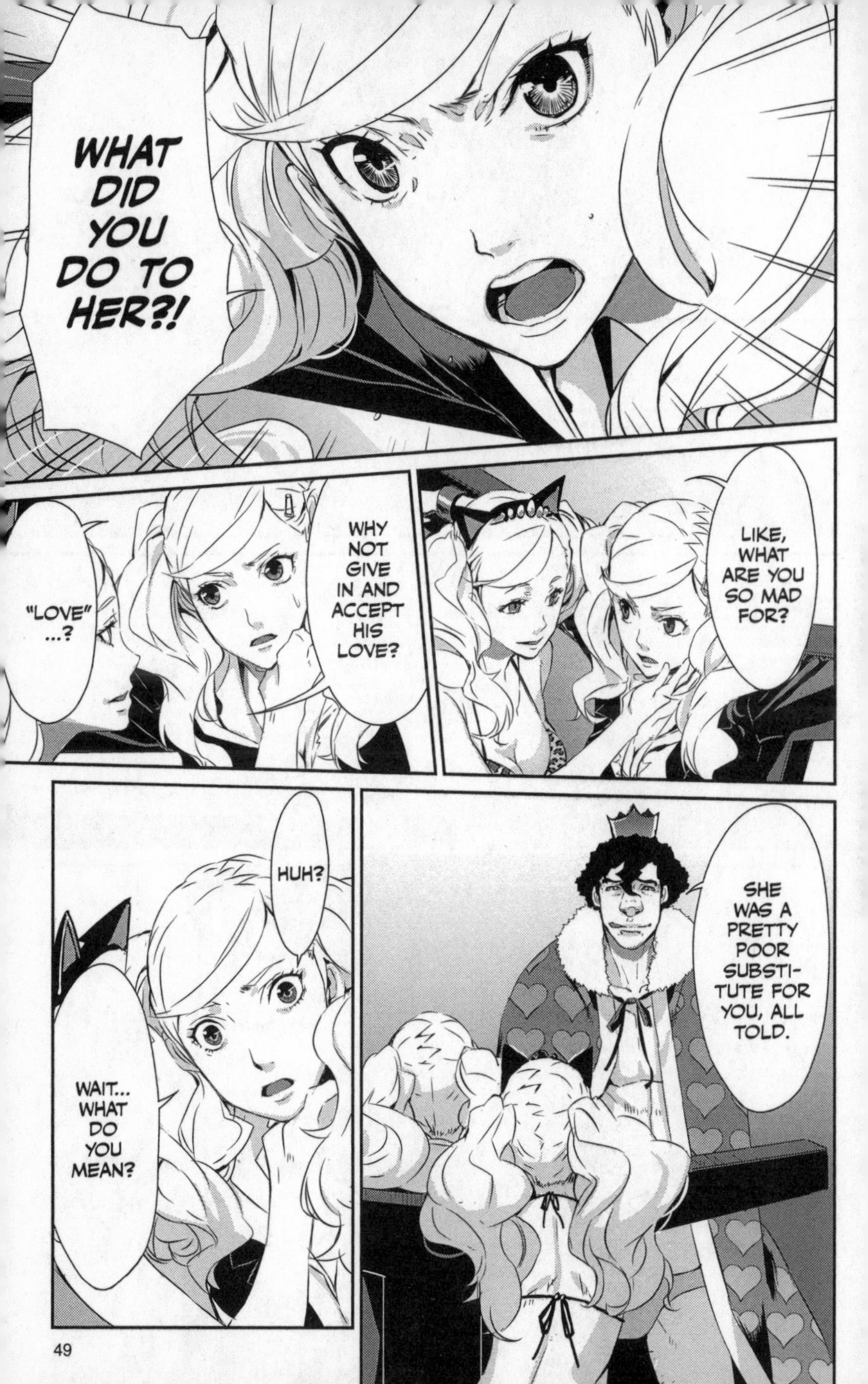
WHAT DID YOU DO TO HER?!
LIKE, WHAT ARE YOU SO MAD FOR?
WHY NOT GIVE IN AND ACCEPT HIS LOVE?
"LOVE" ...?
SHE WAS A PRETTY POOR SUBSTI-TUTE FOR YOU, ALL TOLD.
HUH?
WAIT... WHAT DO YOU MEAN?

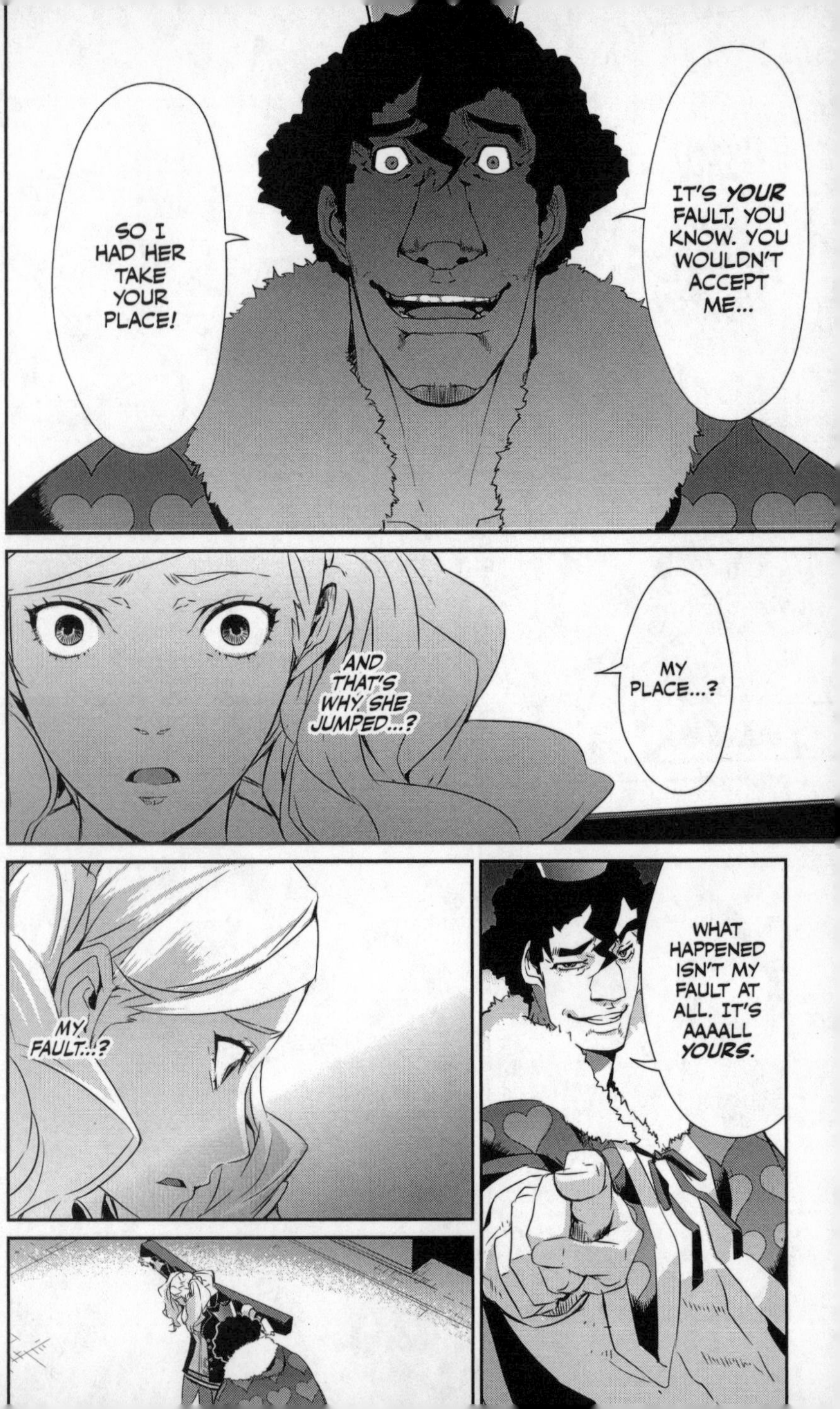
IT'S *YOUR* FAULT, YOU KNOW. YOU WOULDN'T ACCEPT ME...
SO I HAD HER TAKE YOUR PLACE!
MY PLACE...?
AND THAT'S WHY SHE JUMPED...?
WHAT HAPPENED ISN'T MY FAULT AT ALL. IT'S AAAALL *YOURS*.
MY FAULT...?

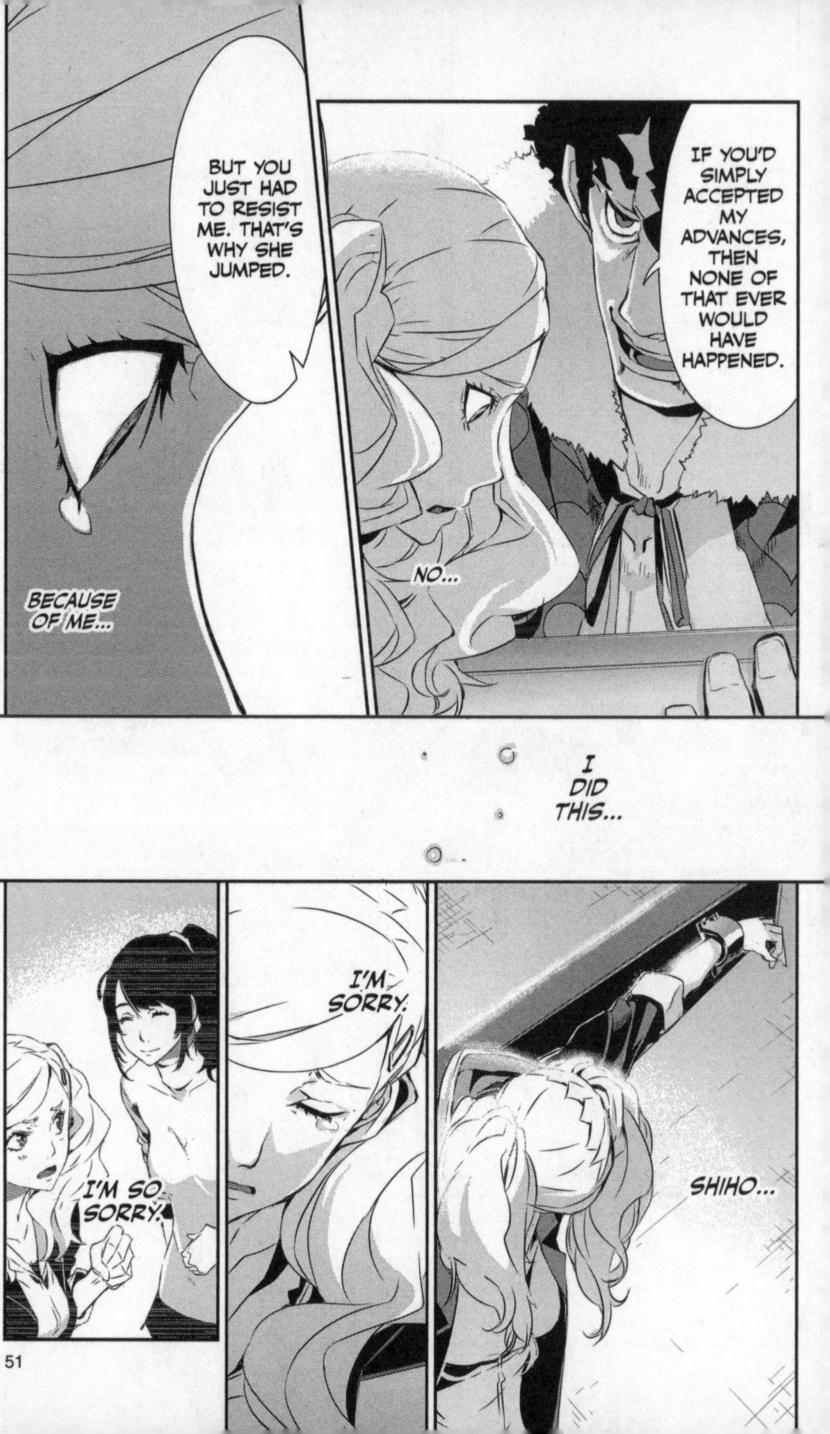
IF YOU'D SIMPLY ACCEPTED MY ADVANCES, THEN NONE OF THAT EVER WOULD HAVE HAPPENED.
NO...
BUT YOU JUST HAD TO RESIST ME. THAT'S WHY SHE JUMPED.
BECAUSE OF ME...
I DID THIS...
SHIHO...
I'M SORRY.
I'M SO SORRY.

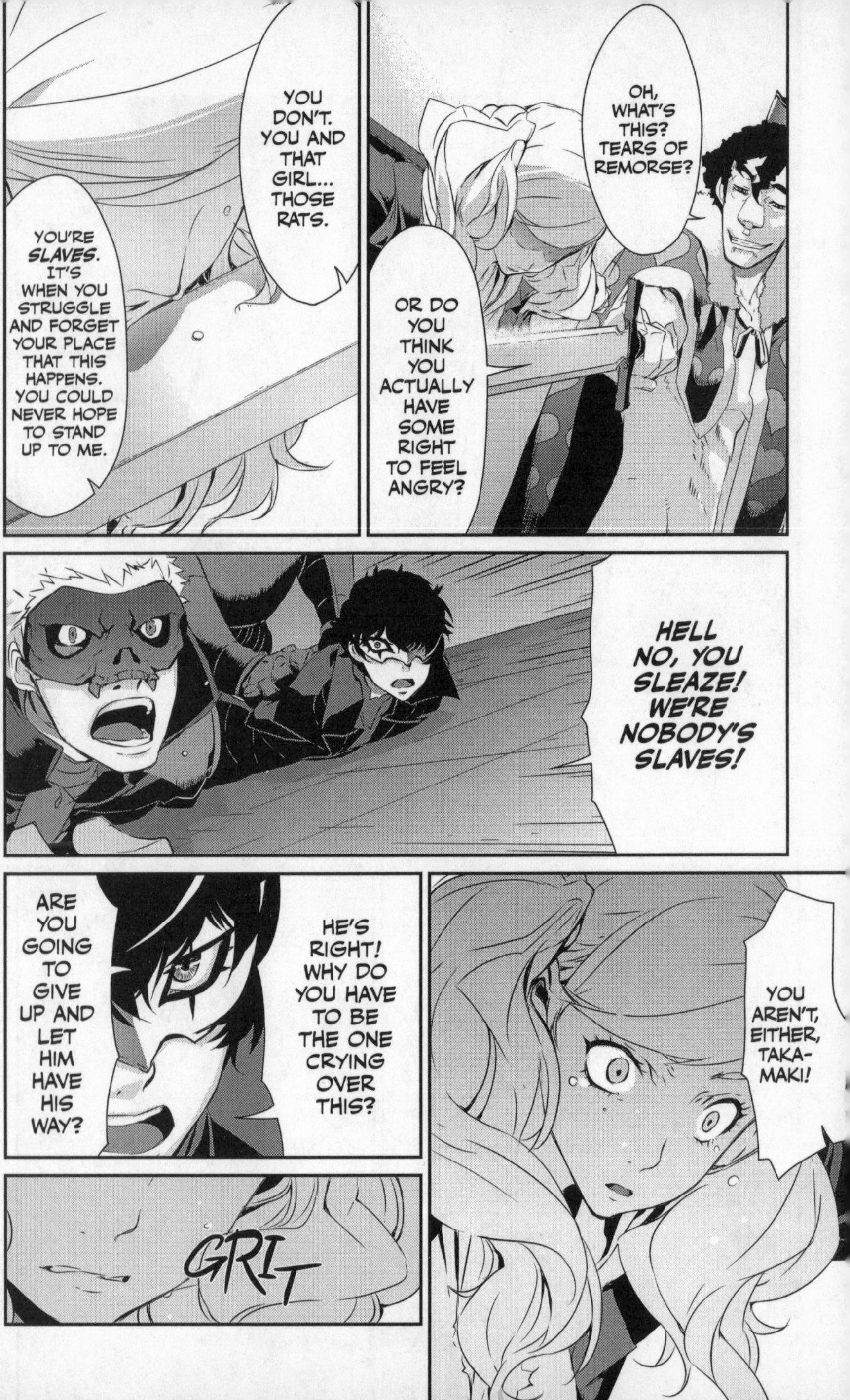
OH, WHAT'S THIS? TEARS OF REMORSE?
OR DO YOU THINK YOU ACTUALLY HAVE SOME RIGHT TO FEEL ANGRY?
YOU DON'T. YOU AND THAT GIRL... THOSE RATS.
YOU'RE *SLAVES*. IT'S WHEN YOU STRUGGLE AND FORGET YOUR PLACE THAT THIS HAPPENS. YOU COULD NEVER HOPE TO STAND UP TO ME.
HELL NO, YOU SLEAZE! WE'RE NOBODY'S SLAVES!
YOU AREN'T, EITHER, TAKAMAKI!
HE'S RIGHT! WHY DO YOU HAVE TO BE THE ONE CRYING OVER THIS?
ARE YOU GOING TO GIVE UP AND LET HIM HAVE HIS WAY?
GRIT

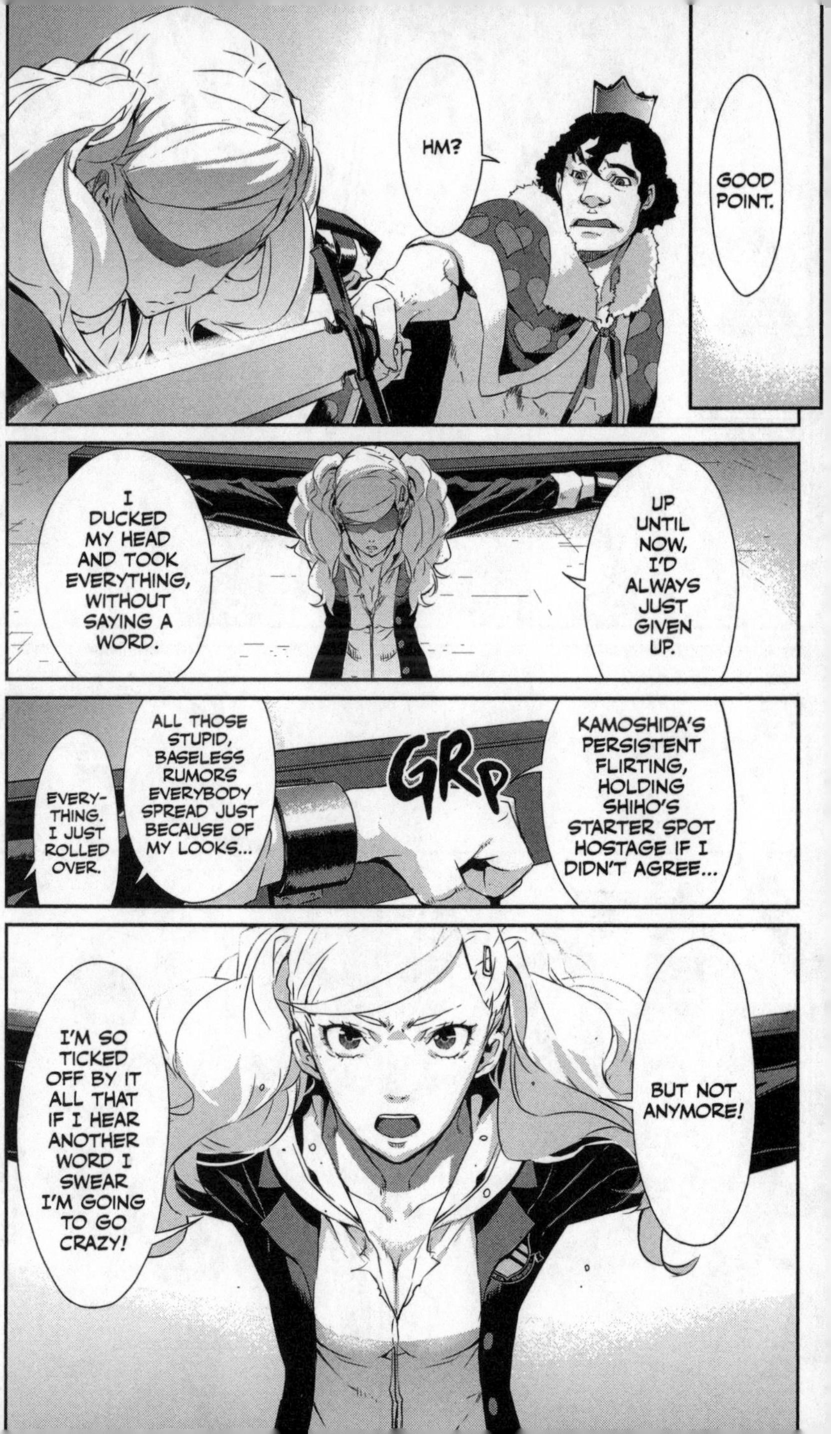
GOOD POINT.
HM?
UP UNTIL NOW, I'D ALWAYS JUST GIVEN UP.
I DUCKED MY HEAD AND TOOK EVERYTHING, WITHOUT SAYING A WORD.
KAMOSHIDA'S PERSISTENT FLIRTING, HOLDING SHIHO'S STARTER SPOT HOSTAGE IF I DIDN'T AGREE...
GRP
ALL THOSE STUPID, BASELESS RUMORS EVERYBODY SPREAD JUST BECAUSE OF MY LOOKS...
EVERY-THING. I JUST ROLLED OVER.
BUT NOT ANYMORE!
I'M SO TICKED OFF BY IT ALL THAT IF I HEAR ANOTHER WORD I SWEAR I'M GOING TO GO CRAZY!

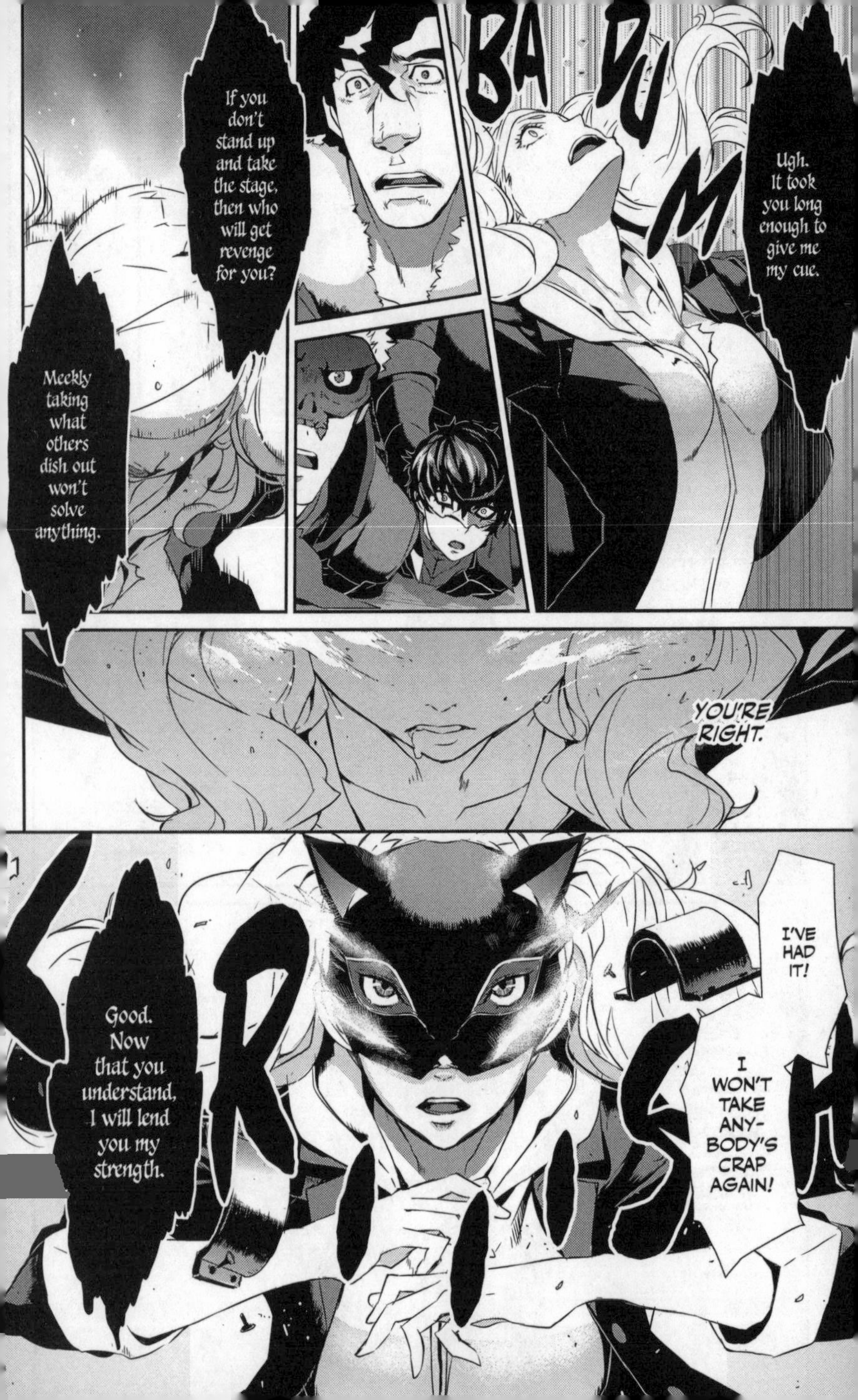
BA DUM
Ugh. It took you long enough to give me my cue.
If you don't stand up and take the stage, then who will get revenge for you?
Meekly taking what others dish out won't solve anything.
YOU'RE RIGHT.
I'VE HAD IT!
I WON'T TAKE ANY-BODY'S CRAP AGAIN!
Good. Now that you understand, I will lend you my strength.

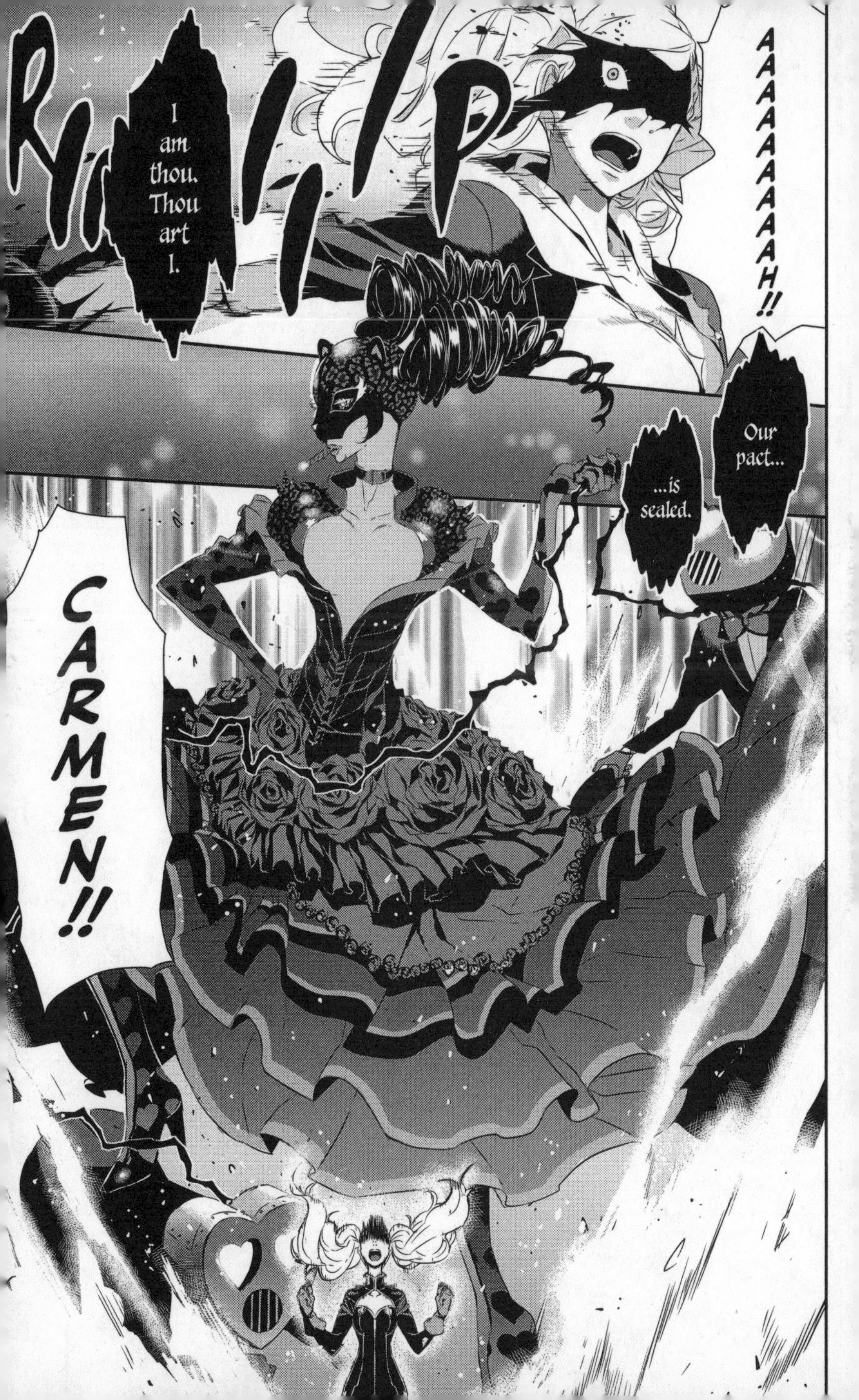
AAAAAAAAAAAH!!
I am thou. Thou art I.
Our pact...
...is sealed.
CARMEN!!

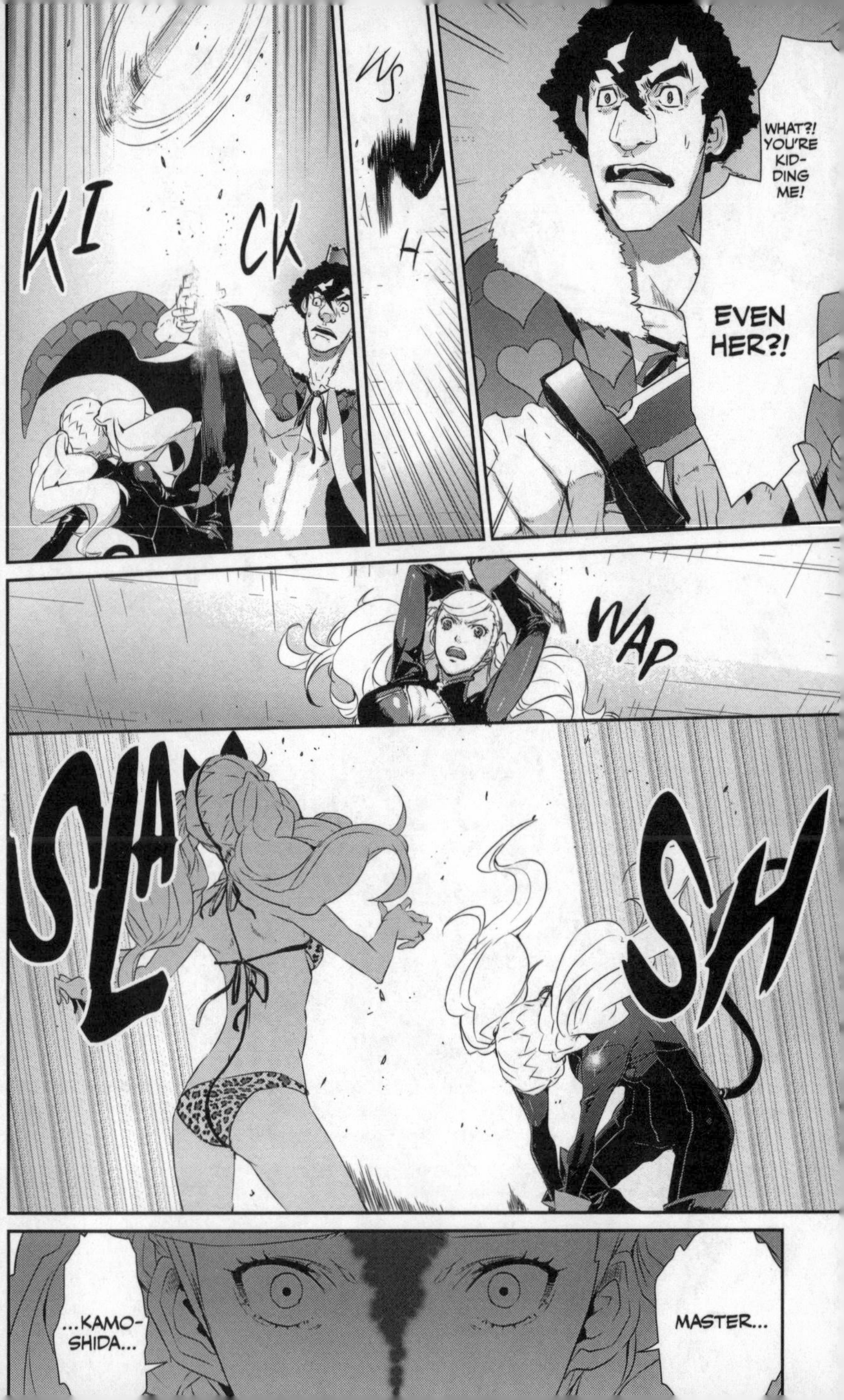
WHAT?! YOU'RE KID-DING ME!
EVEN HER?!
KICK
WAP
SLASH
MASTER...
...KAMO-SHIDA...

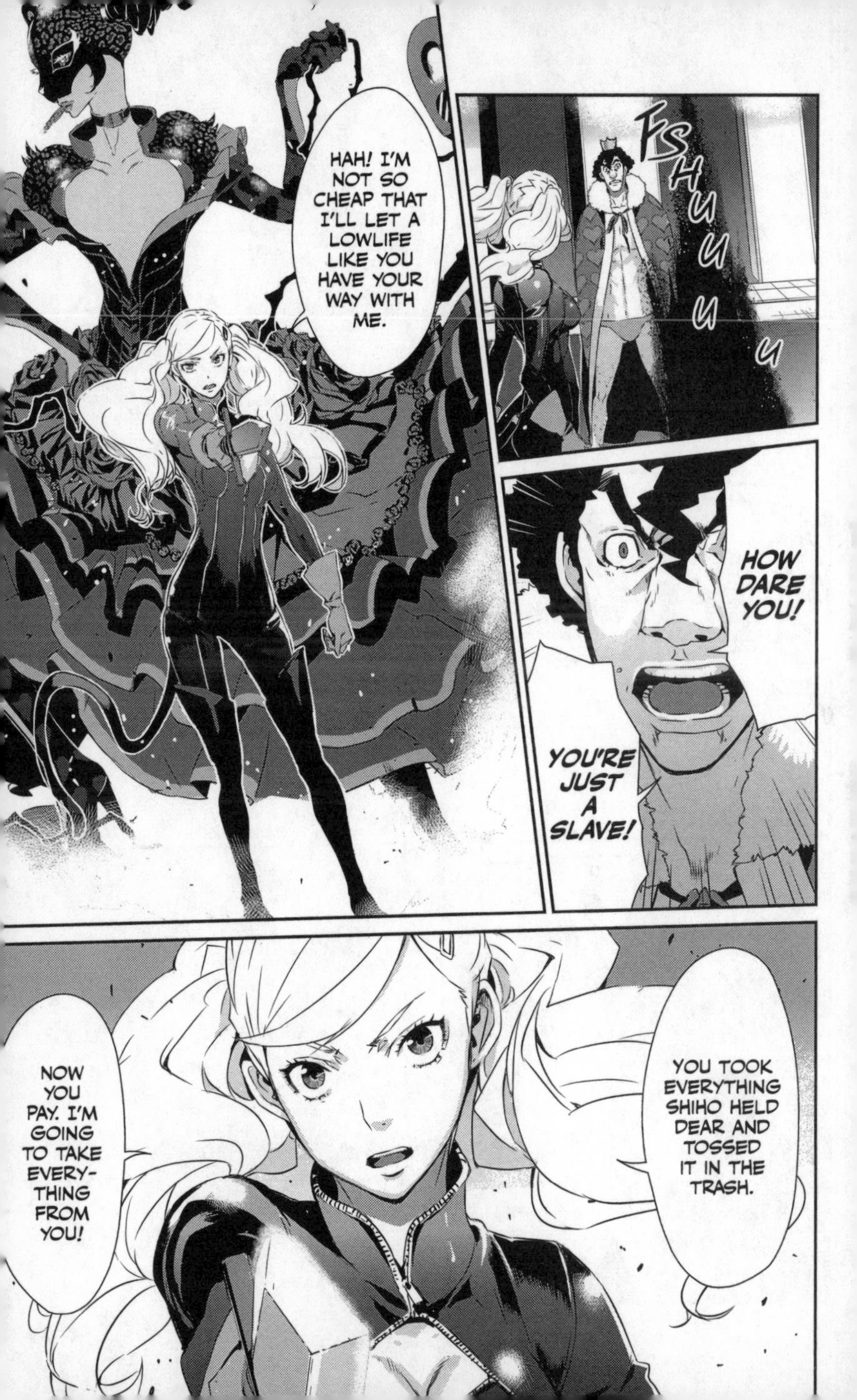
FSHUUUUU
HOW DARE YOU!
YOU'RE JUST A SLAVE!
HAH! I'M NOT SO CHEAP THAT I'LL LET A LOWLIFE LIKE YOU HAVE YOUR WAY WITH ME.
YOU TOOK EVERYTHING SHIHO HELD DEAR AND TOSSED IT IN THE TRASH.
NOW YOU PAY. I'M GOING TO TAKE EVERY-THING FROM YOU!

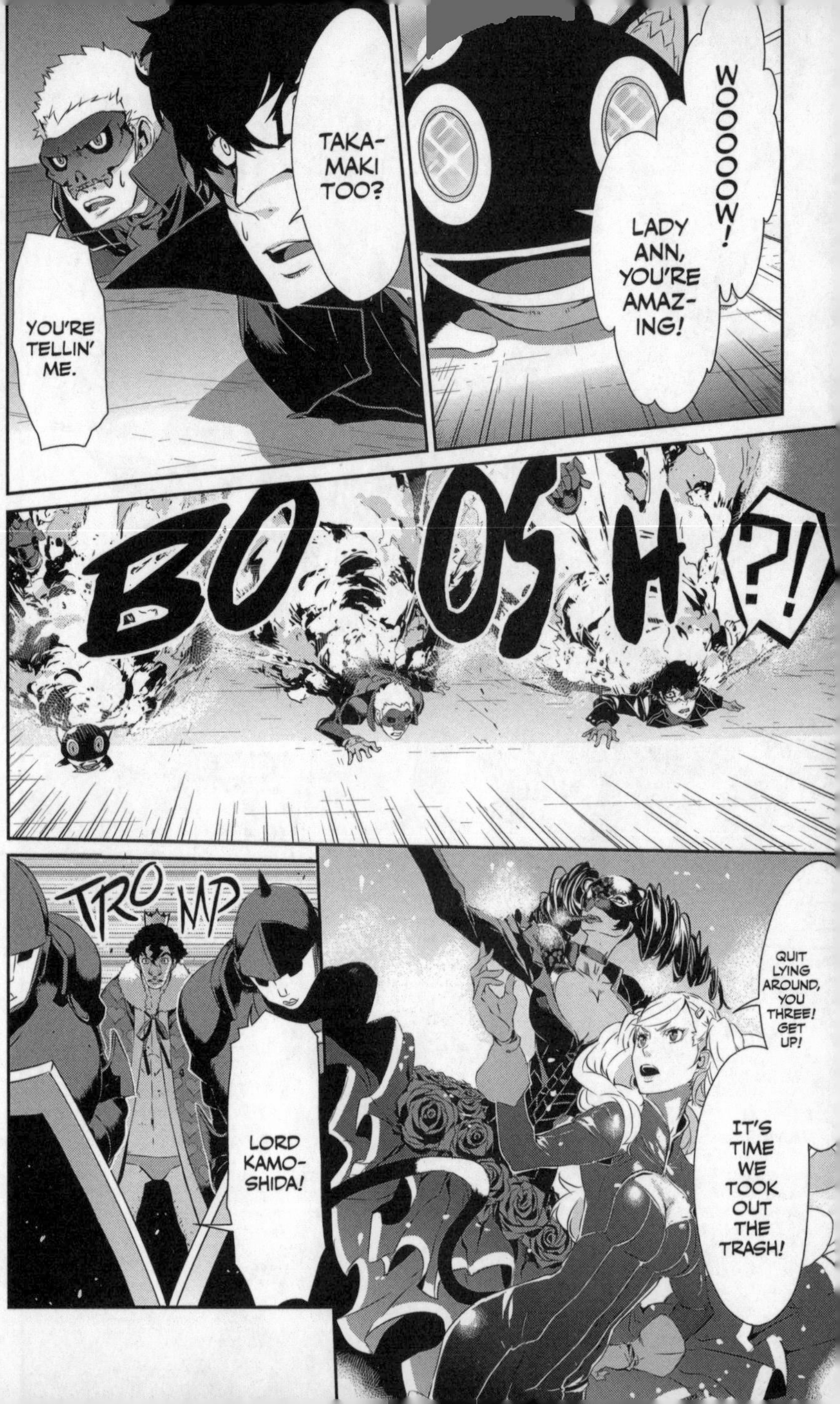
WOOOOOOW!
LADY ANN, YOU'RE AMAZ-ING!
TAKA-MAKI TOO?
YOU'RE TELLIN' ME.
BOOSH
?!
QUIT LYING AROUND, YOU THREE! GET UP!
IT'S TIME WE TOOK OUT THE TRASH!
TROMP
LORD KAMO-SHIDA!

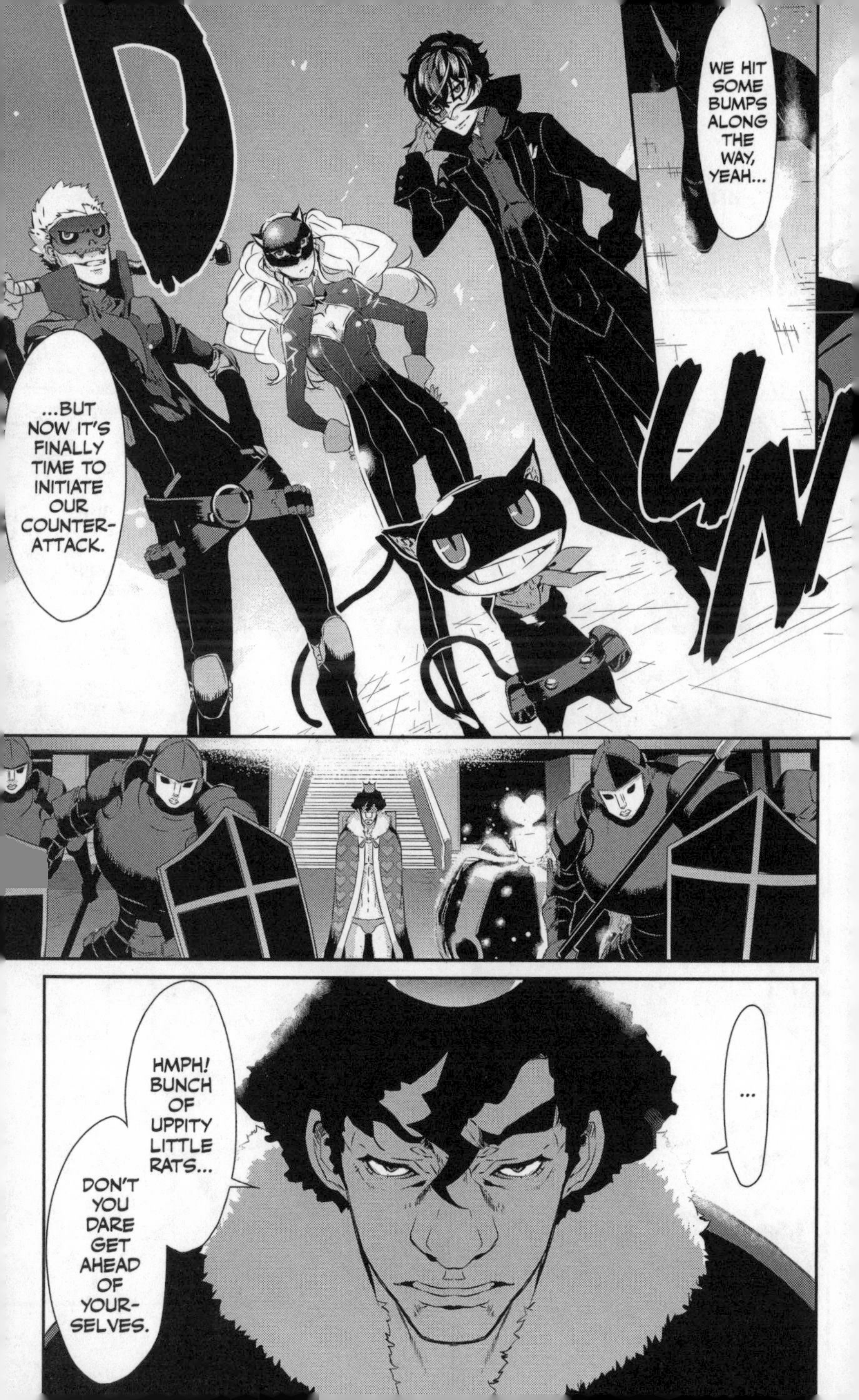
WE HIT SOME BUMPS ALONG THE WAY, YEAH...
...BUT NOW IT'S FINALLY TIME TO INITIATE OUR COUNTER-ATTACK.
...
HMPH! BUNCH OF UPPITY LITTLE RATS...
DON'T YOU DARE GET AHEAD OF YOUR-SELVES.

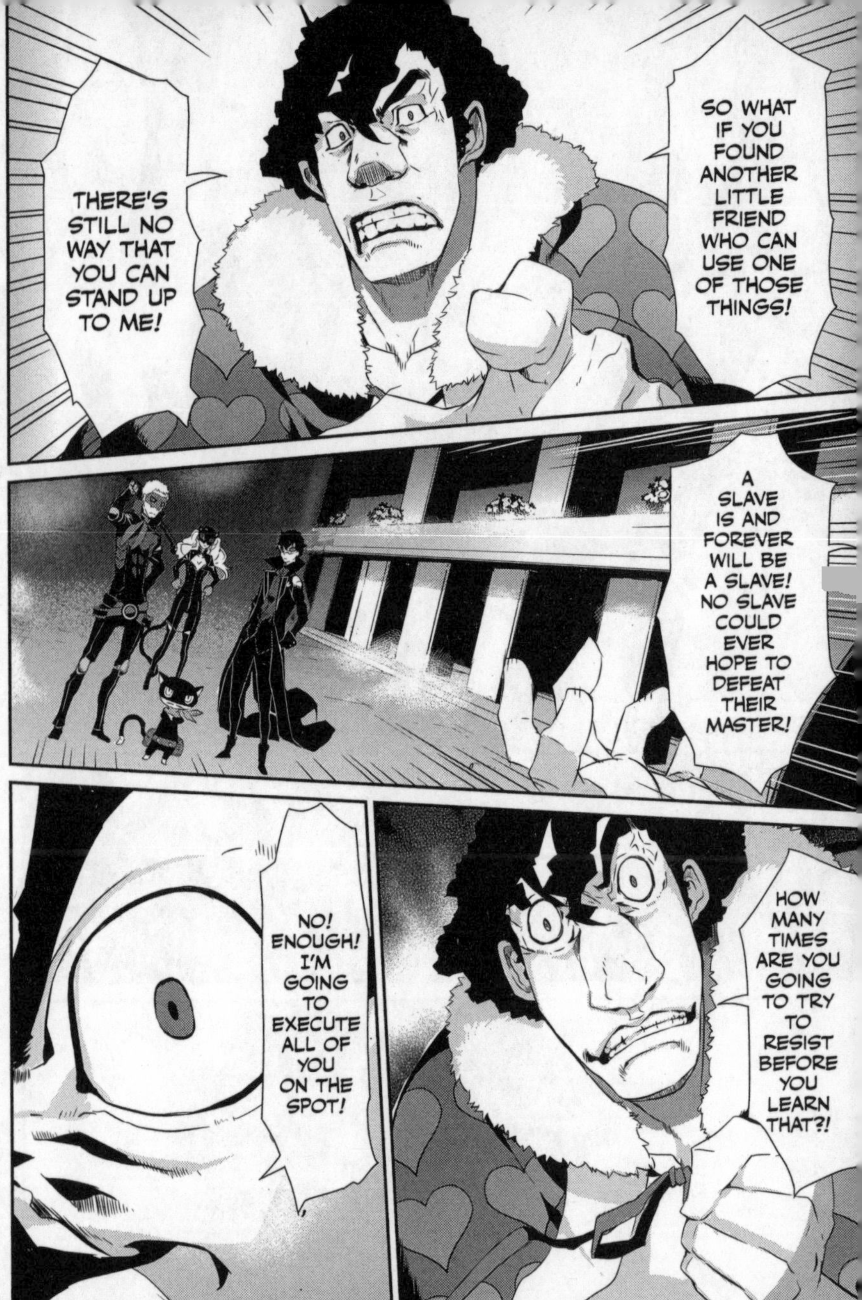
SO WHAT IF YOU FOUND ANOTHER LITTLE FRIEND WHO CAN USE ONE OF THOSE THINGS!
THERE'S STILL NO WAY THAT YOU CAN STAND UP TO ME!
A SLAVE IS AND FOREVER WILL BE A SLAVE! NO SLAVE COULD EVER HOPE TO DEFEAT THEIR MASTER!
HOW MANY TIMES ARE YOU GOING TO TRY TO RESIST BEFORE YOU LEARN THAT?!
NO! ENOUGH! I'M GOING TO EXECUTE ALL OF YOU ON THE SPOT!

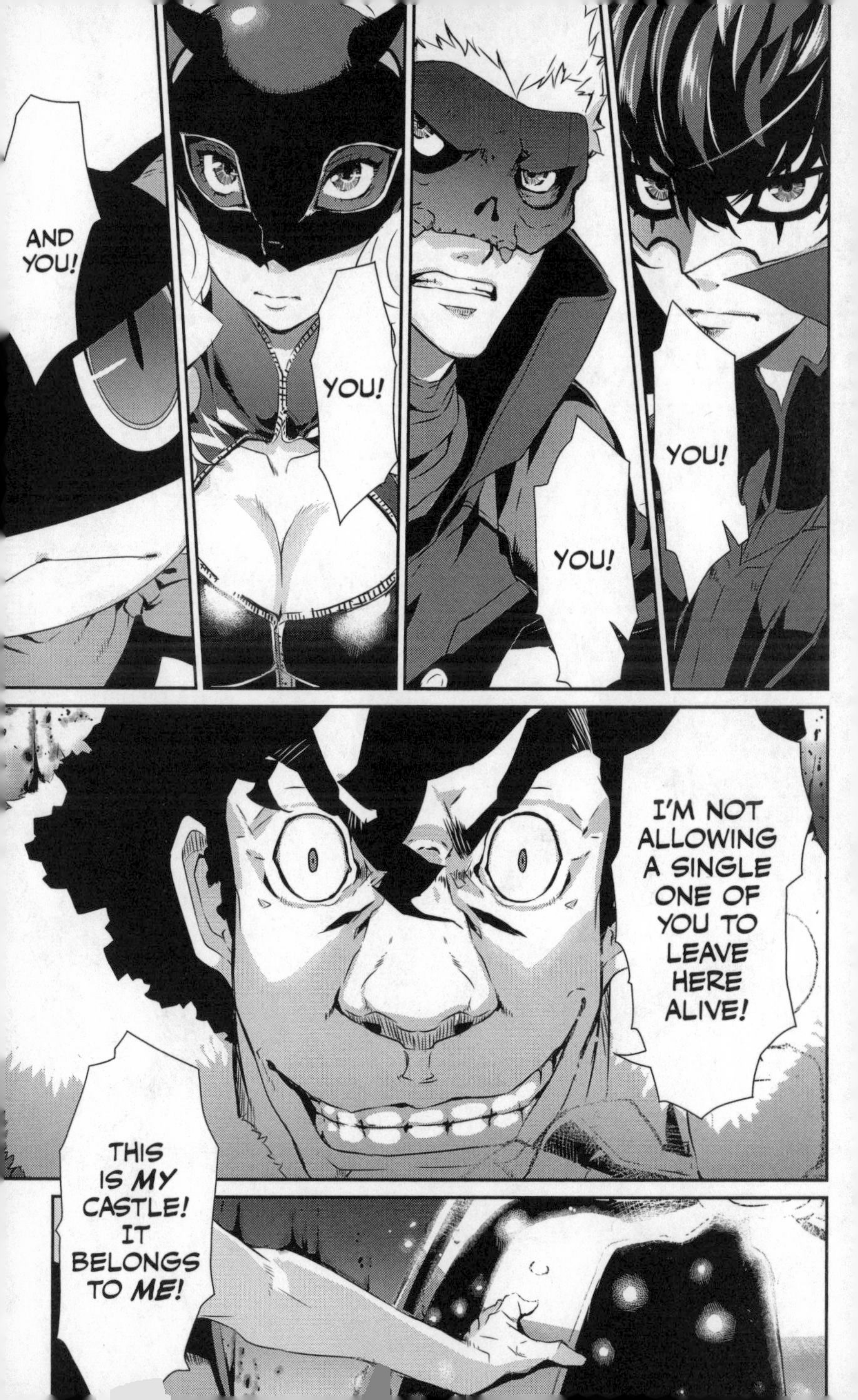
YOU!
YOU!
YOU!
AND YOU!
I'M NOT ALLOWING A SINGLE ONE OF YOU TO LEAVE HERE ALIVE!
THIS IS *MY* CASTLE! IT BELONGS TO *ME*!

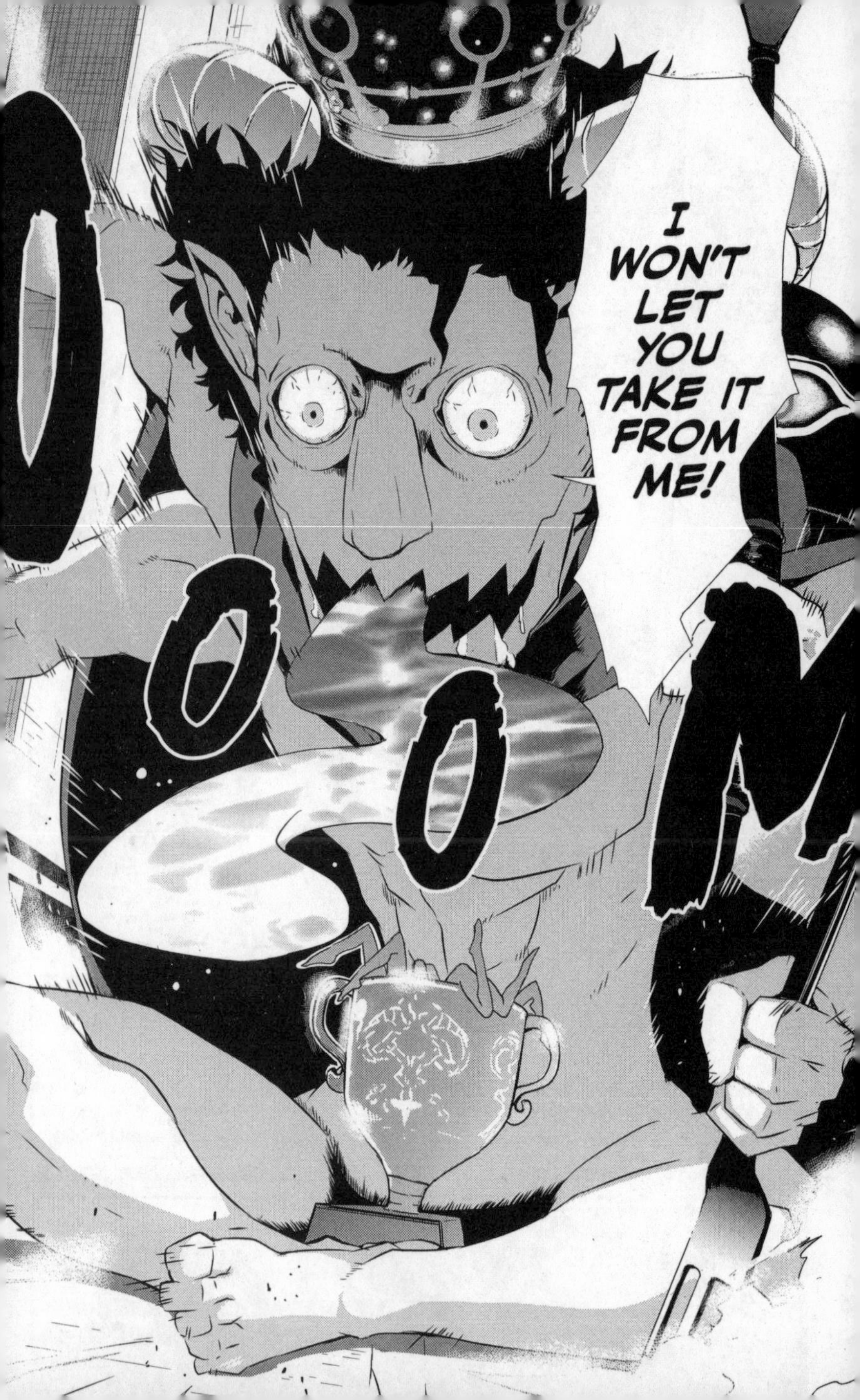
I WON'T LET YOU TAKE IT FROM ME!
OOOM

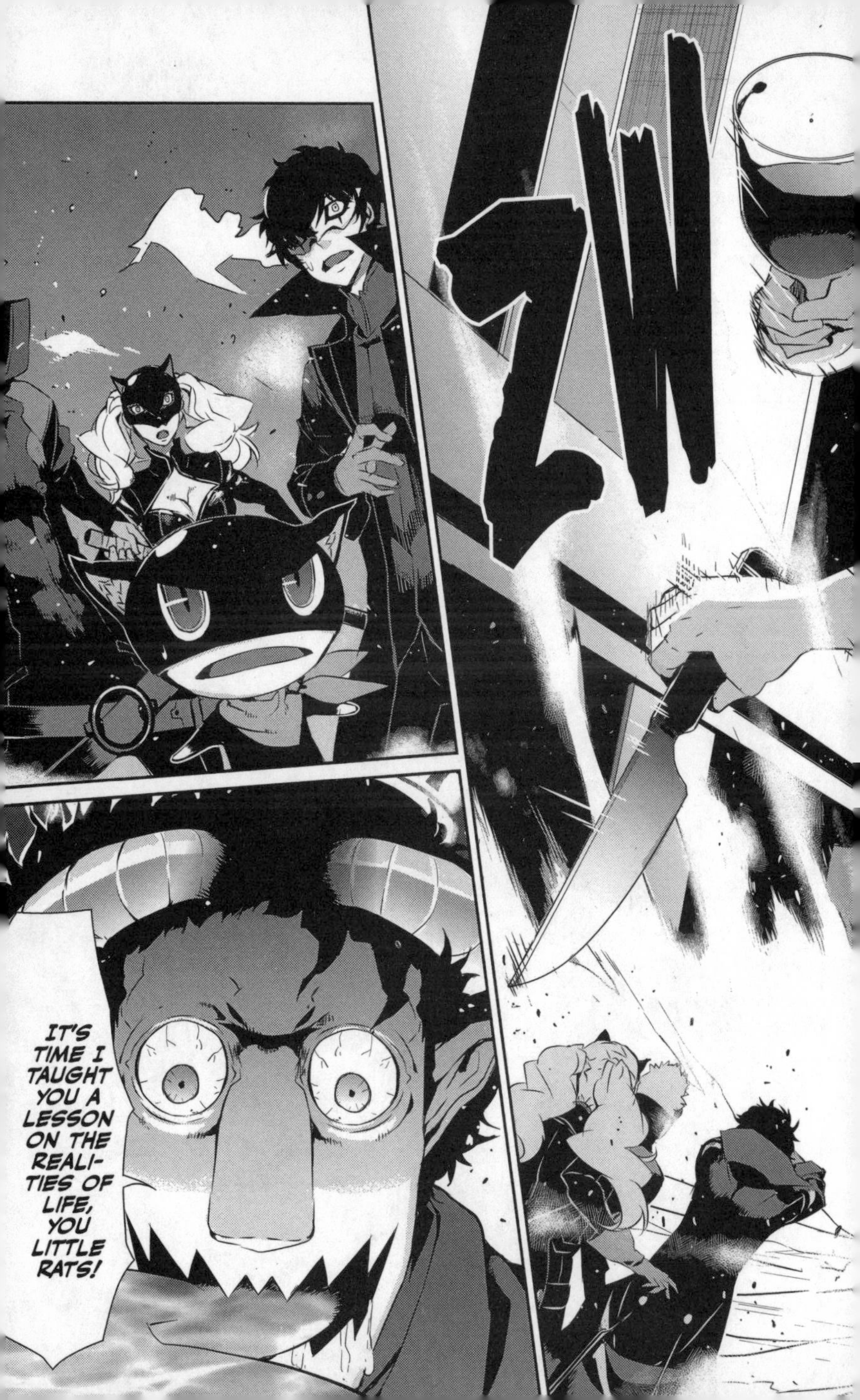
ZW
IT'S TIME I TAUGHT YOU A LESSON ON THE REALI- TIES OF LIFE, YOU LITTLE RATS!

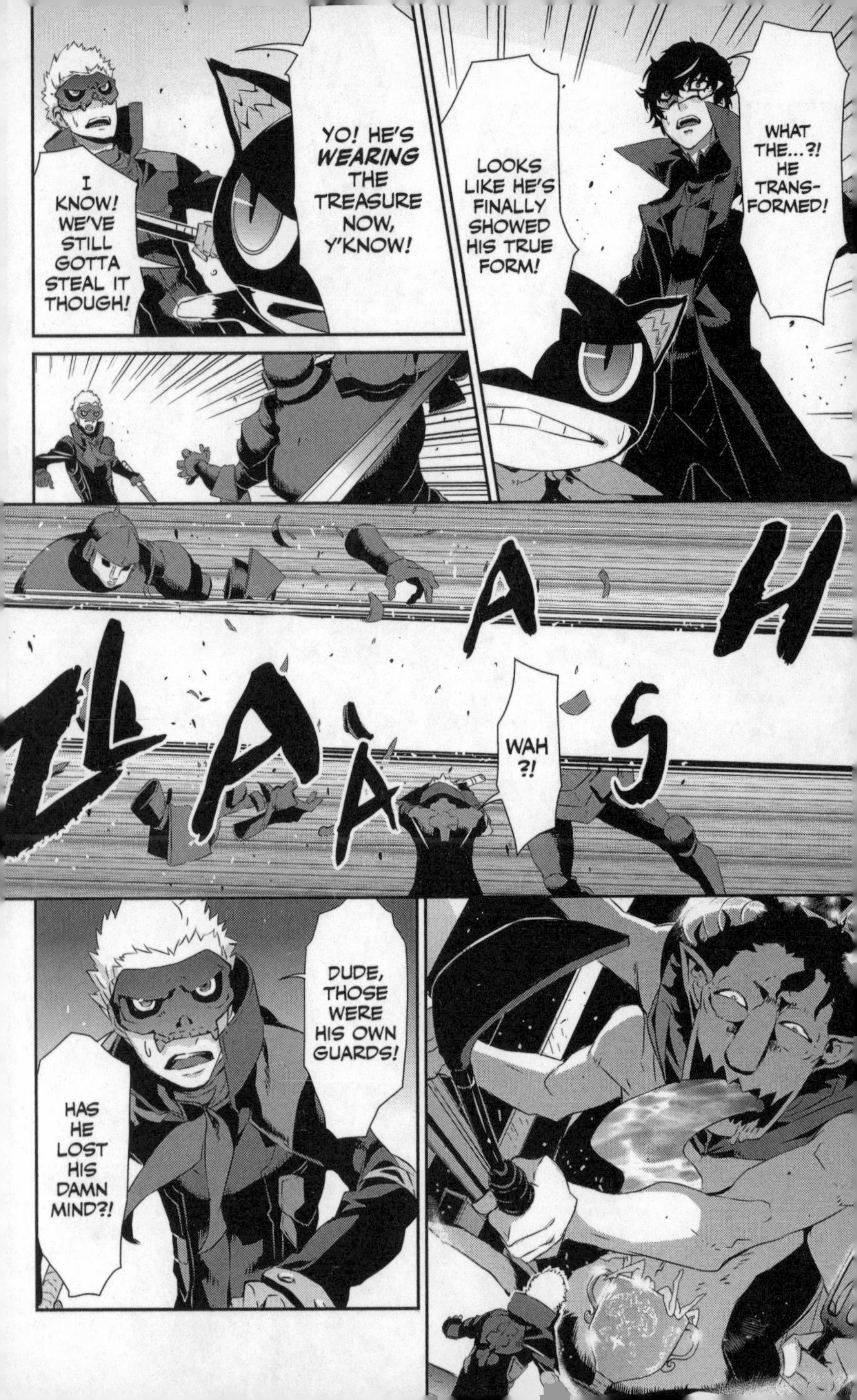
WHAT THE...?! HE TRANS-FORMED!
LOOKS LIKE HE'S FINALLY SHOWED HIS TRUE FORM!
YO! HE'S *WEARING* THE TREASURE NOW, Y'KNOW!
I KNOW! WE'VE STILL GOTTA STEAL IT THOUGH!
ZLAASH
WAH ?!
DUDE, THOSE WERE HIS OWN GUARDS!
HAS HE LOST HIS DAMN MIND?!

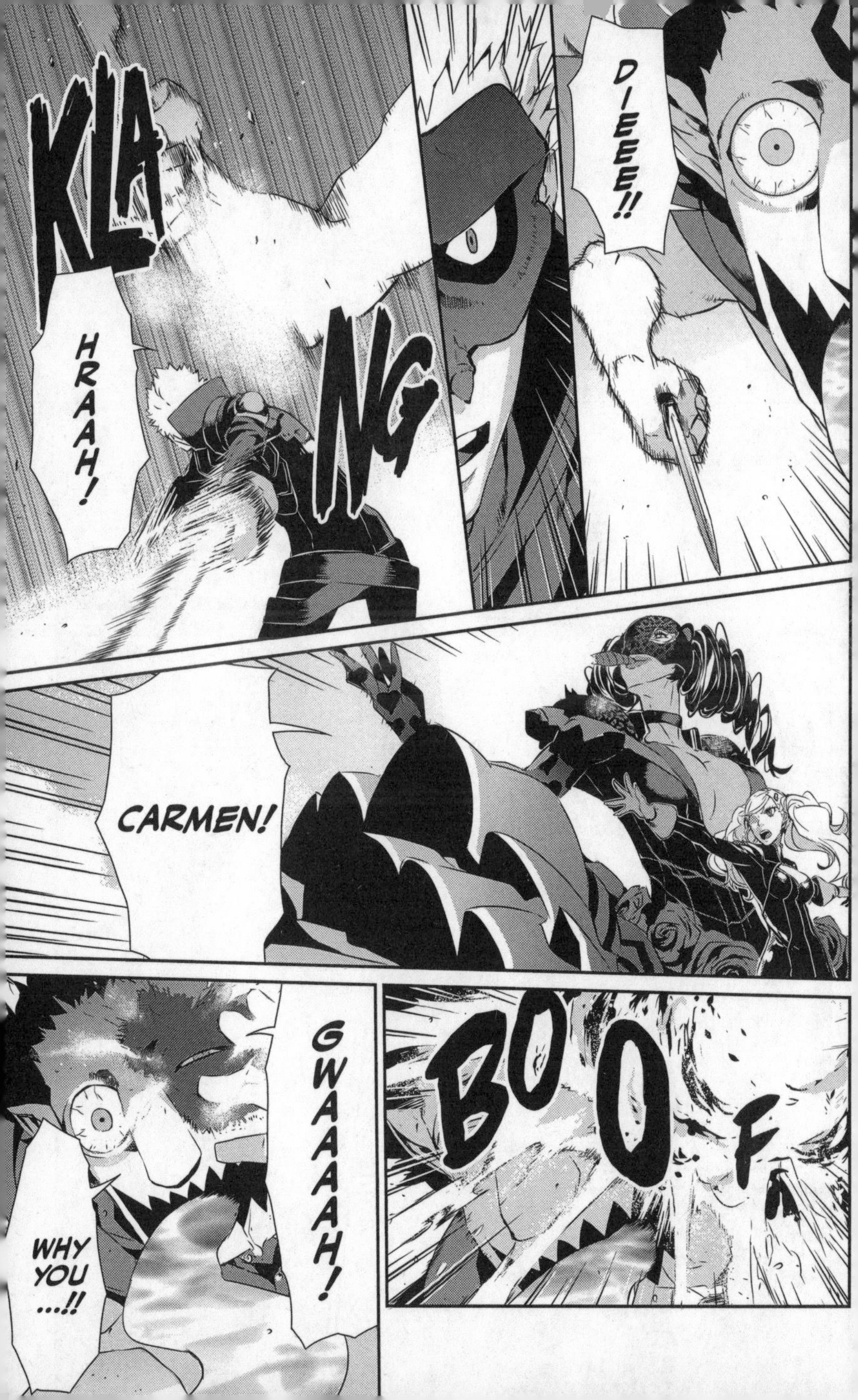
DIEEE!!
KLANG
HRAAAH!
CARMEN!
BOOF
GWAAAAH!
WHY YOU ...!!

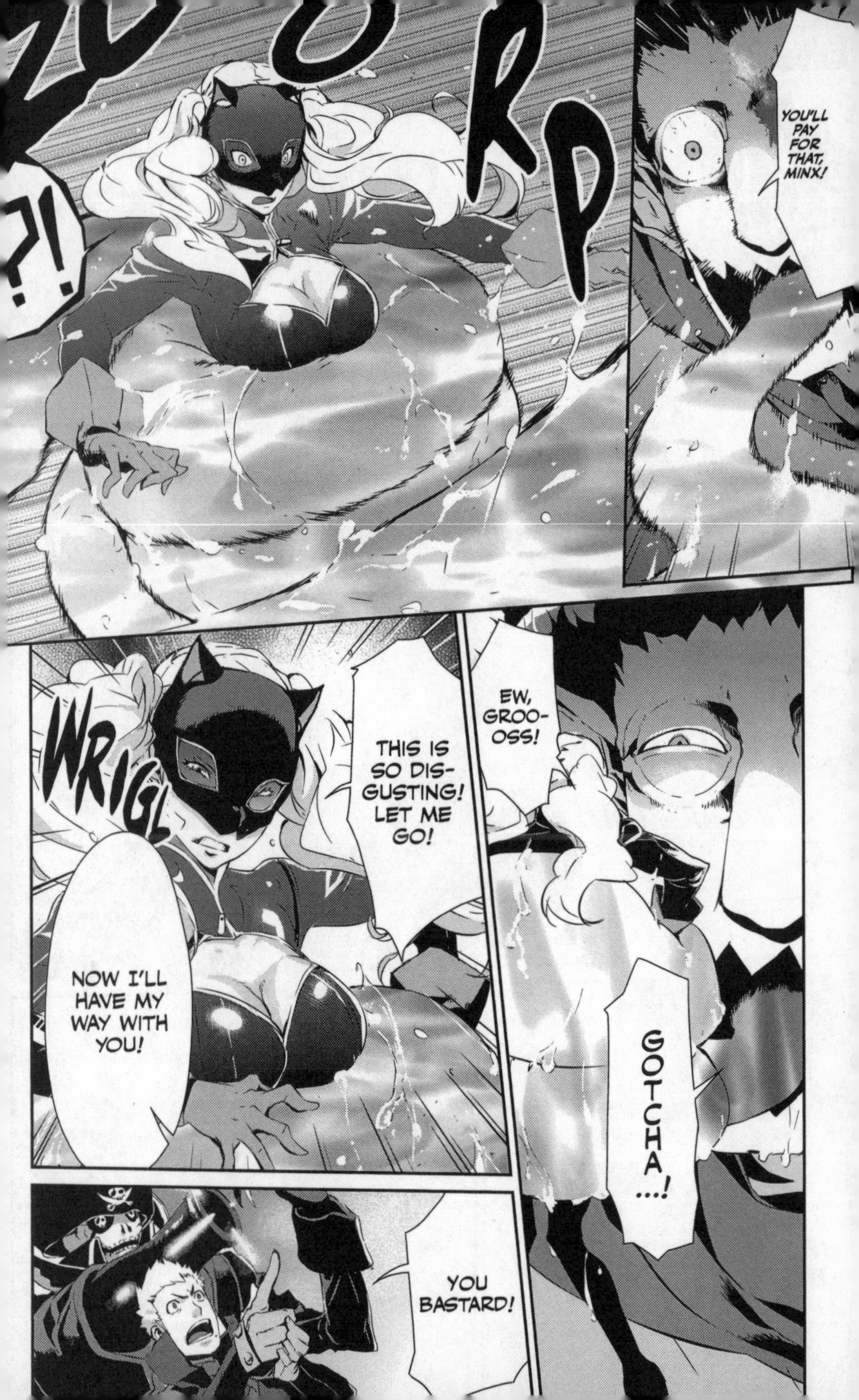
YOU'LL PAY FOR THAT, MINX!
?!
EW, GROO-OSS!
GOTCHA...!
THIS IS SO DIS-GUSTING! LET ME GO!
WRIGL
NOW I'LL HAVE MY WAY WITH YOU!
YOU BASTARD!

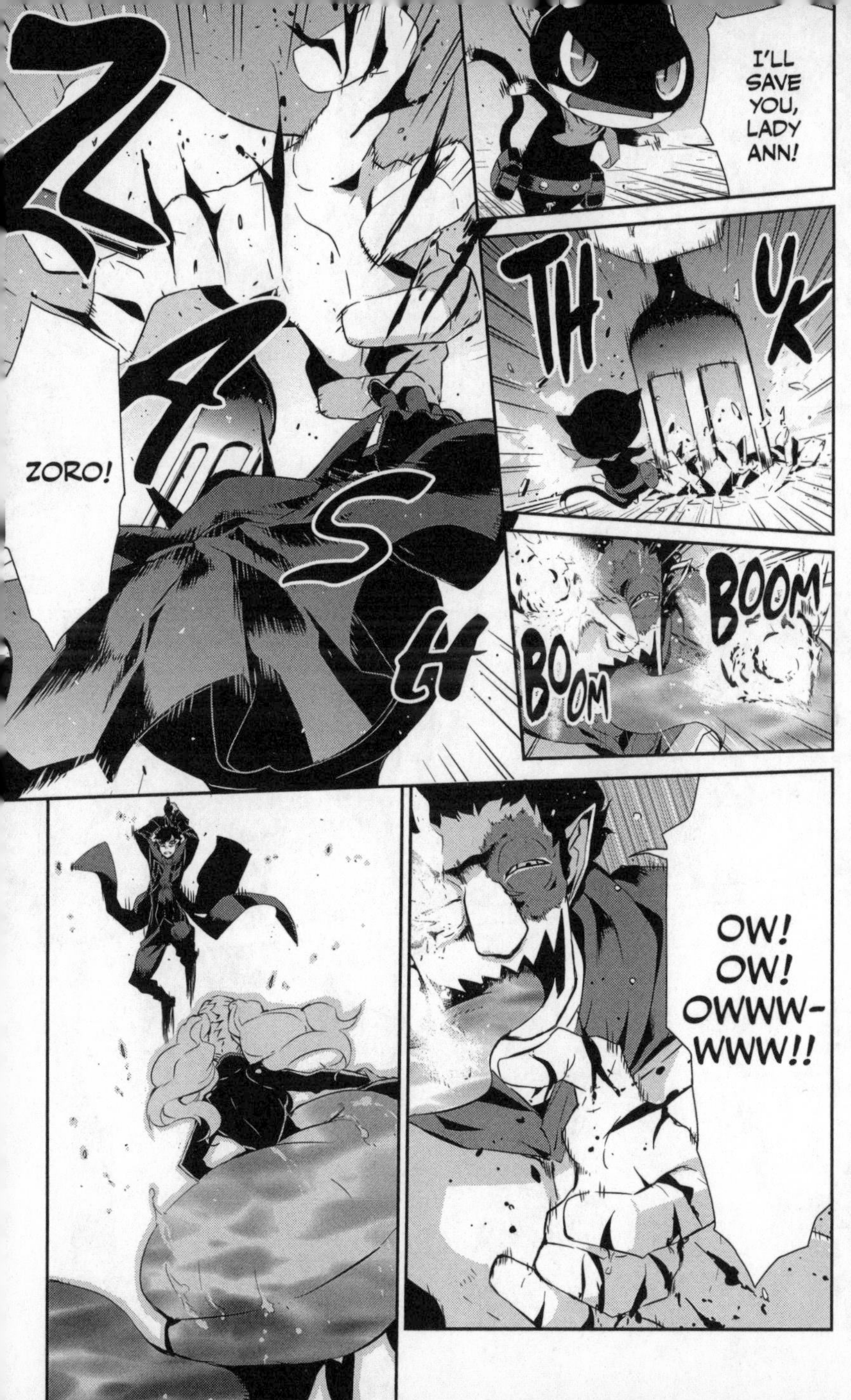
I'LL SAVE YOU, LADY ANN!
THUK
BOOM
BOOM
ZASH
ZORO!
OW! OW! OWWW-WWW!!

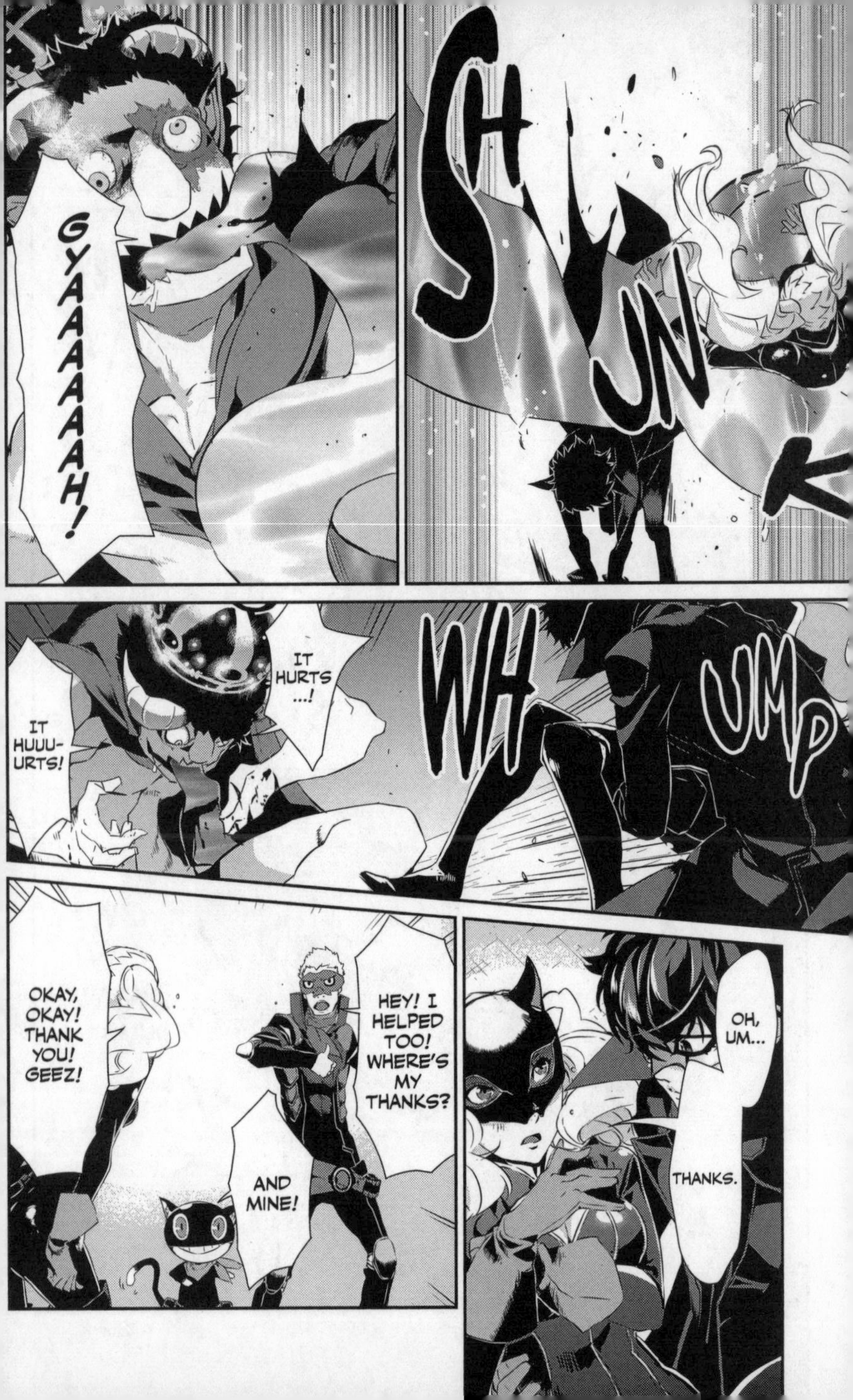
SHUNK
GYAAAAAAAH!
WHUMP
IT HURTS...!
IT HUUU-URTS!
OH, UM...
THANKS.
HEY! I HELPED TOO! WHERE'S MY THANKS?
AND MINE!
OKAY, OKAY! THANK YOU! GEEZ!

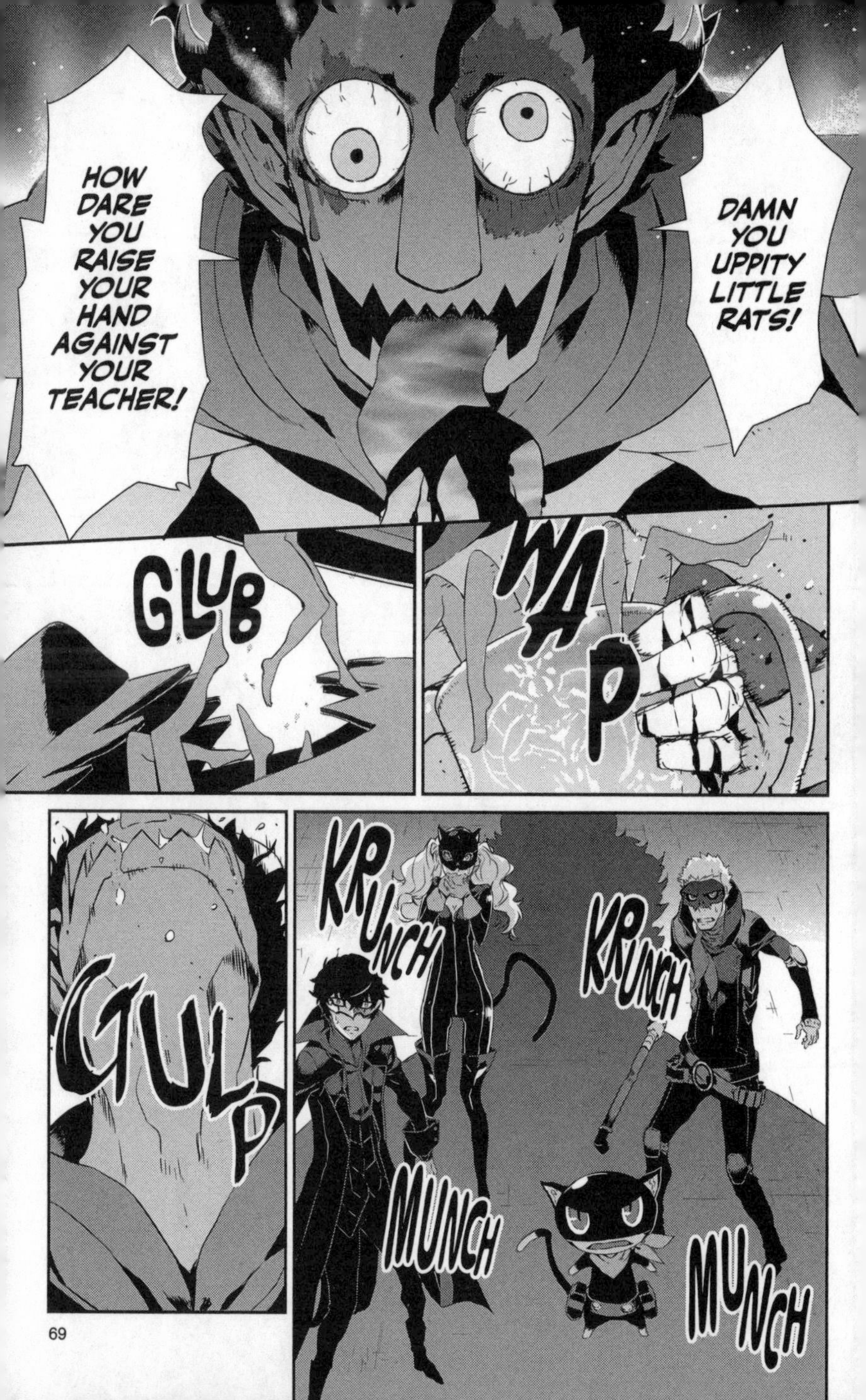
DAMN YOU UPPITY LITTLE RATS!
HOW DARE YOU RAISE YOUR HAND AGAINST YOUR TEACHER!
WAP
GLUB
KRUNCH
KRUNCH
MUNCH
MUNCH
GULP

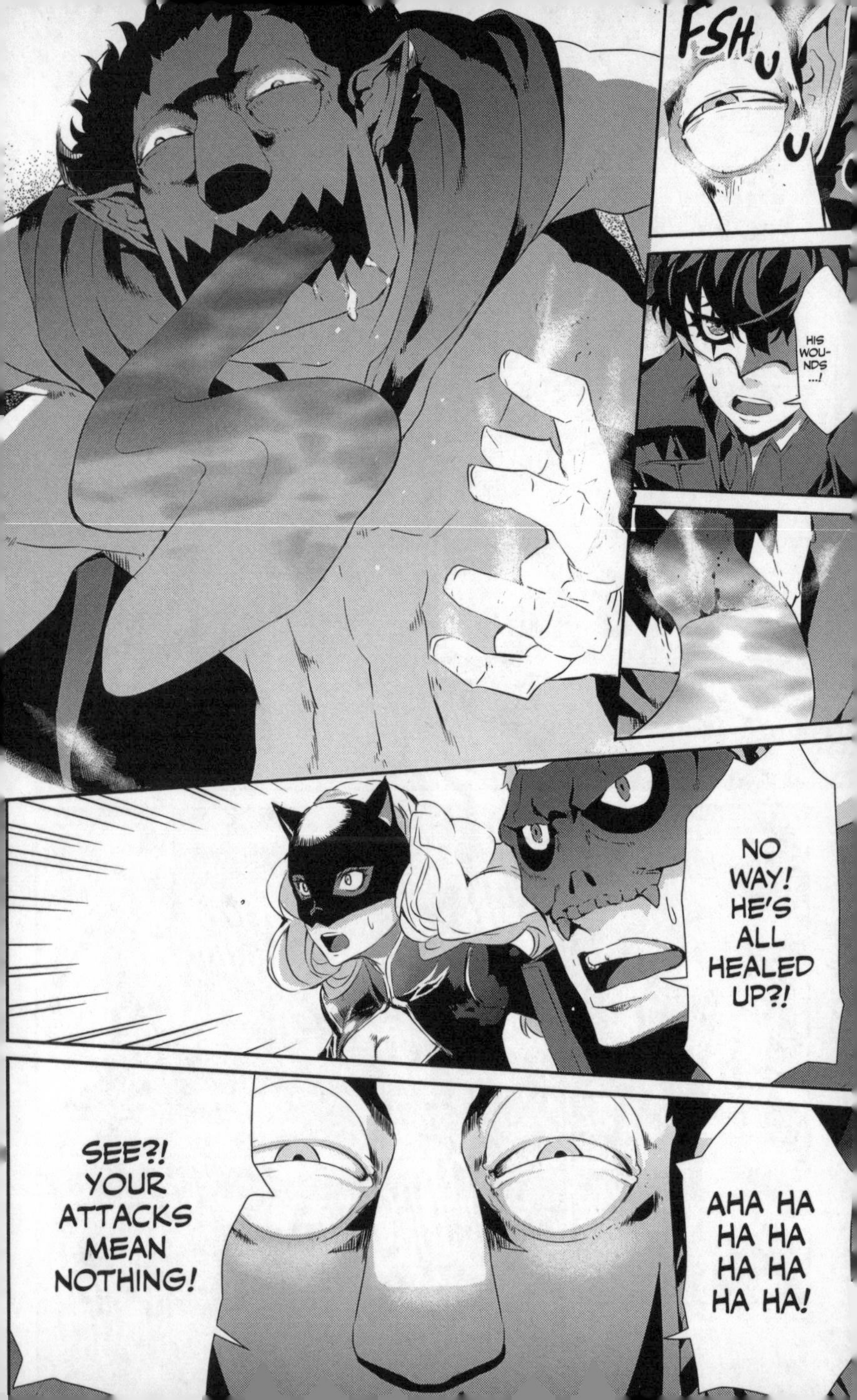
FSHUUU
HIS WOUNDS...!
NO WAY! HE'S ALL HEALED UP?!
AHA HA HA HA HA HA HA HA!
SEE?! YOUR ATTACKS MEAN NOTHING!

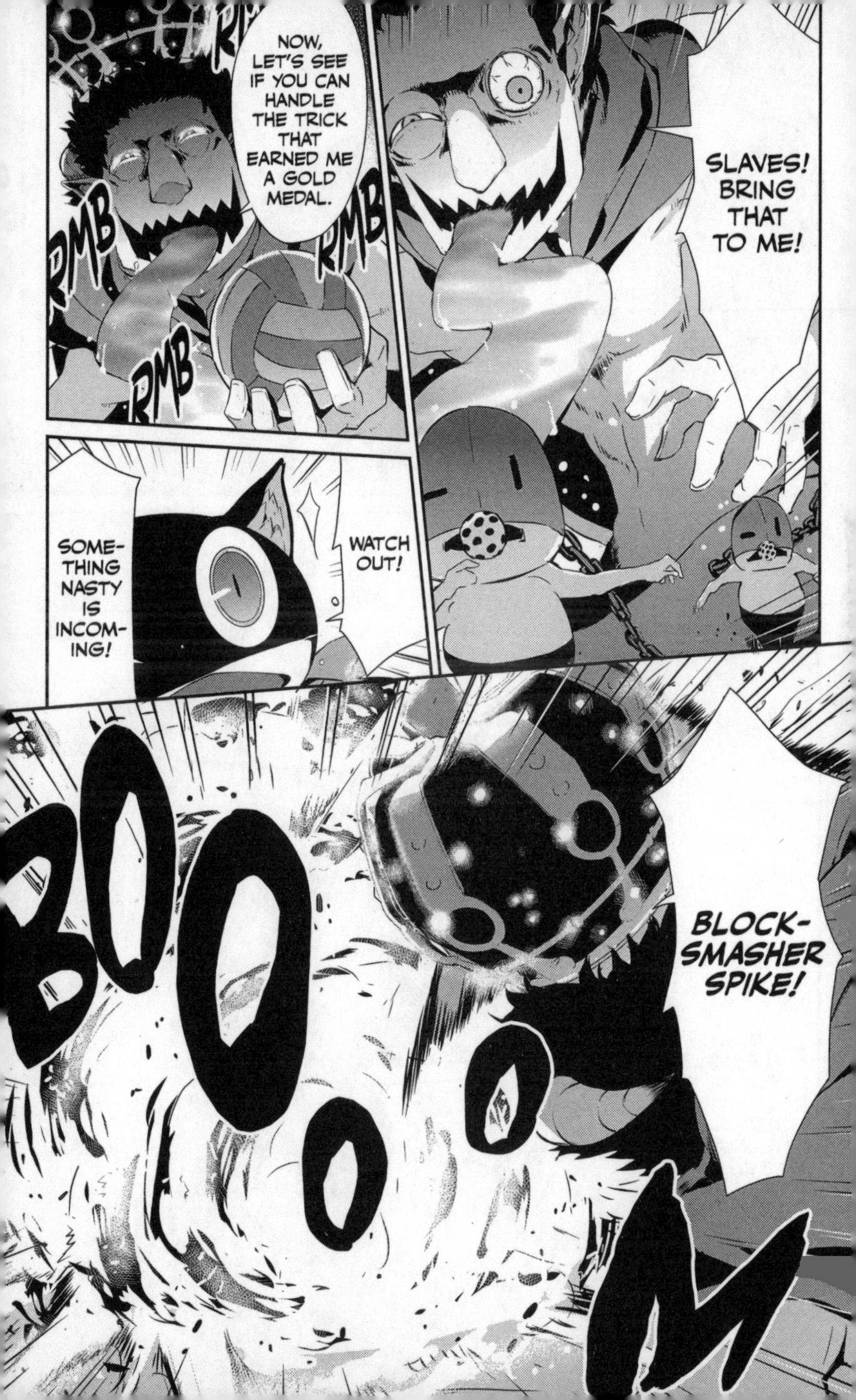
SLAVES! BRING THAT TO ME!
NOW, LET'S SEE IF YOU CAN HANDLE THE TRICK THAT EARNED ME A GOLD MEDAL.
RMB
RMB
RMB
RMB
WATCH OUT!
SOME-THING NASTY IS INCOM-ING!
BLOCK-SMASHER SPIKE!
BOOOOOM

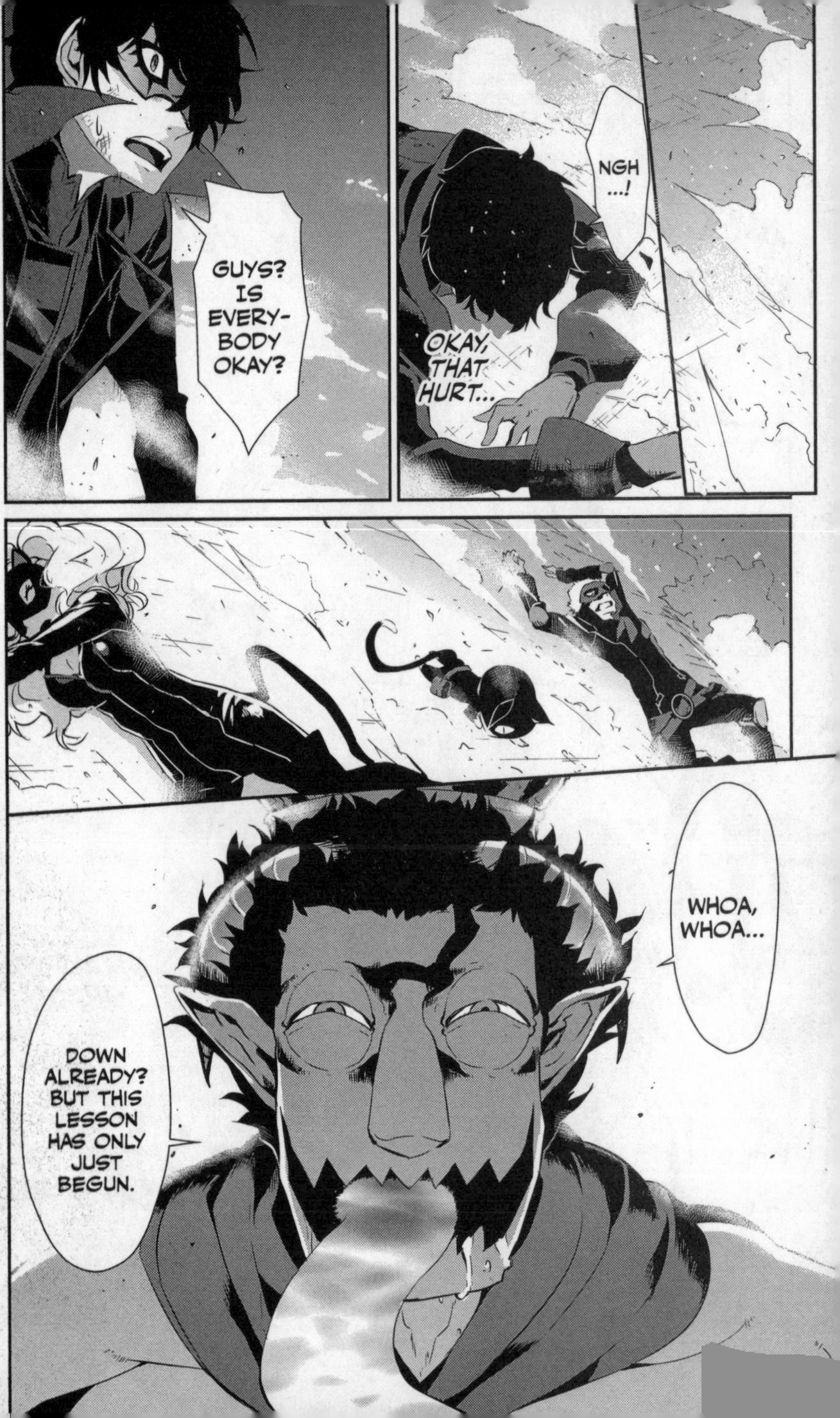
NGH ...!
OKAY, THAT HURT...
GUYS? IS EVERY-BODY OKAY?
WHOA, WHOA...
DOWN ALREADY? BUT THIS LESSON HAS ONLY JUST BEGUN.

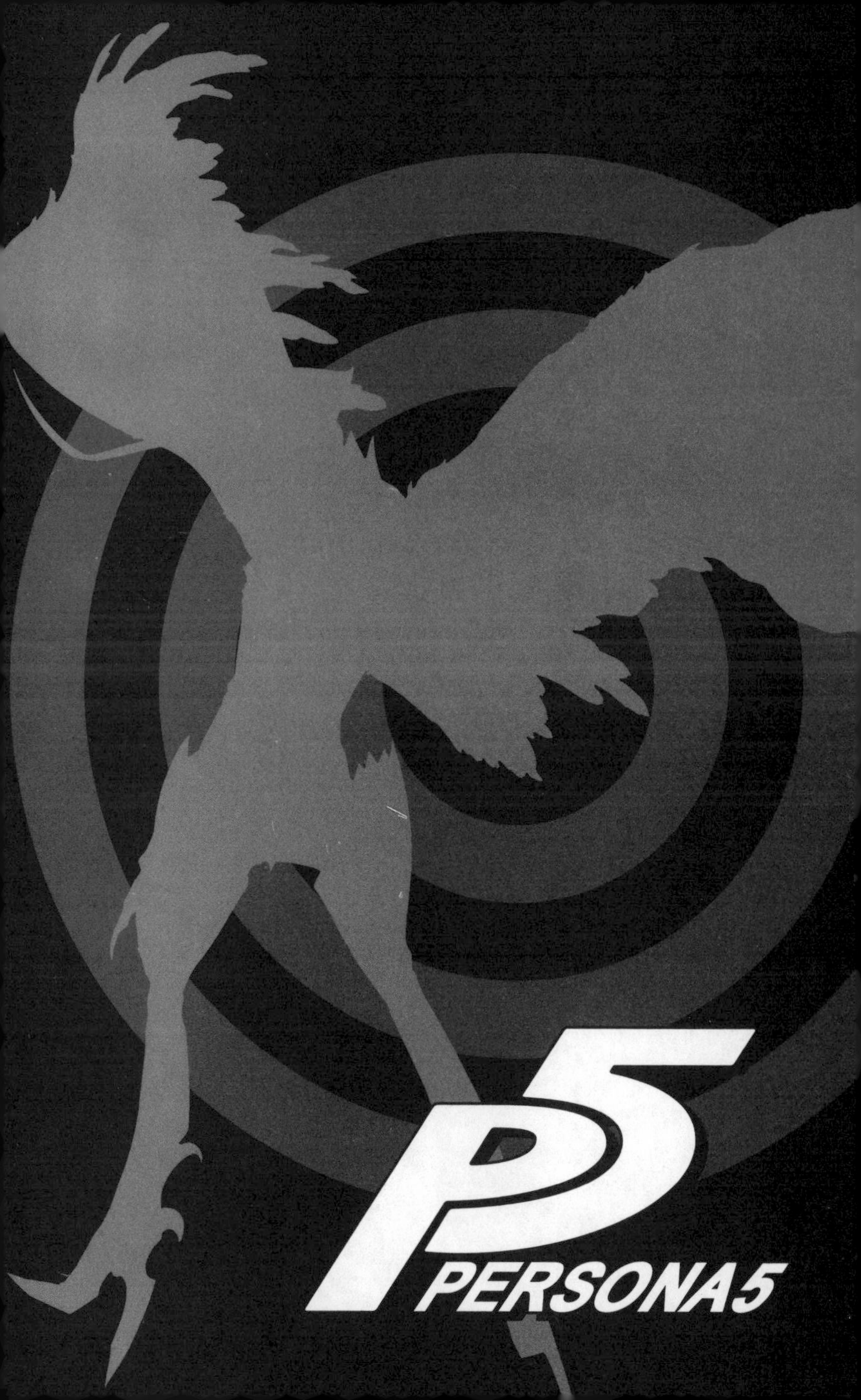
P5
PERSONA5

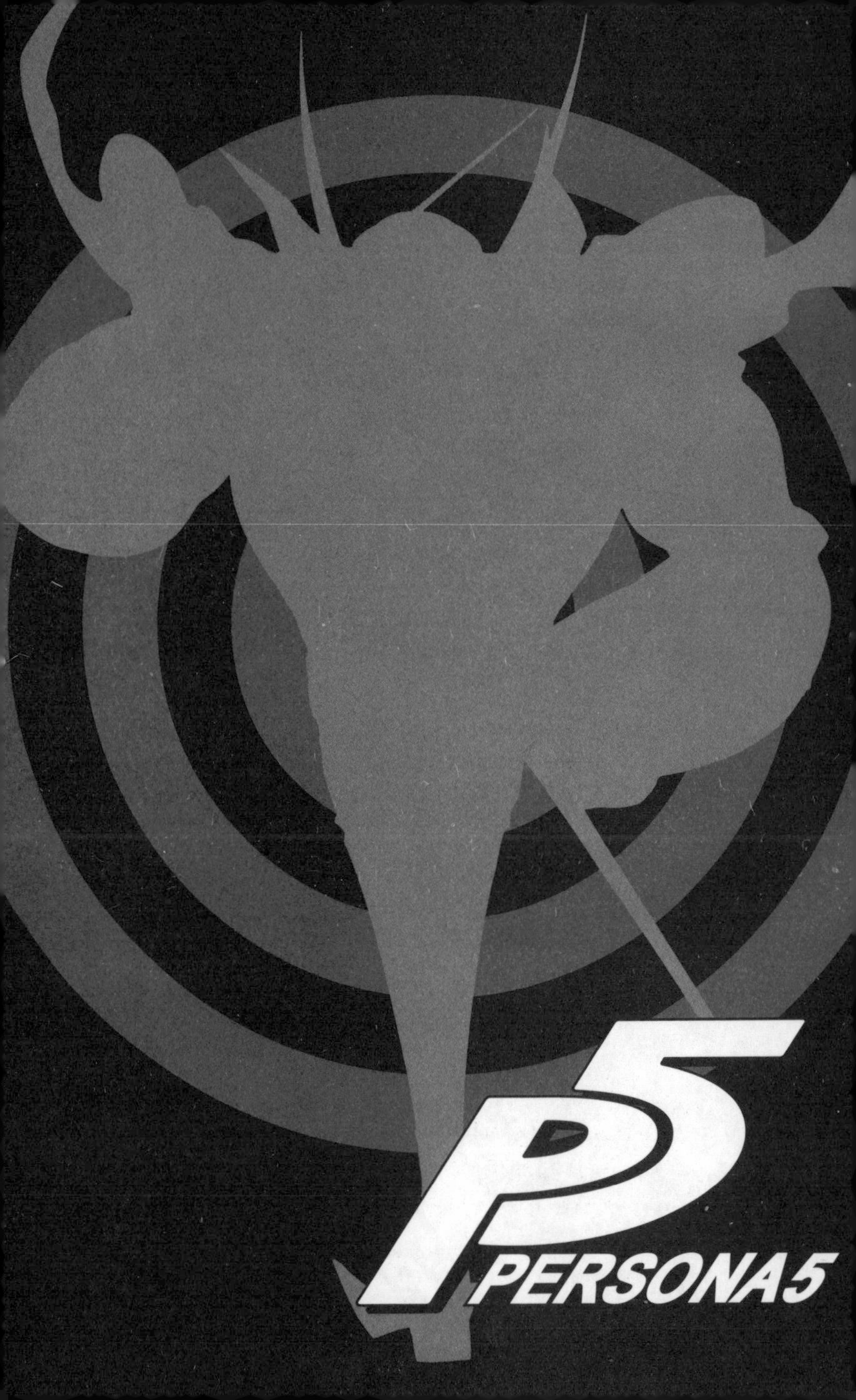
P5
PERSONA5

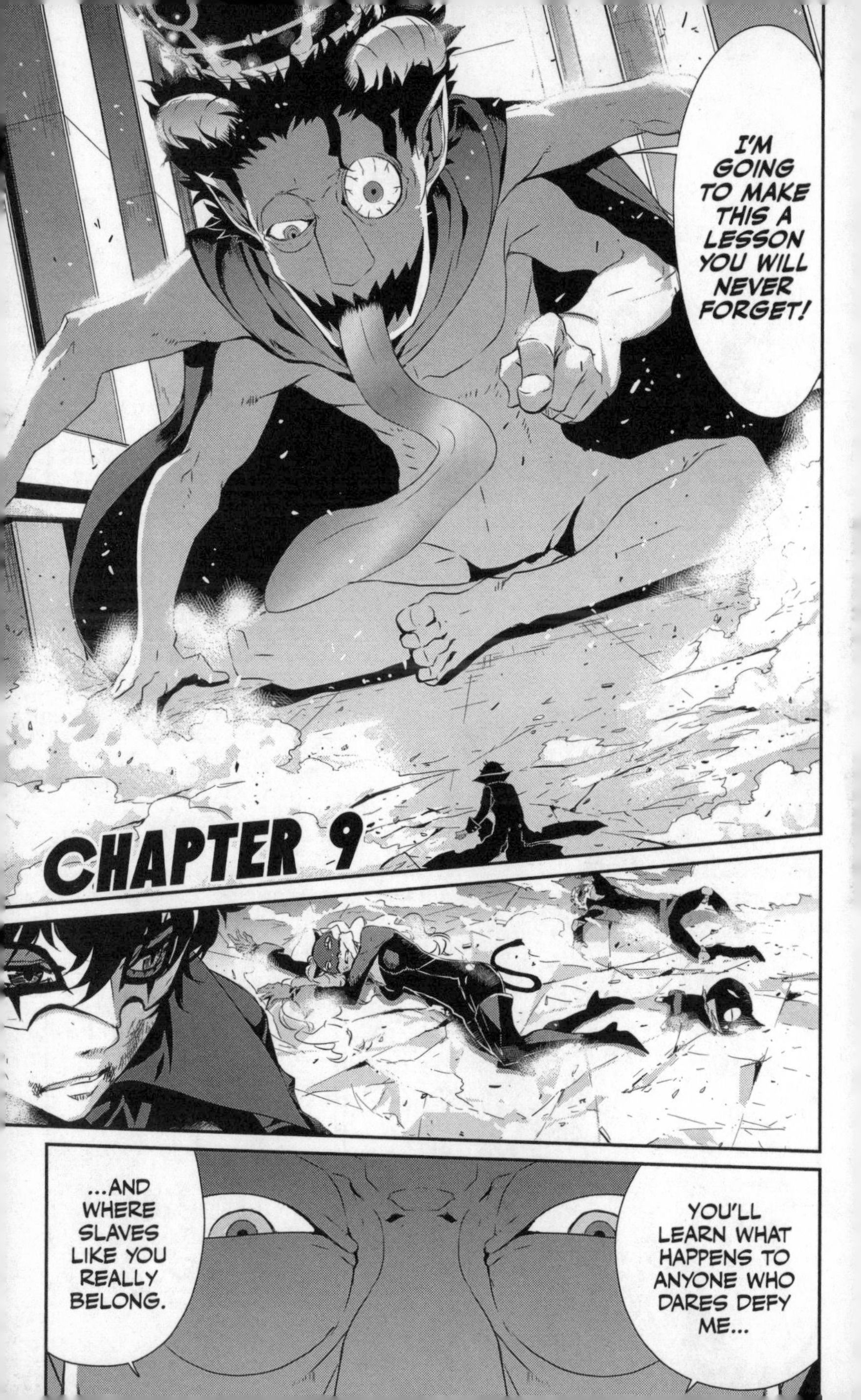
I'M GOING TO MAKE THIS A LESSON YOU WILL NEVER FORGET!
CHAPTER 9
YOU'LL LEARN WHAT HAPPENS TO ANYONE WHO DARES DEFY ME...
...AND WHERE SLAVES LIKE YOU REALLY BELONG.

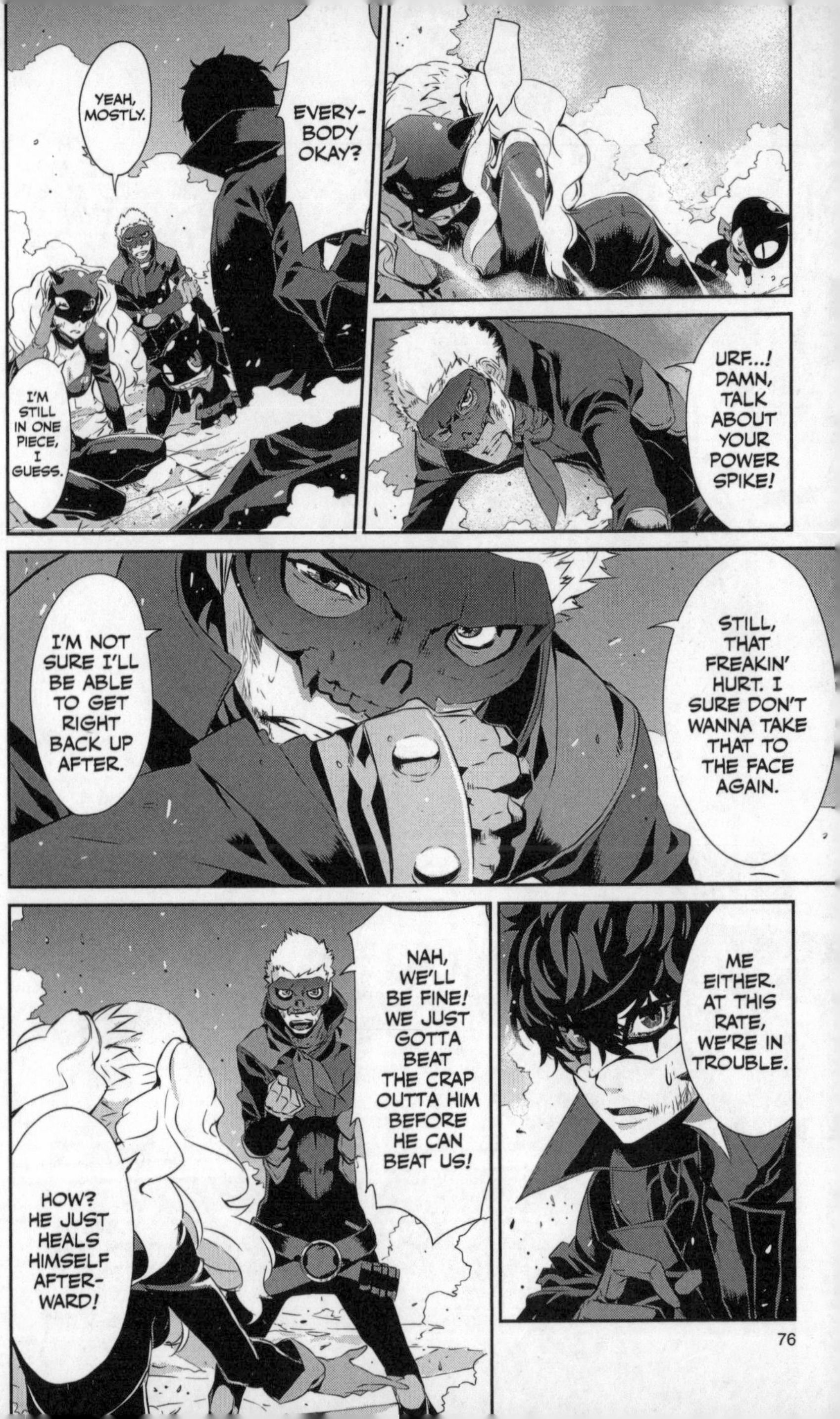
URF...! DAMN, TALK ABOUT YOUR POWER SPIKE!
EVERY-BODY OKAY?
YEAH, MOSTLY.
I'M STILL IN ONE PIECE, I GUESS.
STILL, THAT FREAKIN' HURT. I SURE DON'T WANNA TAKE THAT TO THE FACE AGAIN.
I'M NOT SURE I'LL BE ABLE TO GET RIGHT BACK UP AFTER.
ME EITHER. AT THIS RATE, WE'RE IN TROUBLE.
NAH, WE'LL BE FINE! WE JUST GOTTA BEAT THE CRAP OUTTA HIM BEFORE HE CAN BEAT US!
HOW? HE JUST HEALS HIMSELF AFTER-WARD!

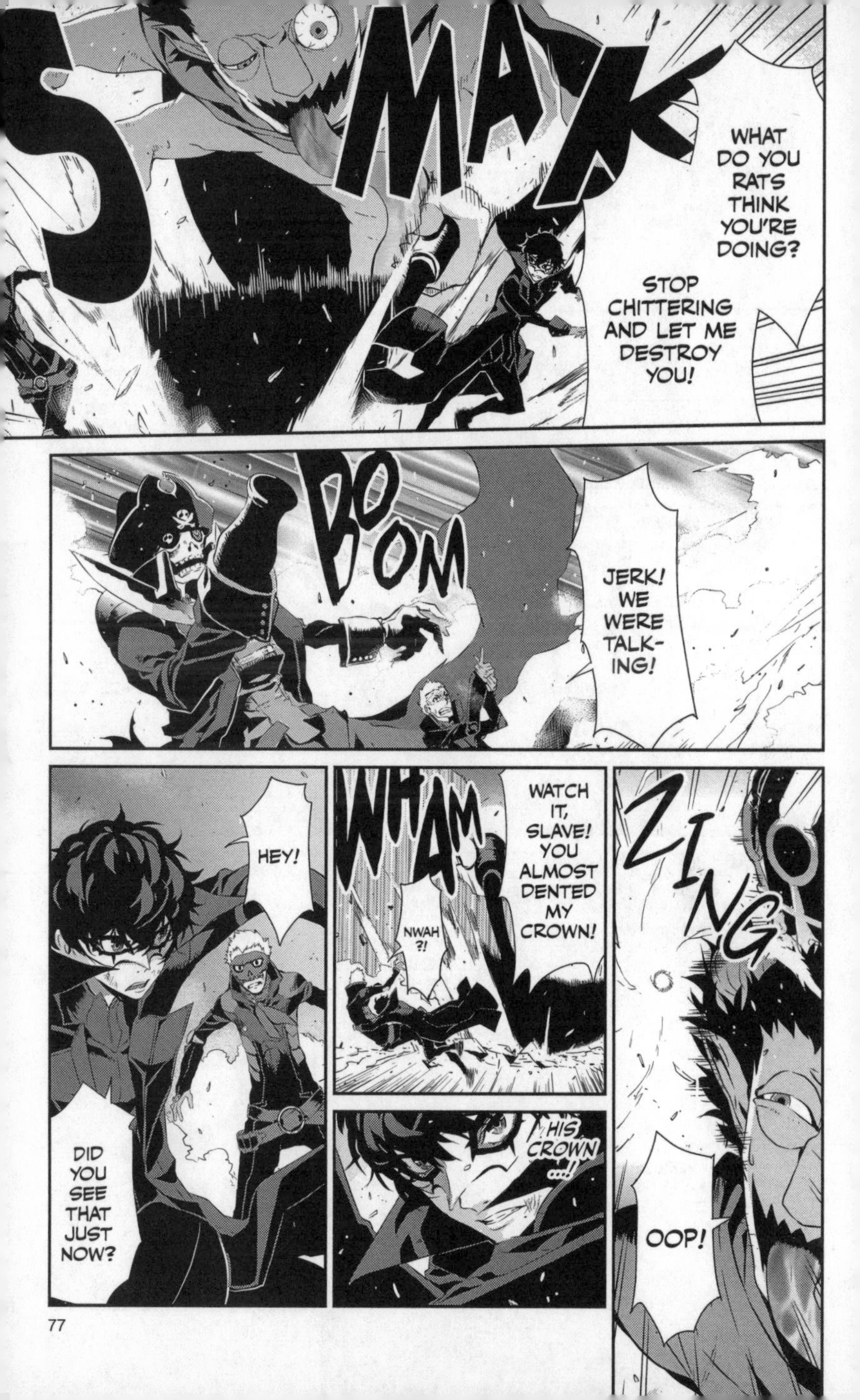
SMAK
WHAT DO YOU RATS THINK YOU'RE DOING?
STOP CHITTERING AND LET ME DESTROY YOU!
BOOM
JERK! WE WERE TALK-ING!
ZING
OOP!
WATCH IT, SLAVE! YOU ALMOST DENTED MY CROWN!
WHAM
NWAH?!
HIS CROWN...!
HEY!
DID YOU SEE THAT JUST NOW?

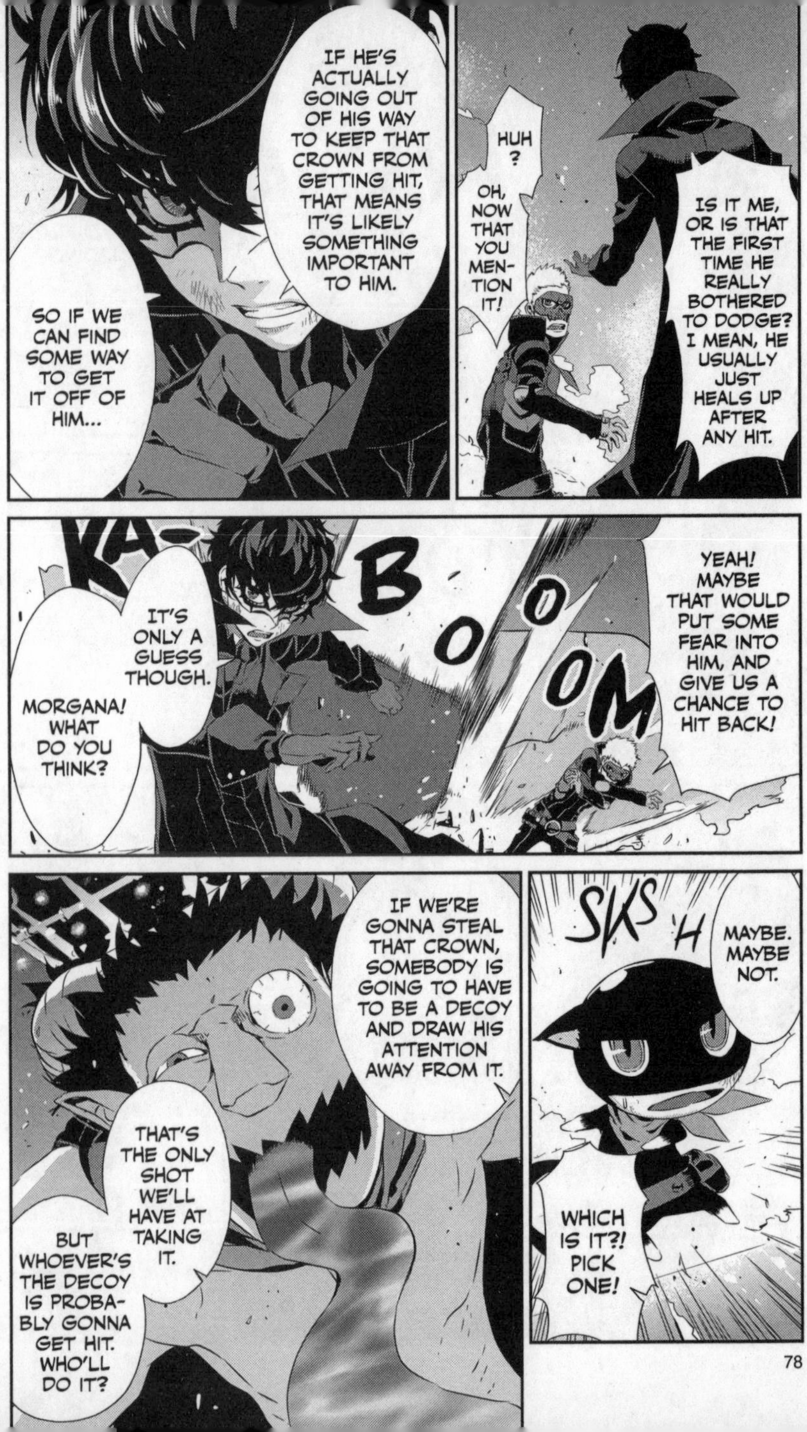
IS IT ME, OR IS THAT THE FIRST TIME HE REALLY BOTHERED TO DODGE? I MEAN, HE USUALLY JUST HEALS UP AFTER ANY HIT.
HUH?
OH, NOW THAT YOU MEN-TION IT!
IF HE'S ACTUALLY GOING OUT OF HIS WAY TO KEEP THAT CROWN FROM GETTING HIT, THAT MEANS IT'S LIKELY SOMETHING IMPORTANT TO HIM.
SO IF WE CAN FIND SOME WAY TO GET IT OFF OF HIM...
YEAH! MAYBE THAT WOULD PUT SOME FEAR INTO HIM, AND GIVE US A CHANCE TO HIT BACK!
BOOOM
IT'S ONLY A GUESS THOUGH.
MORGANA! WHAT DO YOU THINK?
SKSSH
MAYBE. MAYBE NOT.
WHICH IS IT?! PICK ONE!
IF WE'RE GONNA STEAL THAT CROWN, SOMEBODY IS GOING TO HAVE TO BE A DECOY AND DRAW HIS ATTENTION AWAY FROM IT.
THAT'S THE ONLY SHOT WE'LL HAVE AT TAKING IT.
BUT WHOEVER'S THE DECOY IS PROBA-BLY GONNA GET HIT. WHO'LL DO IT?

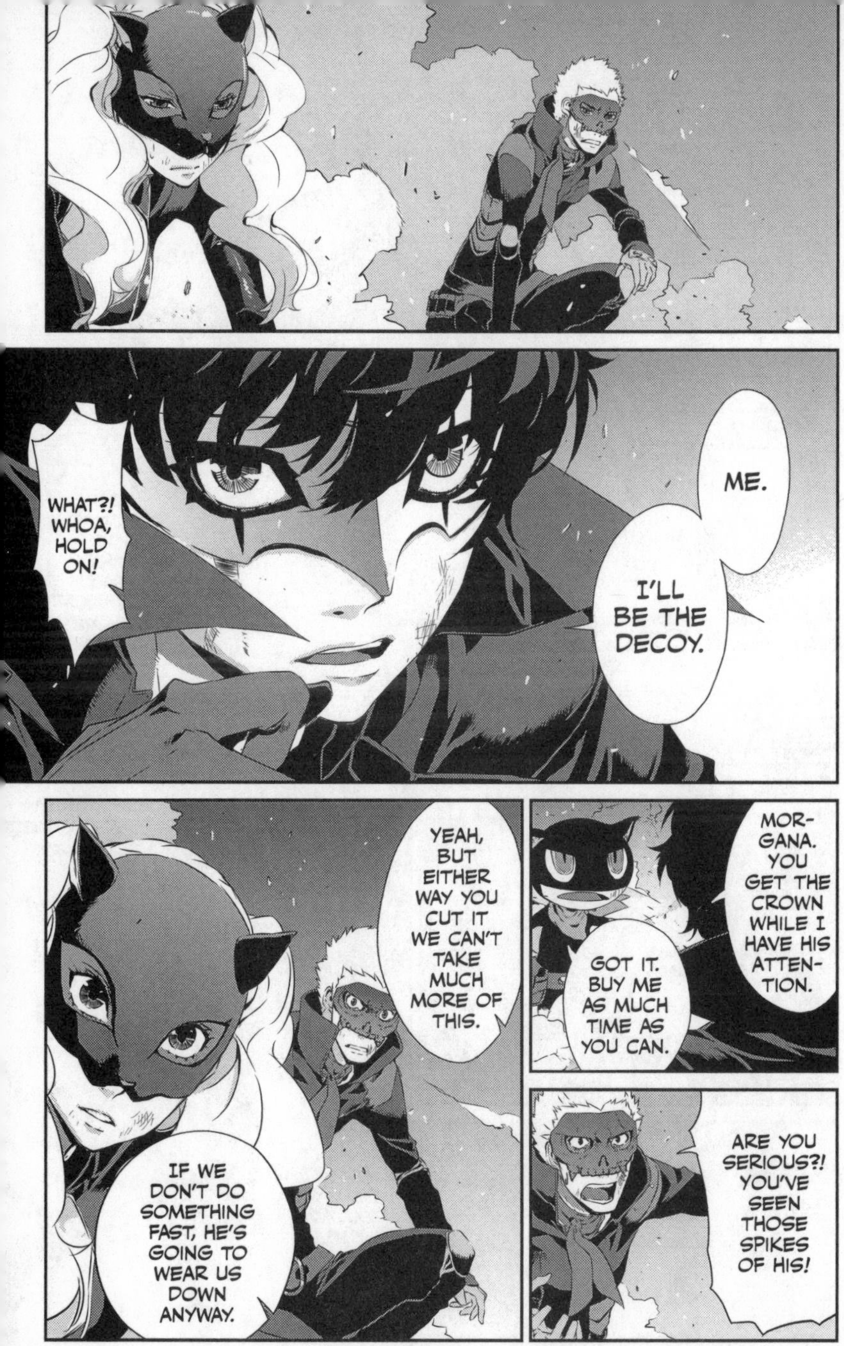
ME.
I'LL BE THE DECOY.
WHAT?! WHOA, HOLD ON!
MORGANA. YOU GET THE CROWN WHILE I HAVE HIS ATTENTION.
GOT IT. BUY ME AS MUCH TIME AS YOU CAN.
ARE YOU SERIOUS?! YOU'VE SEEN THOSE SPIKES OF HIS!
YEAH, BUT EITHER WAY YOU CUT IT WE CAN'T TAKE MUCH MORE OF THIS.
IF WE DON'T DO SOMETHING FAST, HE'S GOING TO WEAR US DOWN ANYWAY.

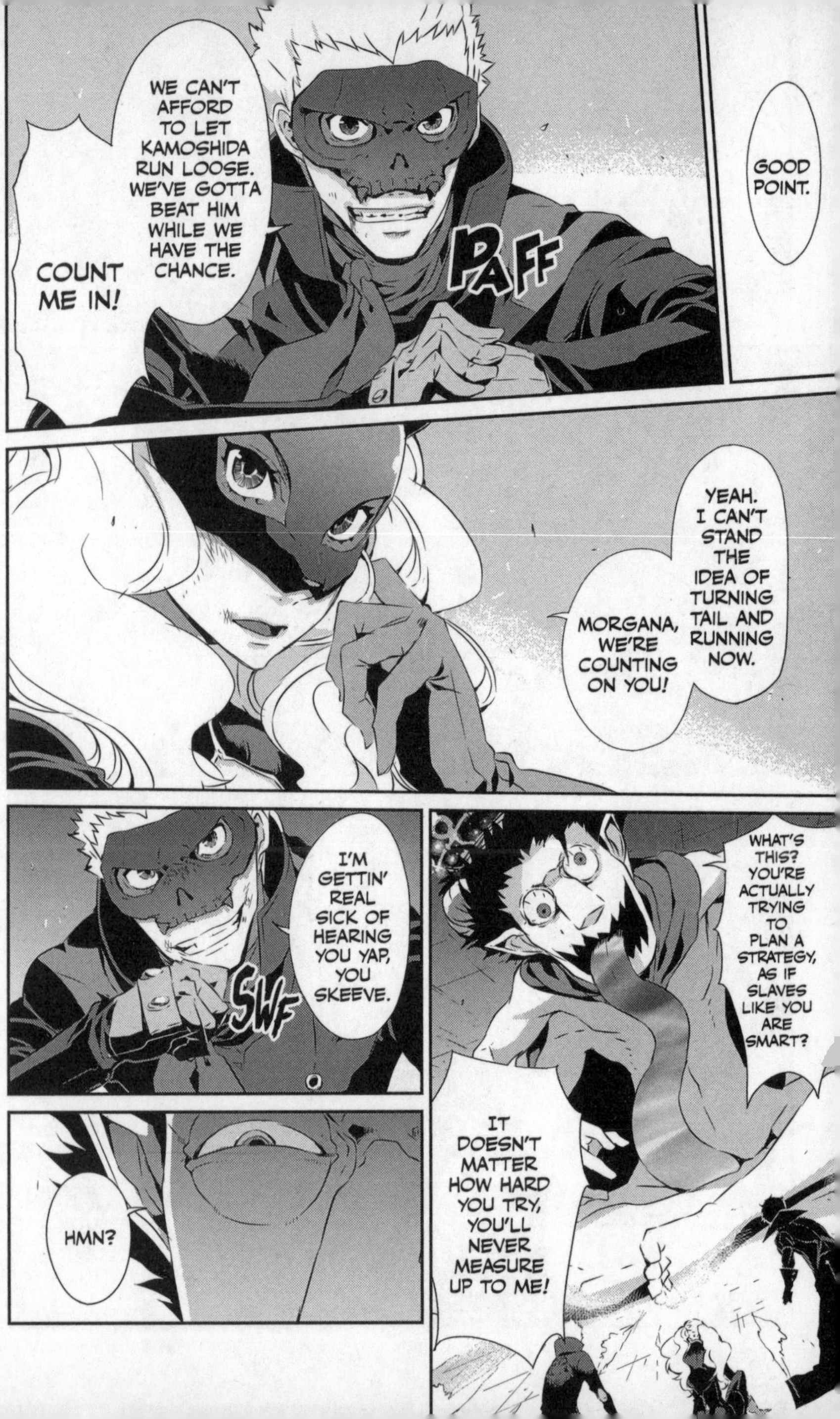
GOOD POINT.
WE CAN'T AFFORD TO LET KAMOSHIDA RUN LOOSE. WE'VE GOTTA BEAT HIM WHILE WE HAVE THE CHANCE.
PAFF
COUNT ME IN!
YEAH. I CAN'T STAND THE IDEA OF TURNING TAIL AND RUNNING NOW.
MORGANA, WE'RE COUNTING ON YOU!
WHAT'S THIS? YOU'RE ACTUALLY TRYING TO PLAN A STRATEGY, AS IF SLAVES LIKE YOU ARE SMART?
IT DOESN'T MATTER HOW HARD YOU TRY, YOU'LL NEVER MEASURE UP TO ME!
I'M GETTIN' REAL SICK OF HEARING YOU YAP, YOU SKEEVE.
SWF
HMN?

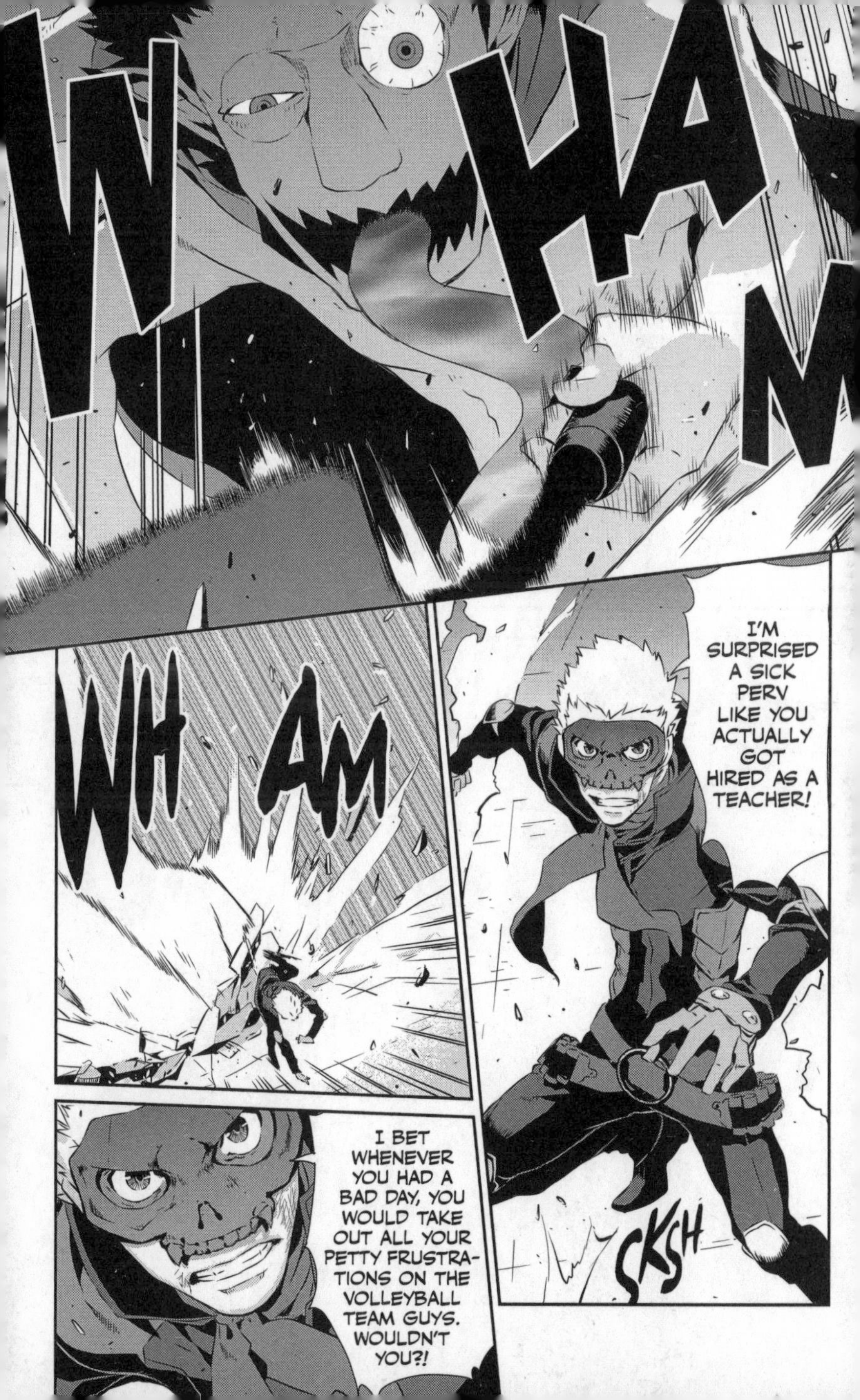
WHAM
I'M SURPRISED A SICK PERV LIKE YOU ACTUALLY GOT HIRED AS A TEACHER!
SKSH
WHAM
I BET WHENEVER YOU HAD A BAD DAY, YOU WOULD TAKE OUT ALL YOUR PETTY FRUSTRATIONS ON THE VOLLEYBALL TEAM GUYS. WOULDN'T YOU?!

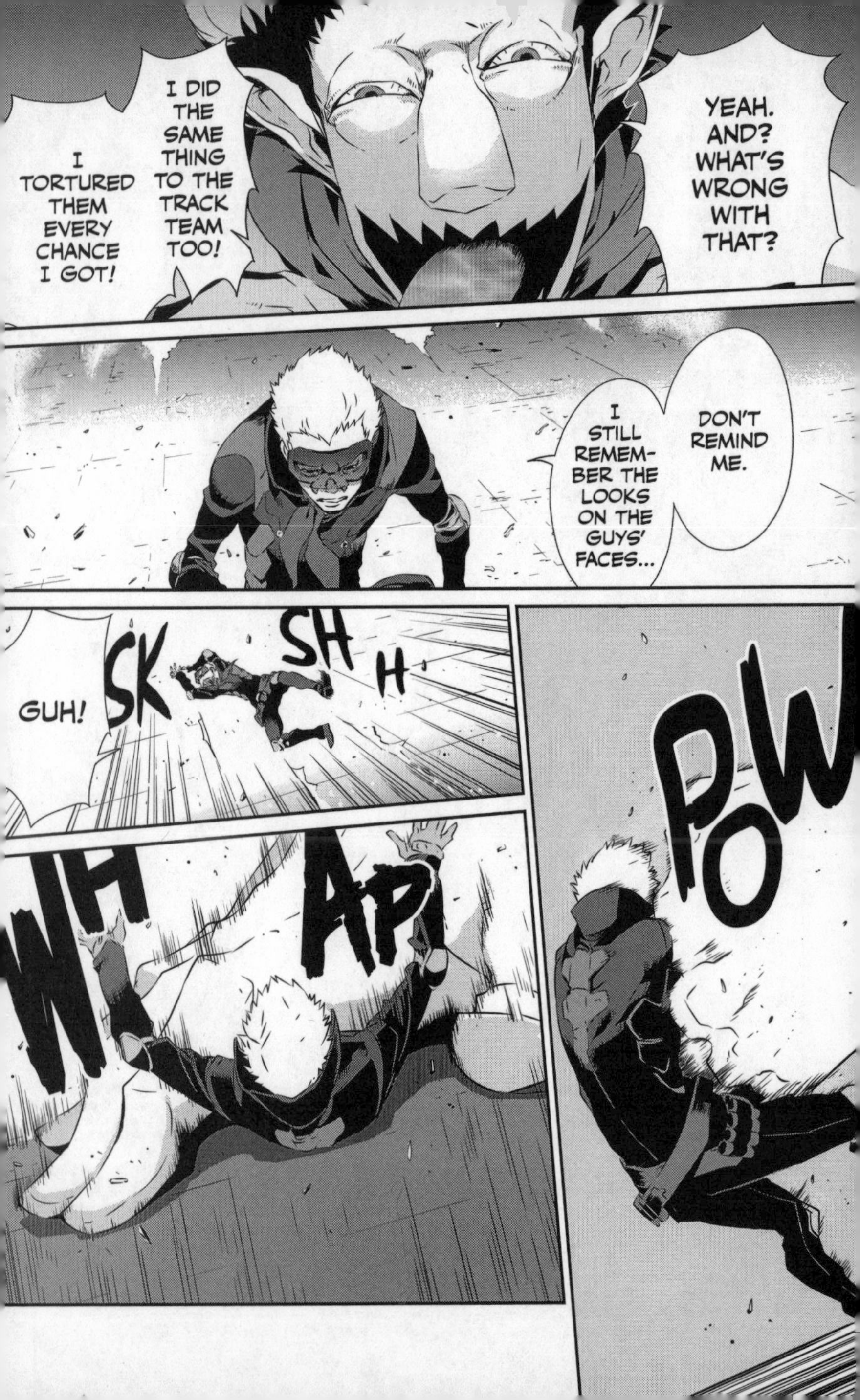
YEAH. AND? WHAT'S WRONG WITH THAT?
I DID THE SAME THING TO THE TRACK TEAM TOO!
I TORTURED THEM EVERY CHANCE I GOT!
DON'T REMIND ME.
I STILL REMEM-BER THE LOOKS ON THE GUYS' FACES...
POW
SKSHH
GUH!
WHAP

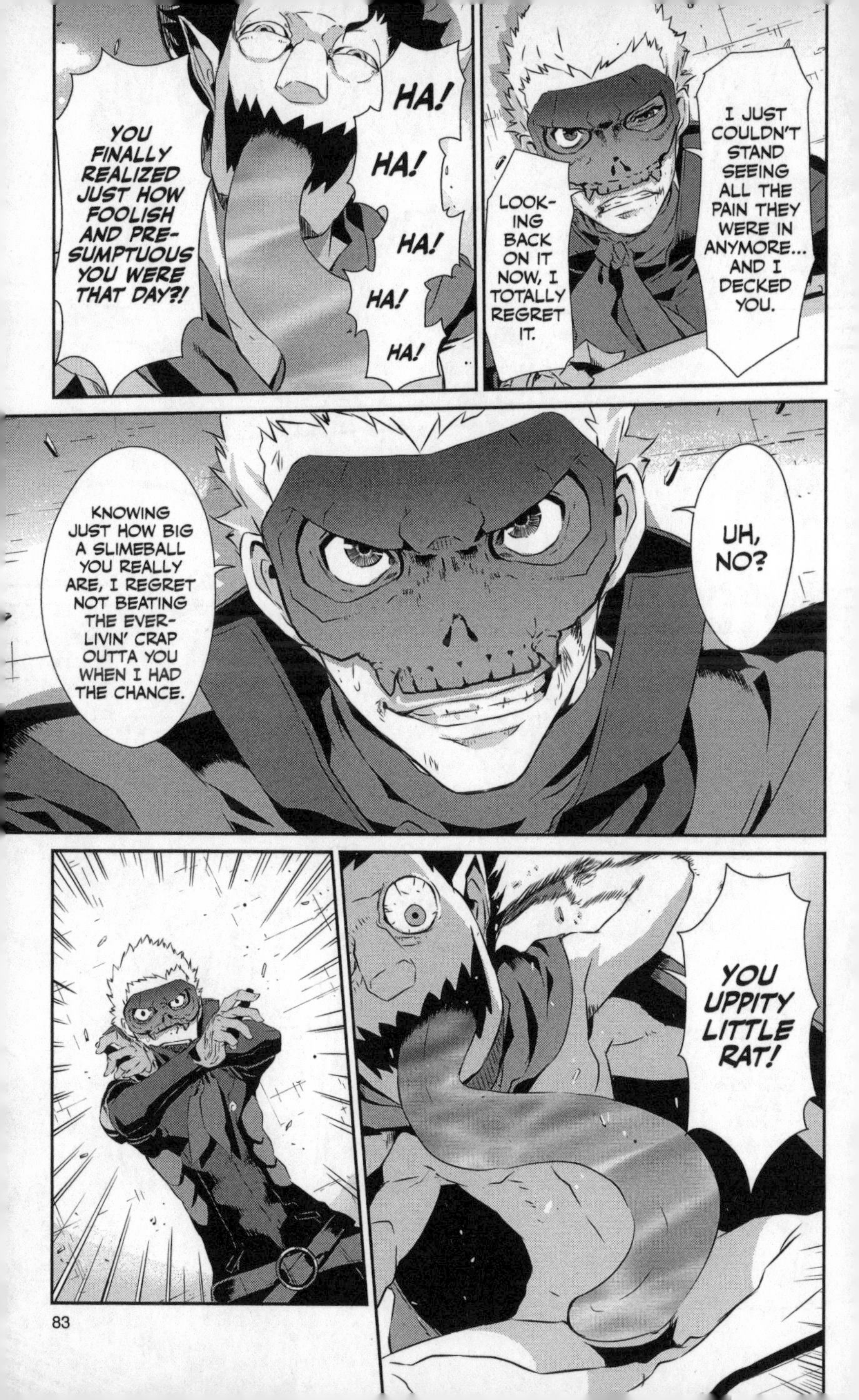
I JUST COULDN'T STAND SEEING ALL THE PAIN THEY WERE IN ANYMORE... AND I DECKED YOU.
LOOKING BACK ON IT NOW, I TOTALLY REGRET IT.
HA! HA! HA! HA! HA!
YOU FINALLY REALIZED JUST HOW FOOLISH AND PRESUMPTUOUS YOU WERE THAT DAY?!
UH, NO?
KNOWING JUST HOW BIG A SLIMEBALL YOU REALLY ARE, I REGRET NOT BEATING THE EVER-LIVIN' CRAP OUTTA YOU WHEN I HAD THE CHANCE.
YOU UPPITY LITTLE RAT!

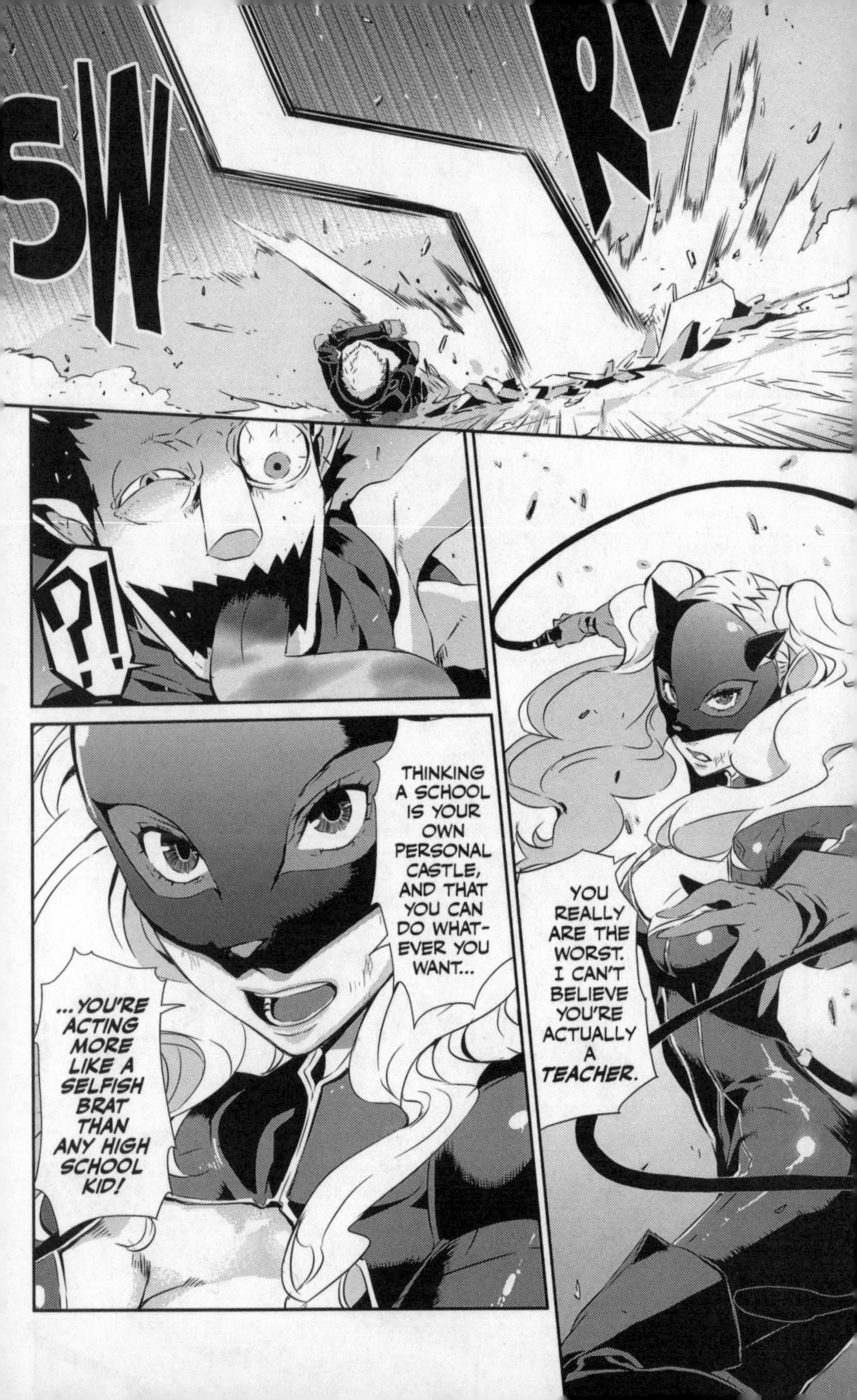
SW
RY
YOU REALLY ARE THE WORST. I CAN'T BELIEVE YOU'RE ACTUALLY A *TEACHER*.
?!
THINKING A SCHOOL IS YOUR OWN PERSONAL CASTLE, AND THAT YOU CAN DO WHAT-EVER YOU WANT...
...YOU'RE ACTING MORE LIKE A SELFISH BRAT THAN ANY HIGH SCHOOL KID!

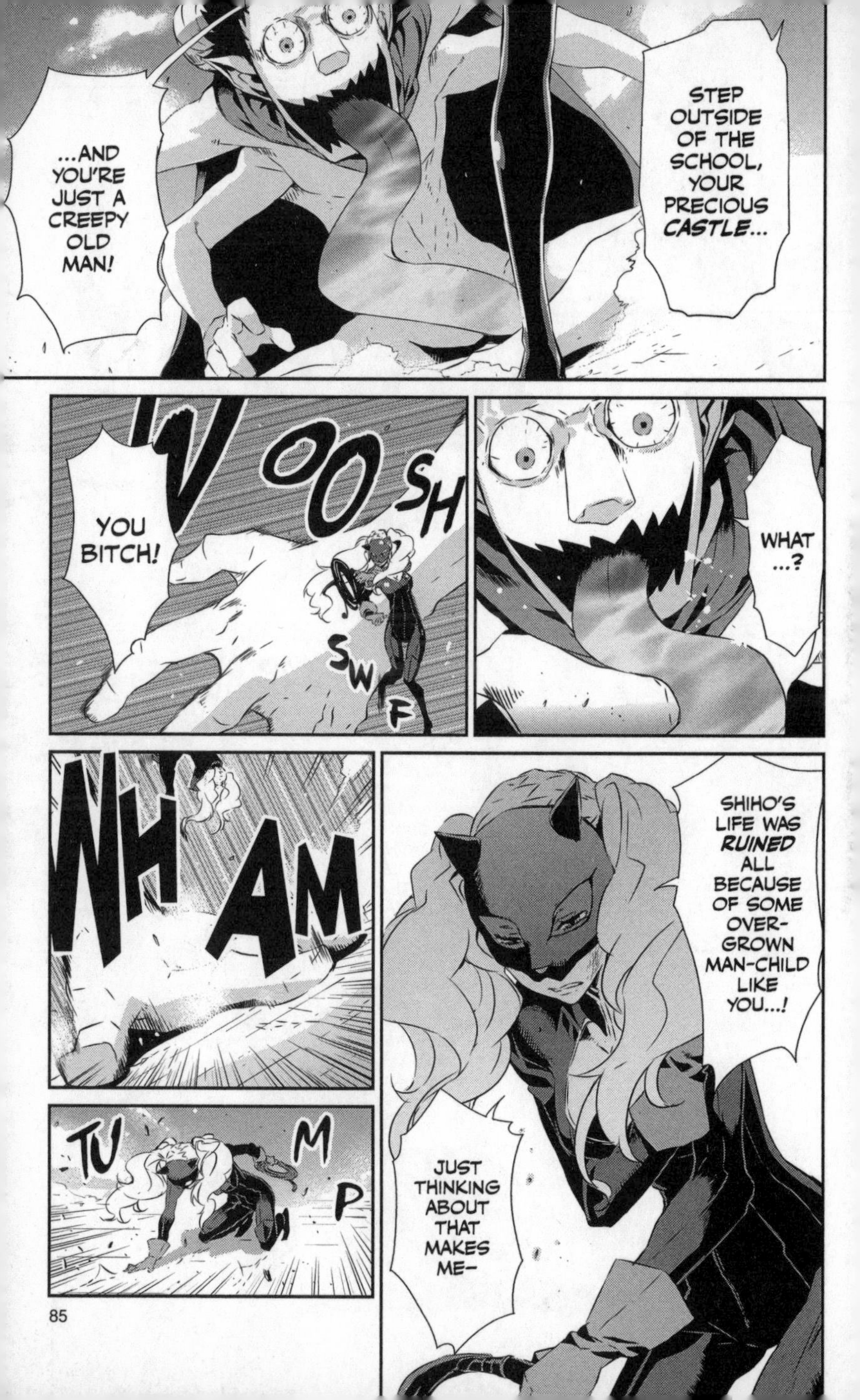
STEP OUTSIDE OF THE SCHOOL, YOUR PRECIOUS *CASTLE*...
...AND YOU'RE JUST A CREEPY OLD MAN!
WHAT ...?
YOU BITCH!
WOOSH
SWF
SHIHO'S LIFE WAS *RUINED* ALL BECAUSE OF SOME OVER-GROWN MAN-CHILD LIKE YOU...!
JUST THINKING ABOUT THAT MAKES ME-
WHAM
TUMP

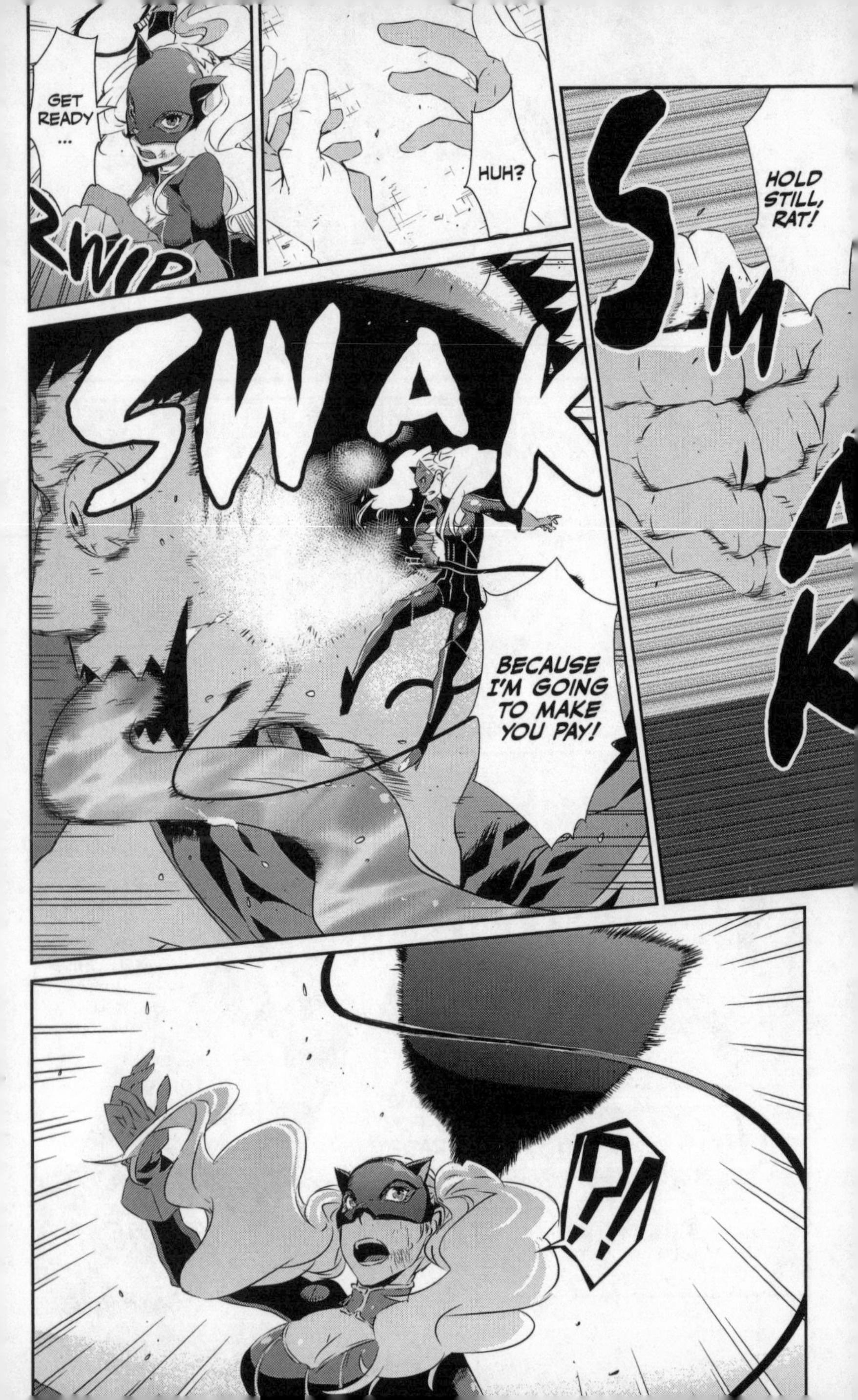
HOLD STILL, RAT!
SMAK
HUH?
GET READY ...
RWIP
SWAK
BECAUSE I'M GOING TO MAKE YOU PAY!
?!

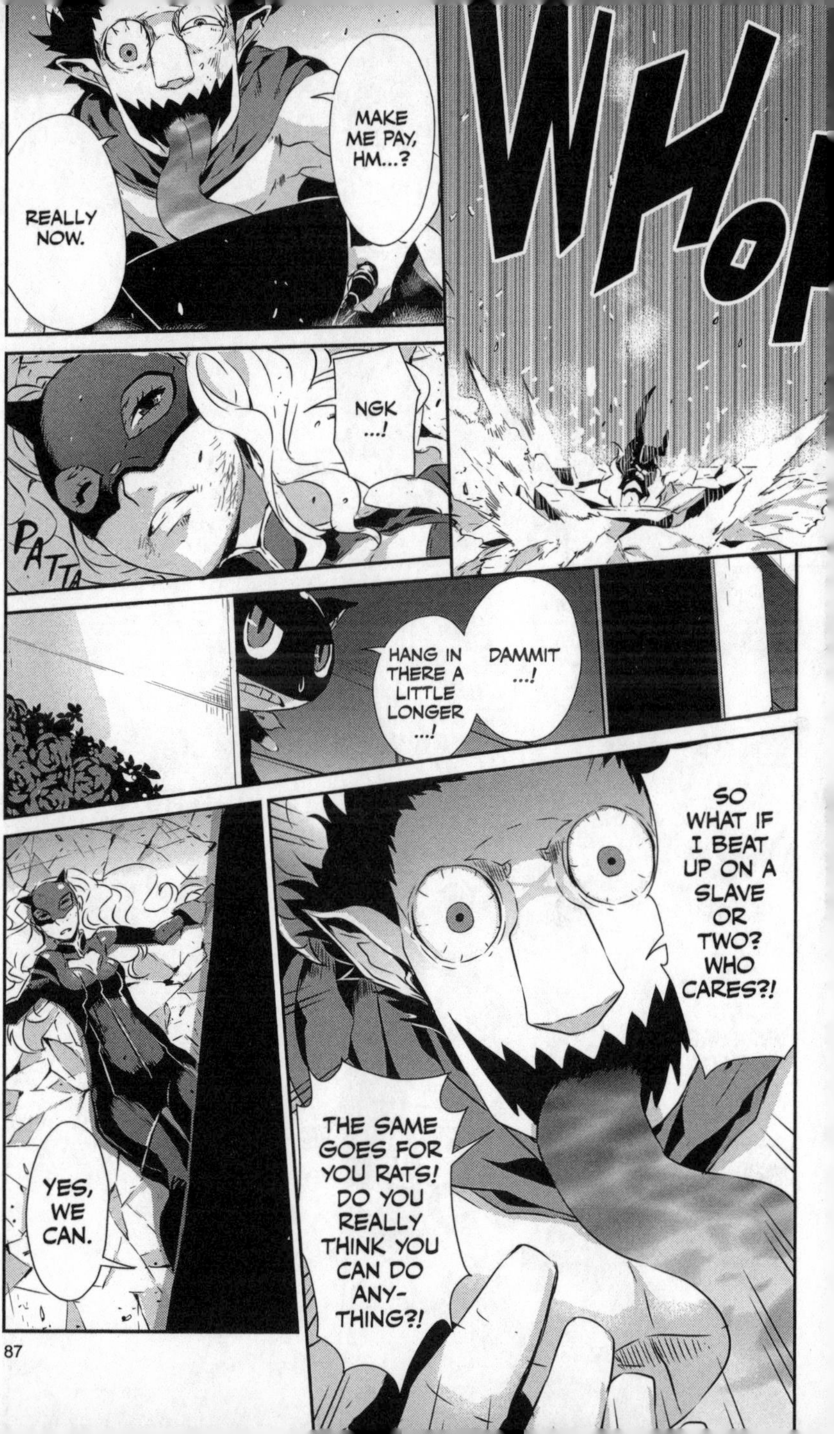
WHOP
MAKE ME PAY, HM...?
REALLY NOW.
NGK ...!
PATTA
DAMMIT ...!
HANG IN THERE A LITTLE LONGER ...!
SO WHAT IF I BEAT UP ON A SLAVE OR TWO? WHO CARES?!
THE SAME GOES FOR YOU RATS! DO YOU REALLY THINK YOU CAN DO ANY-THING?!
YES, WE CAN.

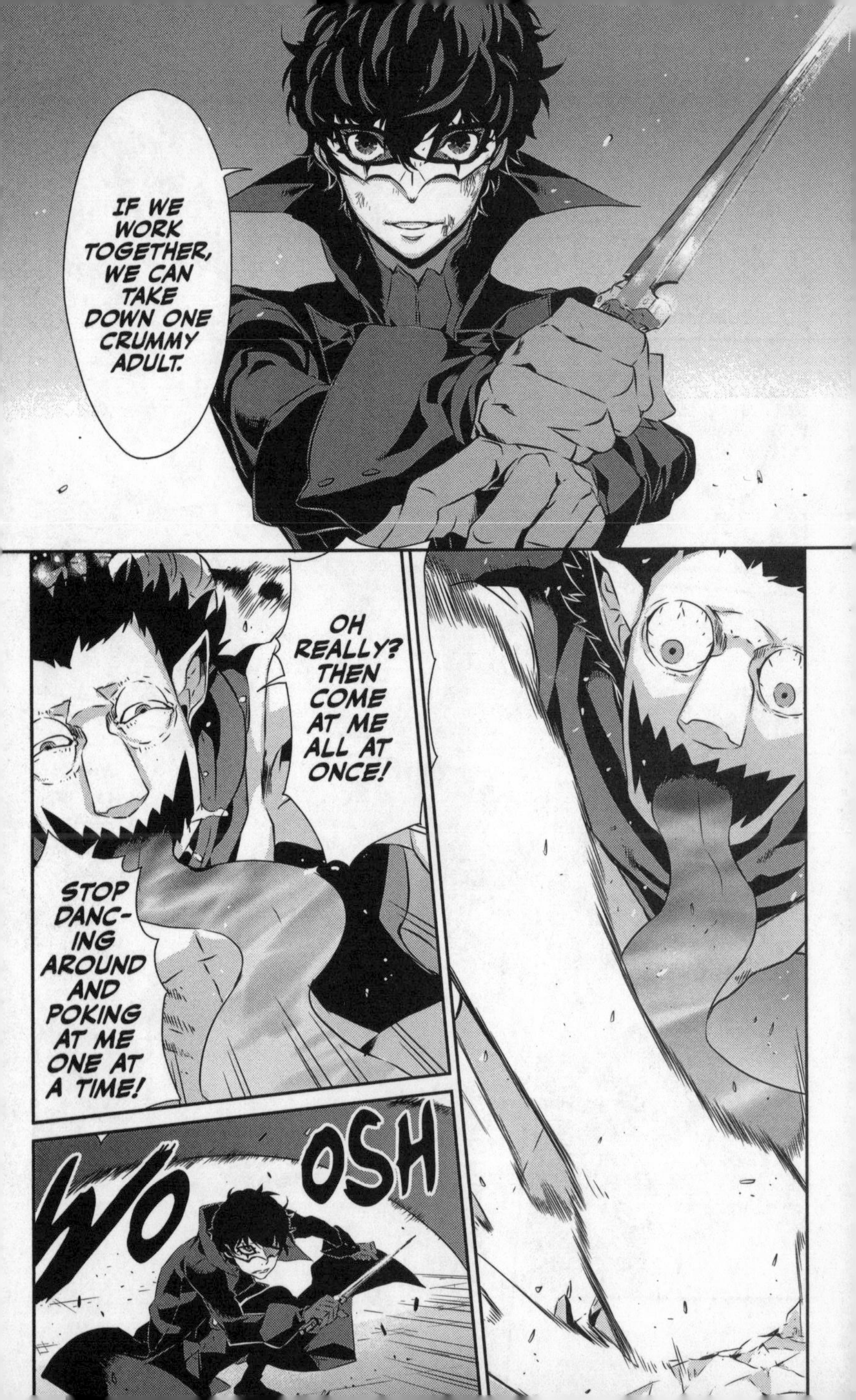
IF WE WORK TOGETHER, WE CAN TAKE DOWN ONE CRUMMY ADULT.
OH REALLY? THEN COME AT ME ALL AT ONCE!
STOP DANC-ING AROUND AND POKING AT ME ONE AT A TIME!
WOOSH

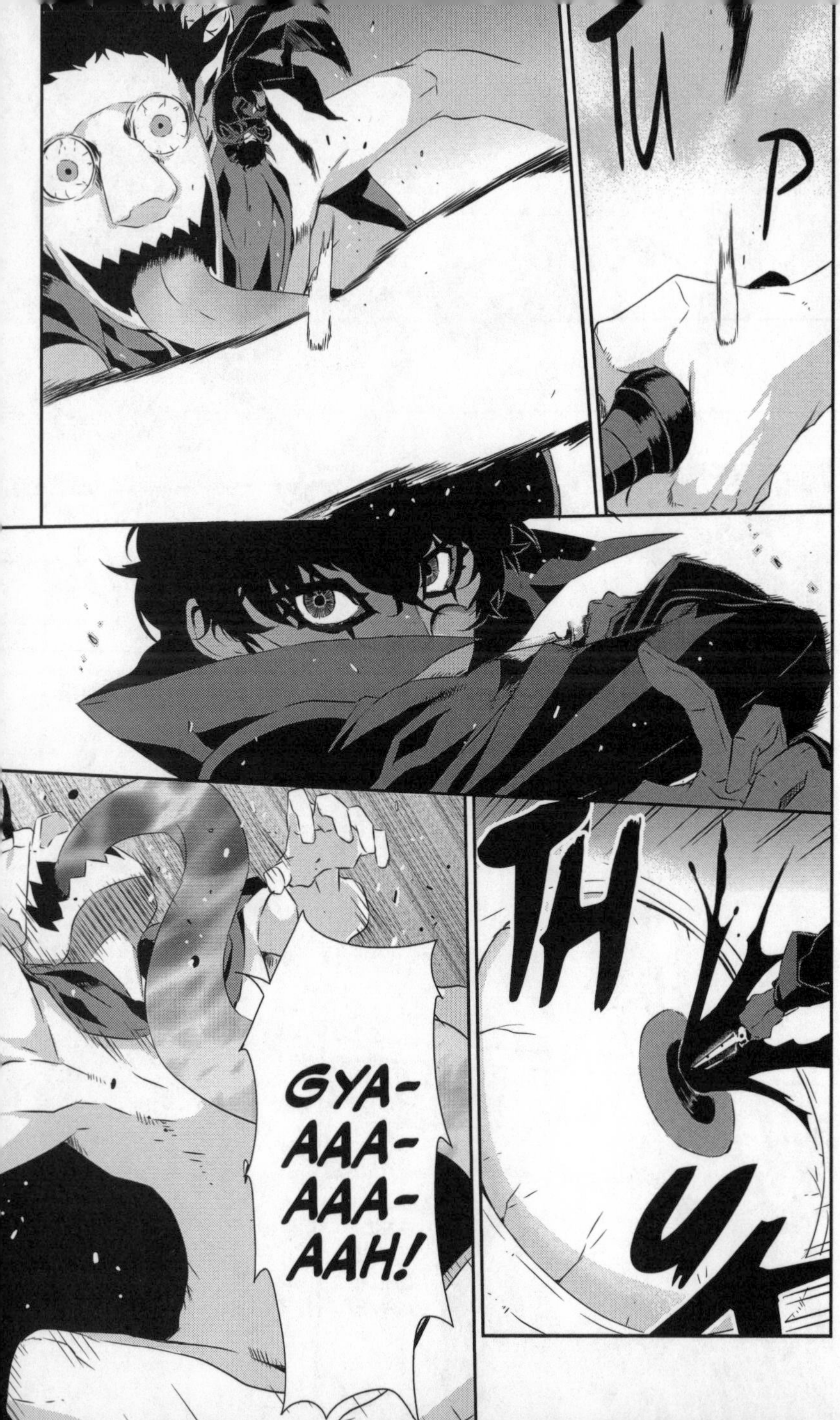
TUP
THUK
GYA-AAA-AAA-AAH!

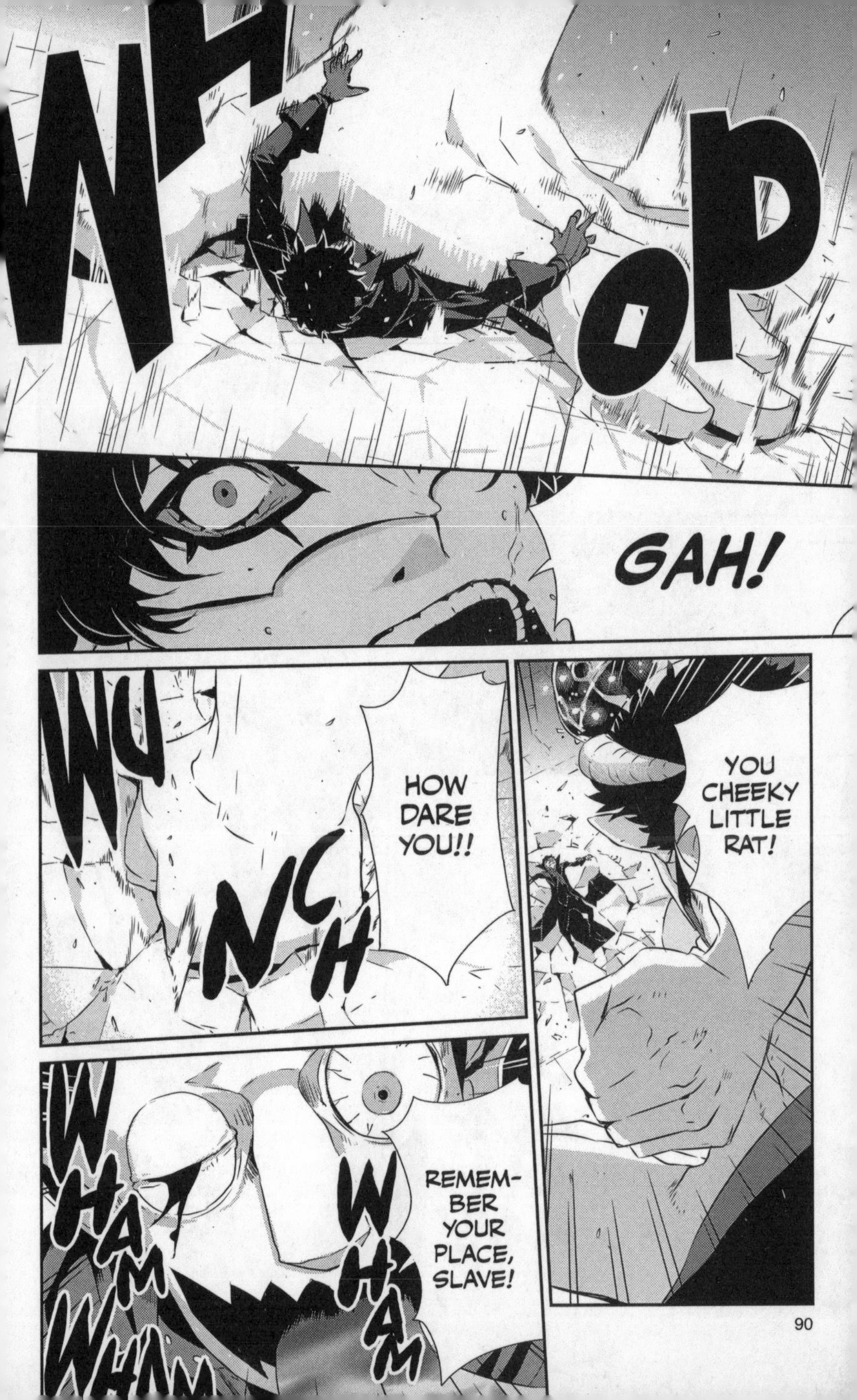
WHOP
GAH!
YOU CHEEKY LITTLE RAT!
HOW DARE YOU!!
WUNCH
WHAM
REMEMBER YOUR PLACE, SLAVE!
WHAM
WHAM

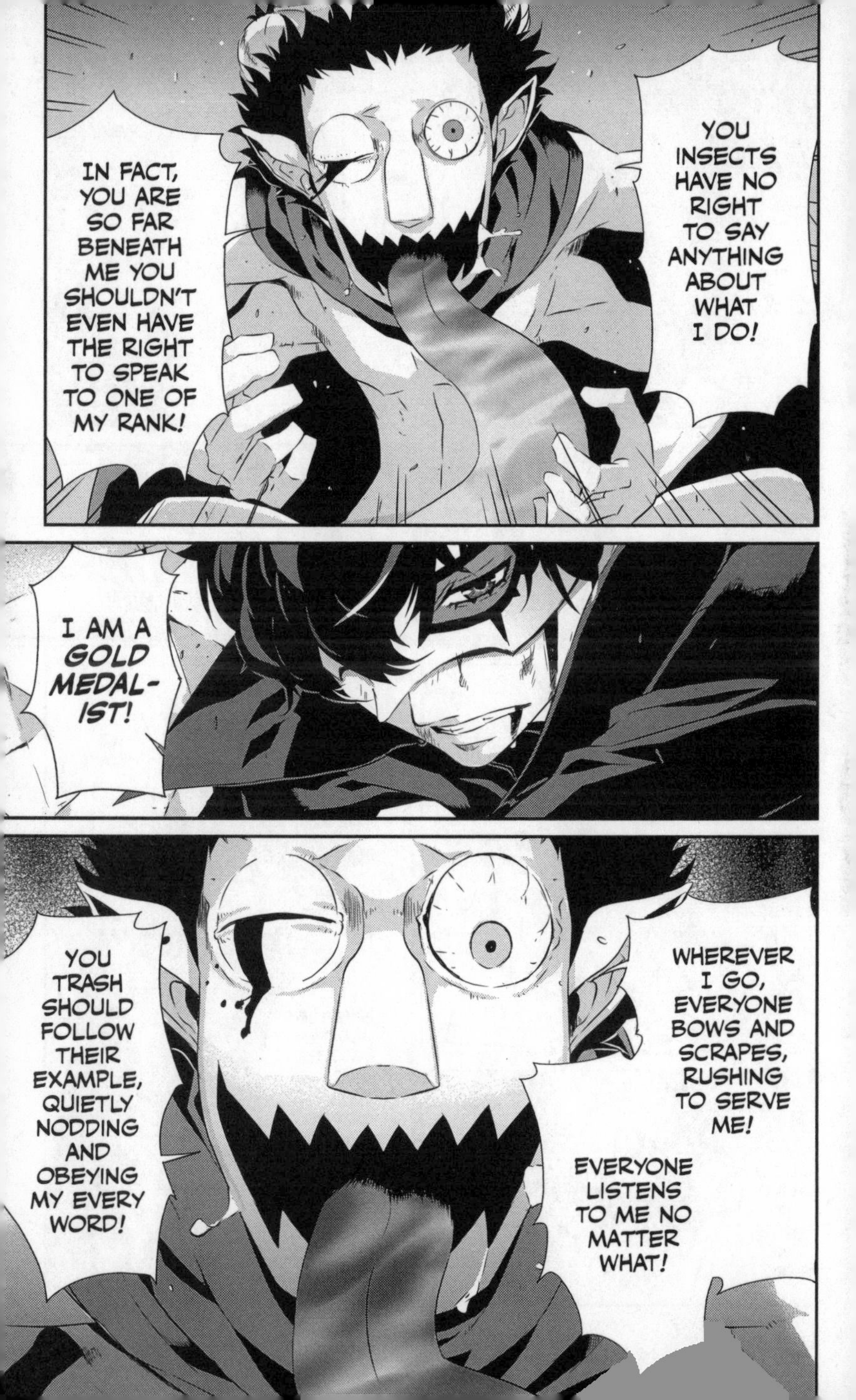
YOU INSECTS HAVE NO RIGHT TO SAY ANYTHING ABOUT WHAT I DO!
IN FACT, YOU ARE SO FAR BENEATH ME YOU SHOULDN'T EVEN HAVE THE RIGHT TO SPEAK TO ONE OF MY RANK!
I AM A *GOLD MEDAL-IST!*
WHEREVER I GO, EVERYONE BOWS AND SCRAPES, RUSHING TO SERVE ME!
EVERYONE LISTENS TO ME NO MATTER WHAT!
YOU TRASH SHOULD FOLLOW THEIR EXAMPLE, QUIETLY NODDING AND OBEYING MY EVERY WORD!

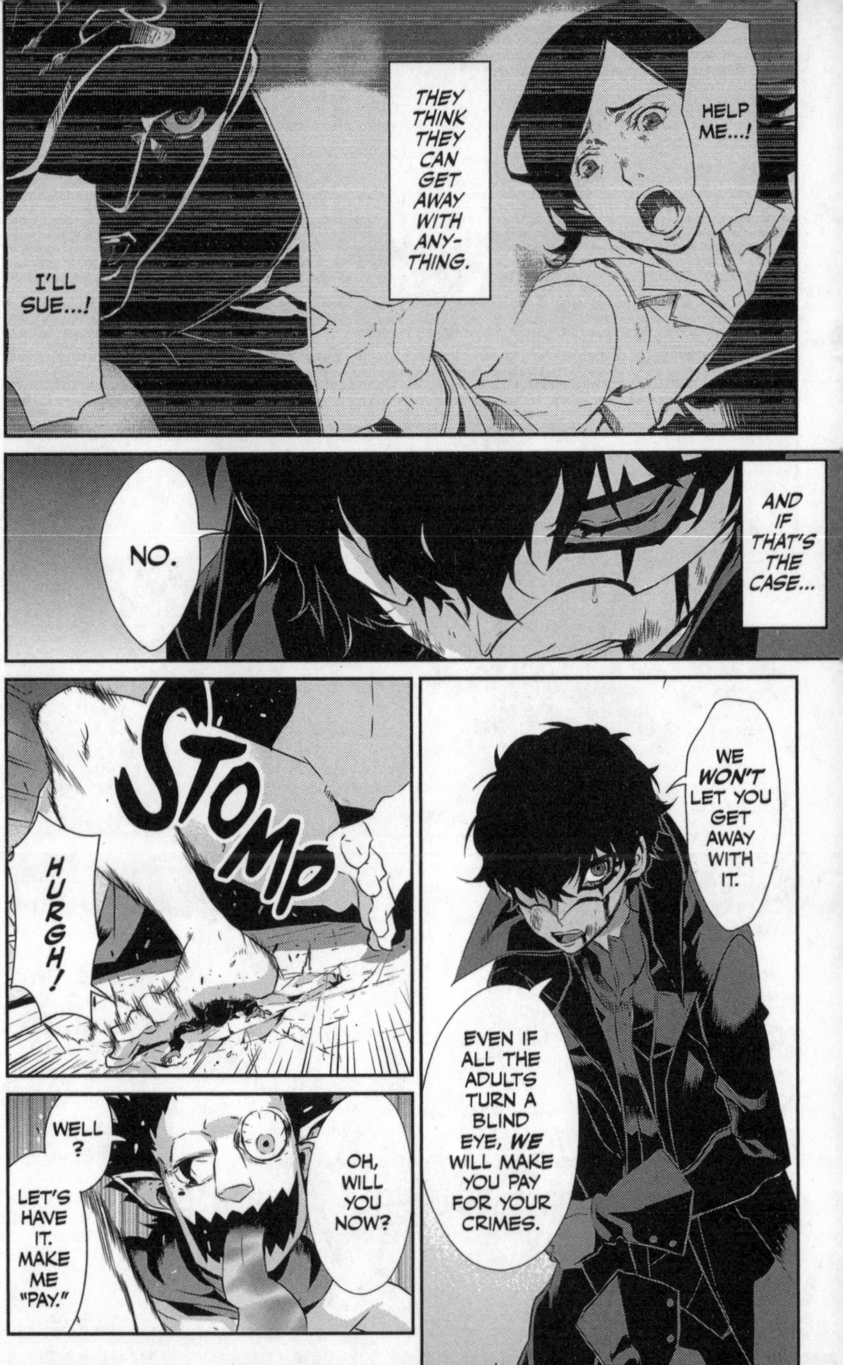
HELP ME...!
THEY THINK THEY CAN GET AWAY WITH ANY-THING.
I'LL SUE...!
AND IF THAT'S THE CASE...
NO.
WE *WON'T* LET YOU GET AWAY WITH IT.
EVEN IF ALL THE ADULTS TURN A BLIND EYE, *WE* WILL MAKE YOU PAY FOR YOUR CRIMES.
STOMP
HURGH!
OH, WILL YOU NOW?
WELL? LET'S HAVE IT. MAKE ME "PAY."

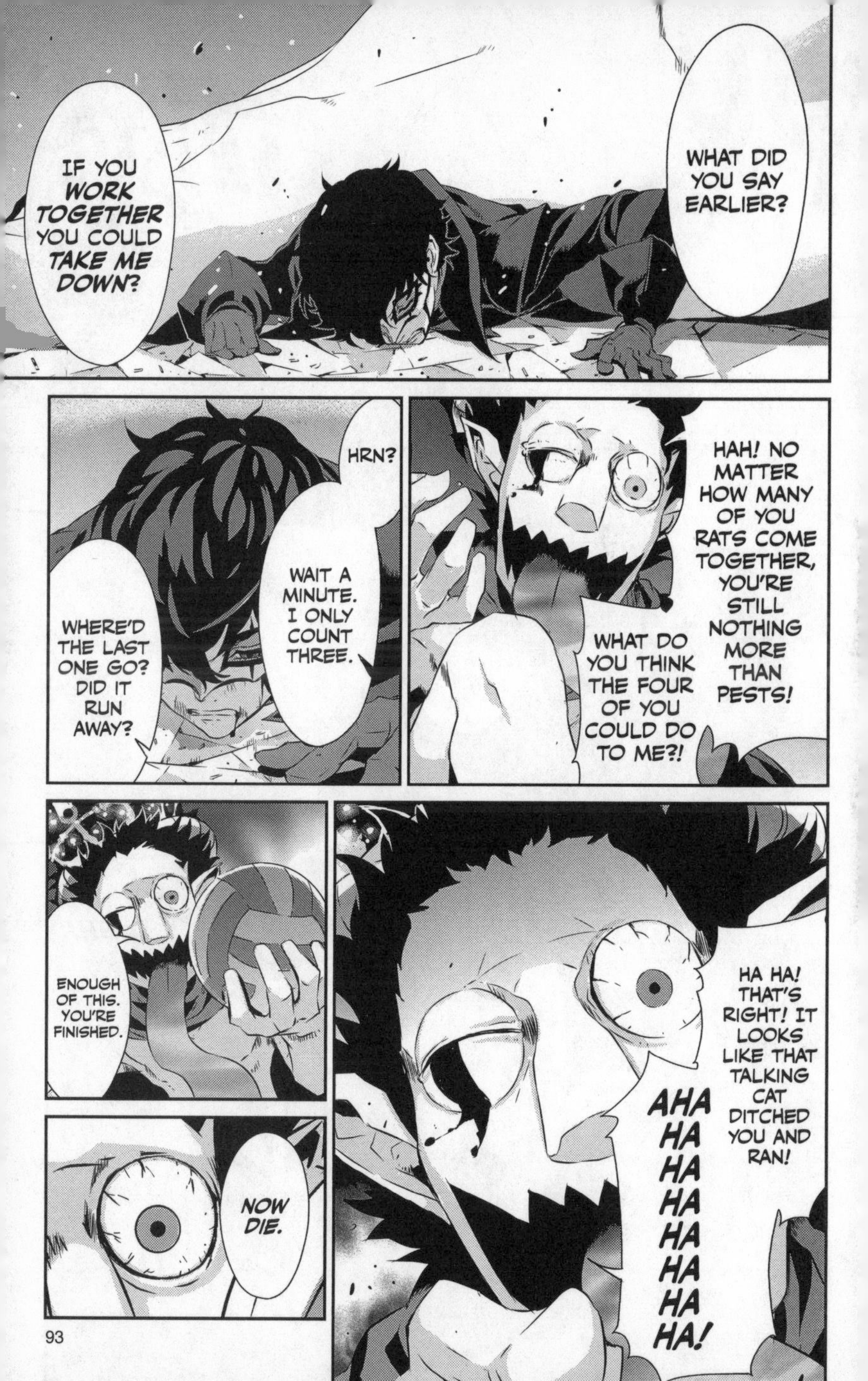
WHAT DID YOU SAY EARLIER?
IF YOU WORK TOGETHER YOU COULD TAKE ME DOWN?
HAH! NO MATTER HOW MANY OF YOU RATS COME TOGETHER, YOU'RE STILL NOTHING MORE THAN PESTS!
WHAT DO YOU THINK THE FOUR OF YOU COULD DO TO ME?!
HRN?
WAIT A MINUTE. I ONLY COUNT THREE.
WHERE'D THE LAST ONE GO? DID IT RUN AWAY?
HA HA! THAT'S RIGHT! IT LOOKS LIKE THAT TALKING CAT DITCHED YOU AND RAN!
AHA HA HA HA HA HA HA HA HA HA!
ENOUGH OF THIS. YOU'RE FINISHED.
NOW DIE.

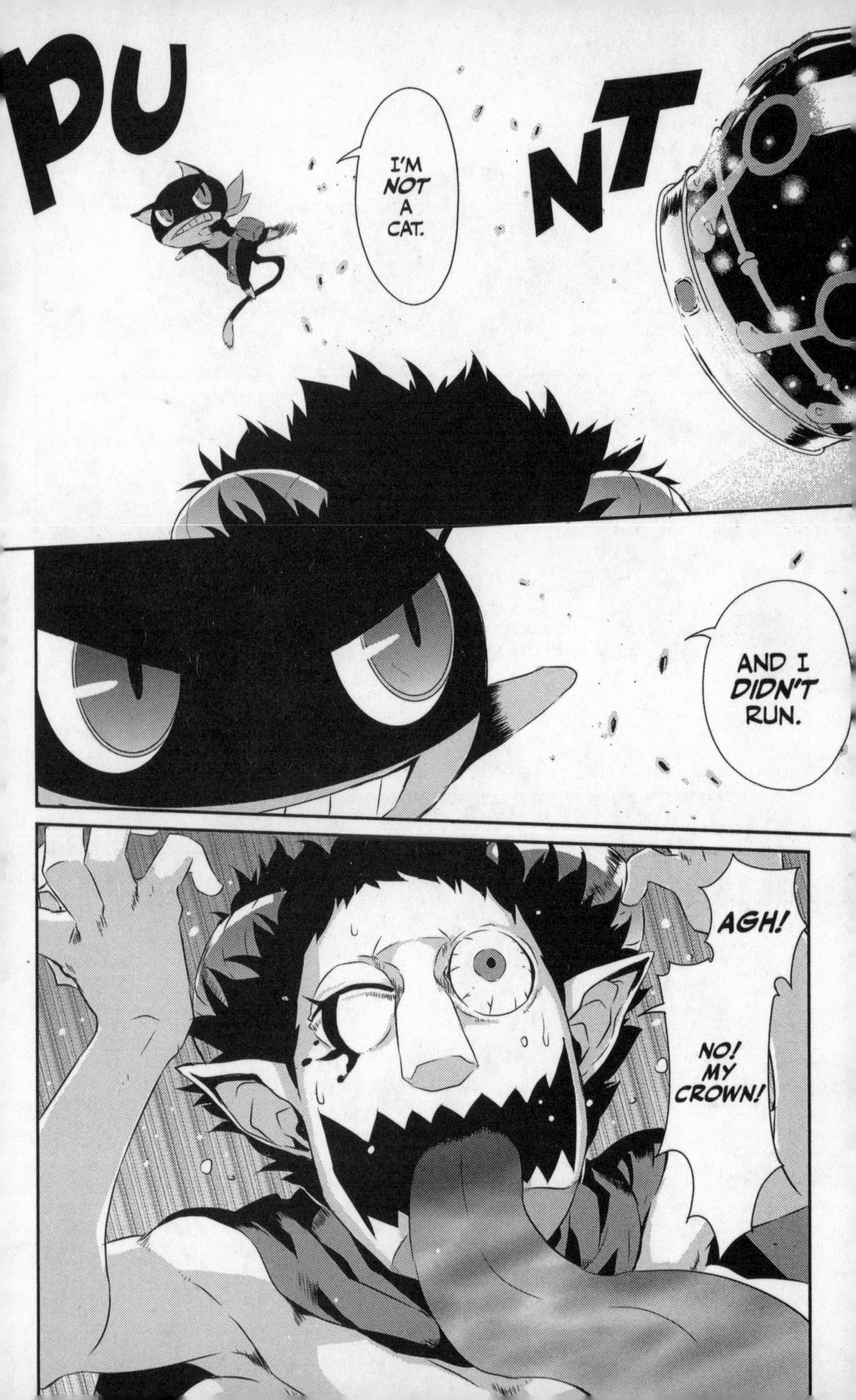
PU
NT
I'M NOT A CAT.
AND I DIDN'T RUN.
AGH!
NO! MY CROWN!

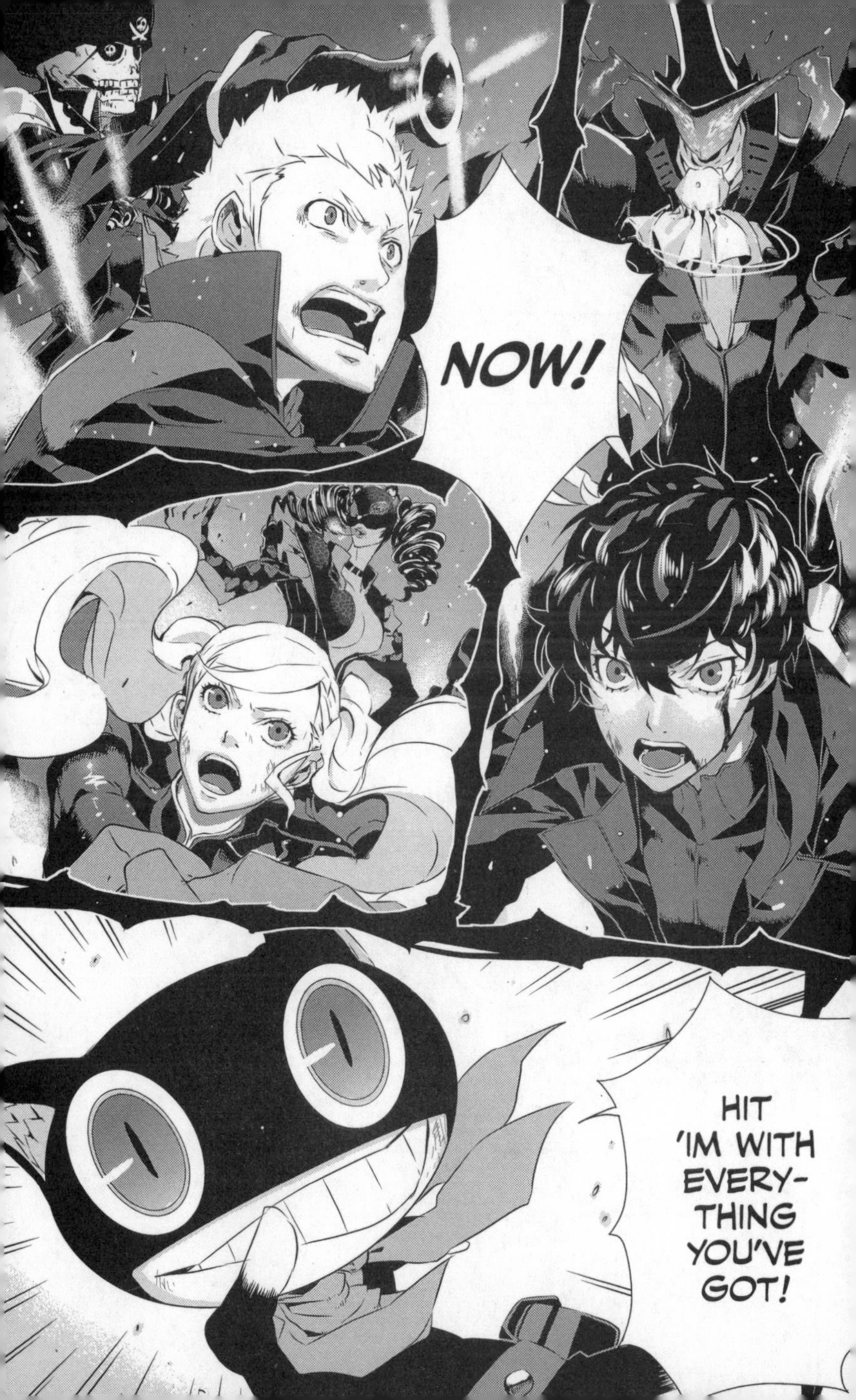
NOW!
HIT 'IM WITH EVERY-THING YOU'VE GOT!

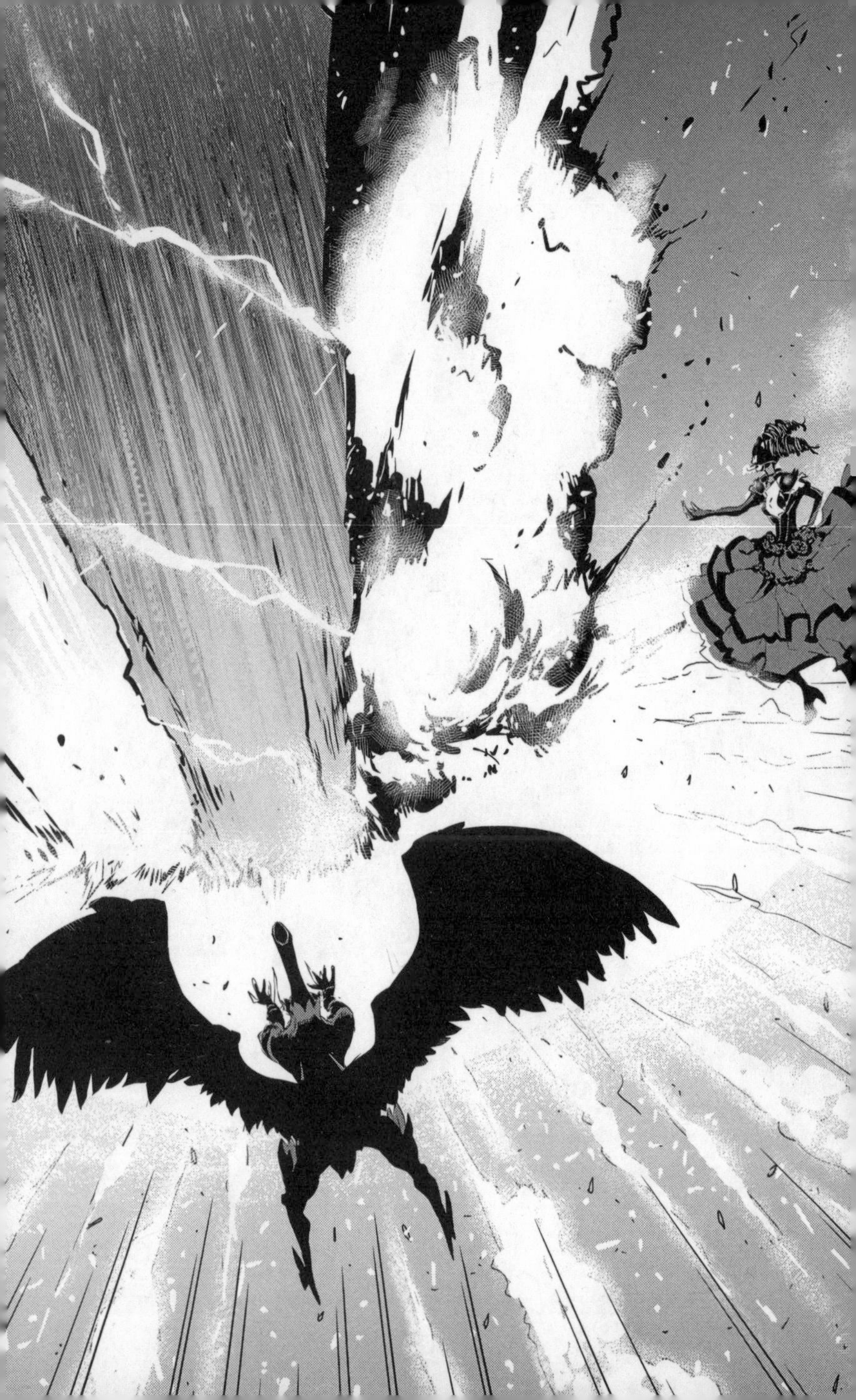

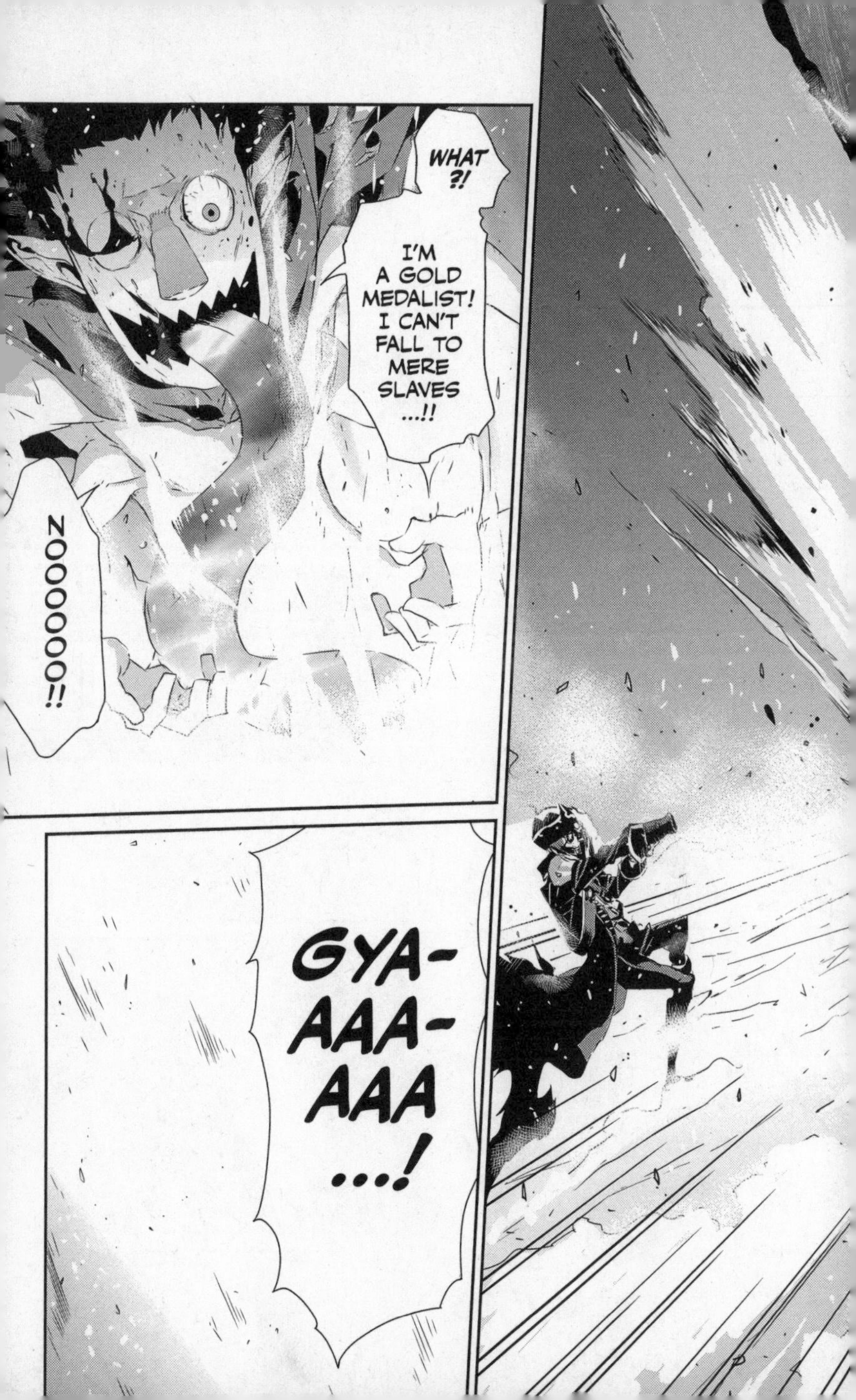
WHAT ?!
I'M A GOLD MEDALIST! I CAN'T FALL TO MERE SLAVES ...!!
NOOOOOOO!!
GYA-AAA-AAA ...!

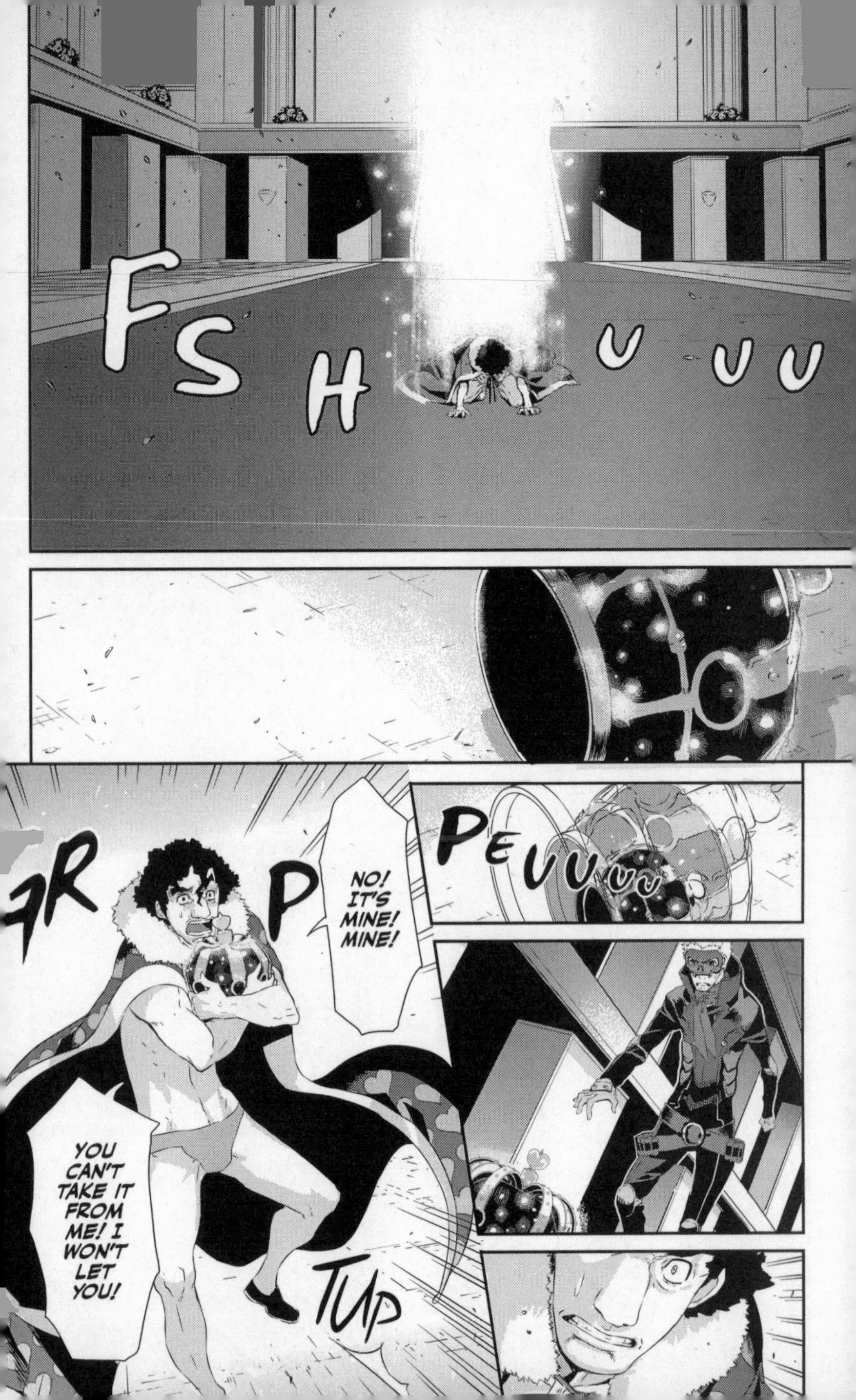
FSHUUUU
PEVUUUU
NO! IT'S MINE! MINE!
YOU CAN'T TAKE IT FROM ME! I WON'T LET YOU!
TUP

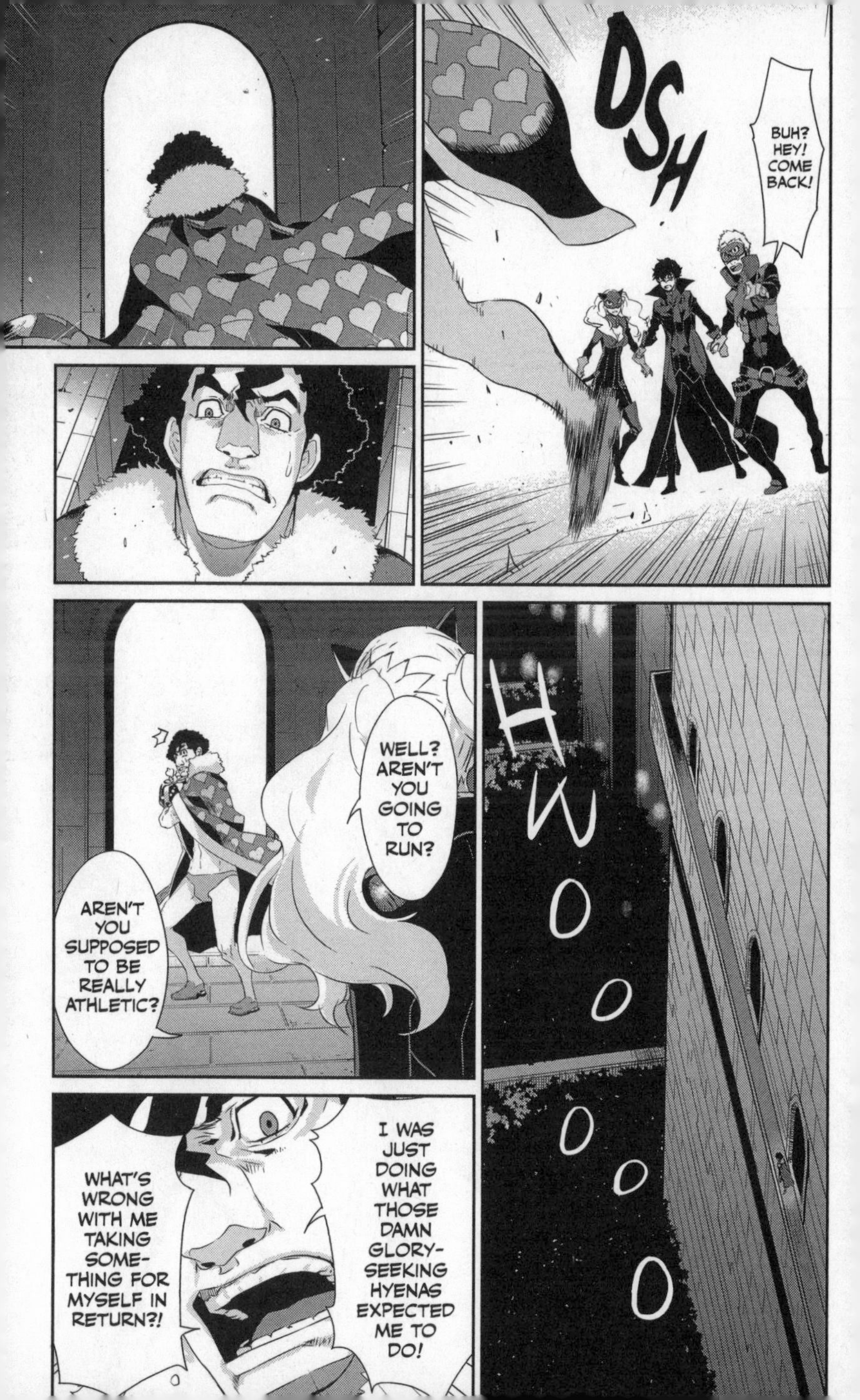
DSH
BUH? HEY! COME BACK!
HWOOOOOO
WELL? AREN'T YOU GOING TO RUN?
AREN'T YOU SUPPOSED TO BE REALLY ATHLETIC?
I WAS JUST DOING WHAT THOSE DAMN GLORY-SEEKING HYENAS EXPECTED ME TO DO!
WHAT'S WRONG WITH ME TAKING SOME-THING FOR MYSELF IN RETURN?!

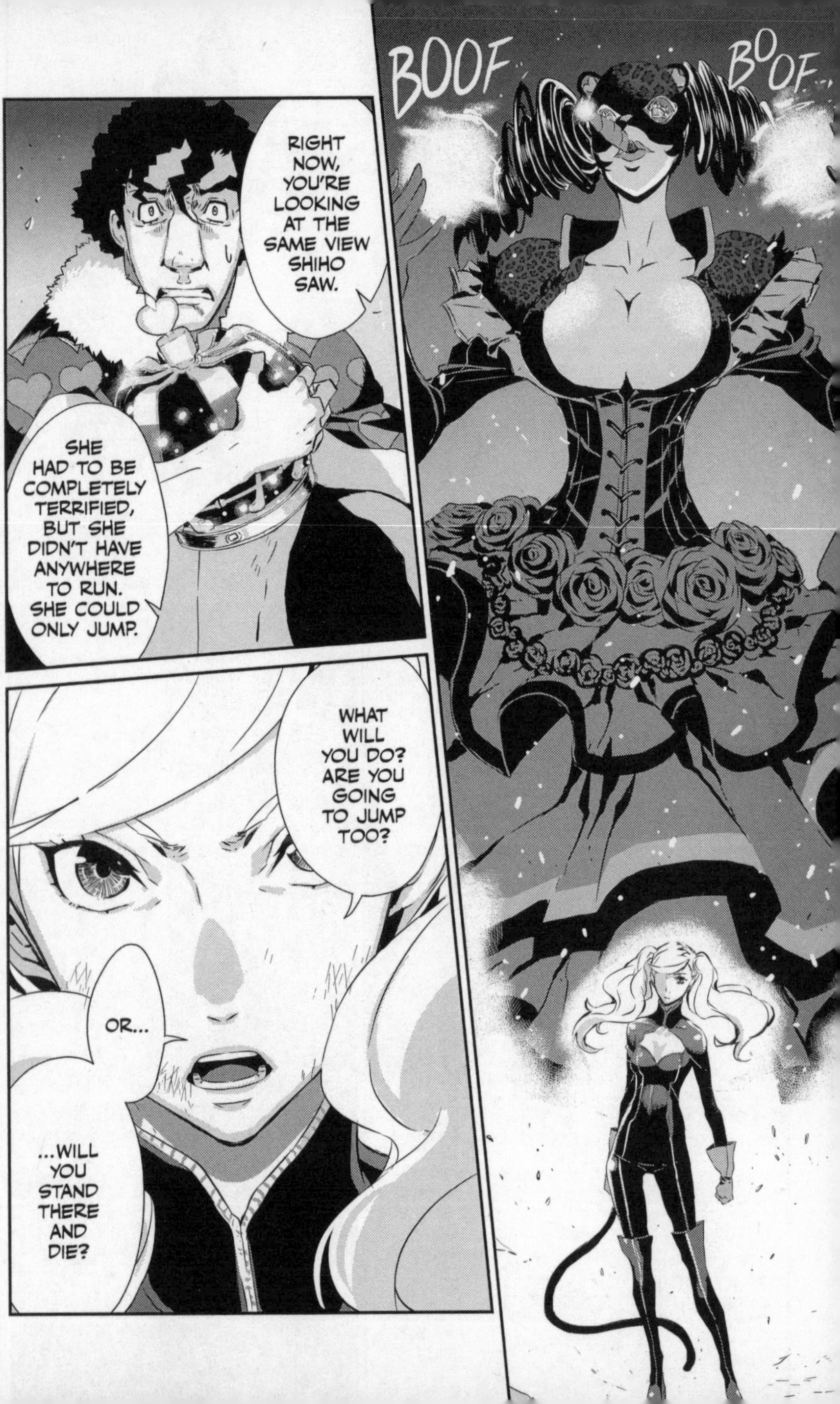
BOOF
BOOF
RIGHT NOW, YOU'RE LOOKING AT THE SAME VIEW SHIHO SAW.
SHE HAD TO BE COMPLETELY TERRIFIED, BUT SHE DIDN'T HAVE ANYWHERE TO RUN. SHE COULD ONLY JUMP.
WHAT WILL YOU DO? ARE YOU GOING TO JUMP TOO?
OR...
...WILL YOU STAND THERE AND DIE?

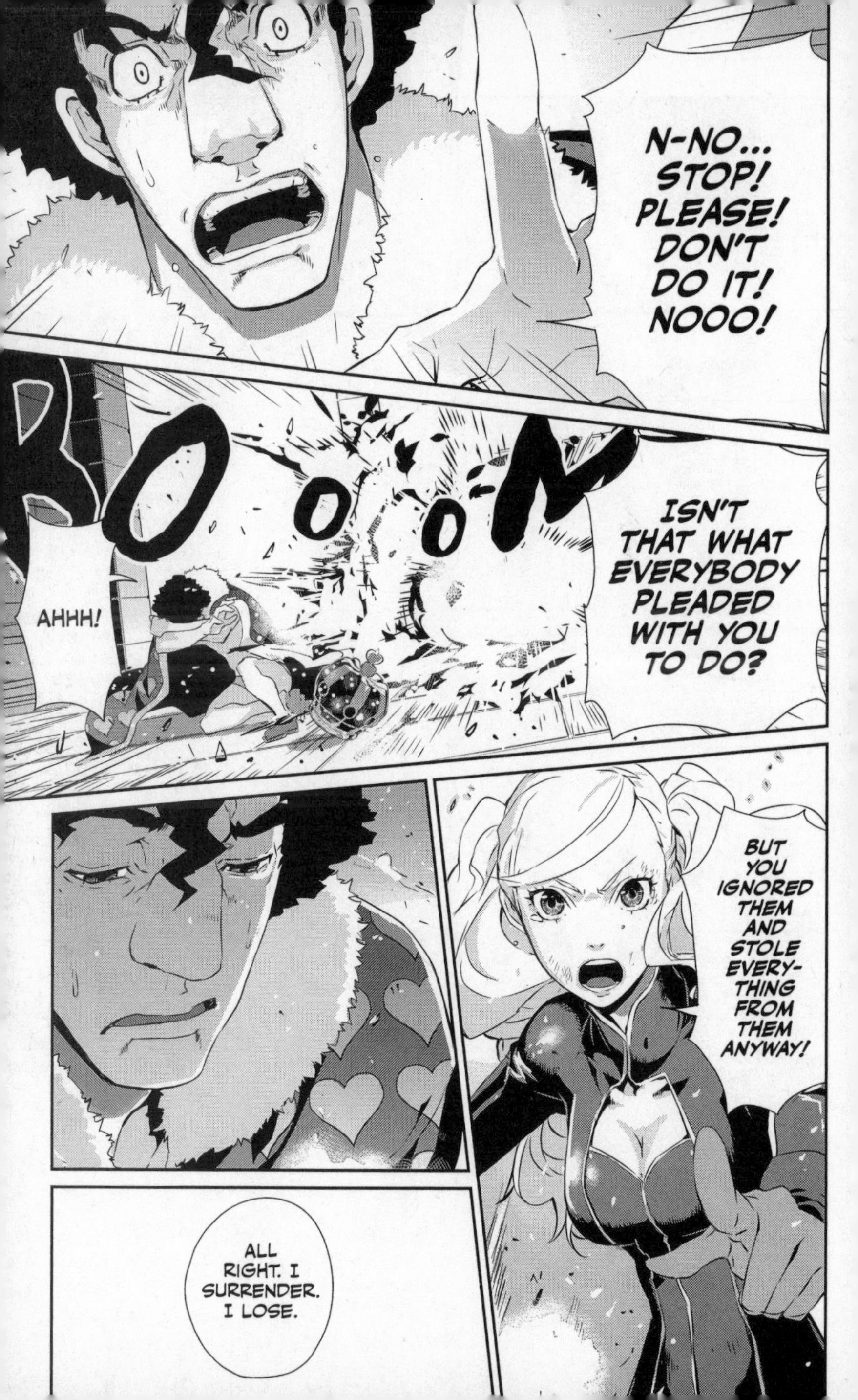

N-NO... STOP! PLEASE! DON'T DO IT! NOOO!
BOOOOM
ISN'T THAT WHAT EVERYBODY PLEADED WITH YOU TO DO?
AHHH!
BUT YOU IGNORED THEM AND STOLE EVERY-THING FROM THEM ANYWAY!
ALL RIGHT. I SURRENDER. I LOSE.

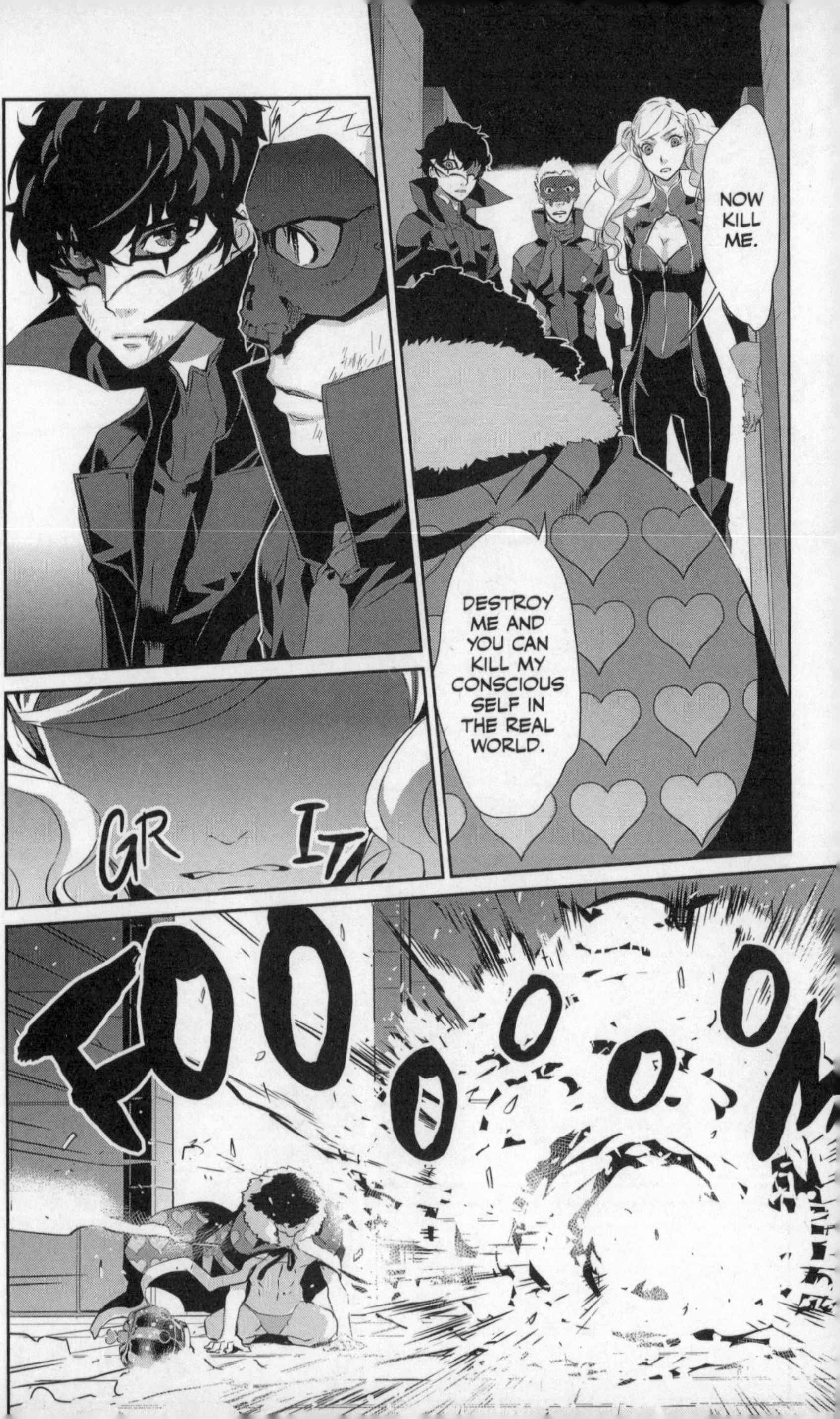
NOW KILL ME.
DESTROY ME AND YOU CAN KILL MY CONSCIOUS SELF IN THE REAL WORLD.
GRIT
TOOOOOOM

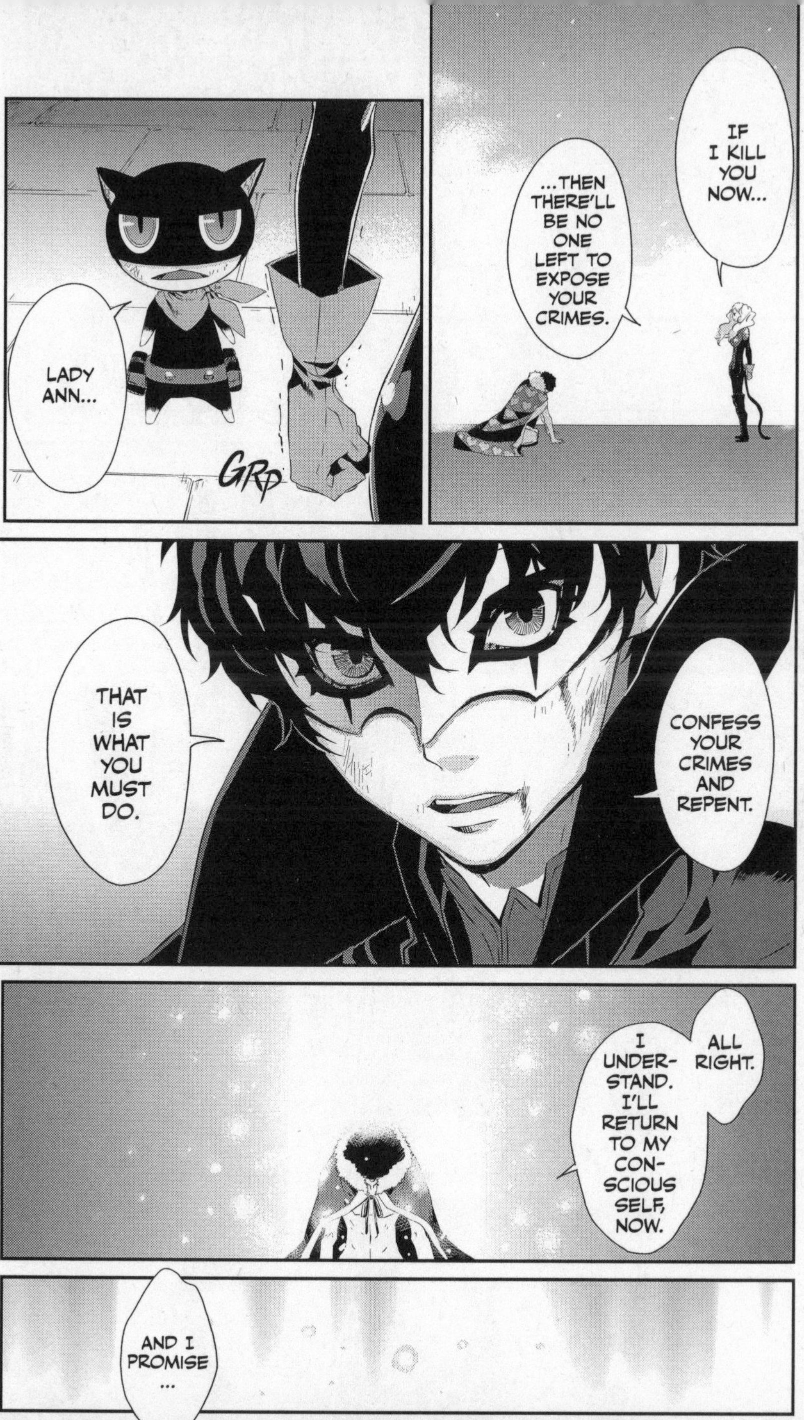
IF I KILL YOU NOW...
...THEN THERE'LL BE NO ONE LEFT TO EXPOSE YOUR CRIMES.
LADY ANN...
GRP
CONFESS YOUR CRIMES AND REPENT.
THAT IS WHAT YOU MUST DO.
ALL RIGHT.
I UNDER-STAND. I'LL RETURN TO MY CON-SCIOUS SELF, NOW.
AND I PROMISE ...

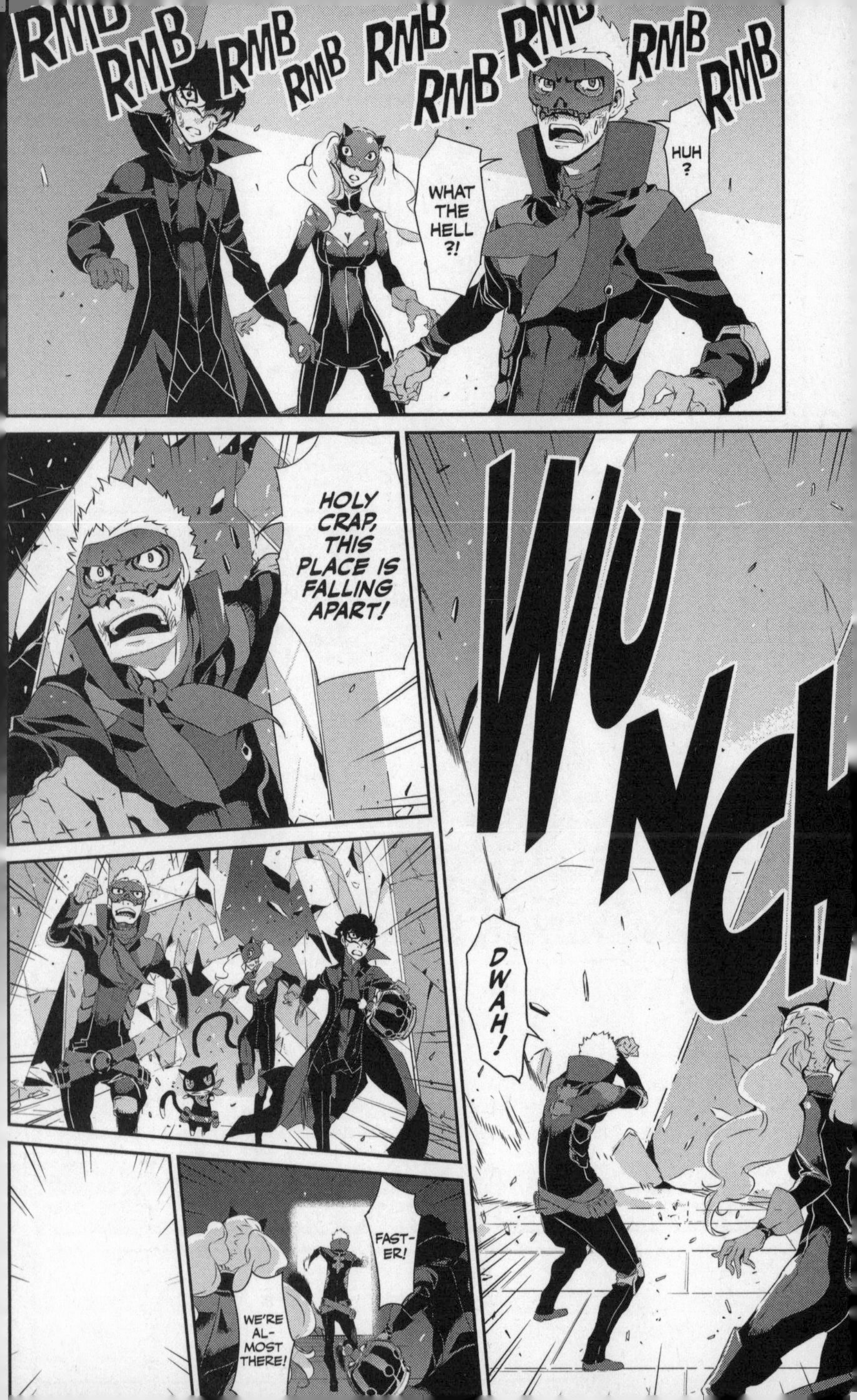
RMB RMB RMB RMB RMB RMB RMB RMB RMB
HUH?
WHAT THE HELL ?!
WUNCH
DWAH!
HOLY CRAP, THIS PLACE IS FALLING APART!
FASTER!
WE'RE AL-MOST THERE!

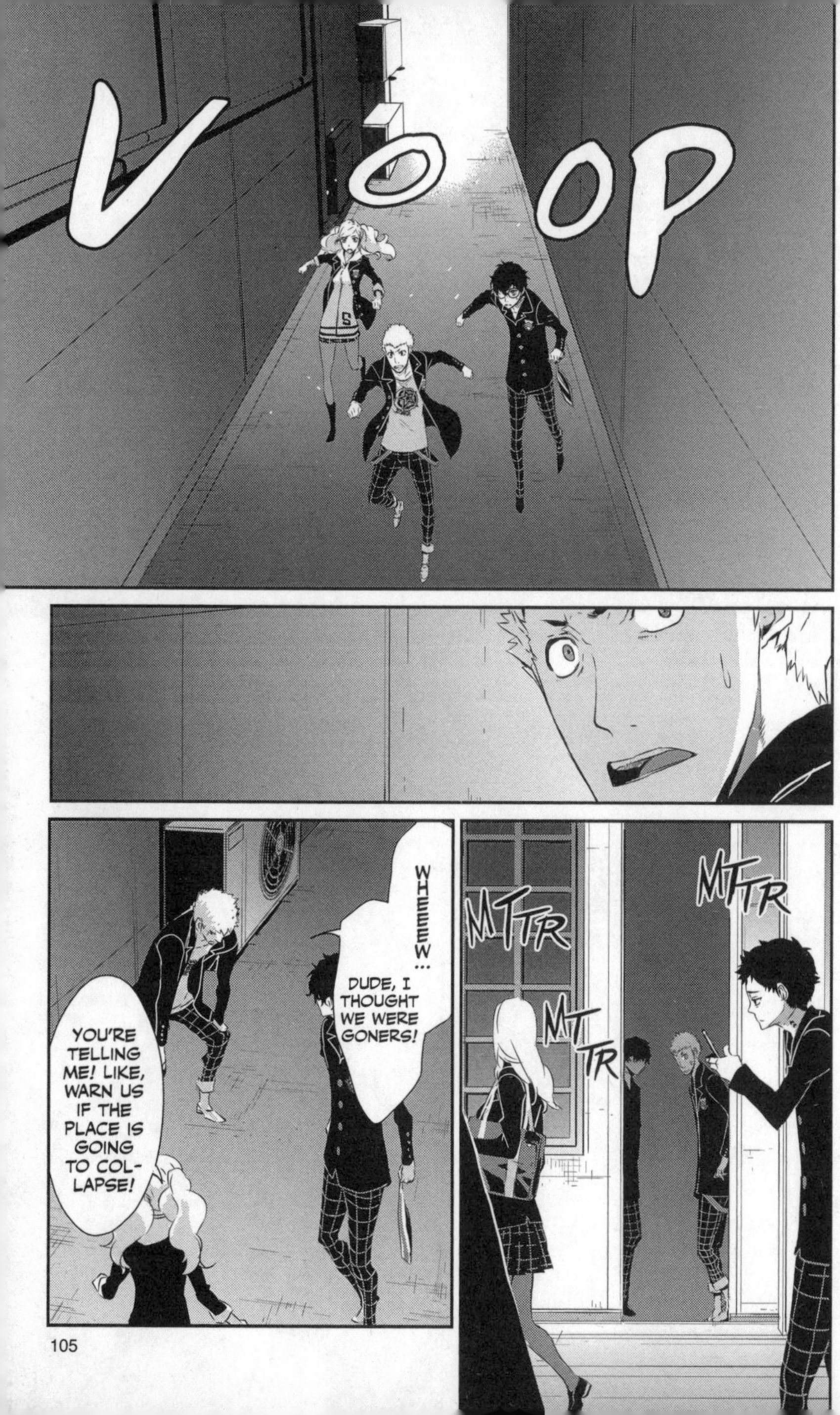
VOOP
MTTR
MTTR
MTTR
WHEEEW...
DUDE, I THOUGHT WE WERE GONERS!
YOU'RE TELLING ME! LIKE, WARN US IF THE PLACE IS GOING TO COL-LAPSE!

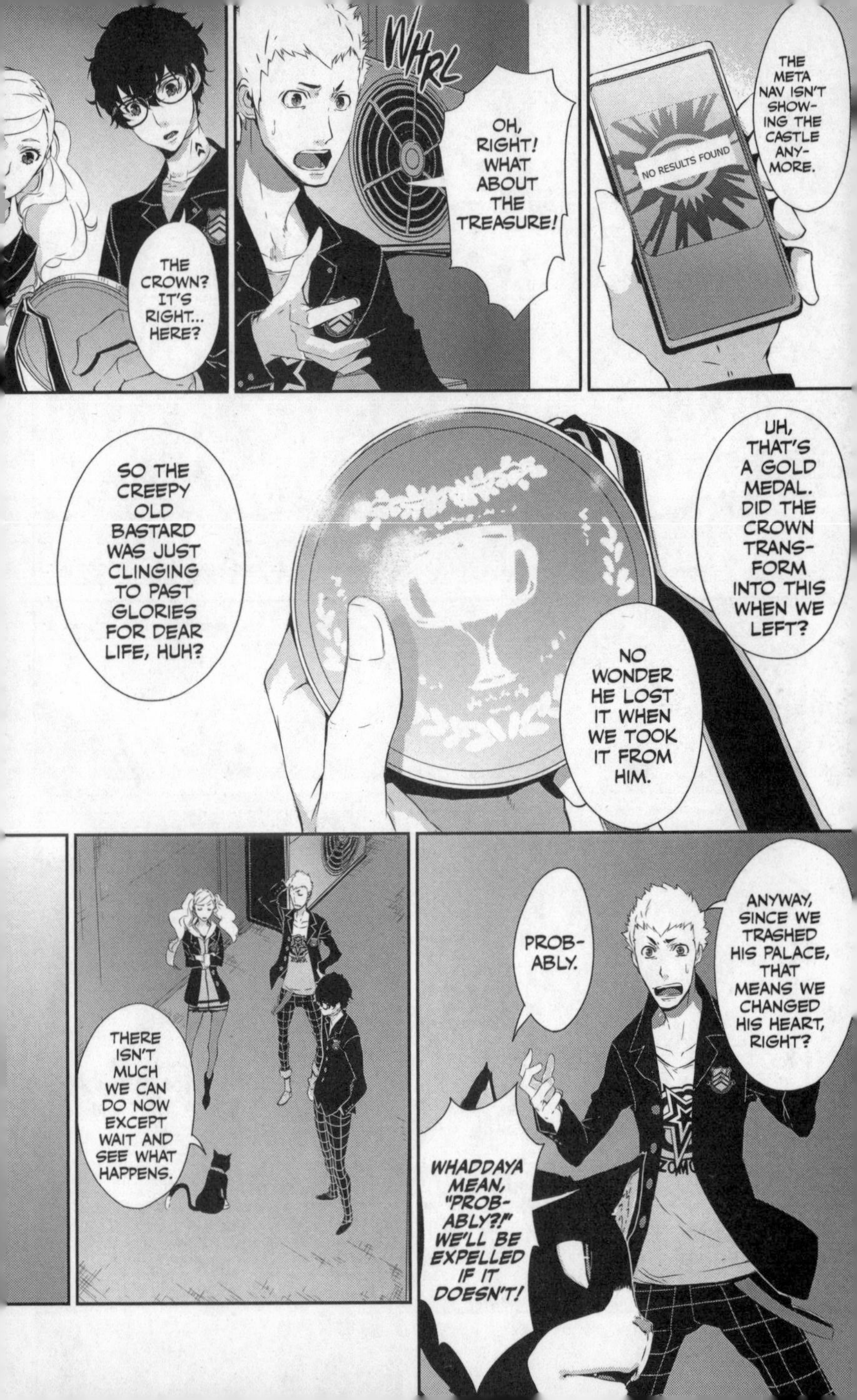

THE META NAV ISN'T SHOWING THE CASTLE ANYMORE.
NO RESULTS FOUND
WHRL
OH, RIGHT! WHAT ABOUT THE TREASURE!
THE CROWN? IT'S RIGHT... HERE?
UH, THAT'S A GOLD MEDAL. DID THE CROWN TRANSFORM INTO THIS WHEN WE LEFT?
SO THE CREEPY OLD BASTARD WAS JUST CLINGING TO PAST GLORIES FOR DEAR LIFE, HUH?
NO WONDER HE LOST IT WHEN WE TOOK IT FROM HIM.
ANYWAY, SINCE WE TRASHED HIS PALACE, THAT MEANS WE CHANGED HIS HEART, RIGHT?
PROBABLY.
WHADDAYA MEAN, "PROBABLY?!" WE'LL BE EXPELLED IF IT DOESN'T!
THERE ISN'T MUCH WE CAN DO NOW EXCEPT WAIT AND SEE WHAT HAPPENS.

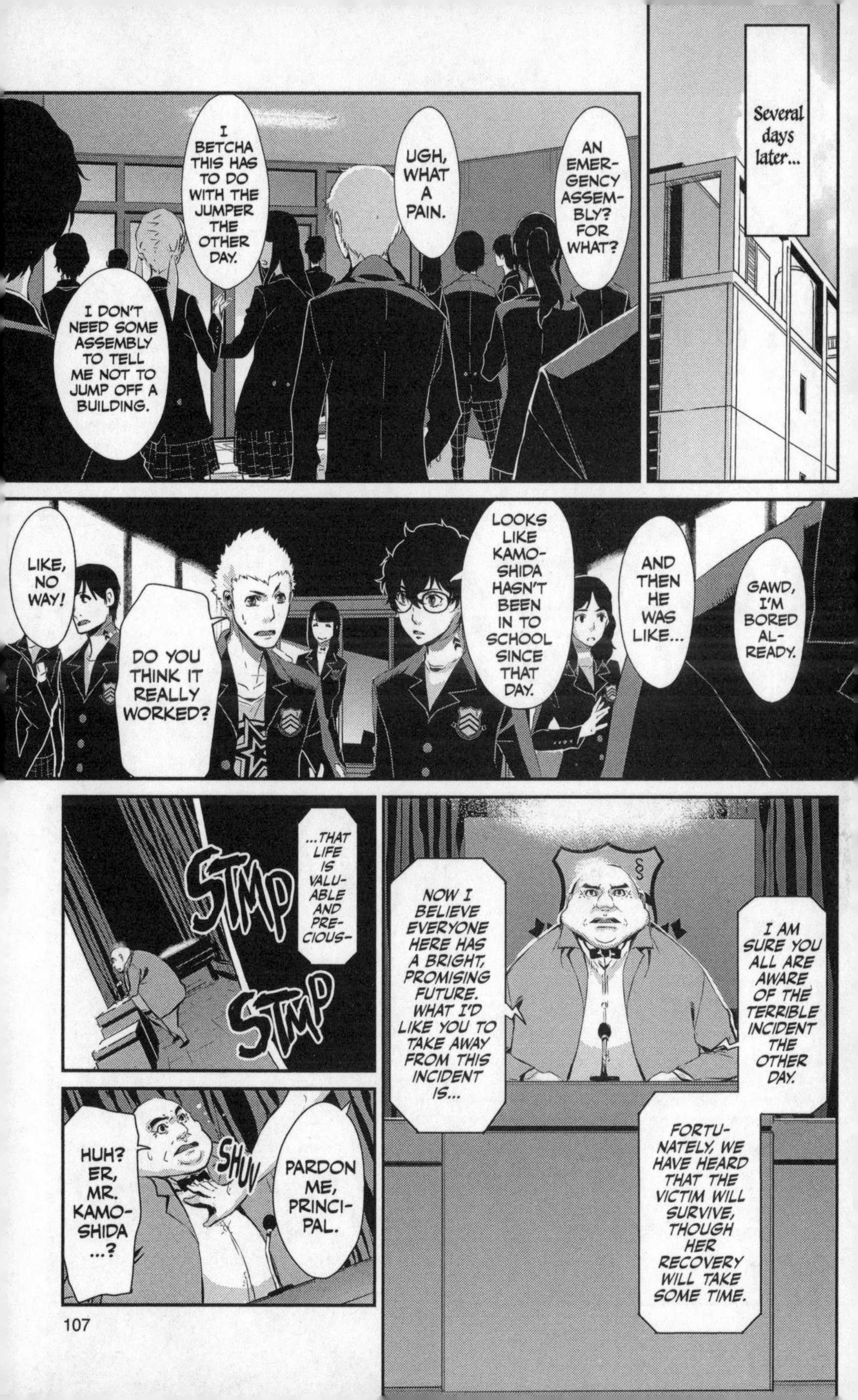
Several days later...
AN EMERGENCY ASSEMBLY? FOR WHAT?
UGH, WHAT A PAIN.
I BETCHA THIS HAS TO DO WITH THE JUMPER THE OTHER DAY.
I DON'T NEED SOME ASSEMBLY TO TELL ME NOT TO JUMP OFF A BUILDING.
GAWD, I'M BORED ALREADY.
AND THEN HE WAS LIKE...
LOOKS LIKE KAMOSHIDA HASN'T BEEN IN TO SCHOOL SINCE THAT DAY.
DO YOU THINK IT REALLY WORKED?
LIKE, NO WAY!
I AM SURE YOU ALL ARE AWARE OF THE TERRIBLE INCIDENT THE OTHER DAY.
FORTUNATELY, WE HAVE HEARD THAT THE VICTIM WILL SURVIVE, THOUGH HER RECOVERY WILL TAKE SOME TIME.
NOW I BELIEVE EVERYONE HERE HAS A BRIGHT, PROMISING FUTURE. WHAT I'D LIKE YOU TO TAKE AWAY FROM THIS INCIDENT IS...
...THAT LIFE IS VALUABLE AND PRECIOUS-
STMP
STMP
PARDON ME, PRINCIPAL.
SHUV
HUH? ER, MR. KAMOSHIDA...?

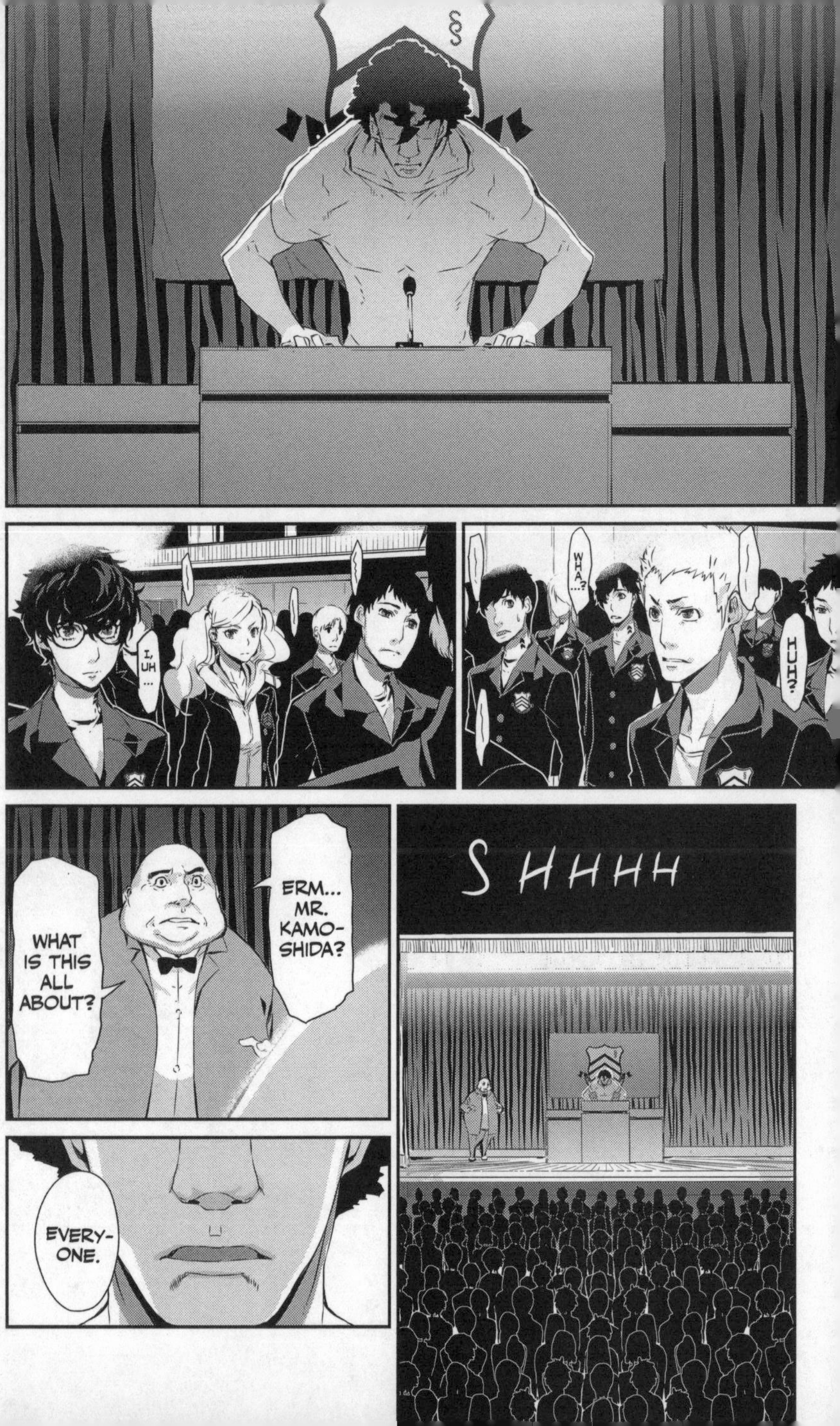
WHA...?
HUH?
I, UH ...
SHHHH
ERM... MR. KAMOSHIDA?
WHAT IS THIS ALL ABOUT?
EVERYONE.

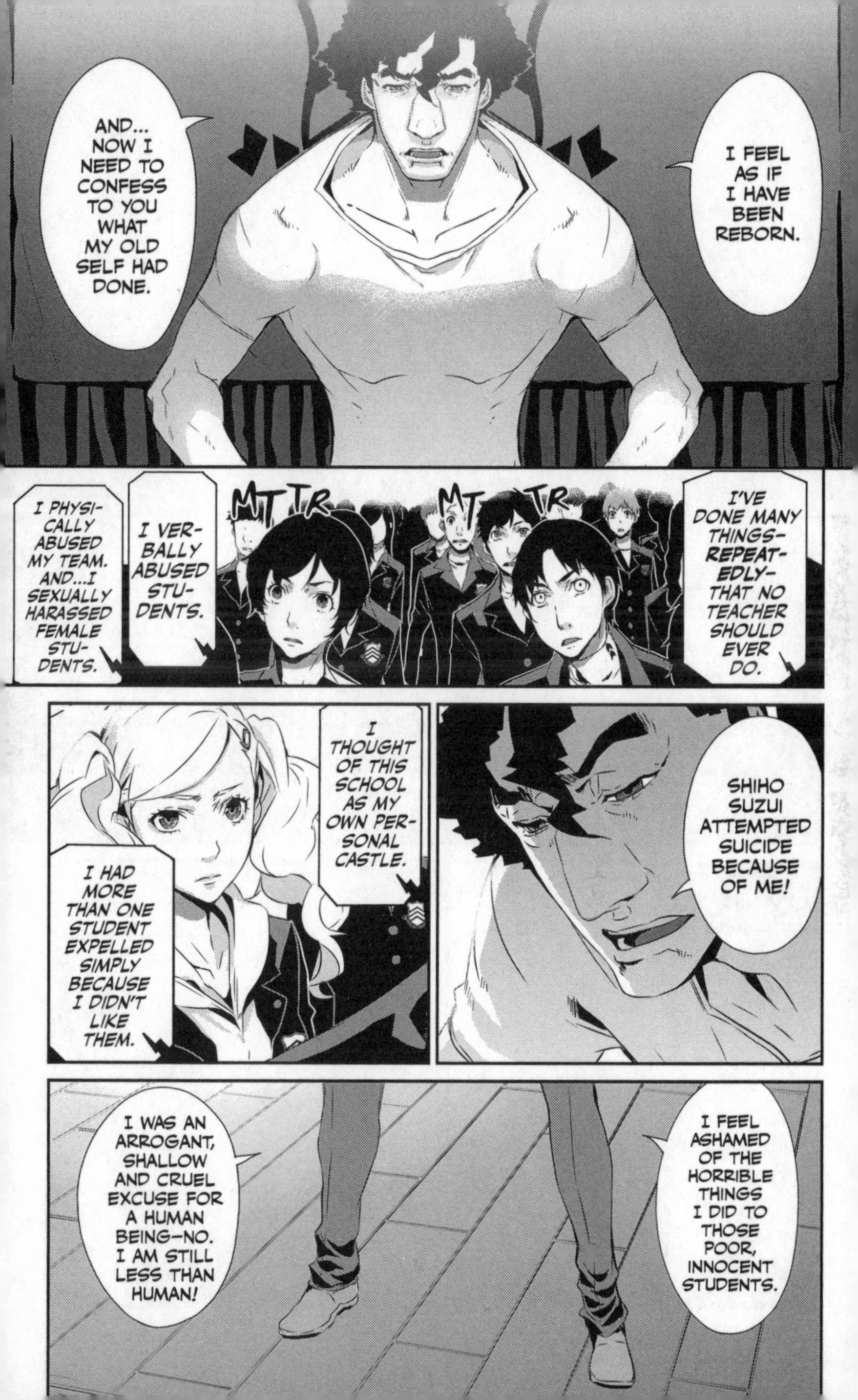
I FEEL AS IF I HAVE BEEN REBORN.
AND... NOW I NEED TO CONFESS TO YOU WHAT MY OLD SELF HAD DONE.
I'VE DONE MANY THINGS—REPEATEDLY—THAT NO TEACHER SHOULD EVER DO.
MT TR
MT TR
I VERBALLY ABUSED STUDENTS.
I PHYSICALLY ABUSED MY TEAM. AND...I SEXUALLY HARASSED FEMALE STUDENTS.
SHIHO SUZUI ATTEMPTED SUICIDE BECAUSE OF ME!
I THOUGHT OF THIS SCHOOL AS MY OWN PERSONAL CASTLE.
I HAD MORE THAN ONE STUDENT EXPELLED SIMPLY BECAUSE I DIDN'T LIKE THEM.
I FEEL ASHAMED OF THE HORRIBLE THINGS I DID TO THOSE POOR, INNOCENT STUDENTS.
I WAS AN ARROGANT, SHALLOW AND CRUEL EXCUSE FOR A HUMAN BEING—NO. I AM STILL LESS THAN HUMAN!

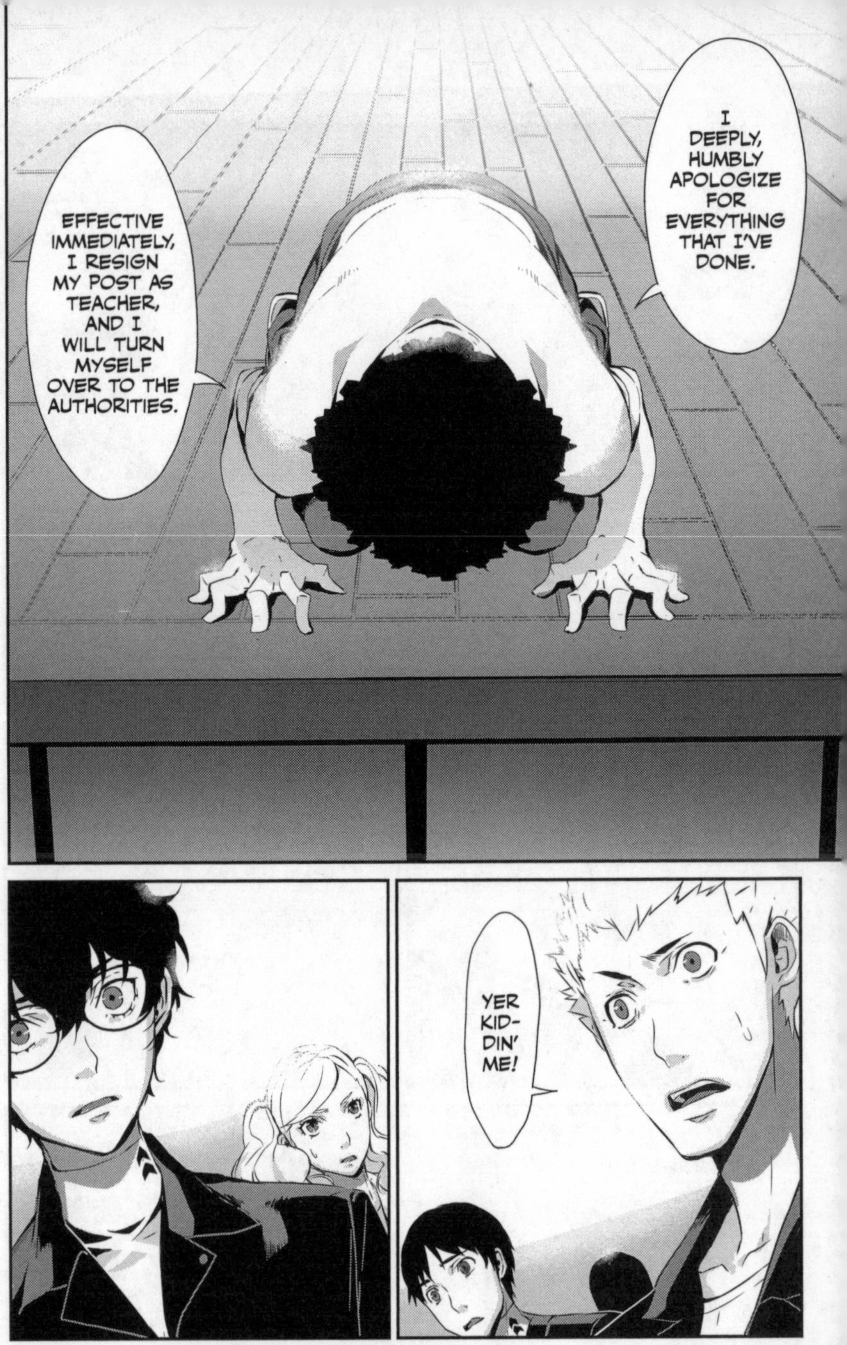
I DEEPLY, HUMBLY APOLOGIZE FOR EVERYTHING THAT I'VE DONE.
EFFECTIVE IMMEDIATELY, I RESIGN MY POST AS TEACHER, AND I WILL TURN MYSELF OVER TO THE AUTHORITIES.
YER KID-DIN' ME!

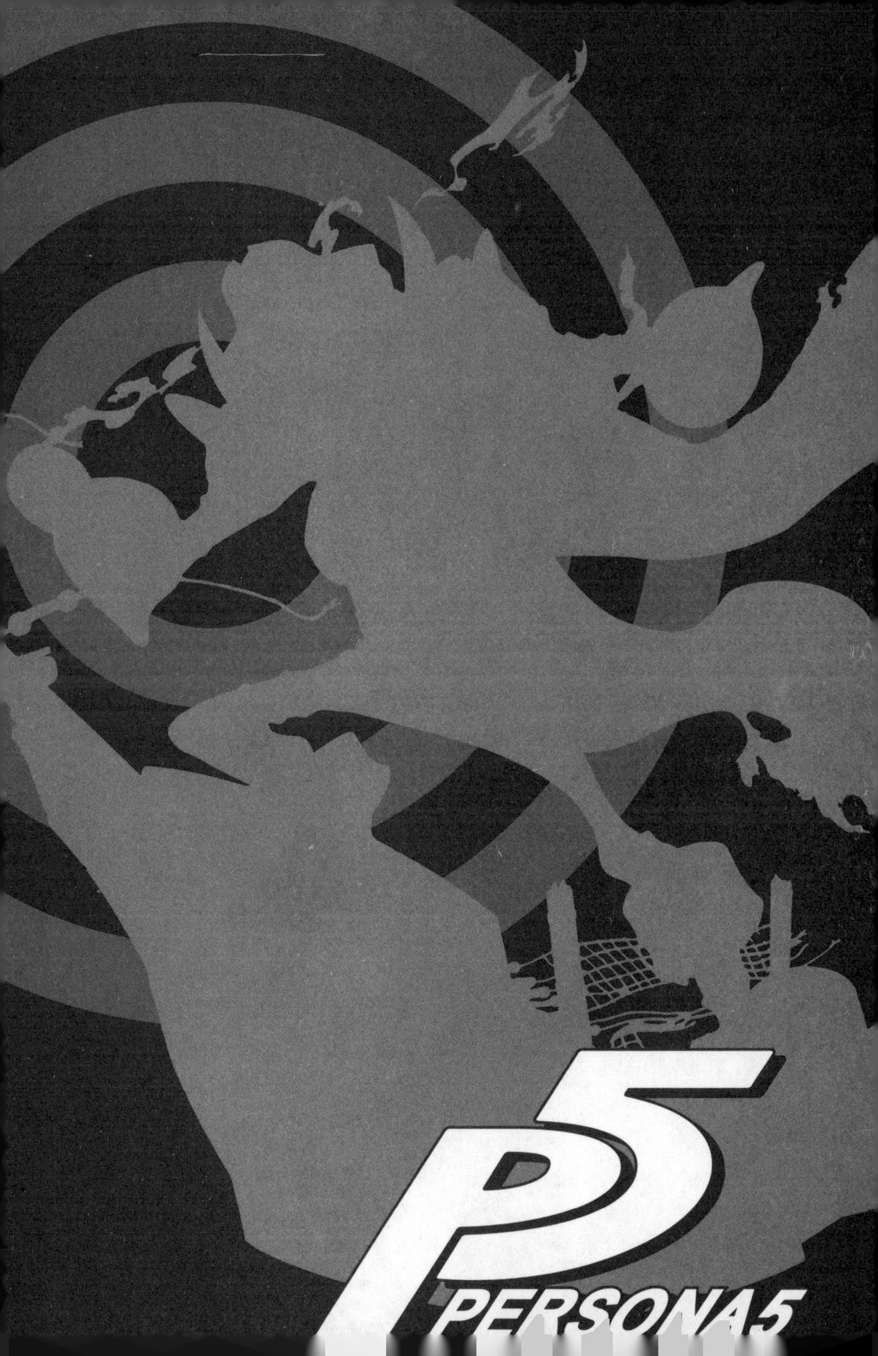
P5
PERSONA5

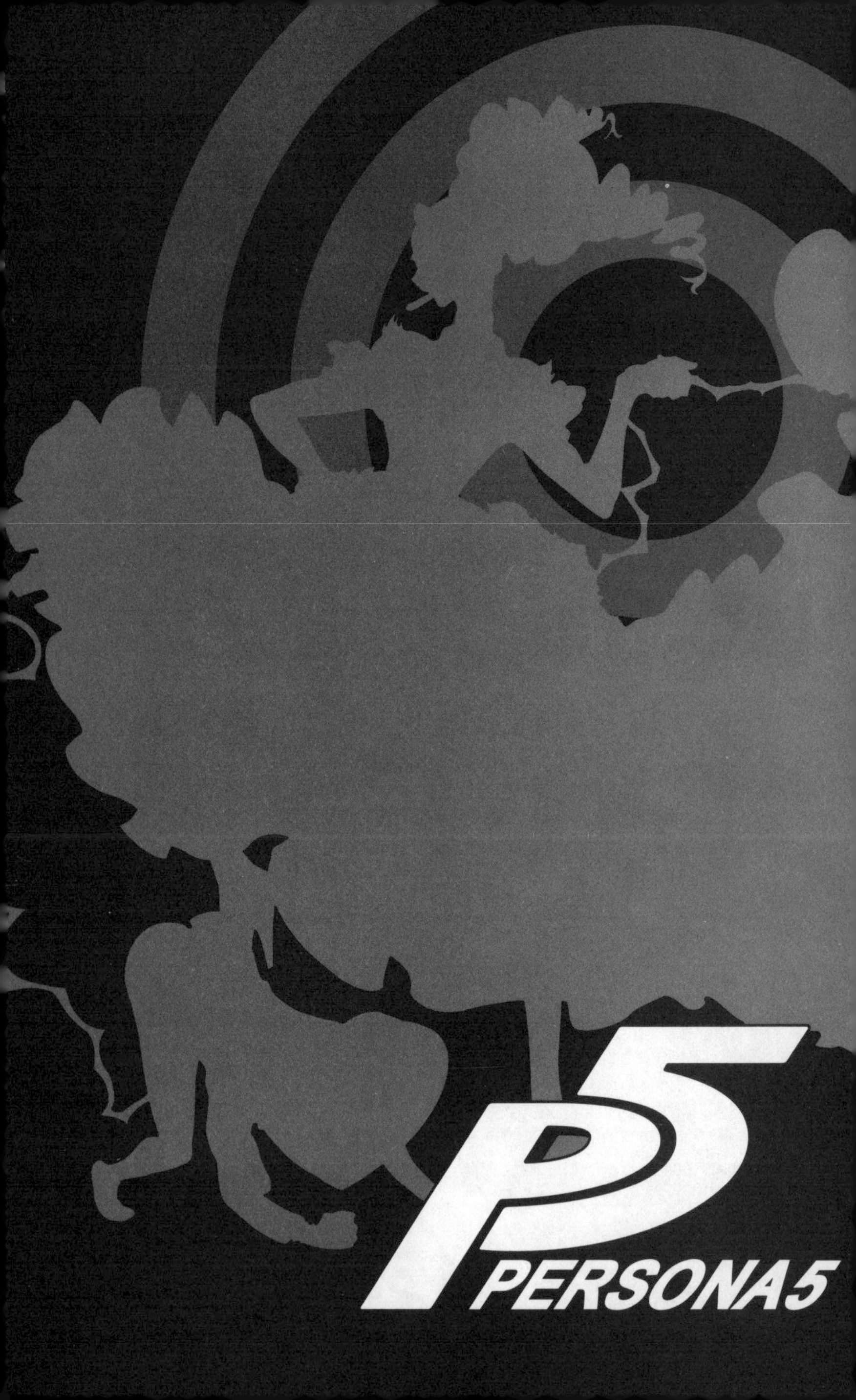
P5
PERSONA5

CHAPTER 10

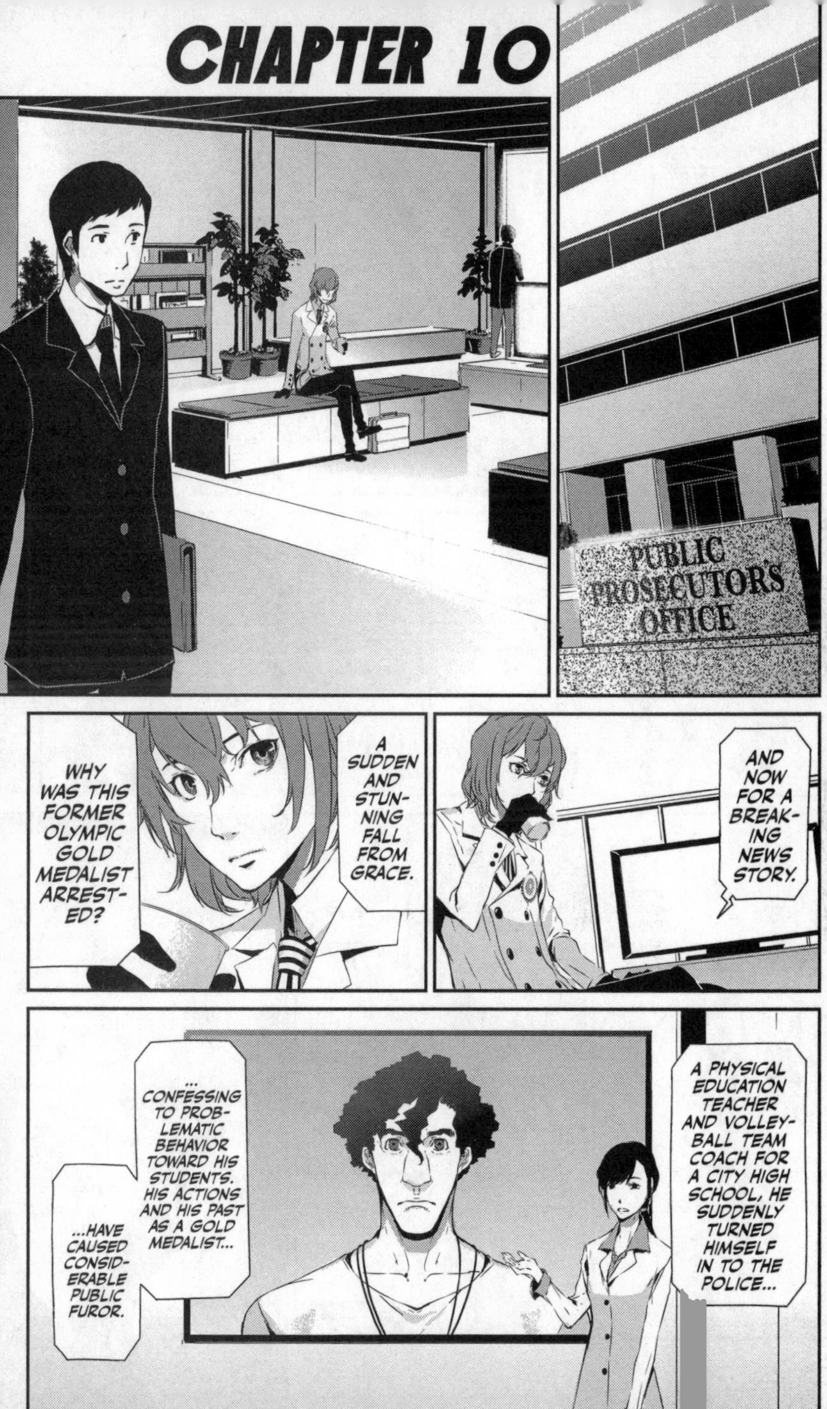
PUBLIC PROSECUTOR'S OFFICE
AND NOW FOR A BREAKING NEWS STORY.
A SUDDEN AND STUNNING FALL FROM GRACE.
WHY WAS THIS FORMER OLYMPIC GOLD MEDALIST ARRESTED?
A PHYSICAL EDUCATION TEACHER AND VOLLEYBALL TEAM COACH FOR A CITY HIGH SCHOOL, HE SUDDENLY TURNED HIMSELF IN TO THE POLICE...
...CONFESSING TO PROBLEMATIC BEHAVIOR TOWARD HIS STUDENTS. HIS ACTIONS AND HIS PAST AS A GOLD MEDALIST...
...HAVE CAUSED CONSIDERABLE PUBLIC FUROR.

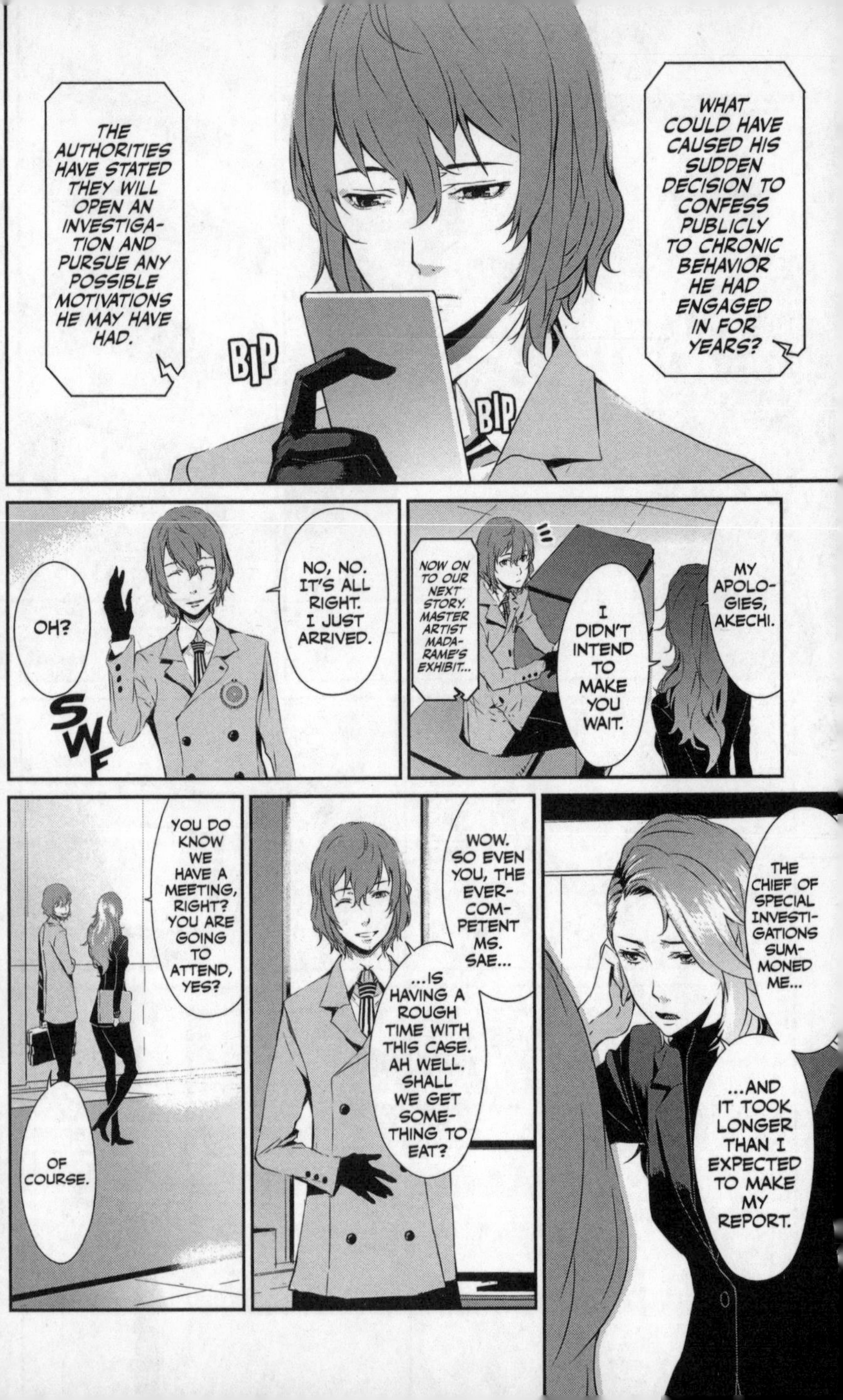
WHAT COULD HAVE CAUSED HIS SUDDEN DECISION TO CONFESS PUBLICLY TO CHRONIC BEHAVIOR HE HAD ENGAGED IN FOR YEARS?
THE AUTHORITIES HAVE STATED THEY WILL OPEN AN INVESTIGATION AND PURSUE ANY POSSIBLE MOTIVATIONS HE MAY HAVE HAD.
BIP
BIP
MY APOLOGIES, AKECHI.
I DIDN'T INTEND TO MAKE YOU WAIT.
NOW ON TO OUR NEXT STORY. MASTER ARTIST MADARAME'S EXHIBIT...
NO, NO. IT'S ALL RIGHT. I JUST ARRIVED.
OH?
SWF
THE CHIEF OF SPECIAL INVESTIGATIONS SUMMONED ME...
...AND IT TOOK LONGER THAN I EXPECTED TO MAKE MY REPORT.
WOW. SO EVEN YOU, THE EVER-COMPETENT MS. SAE...
...IS HAVING A ROUGH TIME WITH THIS CASE. AH WELL. SHALL WE GET SOMETHING TO EAT?
YOU DO KNOW WE HAVE A MEETING, RIGHT? YOU ARE GOING TO ATTEND, YES?
OF COURSE.

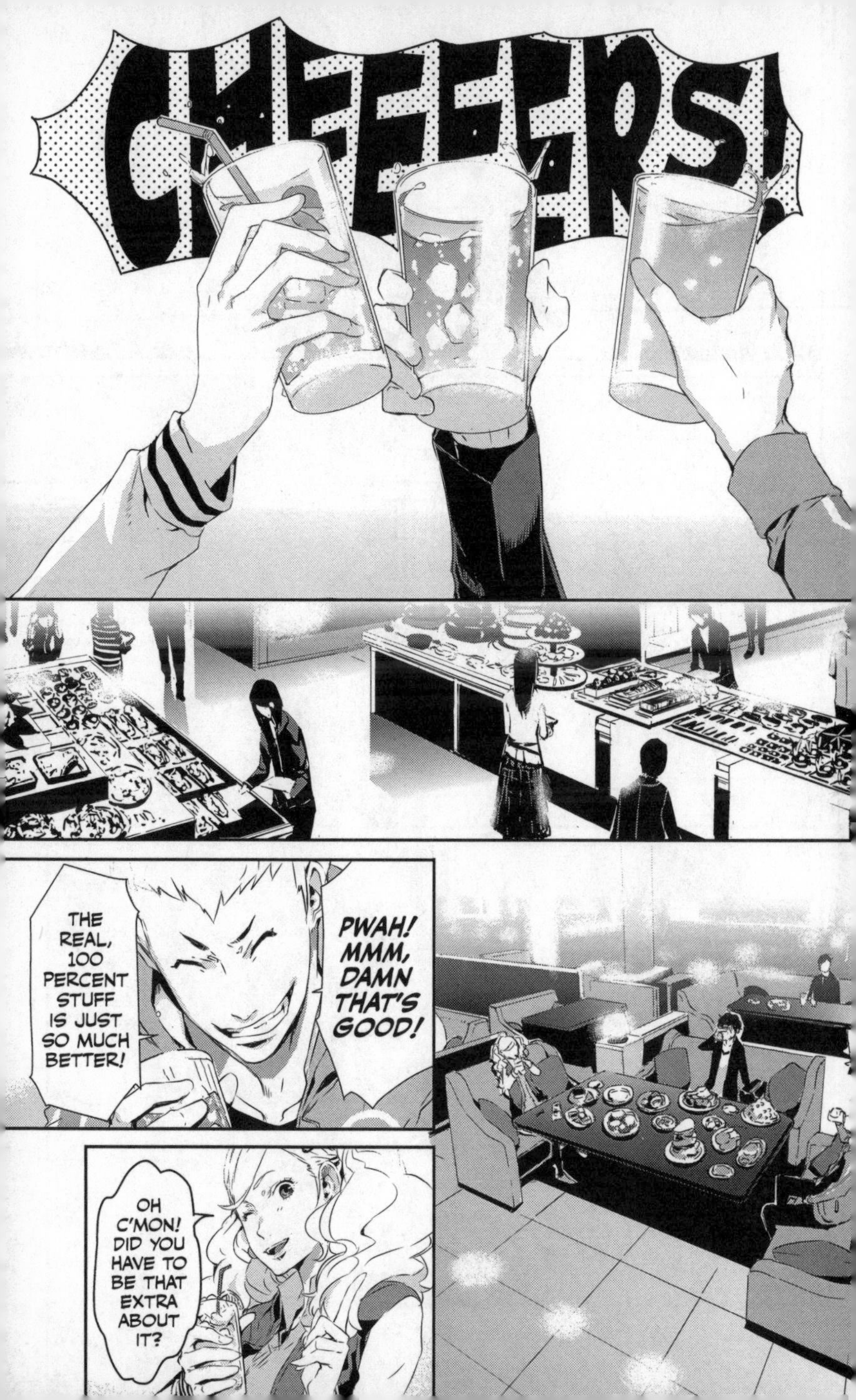
CHEEEERS!
PWAH! MMM, DAMN THAT'S GOOD!
THE REAL, 100 PERCENT STUFF IS JUST SO MUCH BETTER!
OH C'MON! DID YOU HAVE TO BE THAT EXTRA ABOUT IT?

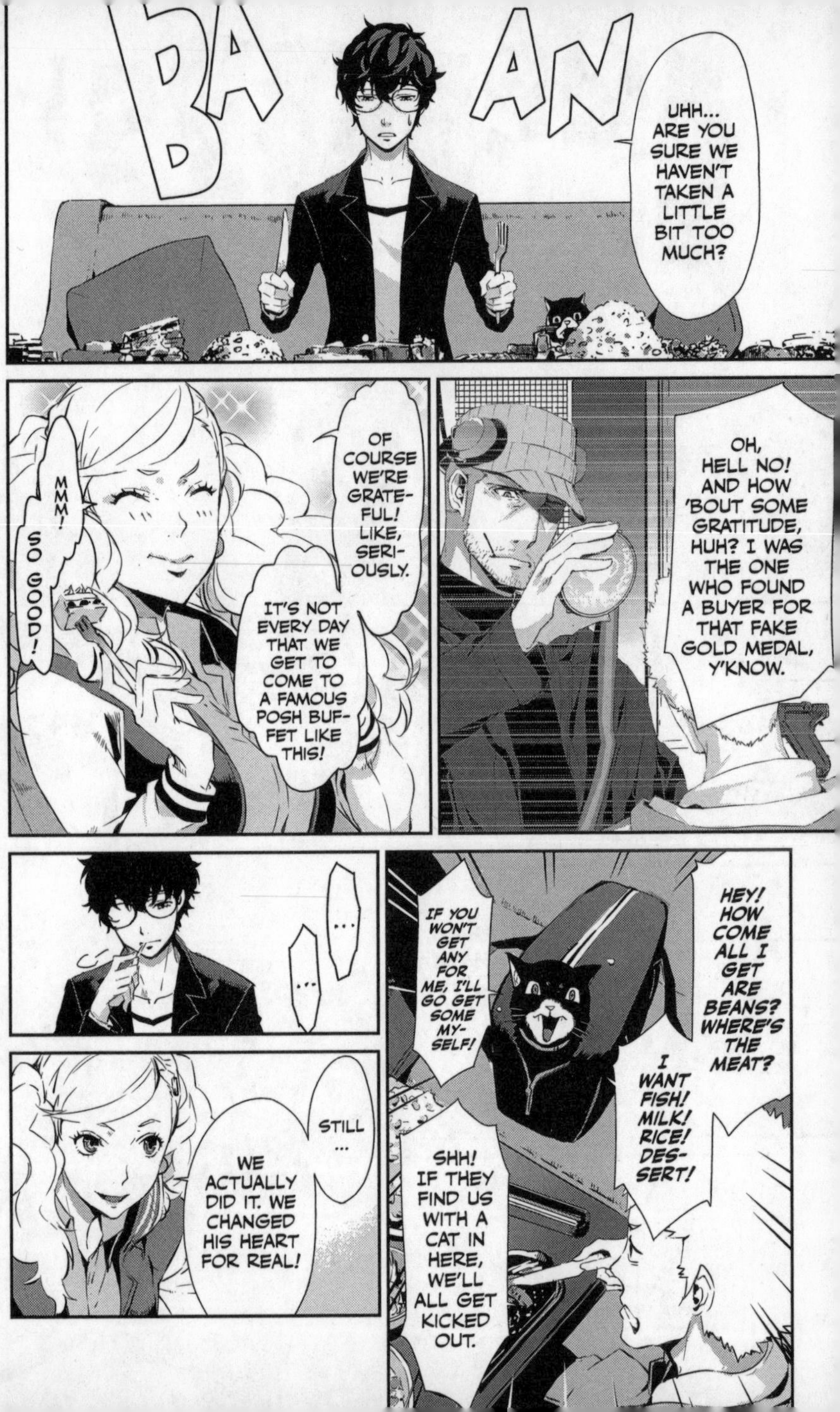
BA
AN
UHH... ARE YOU SURE WE HAVEN'T TAKEN A LITTLE BIT TOO MUCH?
OH, HELL NO! AND HOW 'BOUT SOME GRATITUDE, HUH? I WAS THE ONE WHO FOUND A BUYER FOR THAT FAKE GOLD MEDAL, Y'KNOW.
OF COURSE WE'RE GRATE-FUL! LIKE, SERI-OUSLY.
IT'S NOT EVERY DAY THAT WE GET TO COME TO A FAMOUS POSH BUF-FET LIKE THIS!
MMM! SO GOOD!
HEY! HOW COME ALL I GET ARE BEANS? WHERE'S THE MEAT?
IF YOU WON'T GET ANY FOR ME, I'LL GO GET SOME MY-SELF!
I WANT FISH! MILK! RICE! DES-SERT!
SHH! IF THEY FIND US WITH A CAT IN HERE, WE'LL ALL GET KICKED OUT.
...
...
STILL...
WE ACTUALLY DID IT. WE CHANGED HIS HEART FOR REAL!

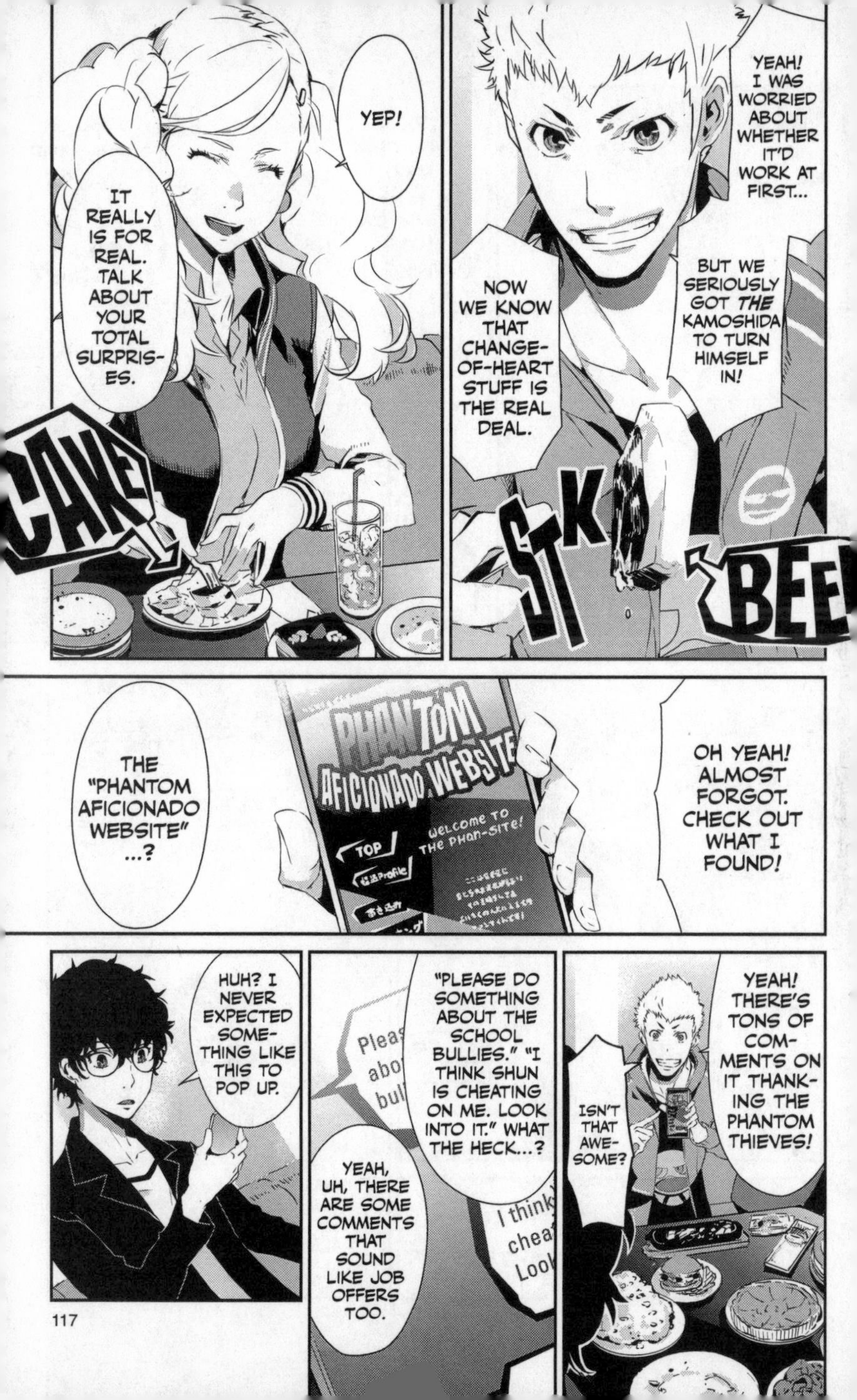
YEAH! I WAS WORRIED ABOUT WHETHER IT'D WORK AT FIRST...
BUT WE SERIOUSLY GOT *THE* KAMOSHIDA TO TURN HIMSELF IN!
NOW WE KNOW THAT CHANGE-OF-HEART STUFF IS THE REAL DEAL.
BEE
STK
YEP!
IT REALLY IS FOR REAL. TALK ABOUT YOUR TOTAL SURPRIS-ES.
CAKE
OH YEAH! ALMOST FORGOT. CHECK OUT WHAT I FOUND!
PHANTOM AFICIONADO WEBSITE
Welcome to the Phan-site!
TOP
THE "PHANTOM AFICIONADO WEBSITE" ...?
YEAH! THERE'S TONS OF COM-MENTS ON IT THANK-ING THE PHANTOM THIEVES!
ISN'T THAT AWE-SOME?
"PLEASE DO SOMETHING ABOUT THE SCHOOL BULLIES." "I THINK SHUN IS CHEATING ON ME. LOOK INTO IT." WHAT THE HECK...?
YEAH, UH, THERE ARE SOME COMMENTS THAT SOUND LIKE JOB OFFERS TOO.
HUH? I NEVER EXPECTED SOME-THING LIKE THIS TO POP UP.

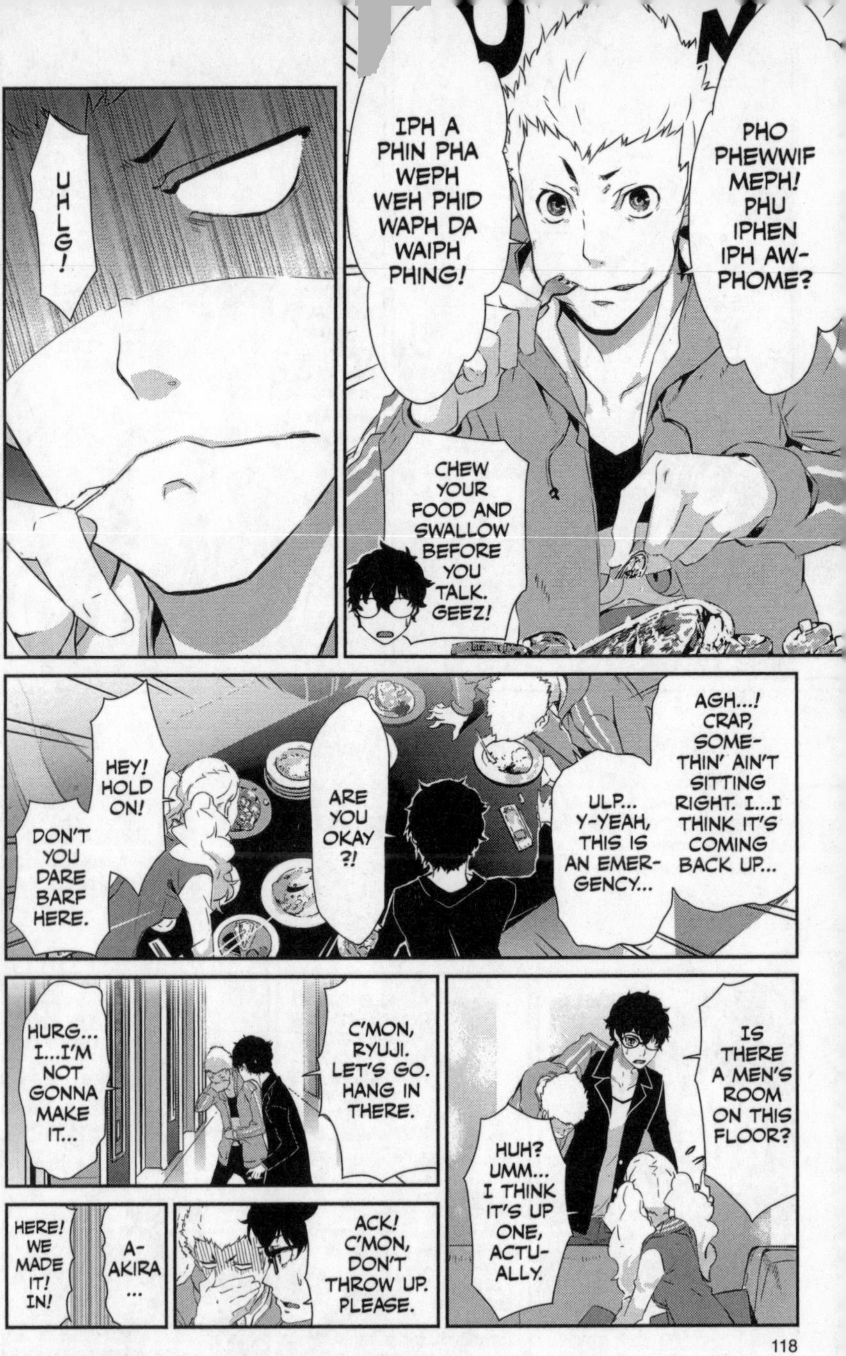
PHO PHEWWIF MEPH! PHU IPHEN IPH AW-PHOME?
IPH A PHIN PHA WEPH WEH PHID WAPH DA WAIPH PHING!
CHEW YOUR FOOD AND SWALLOW BEFORE YOU TALK. GEEZ!
UHLG!
AGH...! CRAP, SOME-THIN' AIN'T SITTING RIGHT. I...I THINK IT'S COMING BACK UP...
ULP... Y-YEAH, THIS IS AN EMER-GENCY...
ARE YOU OKAY?!
HEY! HOLD ON!
DON'T YOU DARE BARF HERE.
IS THERE A MEN'S ROOM ON THIS FLOOR?
HUH? UMM... I THINK IT'S UP ONE, ACTU-ALLY.
C'MON, RYUJI. LET'S GO. HANG IN THERE.
HURG... I...I'M NOT GONNA MAKE IT...
ACK! C'MON, DON'T THROW UP. PLEASE.
A-AKIRA...
HERE! WE MADE IT! IN!

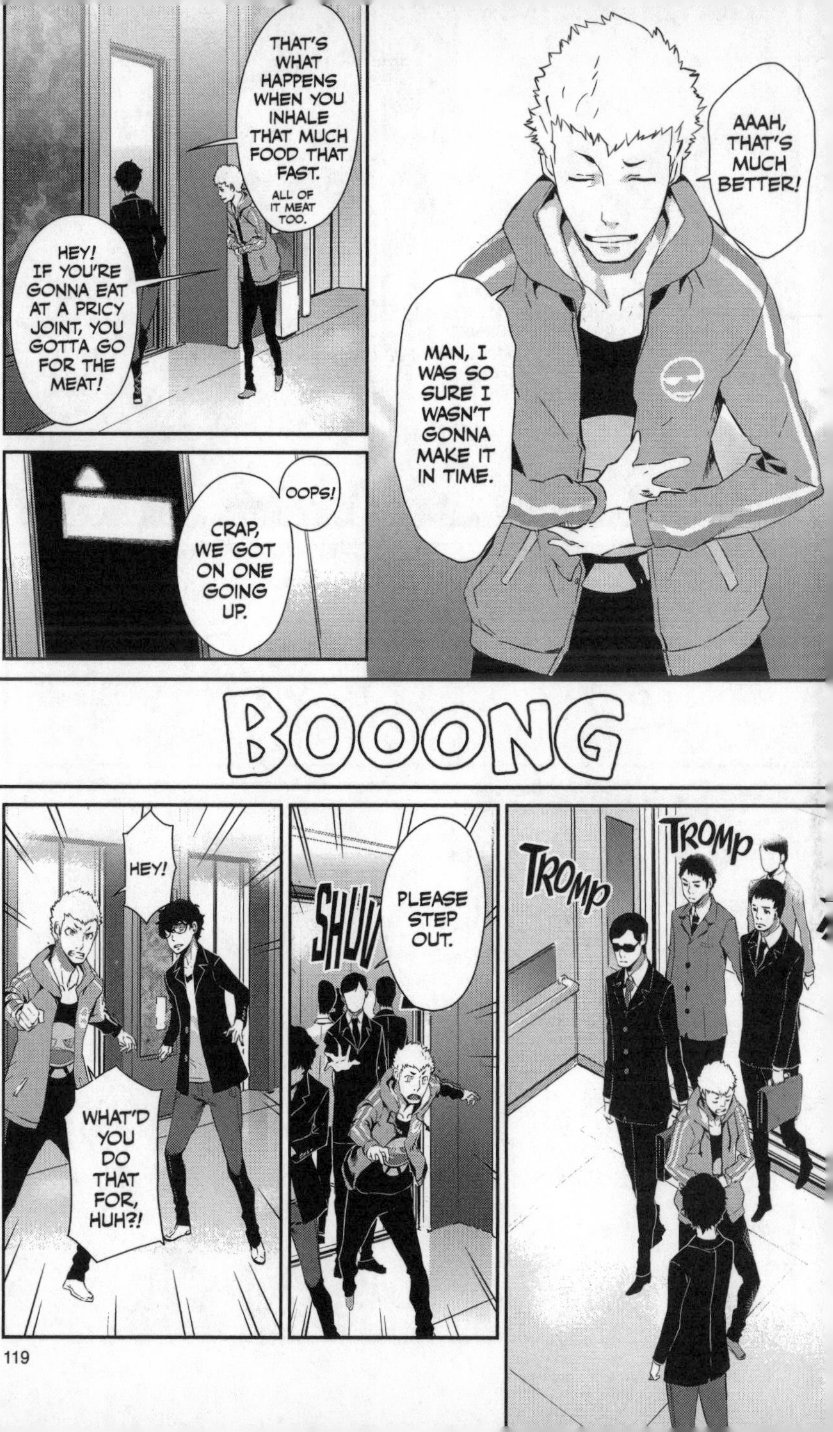
AAAH, THAT'S MUCH BETTER!
MAN, I WAS SO SURE I WASN'T GONNA MAKE IT IN TIME.
THAT'S WHAT HAPPENS WHEN YOU INHALE THAT MUCH FOOD THAT FAST.
ALL OF IT MEAT TOO.
HEY! IF YOU'RE GONNA EAT AT A PRICY JOINT, YOU GOTTA GO FOR THE MEAT!
OOPS!
CRAP, WE GOT ON ONE GOING UP.
BOOONG
TROMP
TROMP
PLEASE STEP OUT.
SHUV
HEY!
WHAT'D YOU DO THAT FOR, HUH?!

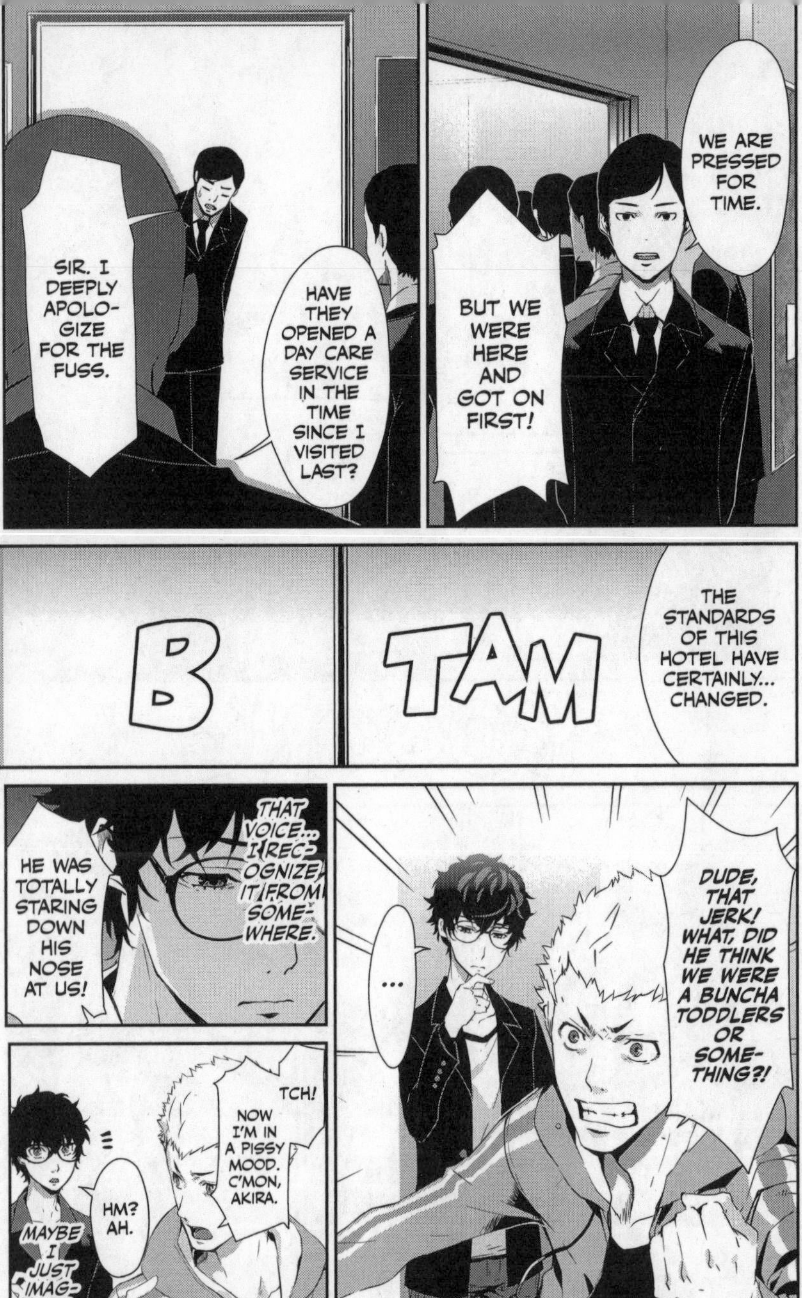
WE ARE PRESSED FOR TIME.
BUT WE WERE HERE AND GOT ON FIRST!
HAVE THEY OPENED A DAY CARE SERVICE IN THE TIME SINCE I VISITED LAST?
SIR. I DEEPLY APOLOGIZE FOR THE FUSS.
THE STANDARDS OF THIS HOTEL HAVE CERTAINLY... CHANGED.
B TAM
DUDE, THAT JERK! WHAT, DID HE THINK WE WERE A BUNCHA TODDLERS OR SOMETHING?!
...
THAT VOICE... I RECOGNIZE IT FROM SOMEWHERE.
HE WAS TOTALLY STARING DOWN HIS NOSE AT US!
TCH!
NOW I'M IN A PISSY MOOD. C'MON, AKIRA.
HM? AH.
MAYBE I JUST IMAGINED IT.

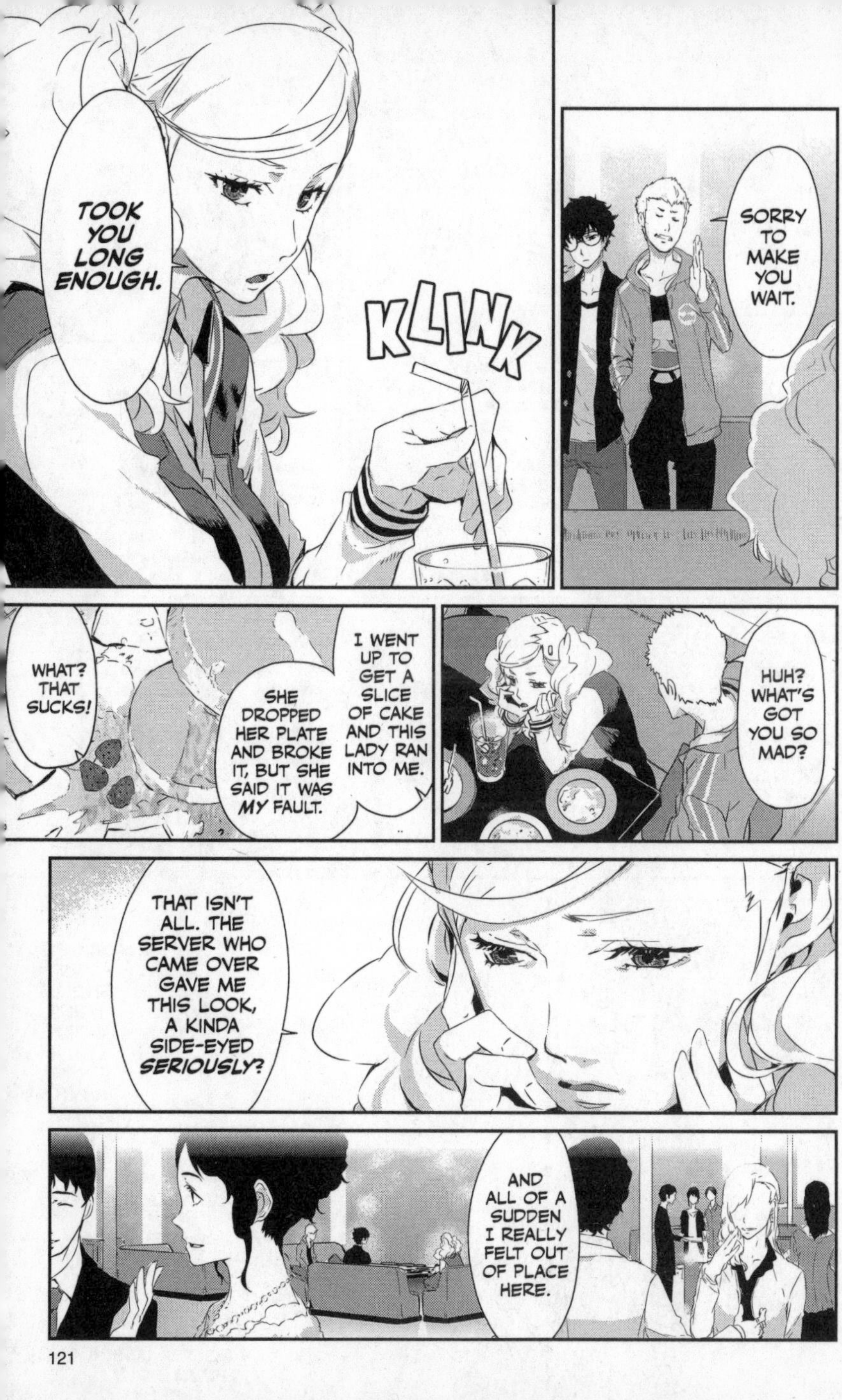
SORRY TO MAKE YOU WAIT.
TOOK YOU LONG ENOUGH.
KLINK
HUH? WHAT'S GOT YOU SO MAD?
I WENT UP TO GET A SLICE OF CAKE AND THIS LADY RAN INTO ME.
SHE DROPPED HER PLATE AND BROKE IT, BUT SHE SAID IT WAS *MY* FAULT.
WHAT? THAT SUCKS!
THAT ISN'T ALL. THE SERVER WHO CAME OVER GAVE ME THIS LOOK, A KINDA SIDE-EYED *SERIOUSLY*?
AND ALL OF A SUDDEN I REALLY FELT OUT OF PLACE HERE.

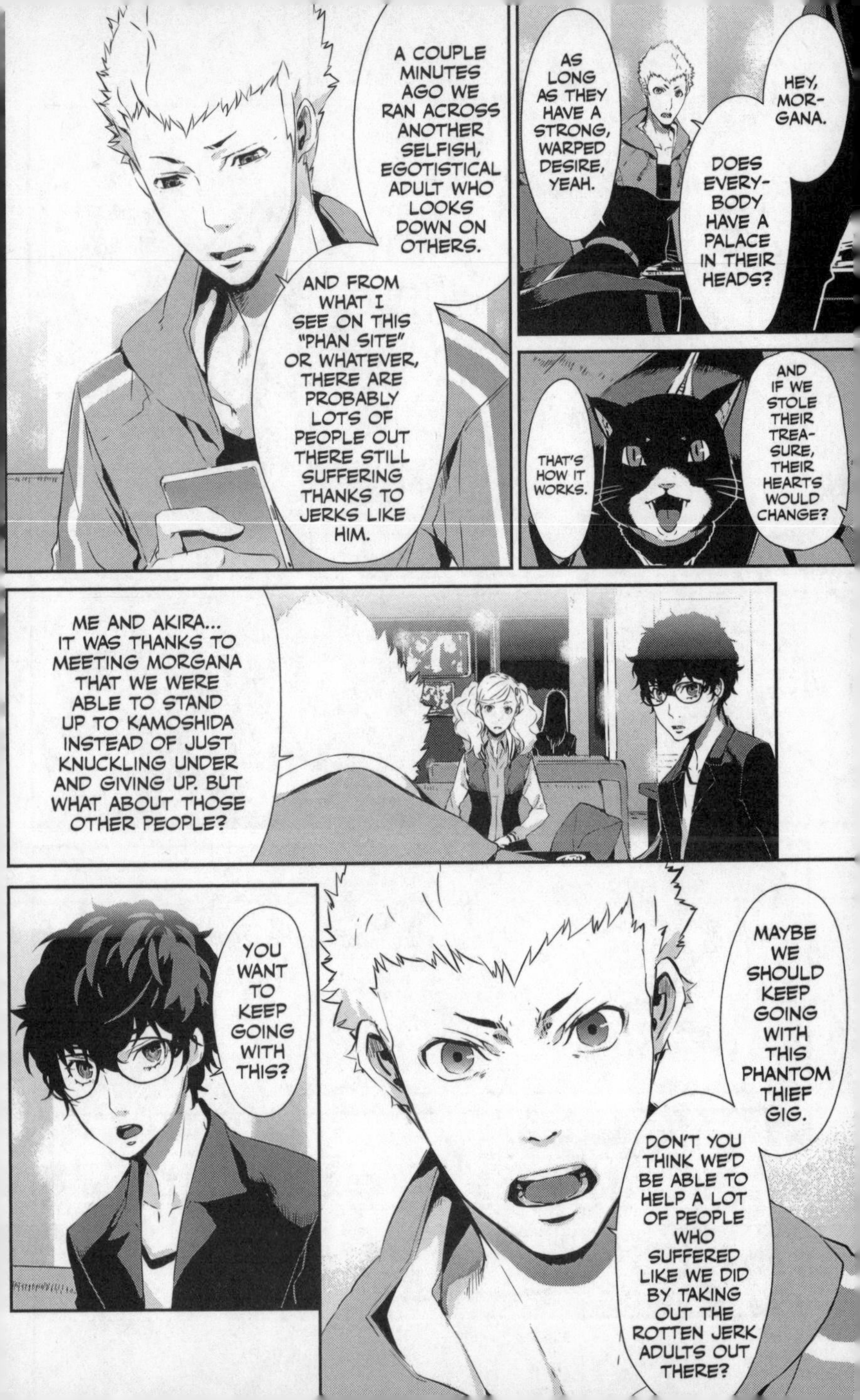
HEY, MORGANA.
DOES EVERYBODY HAVE A PALACE IN THEIR HEADS?
AS LONG AS THEY HAVE A STRONG, WARPED DESIRE, YEAH.
AND IF WE STOLE THEIR TREASURE, THEIR HEARTS WOULD CHANGE?
THAT'S HOW IT WORKS.
A COUPLE MINUTES AGO WE RAN ACROSS ANOTHER SELFISH, EGOTISTICAL ADULT WHO LOOKS DOWN ON OTHERS.
AND FROM WHAT I SEE ON THIS "PHAN SITE" OR WHATEVER, THERE ARE PROBABLY LOTS OF PEOPLE OUT THERE STILL SUFFERING THANKS TO JERKS LIKE HIM.
ME AND AKIRA... IT WAS THANKS TO MEETING MORGANA THAT WE WERE ABLE TO STAND UP TO KAMOSHIDA INSTEAD OF JUST KNUCKLING UNDER AND GIVING UP. BUT WHAT ABOUT THOSE OTHER PEOPLE?
MAYBE WE SHOULD KEEP GOING WITH THIS PHANTOM THIEF GIG.
DON'T YOU THINK WE'D BE ABLE TO HELP A LOT OF PEOPLE WHO SUFFERED LIKE WE DID BY TAKING OUT THE ROTTEN JERK ADULTS OUT THERE?
YOU WANT TO KEEP GOING WITH THIS?

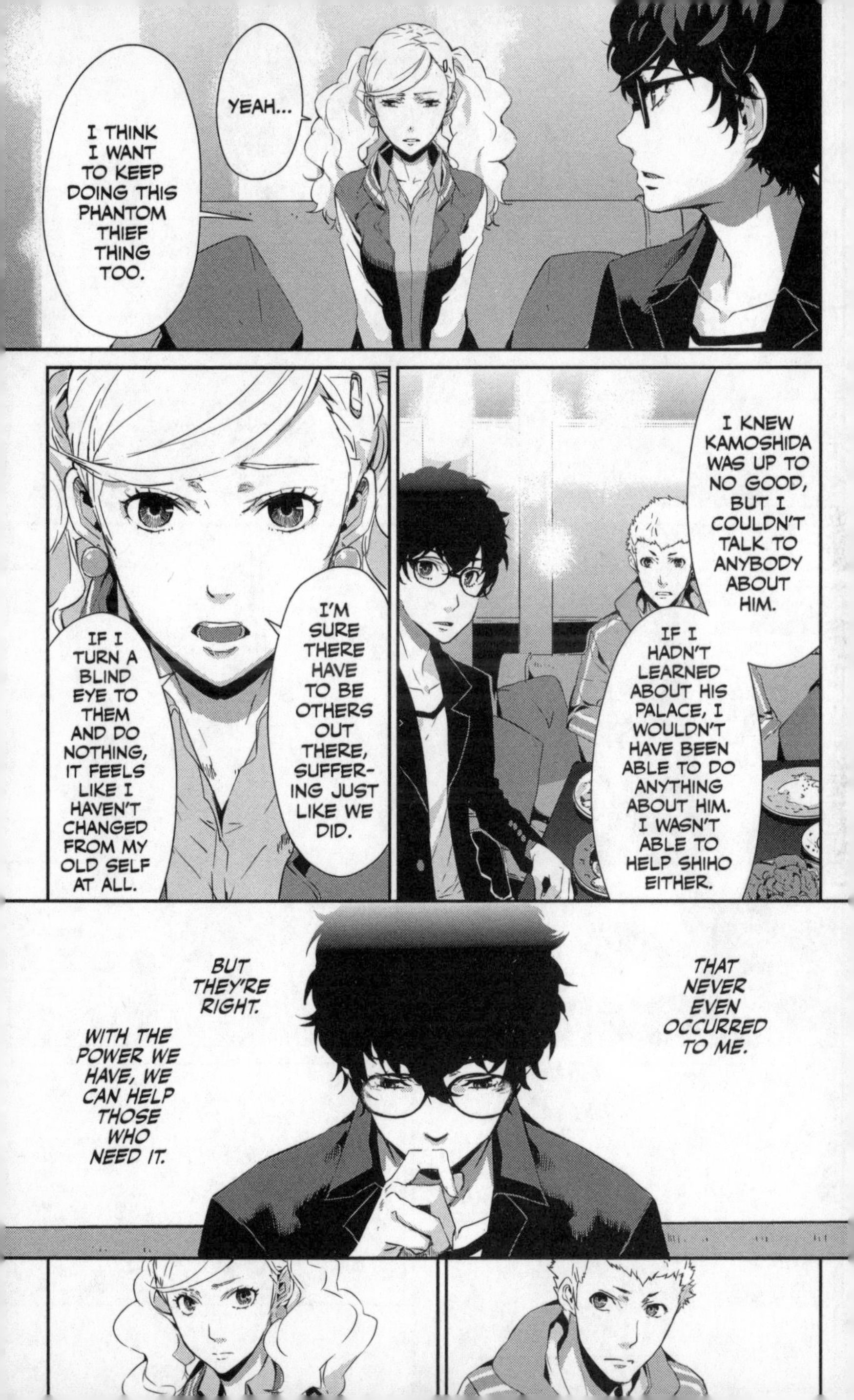
YEAH...
I THINK I WANT TO KEEP DOING THIS PHANTOM THIEF THING TOO.
I KNEW KAMOSHIDA WAS UP TO NO GOOD, BUT I COULDN'T TALK TO ANYBODY ABOUT HIM.
IF I HADN'T LEARNED ABOUT HIS PALACE, I WOULDN'T HAVE BEEN ABLE TO DO ANYTHING ABOUT HIM. I WASN'T ABLE TO HELP SHIHO EITHER.
I'M SURE THERE HAVE TO BE OTHERS OUT THERE, SUFFER-ING JUST LIKE WE DID.
IF I TURN A BLIND EYE TO THEM AND DO NOTHING, IT FEELS LIKE I HAVEN'T CHANGED FROM MY OLD SELF AT ALL.
THAT NEVER EVEN OCCURRED TO ME.
BUT THEY'RE RIGHT.
WITH THE POWER WE HAVE, WE CAN HELP THOSE WHO NEED IT.

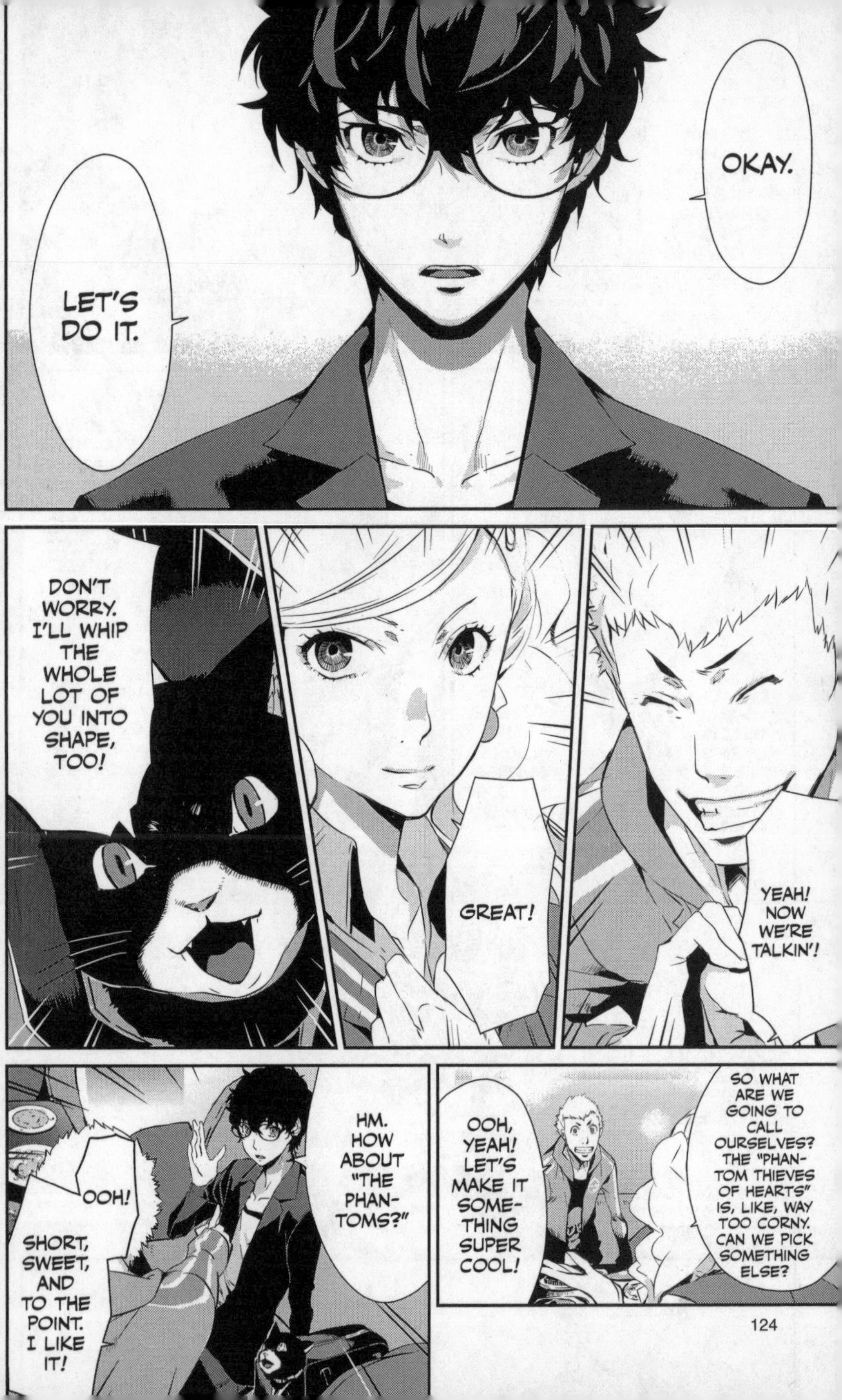
OKAY.
LET'S DO IT.
YEAH! NOW WE'RE TALKIN'!
GREAT!
DON'T WORRY. I'LL WHIP THE WHOLE LOT OF YOU INTO SHAPE, TOO!
SO WHAT ARE WE GOING TO CALL OURSELVES? THE "PHANTOM THIEVES OF HEARTS" IS, LIKE, WAY TOO CORNY. CAN WE PICK SOMETHING ELSE?
OOH, YEAH! LET'S MAKE IT SOMETHING SUPER COOL!
HM. HOW ABOUT "THE PHANTOMS?"
OOH!
SHORT, SWEET, AND TO THE POINT. I LIKE IT!

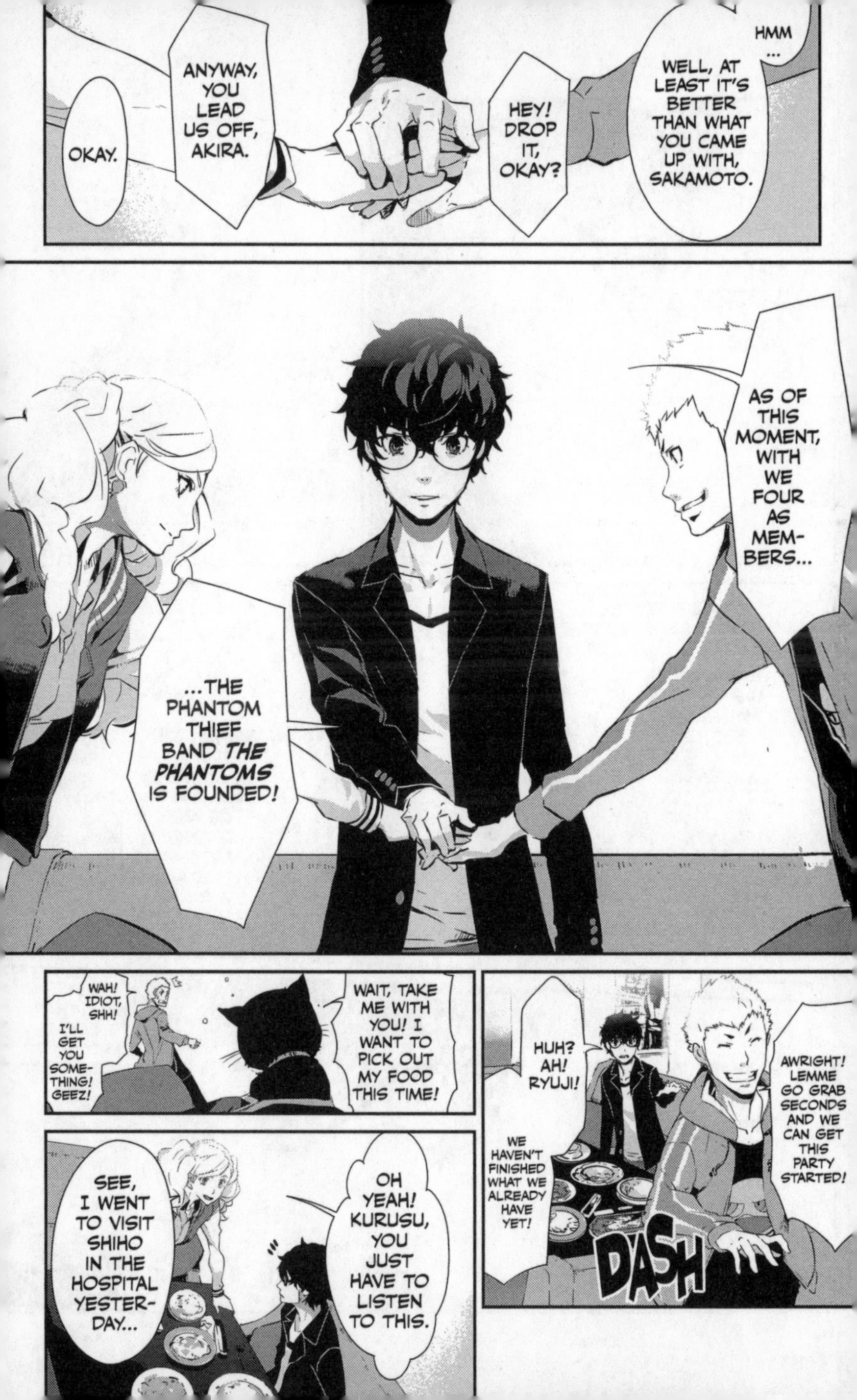
HMM...
WELL, AT LEAST IT'S BETTER THAN WHAT YOU CAME UP WITH, SAKAMOTO.
HEY! DROP IT, OKAY?
ANYWAY, YOU LEAD US OFF, AKIRA.
OKAY.
AS OF THIS MOMENT, WITH WE FOUR AS MEM-BERS...
...THE PHANTOM THIEF BAND *THE PHANTOMS* IS FOUNDED!
AWRIGHT! LEMME GO GRAB SECONDS AND WE CAN GET THIS PARTY STARTED!
HUH? AH! RYUJI!
WE HAVEN'T FINISHED WHAT WE ALREADY HAVE YET!
DASH
WAIT, TAKE ME WITH YOU! I WANT TO PICK OUT MY FOOD THIS TIME!
WAH! IDIOT, SHH!
I'LL GET YOU SOME-THING! GEEZ!
OH YEAH! KURUSU, YOU JUST HAVE TO LISTEN TO THIS.
SEE, I WENT TO VISIT SHIHO IN THE HOSPITAL YESTER-DAY...

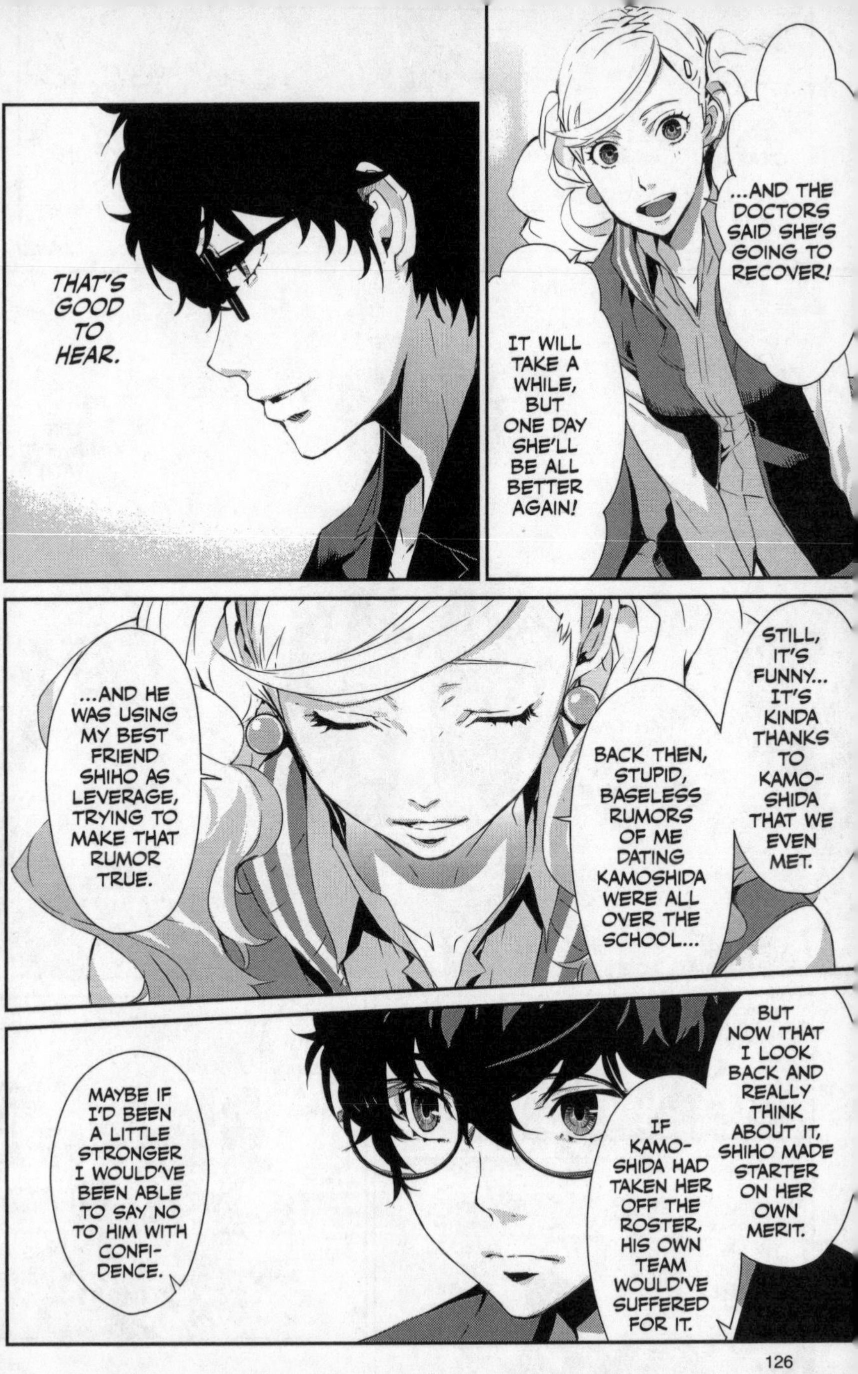
...AND THE DOCTORS SAID SHE'S GOING TO RECOVER!
IT WILL TAKE A WHILE, BUT ONE DAY SHE'LL BE ALL BETTER AGAIN!
THAT'S GOOD TO HEAR.
STILL, IT'S FUNNY... IT'S KINDA THANKS TO KAMOSHIDA THAT WE EVEN MET.
BACK THEN, STUPID, BASELESS RUMORS OF ME DATING KAMOSHIDA WERE ALL OVER THE SCHOOL...
...AND HE WAS USING MY BEST FRIEND SHIHO AS LEVERAGE, TRYING TO MAKE THAT RUMOR TRUE.
BUT NOW THAT I LOOK BACK AND REALLY THINK ABOUT IT, SHIHO MADE STARTER ON HER OWN MERIT.
IF KAMOSHIDA HAD TAKEN HER OFF THE ROSTER, HIS OWN TEAM WOULD'VE SUFFERED FOR IT.
MAYBE IF I'D BEEN A LITTLE STRONGER I WOULD'VE BEEN ABLE TO SAY NO TO HIM WITH CONFIDENCE.

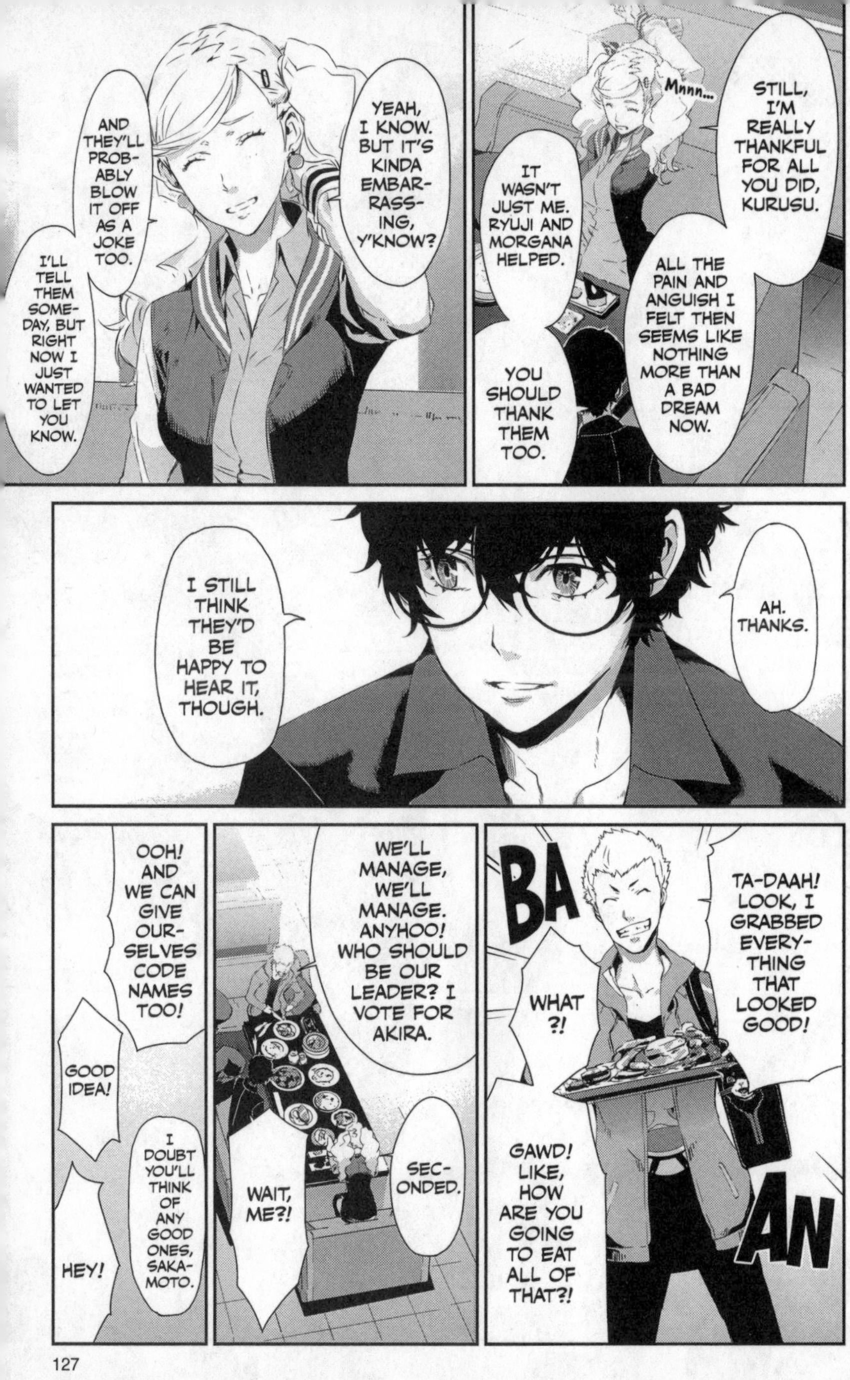
STILL, I'M REALLY THANKFUL FOR ALL YOU DID, KURUSU.
Mnnn...
ALL THE PAIN AND ANGUISH I FELT THEN SEEMS LIKE NOTHING MORE THAN A BAD DREAM NOW.
IT WASN'T JUST ME. RYUJI AND MORGANA HELPED.
YOU SHOULD THANK THEM TOO.
YEAH, I KNOW. BUT IT'S KINDA EMBAR-RASS-ING, Y'KNOW?
AND THEY'LL PROB-ABLY BLOW IT OFF AS A JOKE TOO.
I'LL TELL THEM SOME-DAY, BUT RIGHT NOW I JUST WANTED TO LET YOU KNOW.
AH. THANKS.
I STILL THINK THEY'D BE HAPPY TO HEAR IT, THOUGH.
BA
TA-DAAH! LOOK, I GRABBED EVERY-THING THAT LOOKED GOOD!
WHAT ?!
GAWD! LIKE, HOW ARE YOU GOING TO EAT ALL OF THAT?!
AN
WE'LL MANAGE, WE'LL MANAGE. ANYHOO! WHO SHOULD BE OUR LEADER? I VOTE FOR AKIRA.
SEC-ONDED.
WAIT, ME?!
OOH! AND WE CAN GIVE OUR-SELVES CODE NAMES TOO!
GOOD IDEA!
I DOUBT YOU'LL THINK OF ANY GOOD ONES, SAKA-MOTO.
HEY!

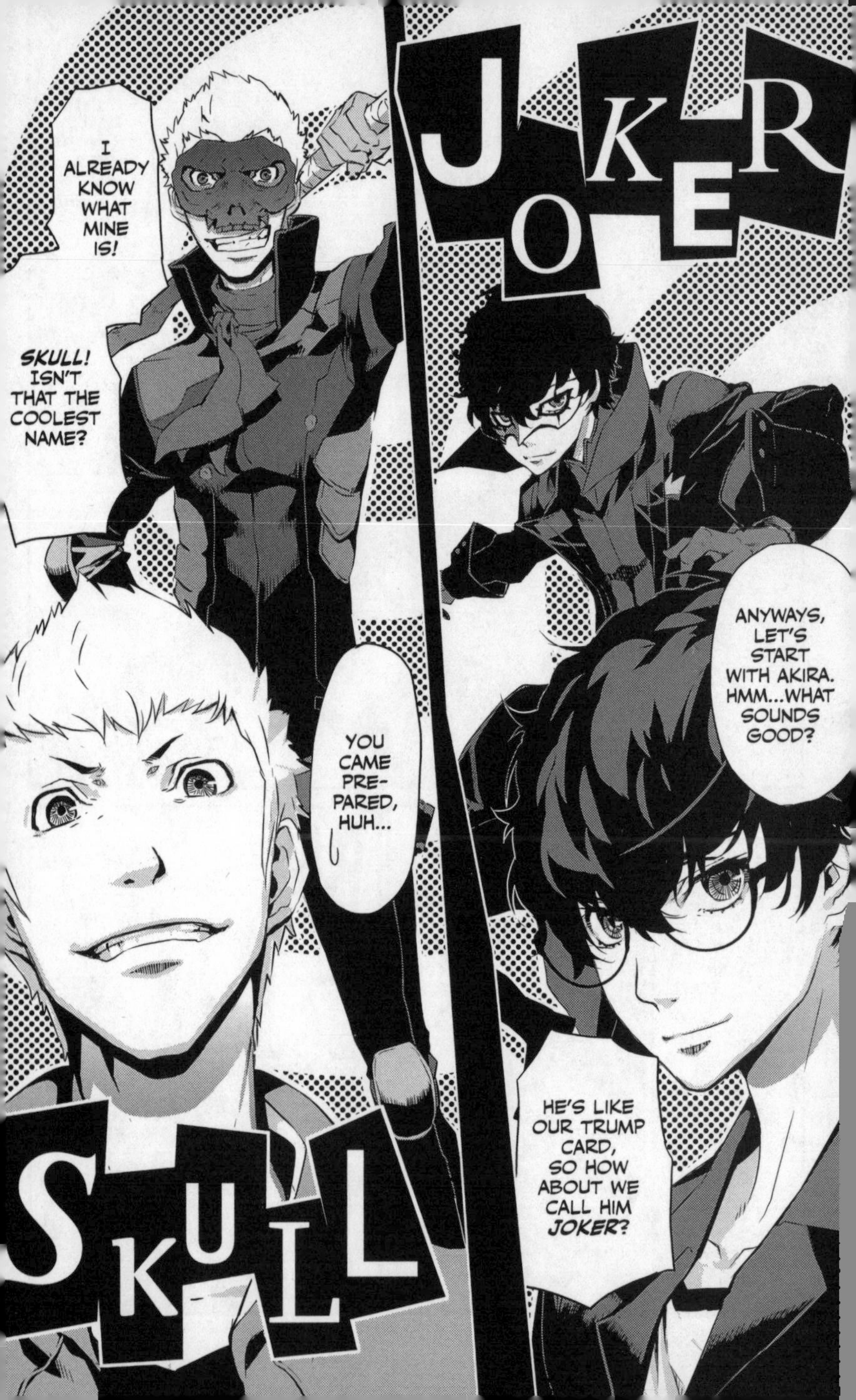
JOKER
ANYWAYS, LET'S START WITH AKIRA. HMM...WHAT SOUNDS GOOD?
HE'S LIKE OUR TRUMP CARD, SO HOW ABOUT WE CALL HIM *JOKER*?
I ALREADY KNOW WHAT MINE IS!
SKULL! ISN'T THAT THE COOLEST NAME?
YOU CAME PRE-PARED, HUH...
SKULL

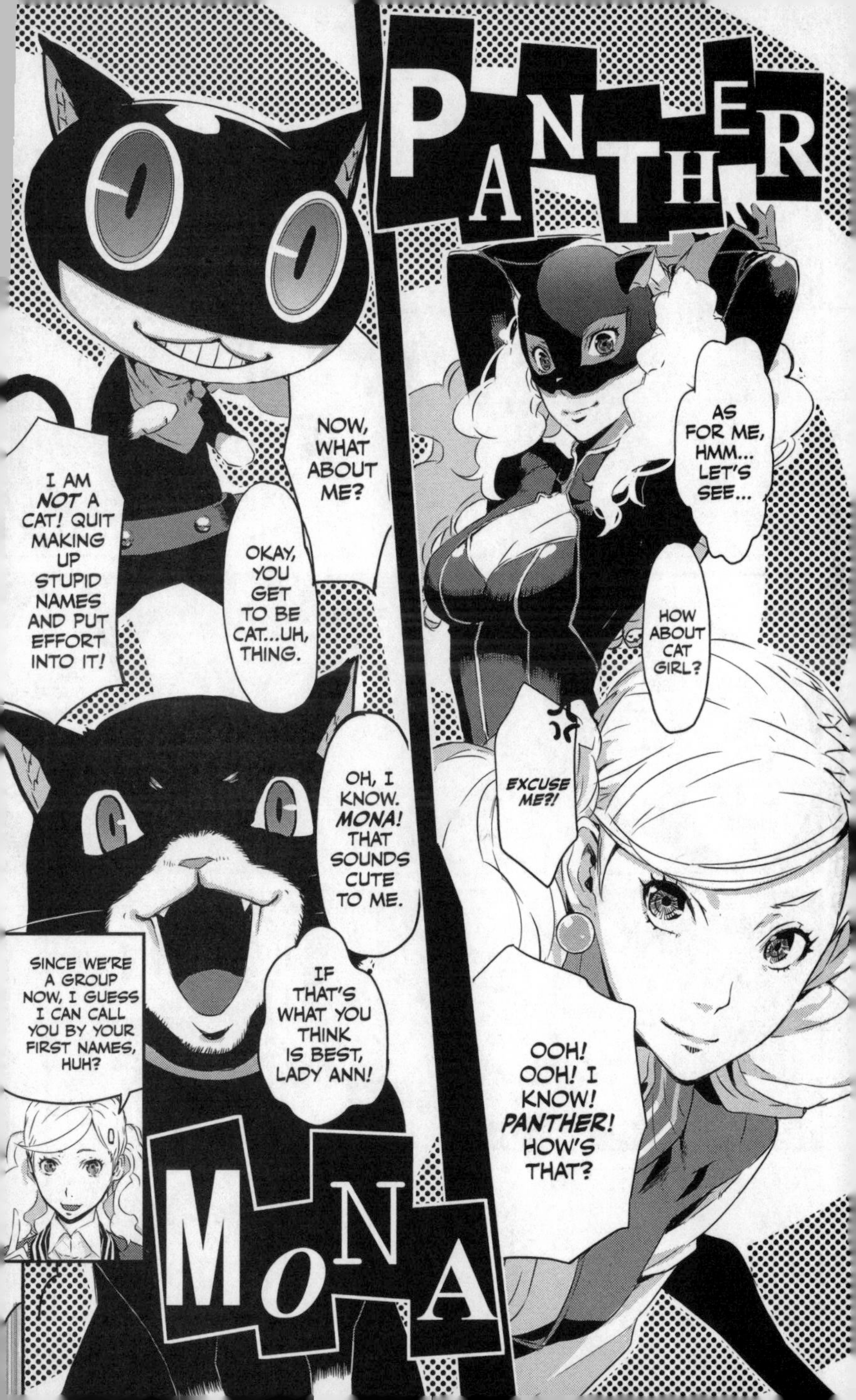
PANTHER
AS FOR ME, HMM... LET'S SEE...
HOW ABOUT CAT GIRL?
EXCUSE ME?!
OOH! OOH! I KNOW! PANTHER! HOW'S THAT?
NOW, WHAT ABOUT ME?
OKAY, YOU GET TO BE CAT...UH, THING.
I AM NOT A CAT! QUIT MAKING UP STUPID NAMES AND PUT EFFORT INTO IT!
OH, I KNOW. MONA! THAT SOUNDS CUTE TO ME.
IF THAT'S WHAT YOU THINK IS BEST, LADY ANN!
SINCE WE'RE A GROUP NOW, I GUESS I CAN CALL YOU BY YOUR FIRST NAMES, HUH?
MONA

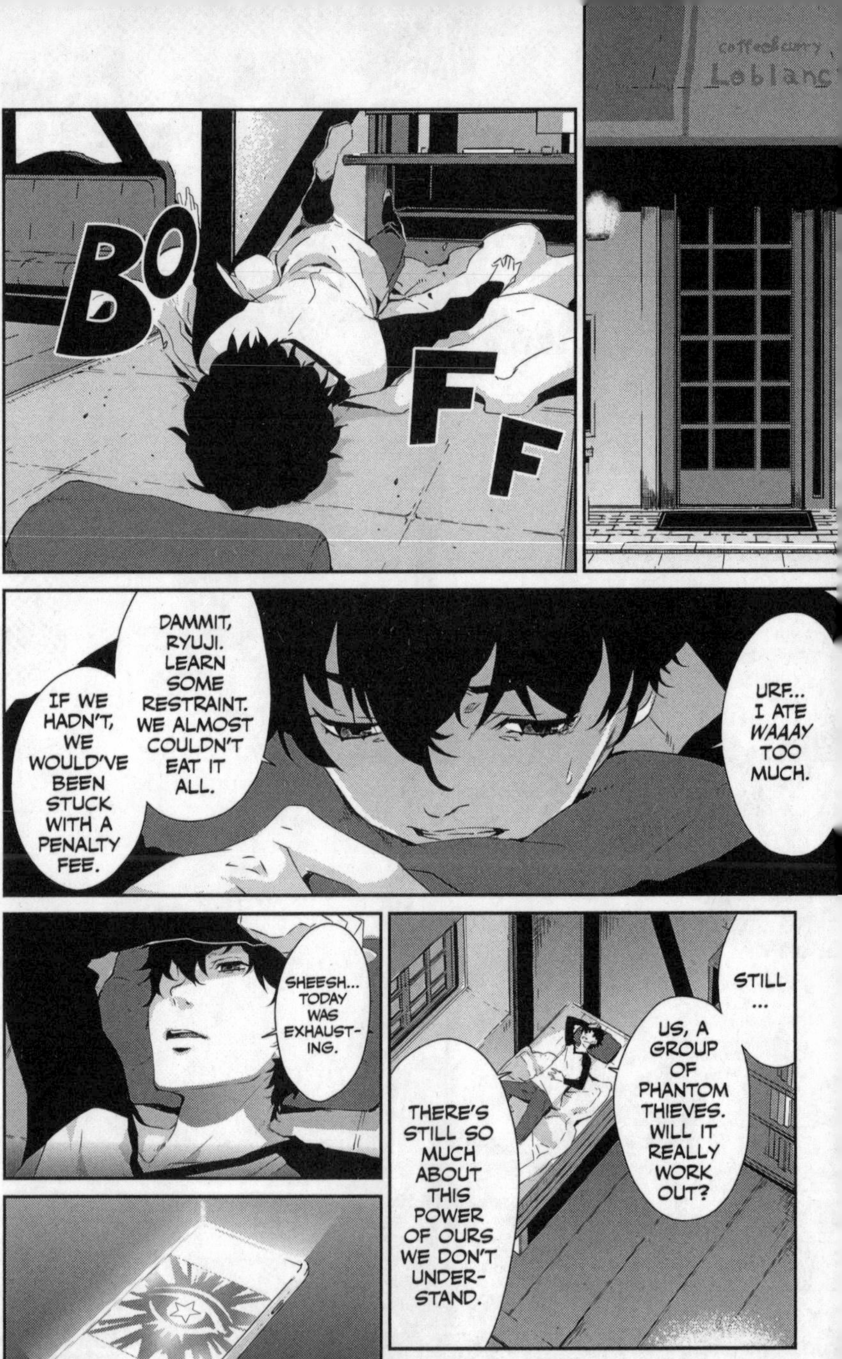
coffee&curry
Leblanc
BOFFF
URF... I ATE WAAAY TOO MUCH.
DAMMIT, RYUJI. LEARN SOME RESTRAINT. WE ALMOST COULDN'T EAT IT ALL.
IF WE HADN'T, WE WOULD'VE BEEN STUCK WITH A PENALTY FEE.
STILL...
US, A GROUP OF PHANTOM THIEVES. WILL IT REALLY WORK OUT?
THERE'S STILL SO MUCH ABOUT THIS POWER OF OURS WE DON'T UNDER-STAND.
SHEESH... TODAY WAS EXHAUST-ING.

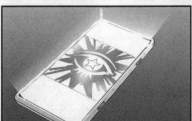

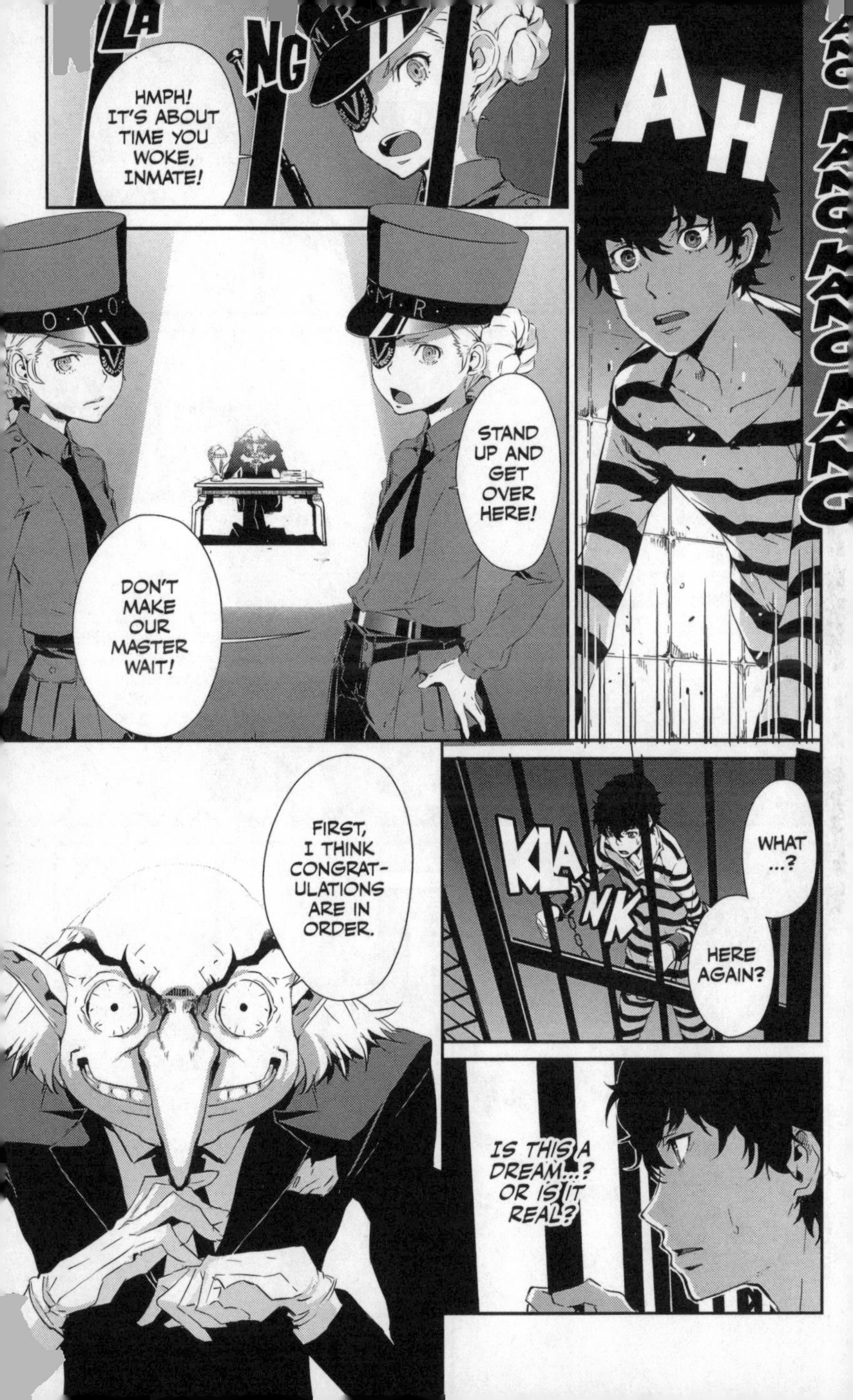
AH
HMPH! IT'S ABOUT TIME YOU WOKE, INMATE!
STAND UP AND GET OVER HERE!
DON'T MAKE OUR MASTER WAIT!
KLANK
WHAT ...?
HERE AGAIN?
IS THIS A DREAM...? OR IS IT REAL?
FIRST, I THINK CONGRAT-ULATIONS ARE IN ORDER.

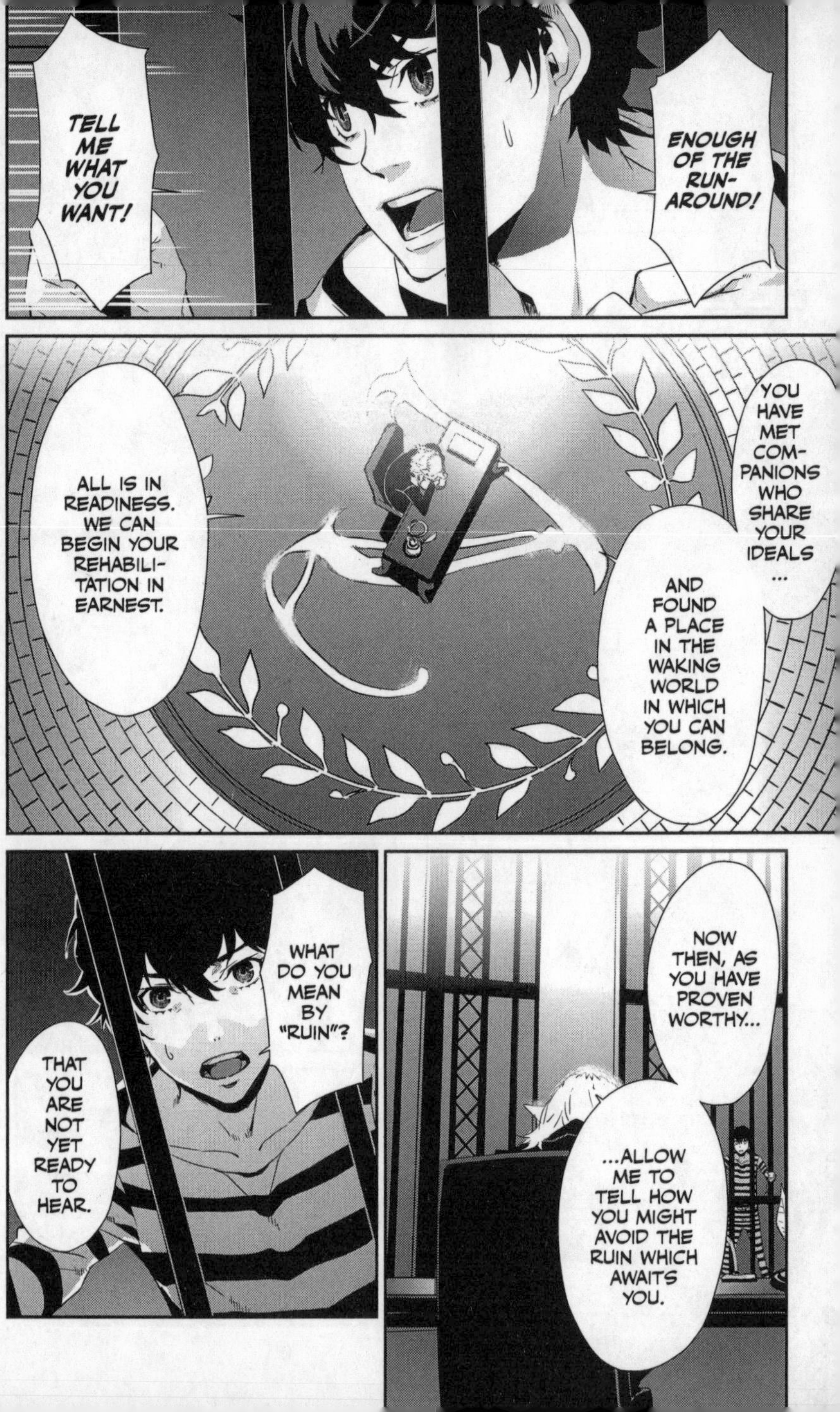
ENOUGH OF THE RUN-AROUND!
TELL ME WHAT YOU WANT!
YOU HAVE MET COMPANIONS WHO SHARE YOUR IDEALS...
AND FOUND A PLACE IN THE WAKING WORLD IN WHICH YOU CAN BELONG.
ALL IS IN READINESS. WE CAN BEGIN YOUR REHABILITATION IN EARNEST.
NOW THEN, AS YOU HAVE PROVEN WORTHY...
...ALLOW ME TO TELL HOW YOU MIGHT AVOID THE RUIN WHICH AWAITS YOU.
WHAT DO YOU MEAN BY "RUIN"?
THAT YOU ARE NOT YET READY TO HEAR.

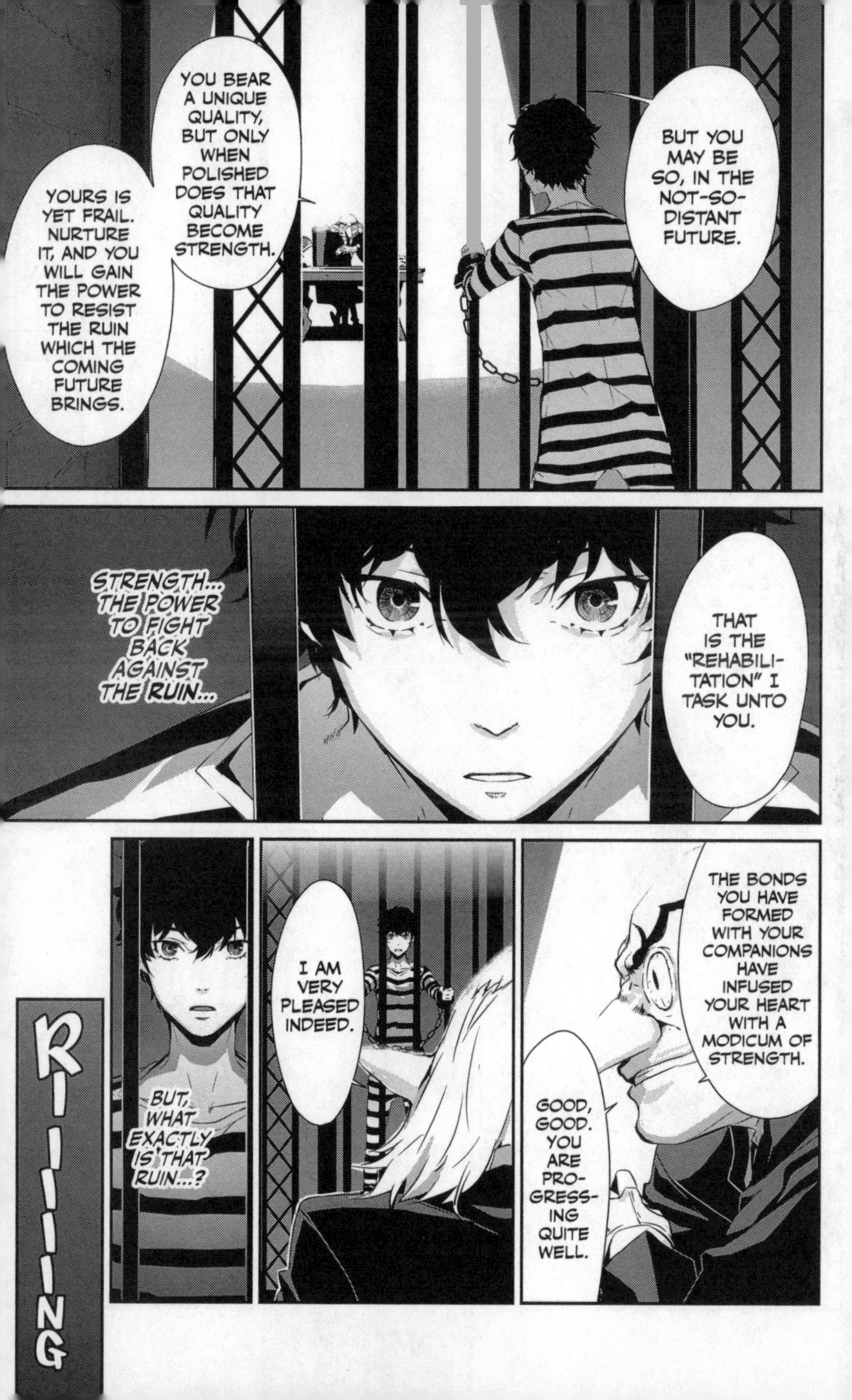
BUT YOU MAY BE SO, IN THE NOT-SO-DISTANT FUTURE.
YOU BEAR A UNIQUE QUALITY, BUT ONLY WHEN POLISHED DOES THAT QUALITY BECOME STRENGTH.
YOURS IS YET FRAIL. NURTURE IT, AND YOU WILL GAIN THE POWER TO RESIST THE RUIN WHICH THE COMING FUTURE BRINGS.
THAT IS THE "REHABILI-TATION" I TASK UNTO YOU.
STRENGTH... THE POWER TO FIGHT BACK AGAINST THE RUIN...
THE BONDS YOU HAVE FORMED WITH YOUR COMPANIONS HAVE INFUSED YOUR HEART WITH A MODICUM OF STRENGTH.
GOOD, GOOD. YOU ARE PRO-GRESS-ING QUITE WELL.
I AM VERY PLEASED INDEED.
BUT, WHAT EXACTLY IS THAT RUIN...?
RIIIIIIIING

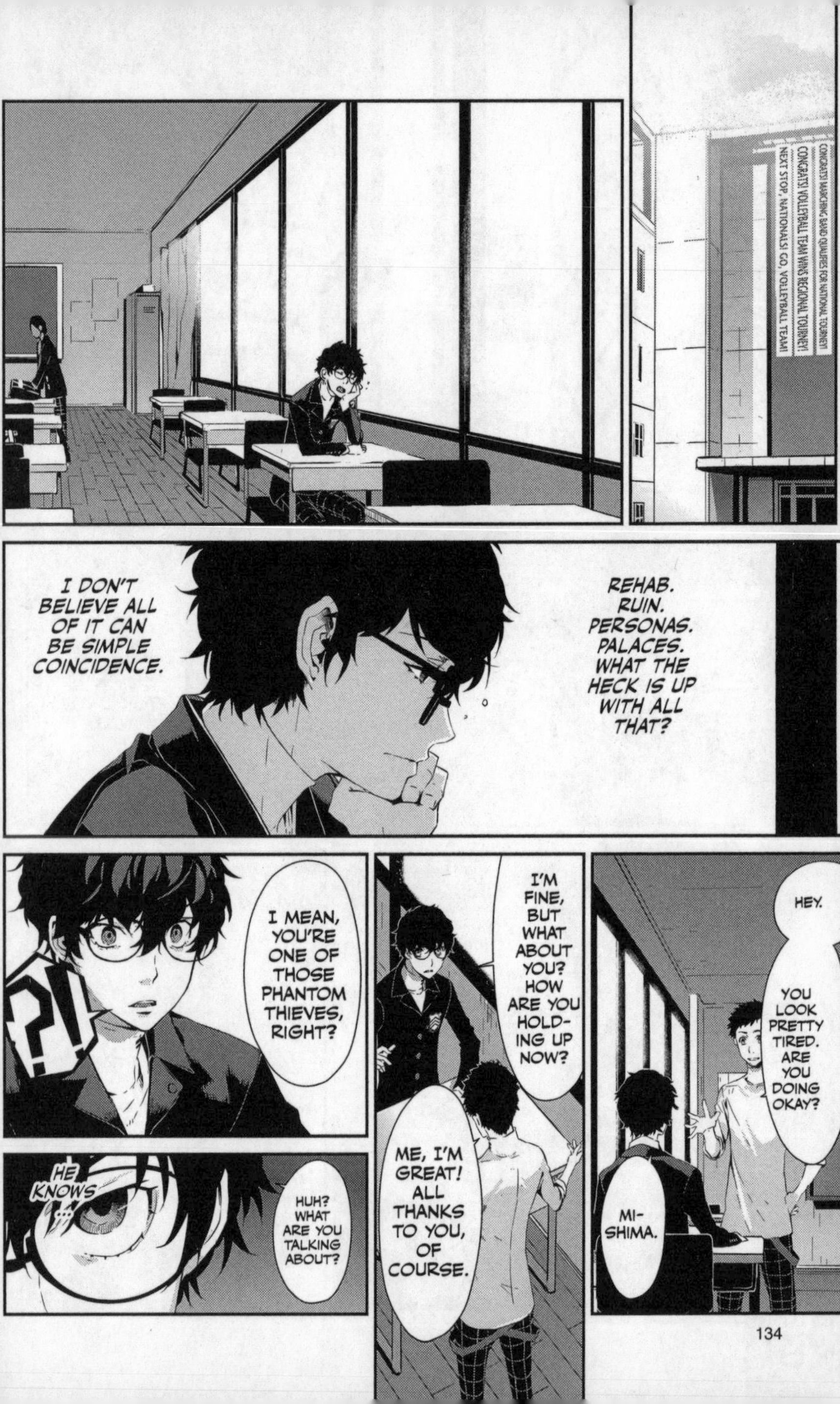
CONGRATS! MARCHING BAND QUALIFIES FOR NATIONAL TOURNEY!
CONGRATS! VOLLEYBALL TEAM WINS REGIONAL TOURNEY!
NEXT STOP, NATIONALS! GO, VOLLEYBALL TEAM!
REHAB. RUIN. PERSONAS. PALACES. WHAT THE HECK IS UP WITH ALL THAT?
I DON'T BELIEVE ALL OF IT CAN BE SIMPLE COINCIDENCE.
HEY.
YOU LOOK PRETTY TIRED. ARE YOU DOING OKAY?
MI-SHIMA.
I'M FINE, BUT WHAT ABOUT YOU? HOW ARE YOU HOLDING UP NOW?
ME, I'M GREAT! ALL THANKS TO YOU, OF COURSE.
I MEAN, YOU'RE ONE OF THOSE PHANTOM THIEVES, RIGHT?
?!
HUH? WHAT ARE YOU TALKING ABOUT?
HE KNOWS...

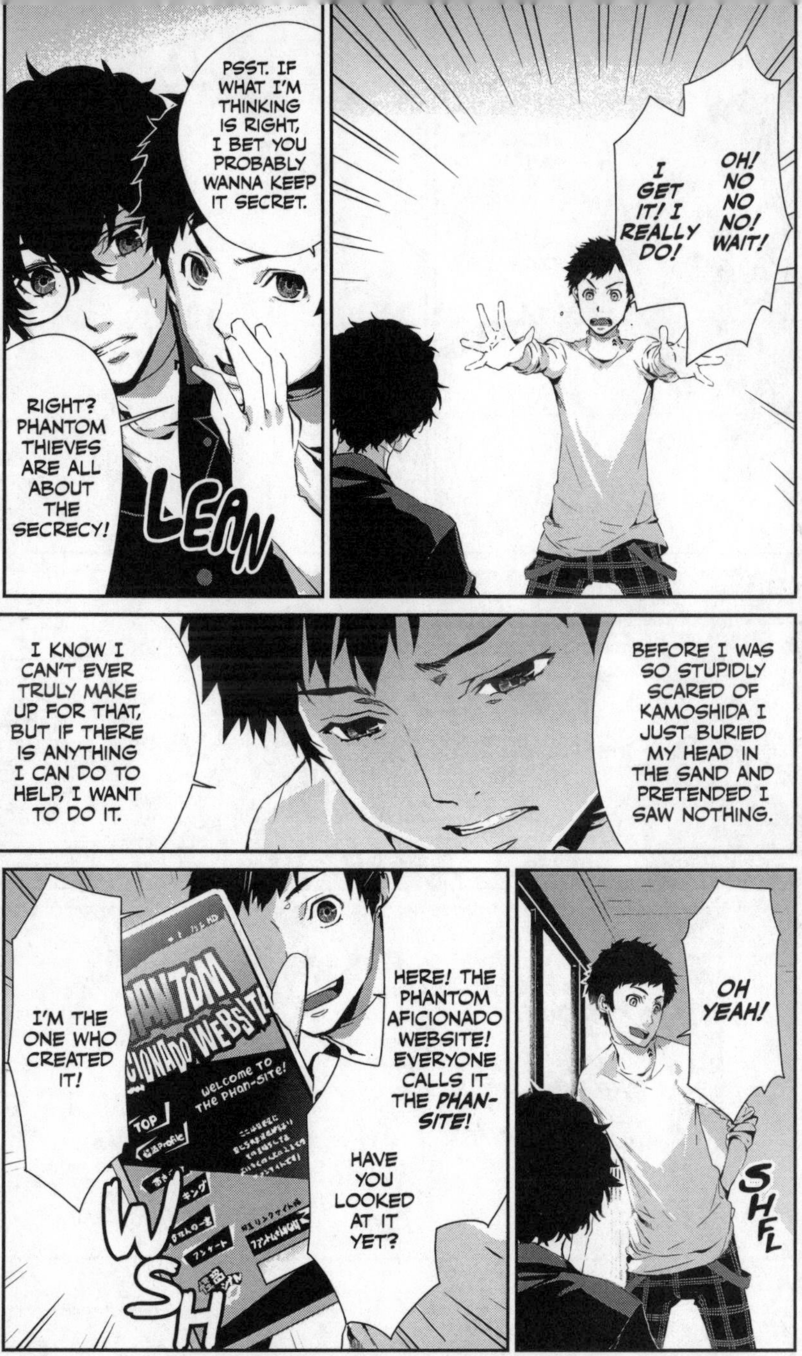
OH! NO NO NO! WAIT!
I GET IT! I REALLY DO!
PSST. IF WHAT I'M THINKING IS RIGHT, I BET YOU PROBABLY WANNA KEEP IT SECRET.
RIGHT? PHANTOM THIEVES ARE ALL ABOUT THE SECRECY!
LEAN
BEFORE I WAS SO STUPIDLY SCARED OF KAMOSHIDA I JUST BURIED MY HEAD IN THE SAND AND PRETENDED I SAW NOTHING.
I KNOW I CAN'T EVER TRULY MAKE UP FOR THAT, BUT IF THERE IS ANYTHING I CAN DO TO HELP, I WANT TO DO IT.
OH YEAH!
SHFL
HERE! THE PHANTOM AFICIONADO WEBSITE! EVERYONE CALLS IT THE *PHAN-SITE*!
HAVE YOU LOOKED AT IT YET?
Welcome to the Phan-site!
TOP
I'M THE ONE WHO CREATED IT!
WSH

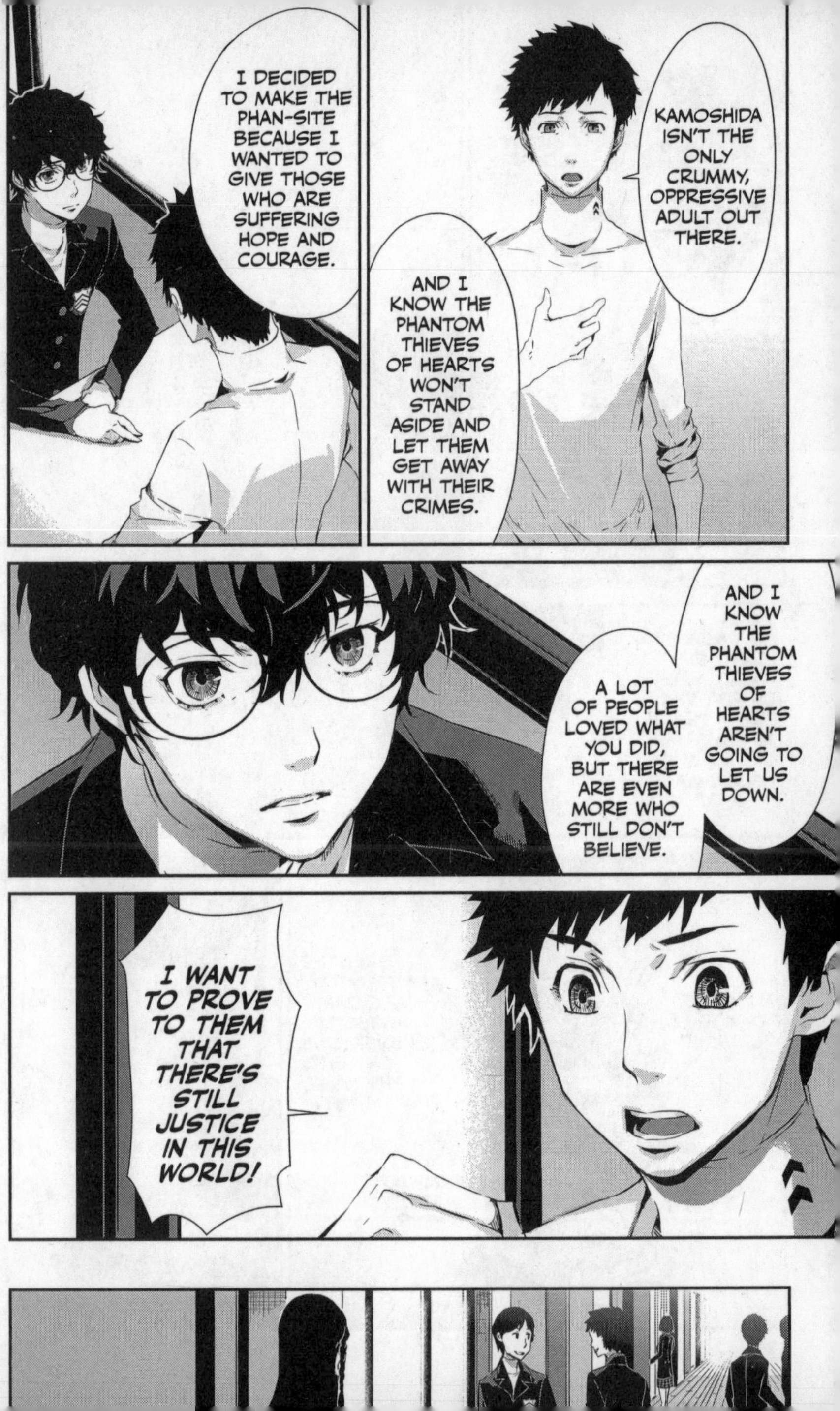
KAMOSHIDA ISN'T THE ONLY CRUMMY, OPPRESSIVE ADULT OUT THERE.
AND I KNOW THE PHANTOM THIEVES OF HEARTS WON'T STAND ASIDE AND LET THEM GET AWAY WITH THEIR CRIMES.
I DECIDED TO MAKE THE PHAN-SITE BECAUSE I WANTED TO GIVE THOSE WHO ARE SUFFERING HOPE AND COURAGE.
AND I KNOW THE PHANTOM THIEVES OF HEARTS AREN'T GOING TO LET US DOWN.
A LOT OF PEOPLE LOVED WHAT YOU DID, BUT THERE ARE EVEN MORE WHO STILL DON'T BELIEVE.
I WANT TO PROVE TO THEM THAT THERE'S STILL JUSTICE IN THIS WORLD!

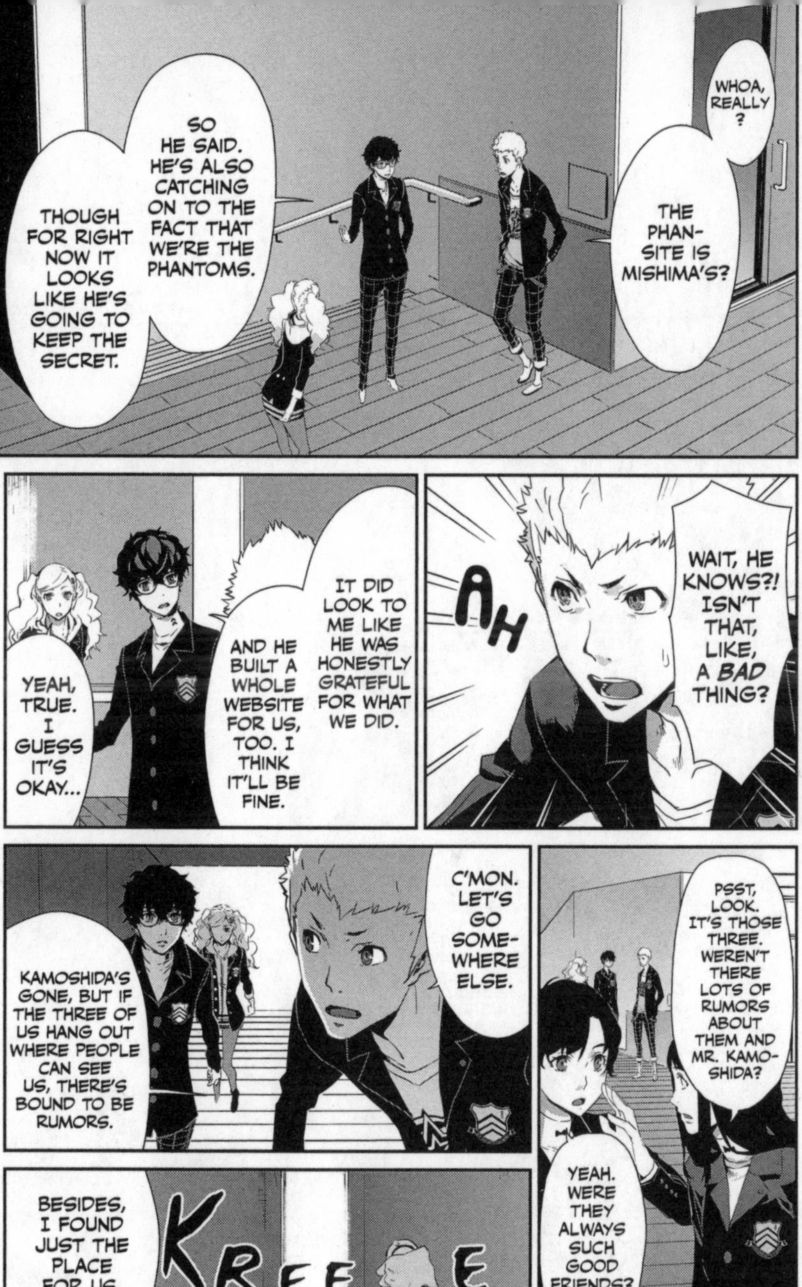
WHOA, REALLY?
THE PHAN-SITE IS MISHIMA'S?
SO HE SAID. HE'S ALSO CATCHING ON TO THE FACT THAT WE'RE THE PHANTOMS.
THOUGH FOR RIGHT NOW IT LOOKS LIKE HE'S GOING TO KEEP THE SECRET.
WAIT, HE KNOWS?! ISN'T THAT, LIKE, A *BAD* THING?
AH
IT DID LOOK TO ME LIKE HE WAS HONESTLY GRATEFUL FOR WHAT WE DID.
AND HE BUILT A WHOLE WEBSITE FOR US, TOO. I THINK IT'LL BE FINE.
YEAH, TRUE. I GUESS IT'S OKAY...
PSST, LOOK. IT'S THOSE THREE. WEREN'T THERE LOTS OF RUMORS ABOUT THEM AND MR. KAMOSHIDA?
YEAH. WERE THEY ALWAYS SUCH GOOD FRIENDS?
C'MON. LET'S GO SOMEWHERE ELSE.
KAMOSHIDA'S GONE, BUT IF THE THREE OF US HANG OUT WHERE PEOPLE CAN SEE US, THERE'S BOUND TO BE RUMORS.
KREE E
BESIDES, I FOUND JUST THE PLACE FOR US.

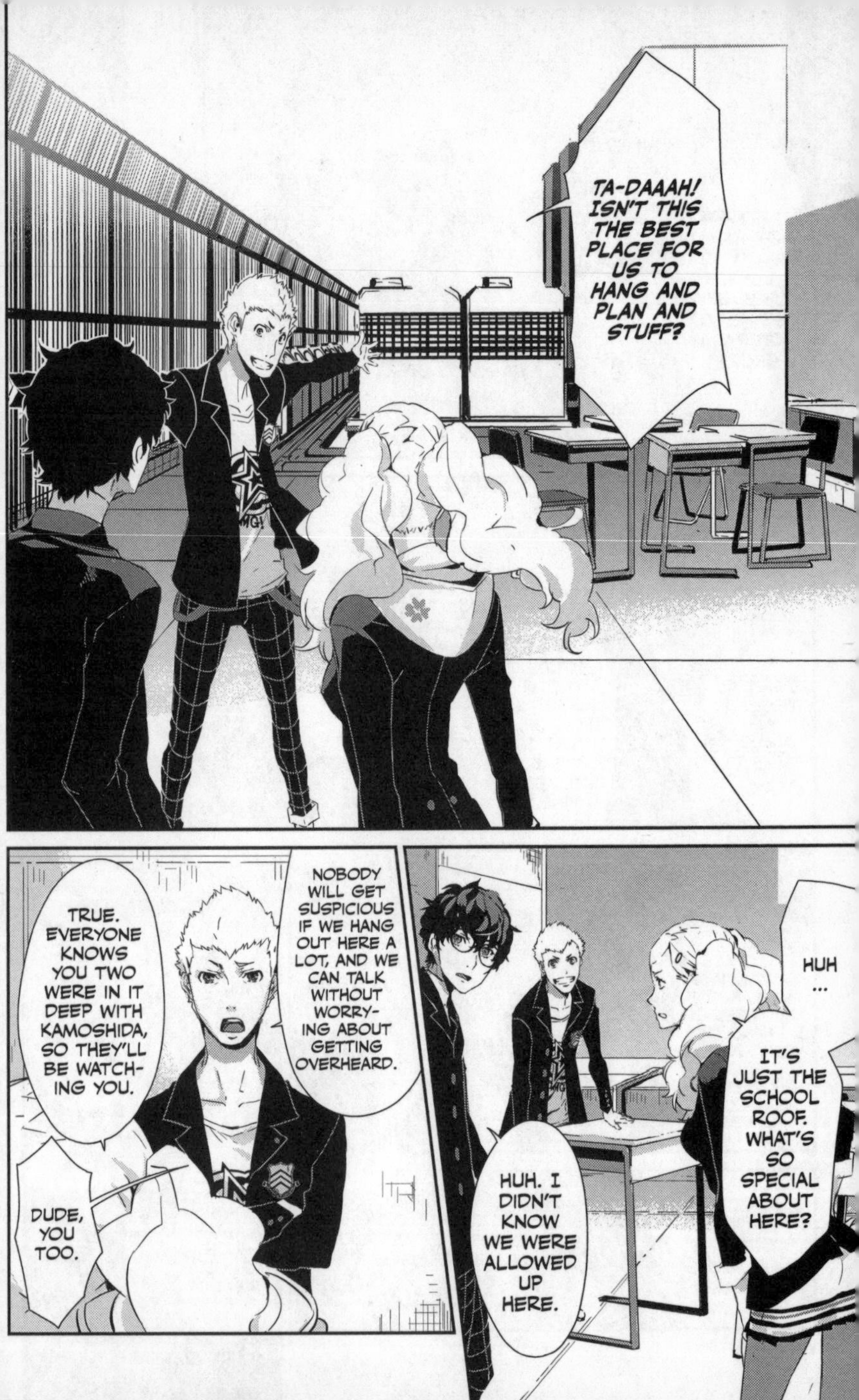
TA-DAAAH! ISN'T THIS THE BEST PLACE FOR US TO HANG AND PLAN AND STUFF?
HUH ...
IT'S JUST THE SCHOOL ROOF. WHAT'S SO SPECIAL ABOUT HERE?
HUH. I DIDN'T KNOW WE WERE ALLOWED UP HERE.
NOBODY WILL GET SUSPICIOUS IF WE HANG OUT HERE A LOT, AND WE CAN TALK WITHOUT WORRYING ABOUT GETTING OVERHEARD.
TRUE. EVERYONE KNOWS YOU TWO WERE IN IT DEEP WITH KAMOSHIDA, SO THEY'LL BE WATCHING YOU.
DUDE, YOU TOO.

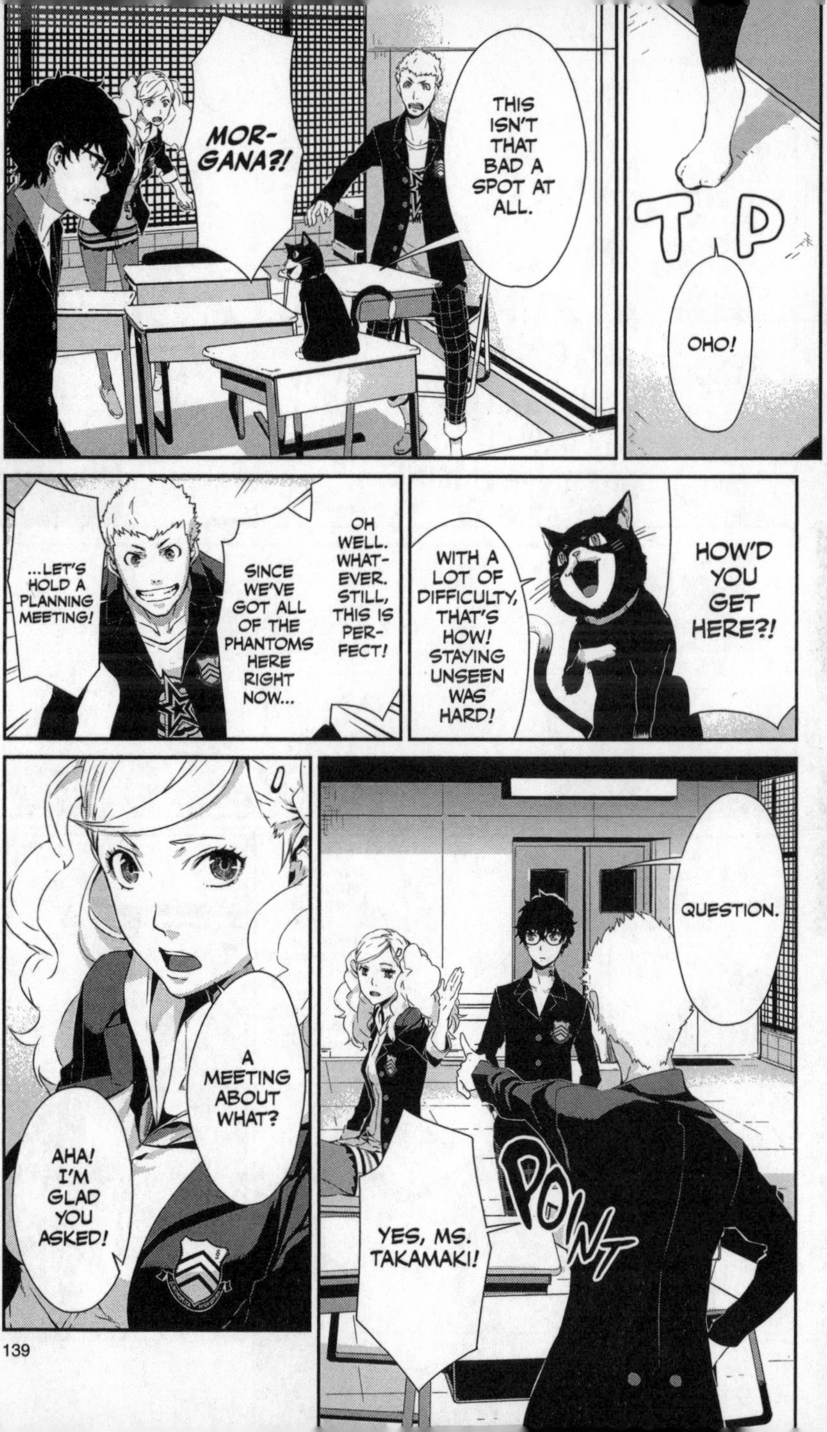
T P
OHO!
THIS ISN'T THAT BAD A SPOT AT ALL.
MOR-GANA?!
HOW'D YOU GET HERE?!
WITH A LOT OF DIFFICULTY, THAT'S HOW! STAYING UNSEEN WAS HARD!
OH WELL. WHAT-EVER. STILL, THIS IS PER-FECT!
SINCE WE'VE GOT ALL OF THE PHANTOMS HERE RIGHT NOW...
...LET'S HOLD A PLANNING MEETING!
QUESTION.
YES, MS. TAKAMAKI!
POINT
A MEETING ABOUT WHAT?
AHA! I'M GLAD YOU ASKED!

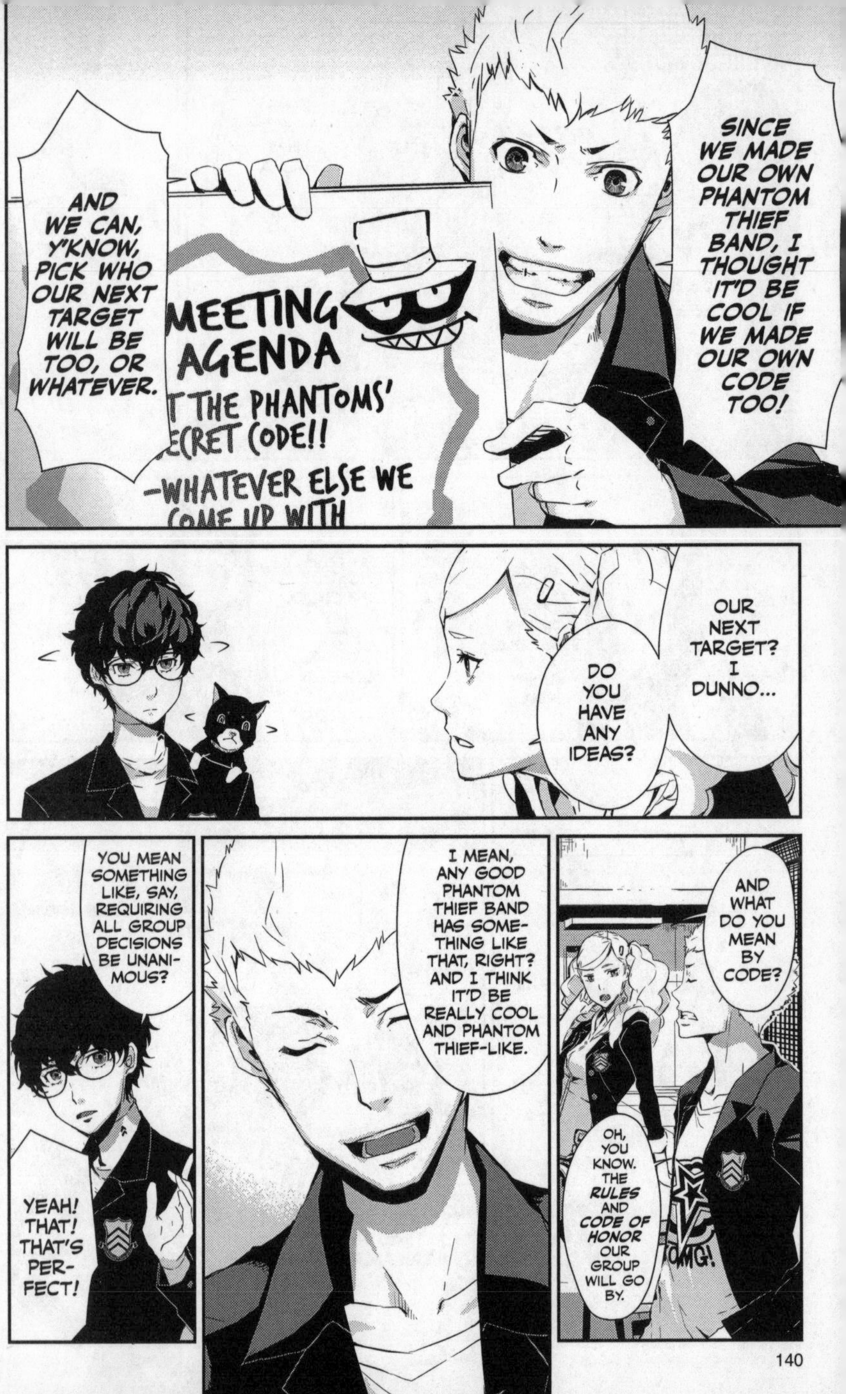
SINCE WE MADE OUR OWN PHANTOM THIEF BAND, I THOUGHT IT'D BE COOL IF WE MADE OUR OWN CODE TOO!
AND WE CAN, Y'KNOW, PICK WHO OUR NEXT TARGET WILL BE TOO, OR WHATEVER.
MEETING AGENDA
-WHATEVER ELSE WE
OUR NEXT TARGET? I DUNNO...
DO YOU HAVE ANY IDEAS?
AND WHAT DO YOU MEAN BY CODE?
OH, YOU KNOW. THE *RULES* AND *CODE OF HONOR* OUR GROUP WILL GO BY.
I MEAN, ANY GOOD PHANTOM THIEF BAND HAS SOME-THING LIKE THAT, RIGHT? AND I THINK IT'D BE REALLY COOL AND PHANTOM THIEF-LIKE.
YOU MEAN SOMETHING LIKE, SAY, REQUIRING ALL GROUP DECISIONS BE UNANI-MOUS?
YEAH! THAT! THAT'S PER-FECT!

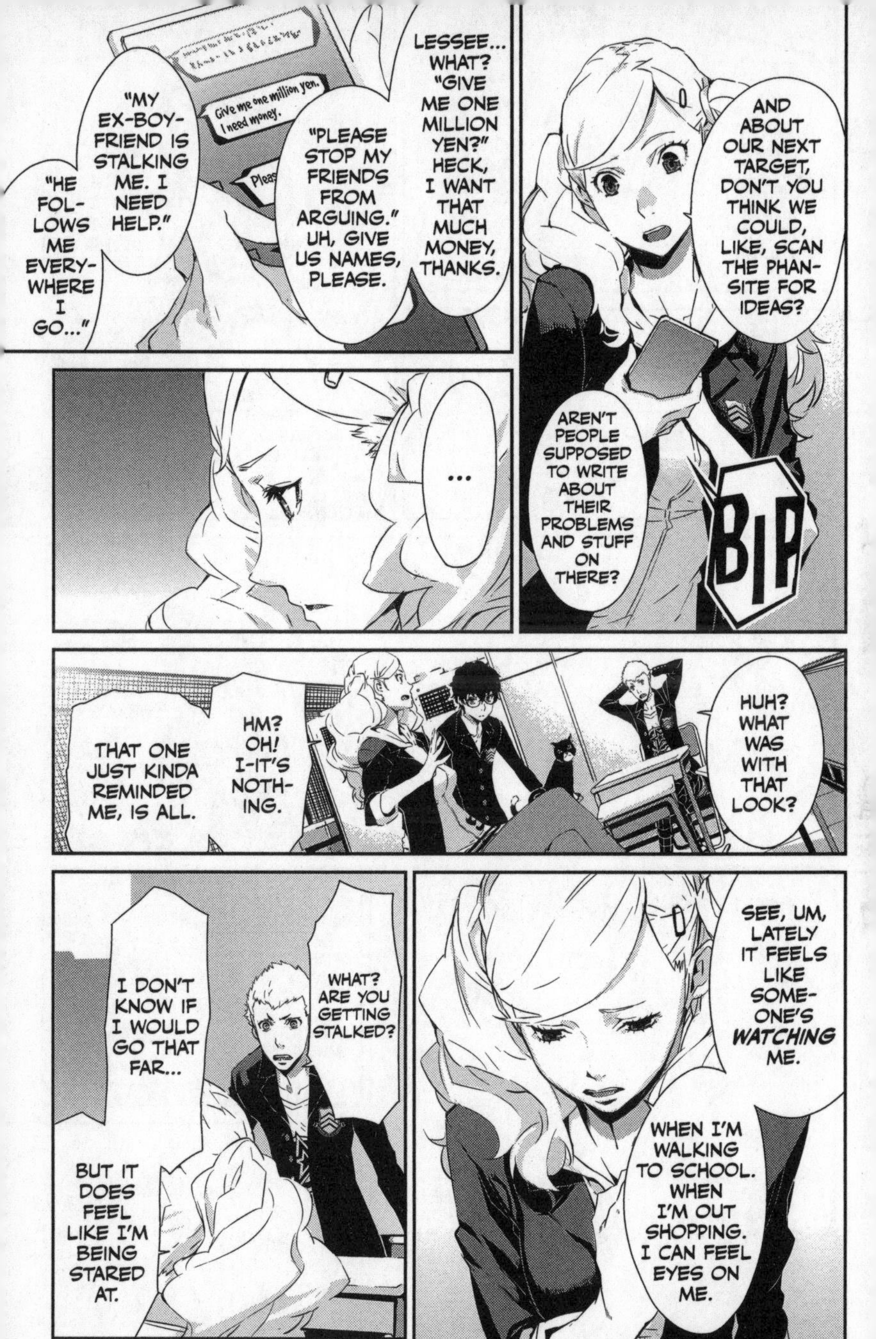
AND ABOUT OUR NEXT TARGET, DON'T YOU THINK WE COULD, LIKE, SCAN THE PHAN-SITE FOR IDEAS?
AREN'T PEOPLE SUPPOSED TO WRITE ABOUT THEIR PROBLEMS AND STUFF ON THERE?
BIP
LESSEE... WHAT? "GIVE ME ONE MILLION YEN?" HECK, I WANT THAT MUCH MONEY, THANKS.
Give me one million yen. I need money.
Pleas
"PLEASE STOP MY FRIENDS FROM ARGUING." UH, GIVE US NAMES, PLEASE.
"MY EX-BOY-FRIEND IS STALKING ME. I NEED HELP."
"HE FOL-LOWS ME EVERY-WHERE I GO..."
...
HUH? WHAT WAS WITH THAT LOOK?
HM? OH! I-IT'S NOTH-ING.
THAT ONE JUST KINDA REMINDED ME, IS ALL.
SEE, UM, LATELY IT FEELS LIKE SOME-ONE'S *WATCHING* ME.
WHEN I'M WALKING TO SCHOOL. WHEN I'M OUT SHOPPING. I CAN FEEL EYES ON ME.
WHAT? ARE YOU GETTING STALKED?
I DON'T KNOW IF I WOULD GO THAT FAR...
BUT IT DOES FEEL LIKE I'M BEING STARED AT.

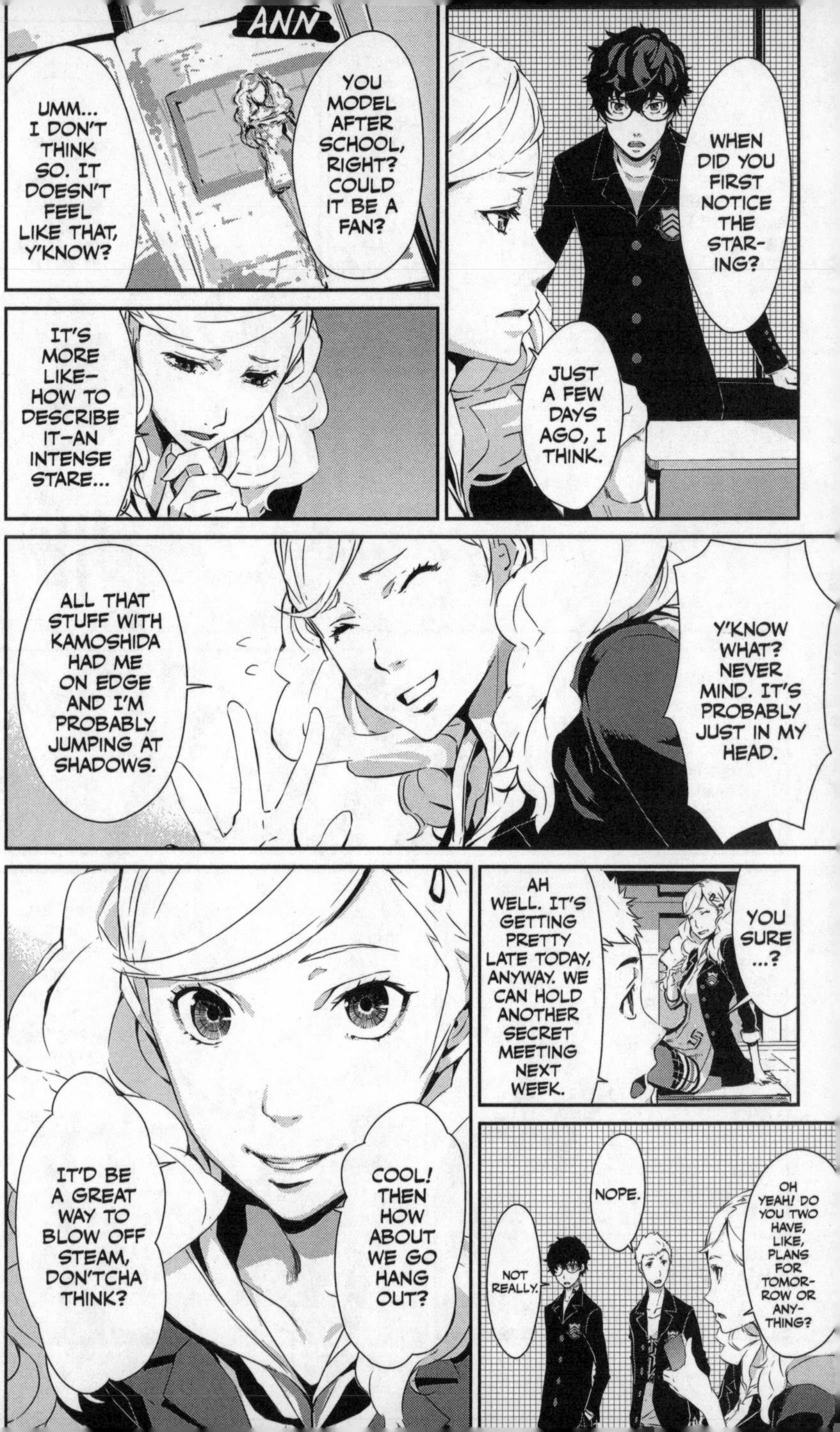
WHEN DID YOU FIRST NOTICE THE STAR-ING?
JUST A FEW DAYS AGO, I THINK.
ANN
YOU MODEL AFTER SCHOOL, RIGHT? COULD IT BE A FAN?
UMM... I DON'T THINK SO. IT DOESN'T FEEL LIKE THAT, Y'KNOW?
IT'S MORE LIKE—HOW TO DESCRIBE IT—AN INTENSE STARE...
Y'KNOW WHAT? NEVER MIND. IT'S PROBABLY JUST IN MY HEAD.
ALL THAT STUFF WITH KAMOSHIDA HAD ME ON EDGE AND I'M PROBABLY JUMPING AT SHADOWS.
YOU SURE ...?
AH WELL. IT'S GETTING PRETTY LATE TODAY, ANYWAY. WE CAN HOLD ANOTHER SECRET MEETING NEXT WEEK.
OH YEAH! DO YOU TWO HAVE, LIKE, PLANS FOR TOMOR-ROW OR ANY-THING?
NOPE.
NOT REALLY.
COOL! THEN HOW ABOUT WE GO HANG OUT?
IT'D BE A GREAT WAY TO BLOW OFF STEAM, DON'TCHA THINK?

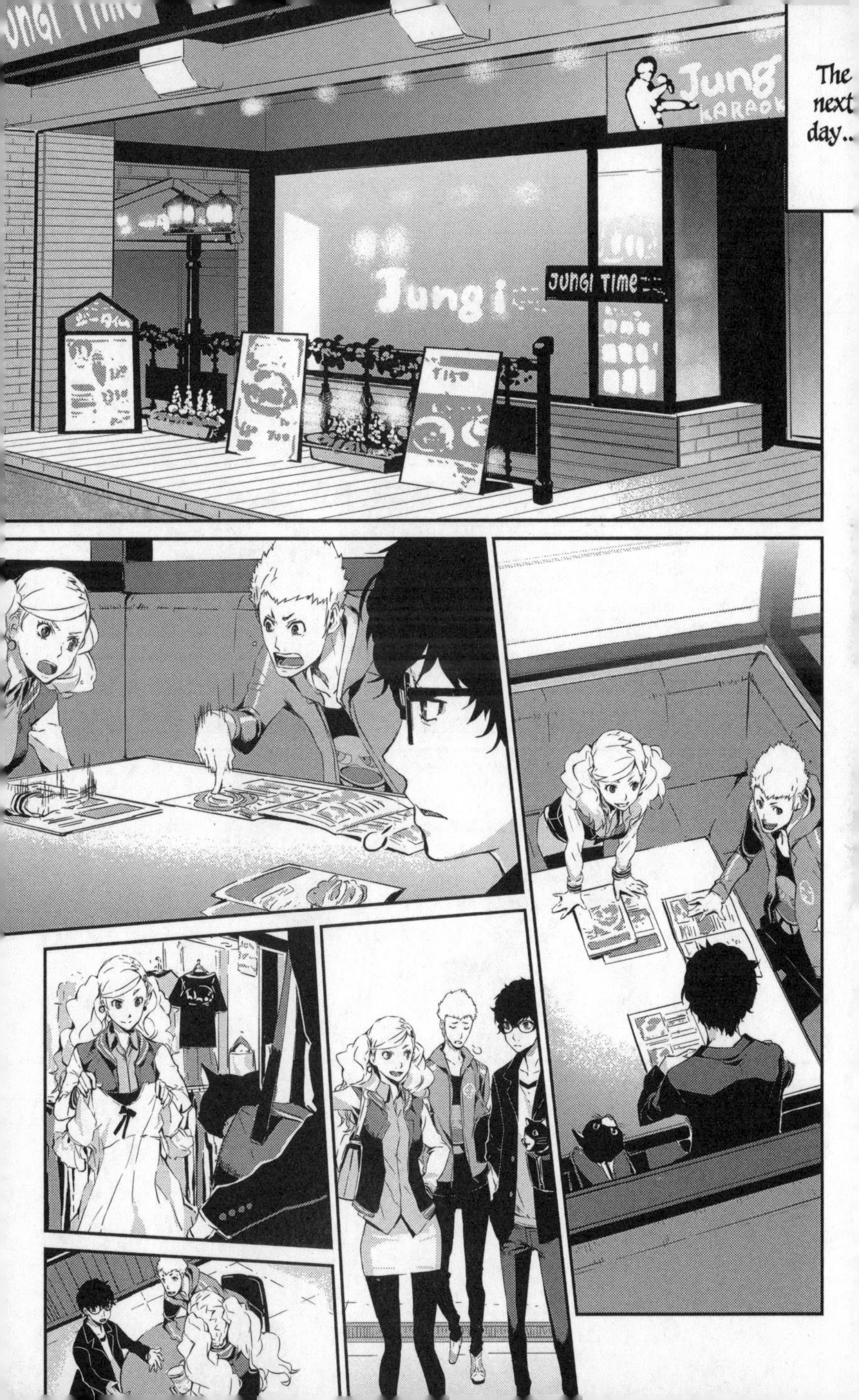
The next day..
Jungi
JUNGI TIME

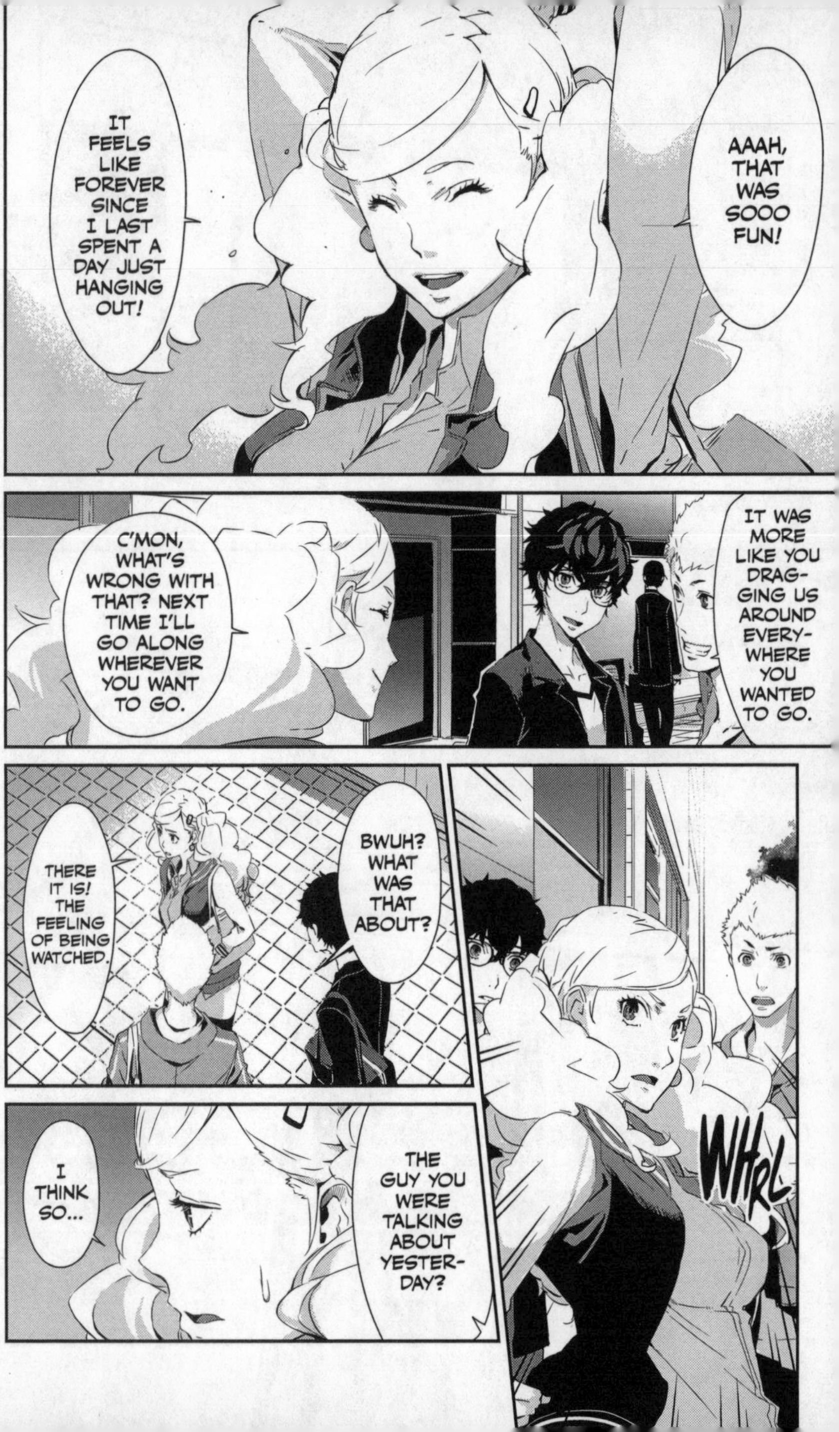
AAAH, THAT WAS SOOO FUN!
IT FEELS LIKE FOREVER SINCE I LAST SPENT A DAY JUST HANGING OUT!
IT WAS MORE LIKE YOU DRAG-GING US AROUND EVERY-WHERE YOU WANTED TO GO.
C'MON, WHAT'S WRONG WITH THAT? NEXT TIME I'LL GO ALONG WHEREVER YOU WANT TO GO.
WHRL
BWUH? WHAT WAS THAT ABOUT?
THERE IT IS! THE FEELING OF BEING WATCHED.
THE GUY YOU WERE TALKING ABOUT YESTER-DAY?
I THINK SO...

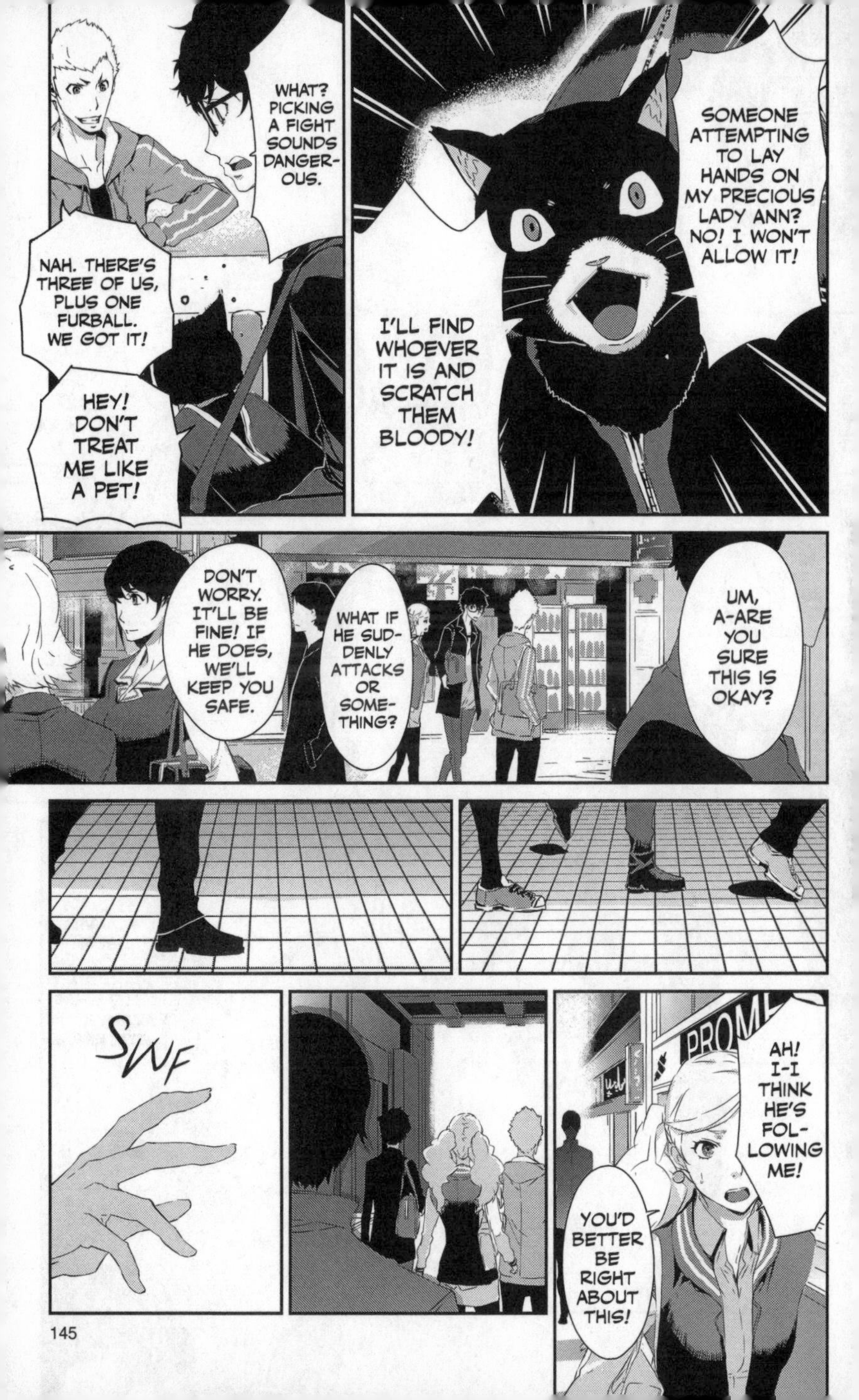
SOMEONE ATTEMPTING TO LAY HANDS ON MY PRECIOUS LADY ANN? NO! I WON'T ALLOW IT!
I'LL FIND WHOEVER IT IS AND SCRATCH THEM BLOODY!
WHAT? PICKING A FIGHT SOUNDS DANGER-OUS.
NAH. THERE'S THREE OF US, PLUS ONE FURBALL. WE GOT IT!
HEY! DON'T TREAT ME LIKE A PET!
UM, A-ARE YOU SURE THIS IS OKAY?
WHAT IF HE SUD-DENLY ATTACKS OR SOME-THING?
DON'T WORRY. IT'LL BE FINE! IF HE DOES, WE'LL KEEP YOU SAFE.
AH! I-I THINK HE'S FOL-LOWING ME!
YOU'D BETTER BE RIGHT ABOUT THIS!
SWF

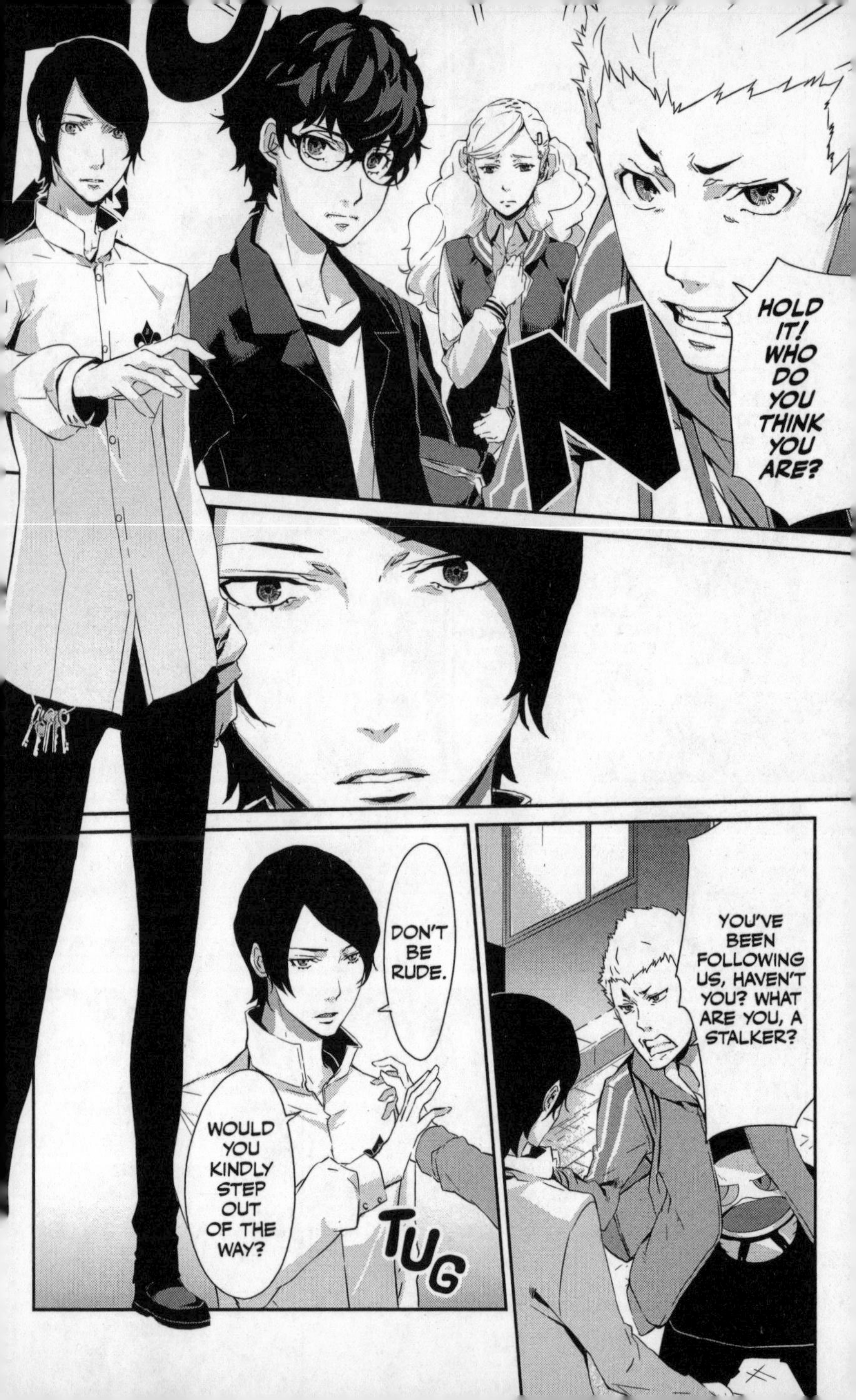
HOLD IT! WHO DO YOU THINK YOU ARE?
YOU'VE BEEN FOLLOWING US, HAVEN'T YOU? WHAT ARE YOU, A STALKER?
DON'T BE RUDE.
WOULD YOU KINDLY STEP OUT OF THE WAY?
TUG

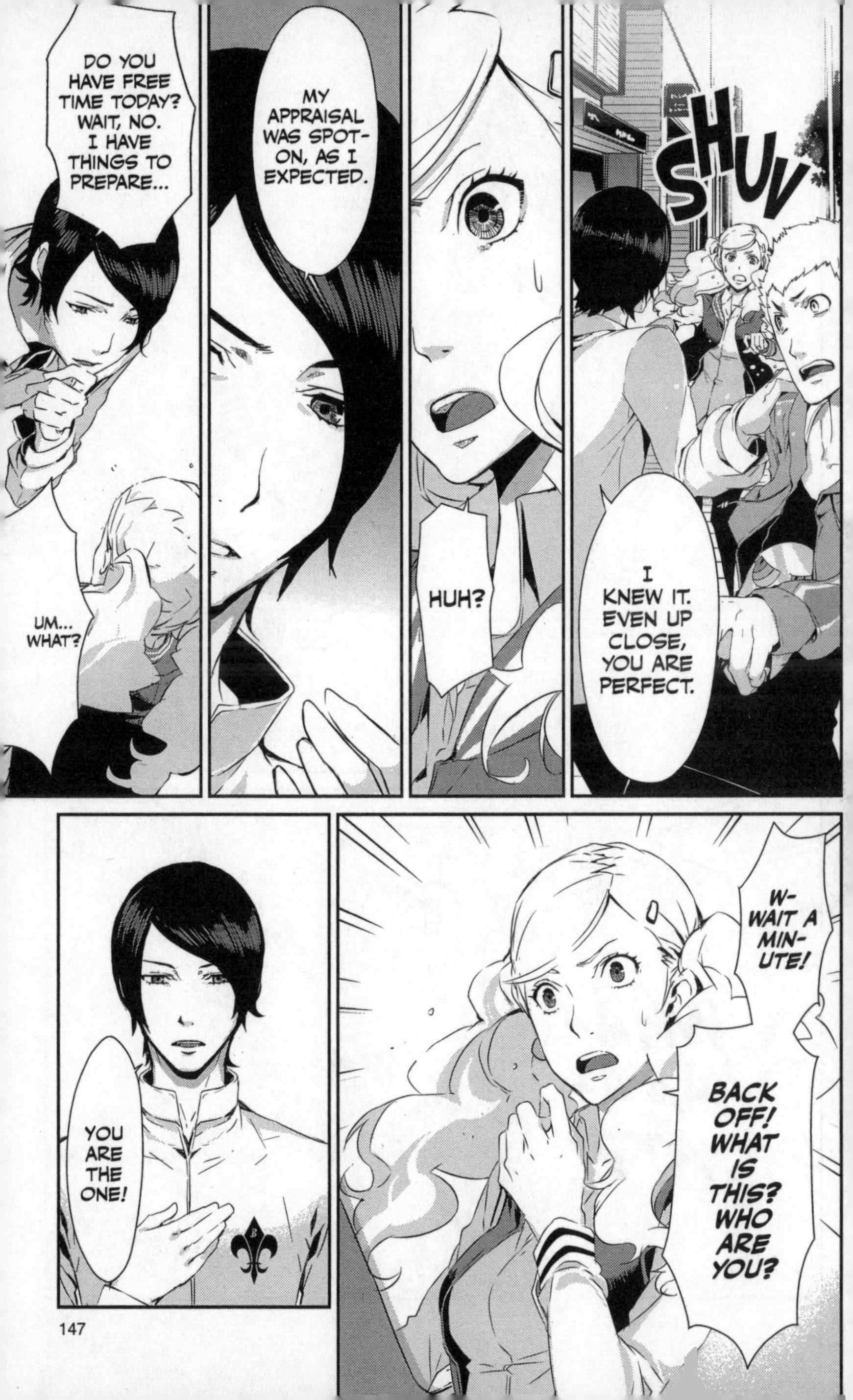
SHUV
I KNEW IT. EVEN UP CLOSE, YOU ARE PERFECT.
HUH?
MY APPRAISAL WAS SPOT-ON, AS I EXPECTED.
DO YOU HAVE FREE TIME TODAY? WAIT, NO. I HAVE THINGS TO PREPARE...
UM... WHAT?
W-WAIT A MINUTE!
BACK OFF! WHAT IS THIS? WHO ARE YOU?
YOU ARE THE ONE!

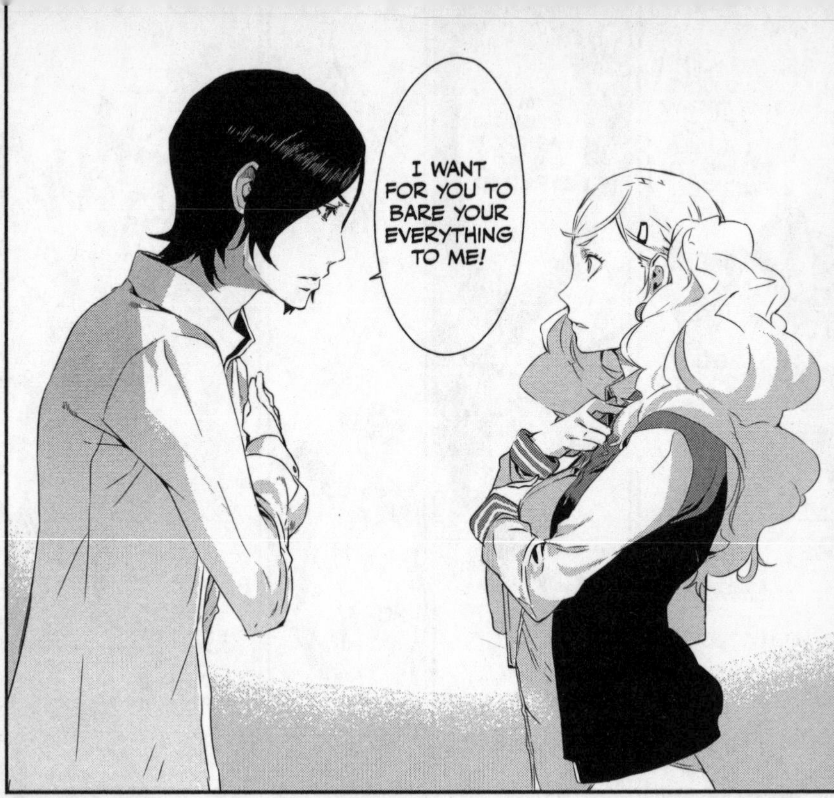
I WANT FOR YOU TO BARE YOUR EVERYTHING TO ME!

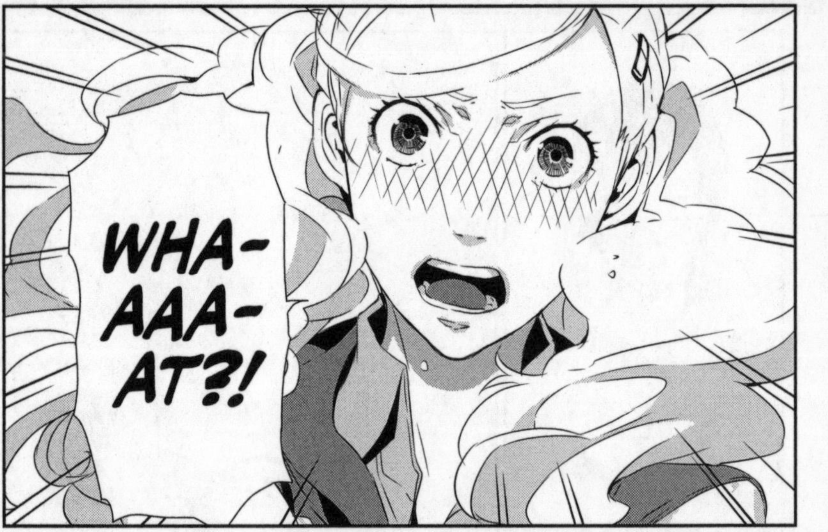
WHA-AAA-AT?!

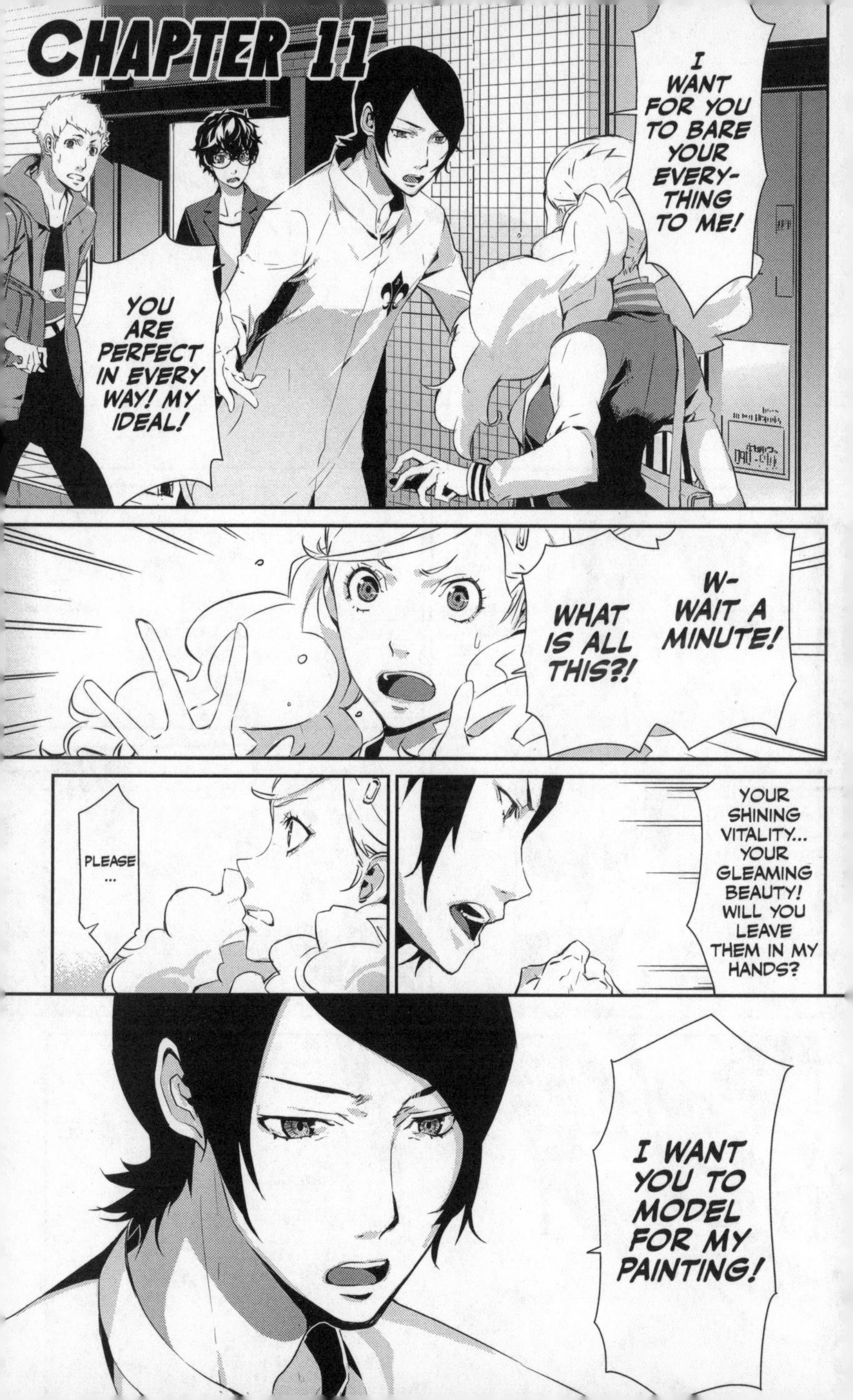
CHAPTER 11
I WANT FOR YOU TO BARE YOUR EVERYTHING TO ME!
YOU ARE PERFECT IN EVERY WAY! MY IDEAL!
W- WAIT A MINUTE!
WHAT IS ALL THIS?!
YOUR SHINING VITALITY... YOUR GLEAMING BEAUTY! WILL YOU LEAVE THEM IN MY HANDS?
PLEASE...
I WANT YOU TO MODEL FOR MY PAINTING!

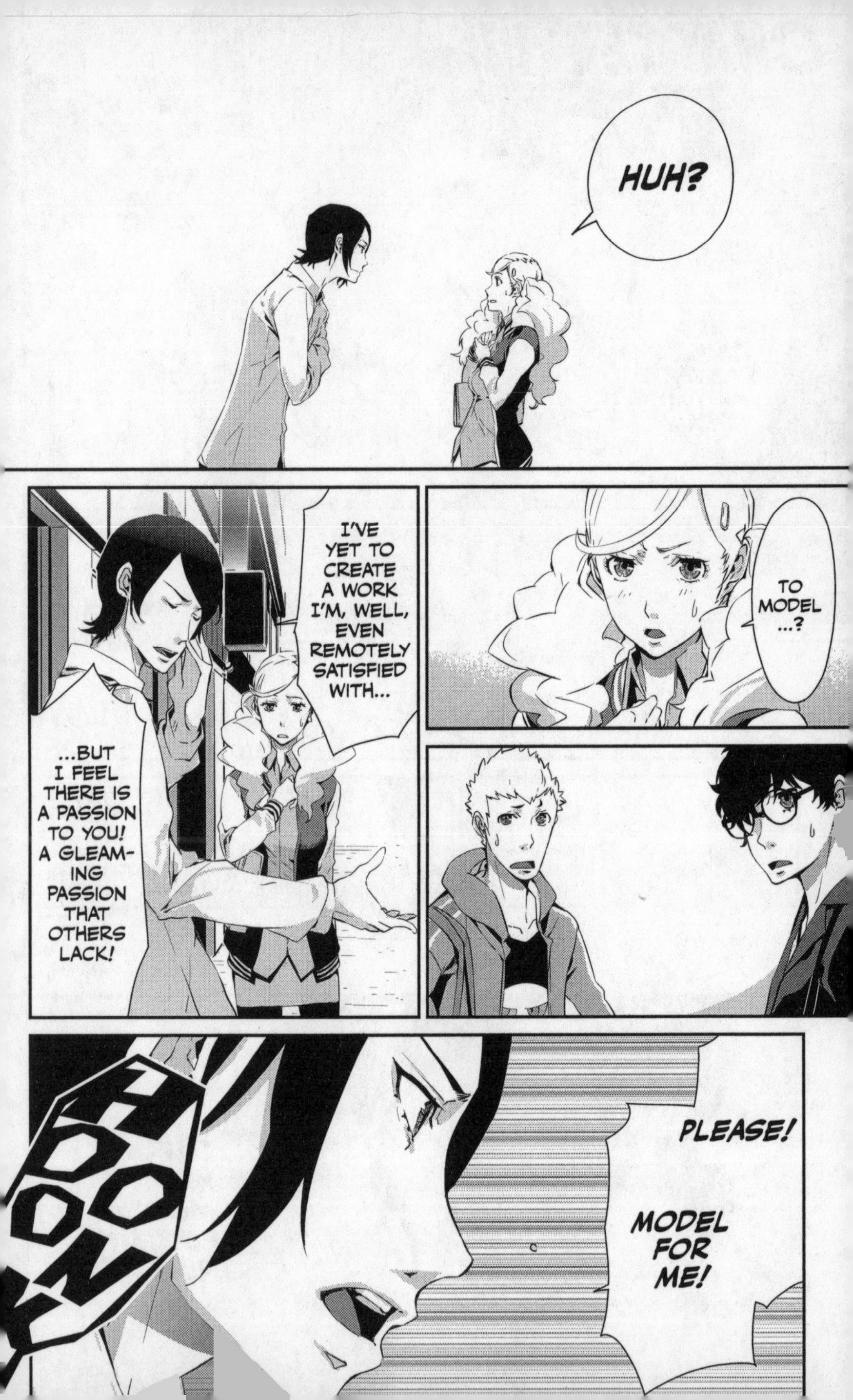
HUH?
TO MODEL ...?
I'VE YET TO CREATE A WORK I'M, WELL, EVEN REMOTELY SATISFIED WITH...
...BUT I FEEL THERE IS A PASSION TO YOU! A GLEAM-ING PASSION THAT OTHERS LACK!
PLEASE!
MODEL FOR ME!

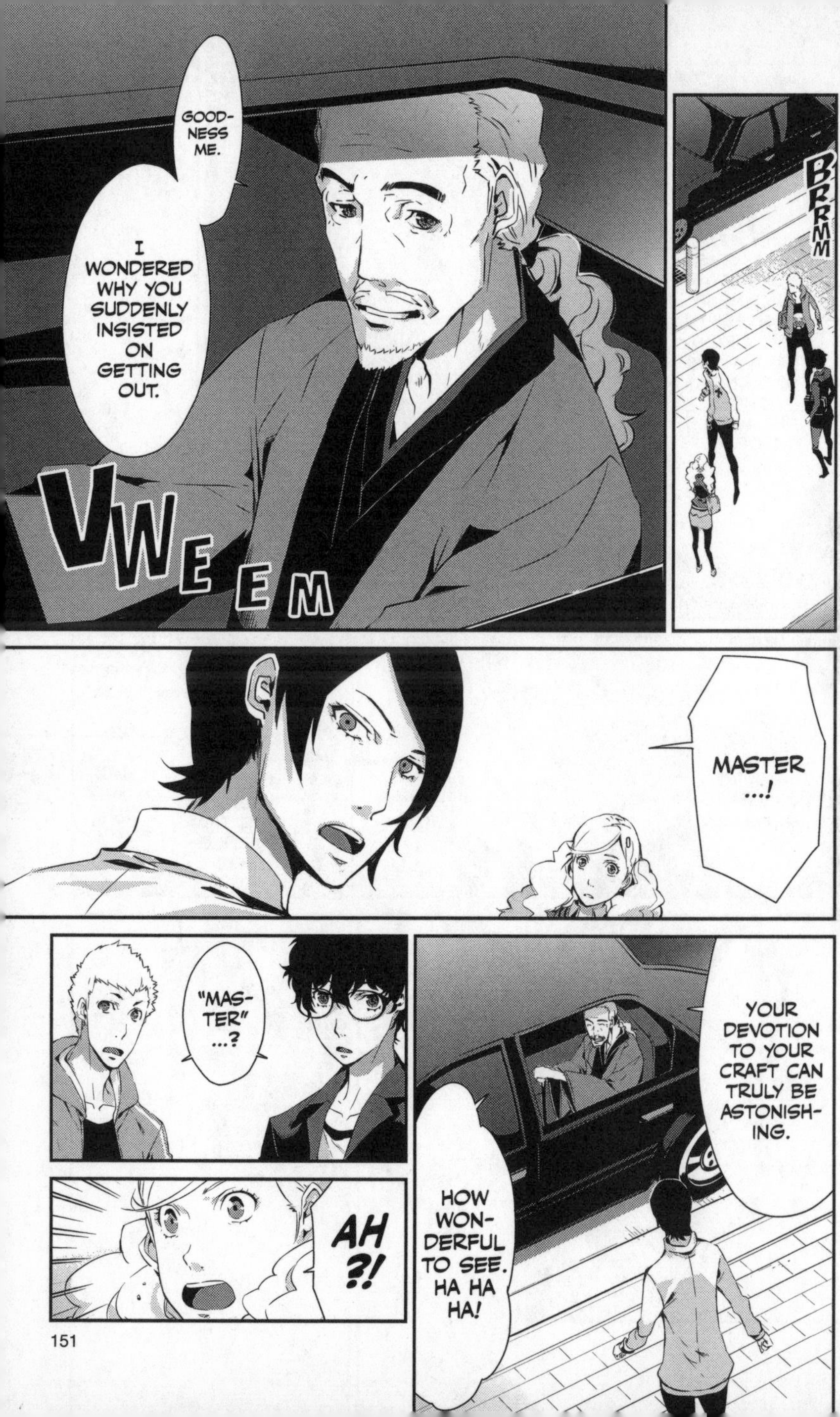
BRRMM
GOOD-NESS ME.
I WONDERED WHY YOU SUDDENLY INSISTED ON GETTING OUT.
VWEEM
MASTER ...!
YOUR DEVOTION TO YOUR CRAFT CAN TRULY BE ASTONISH-ING.
HOW WON-DERFUL TO SEE. HA HA HA!
"MAS-TER" ...?
AH ?!

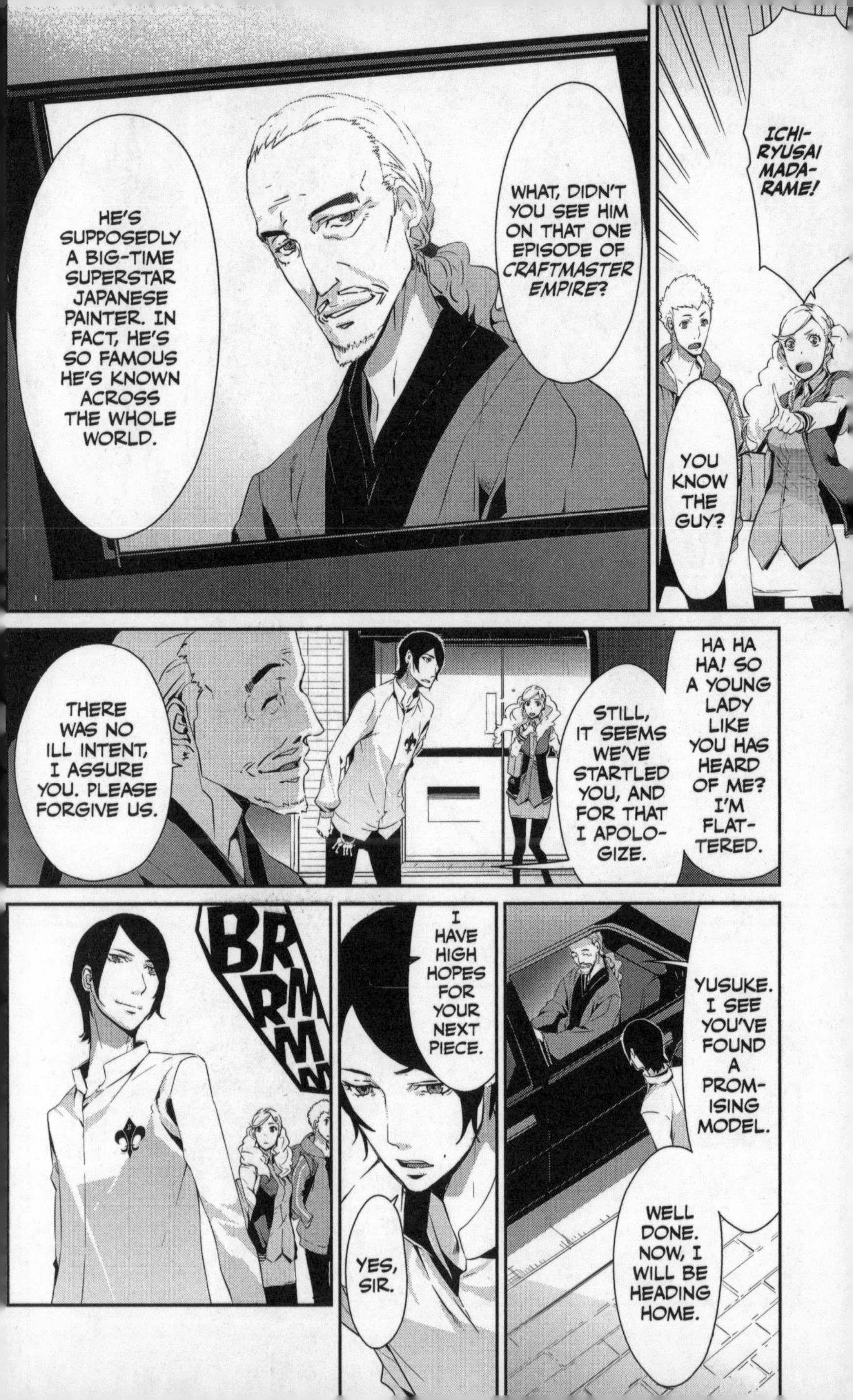
ICHI-RYUSAI MADARAME!
YOU KNOW THE GUY?
WHAT, DIDN'T YOU SEE HIM ON THAT ONE EPISODE OF *CRAFTMASTER EMPIRE*?
HE'S SUPPOSEDLY A BIG-TIME SUPERSTAR JAPANESE PAINTER. IN FACT, HE'S SO FAMOUS HE'S KNOWN ACROSS THE WHOLE WORLD.
HA HA HA! SO A YOUNG LADY LIKE YOU HAS HEARD OF ME? I'M FLATTERED.
STILL, IT SEEMS WE'VE STARTLED YOU, AND FOR THAT I APOLOGIZE.
THERE WAS NO ILL INTENT, I ASSURE YOU. PLEASE FORGIVE US.
YUSUKE. I SEE YOU'VE FOUND A PROMISING MODEL.
WELL DONE. NOW, I WILL BE HEADING HOME.
I HAVE HIGH HOPES FOR YOUR NEXT PIECE.
YES, SIR.
BRRMM

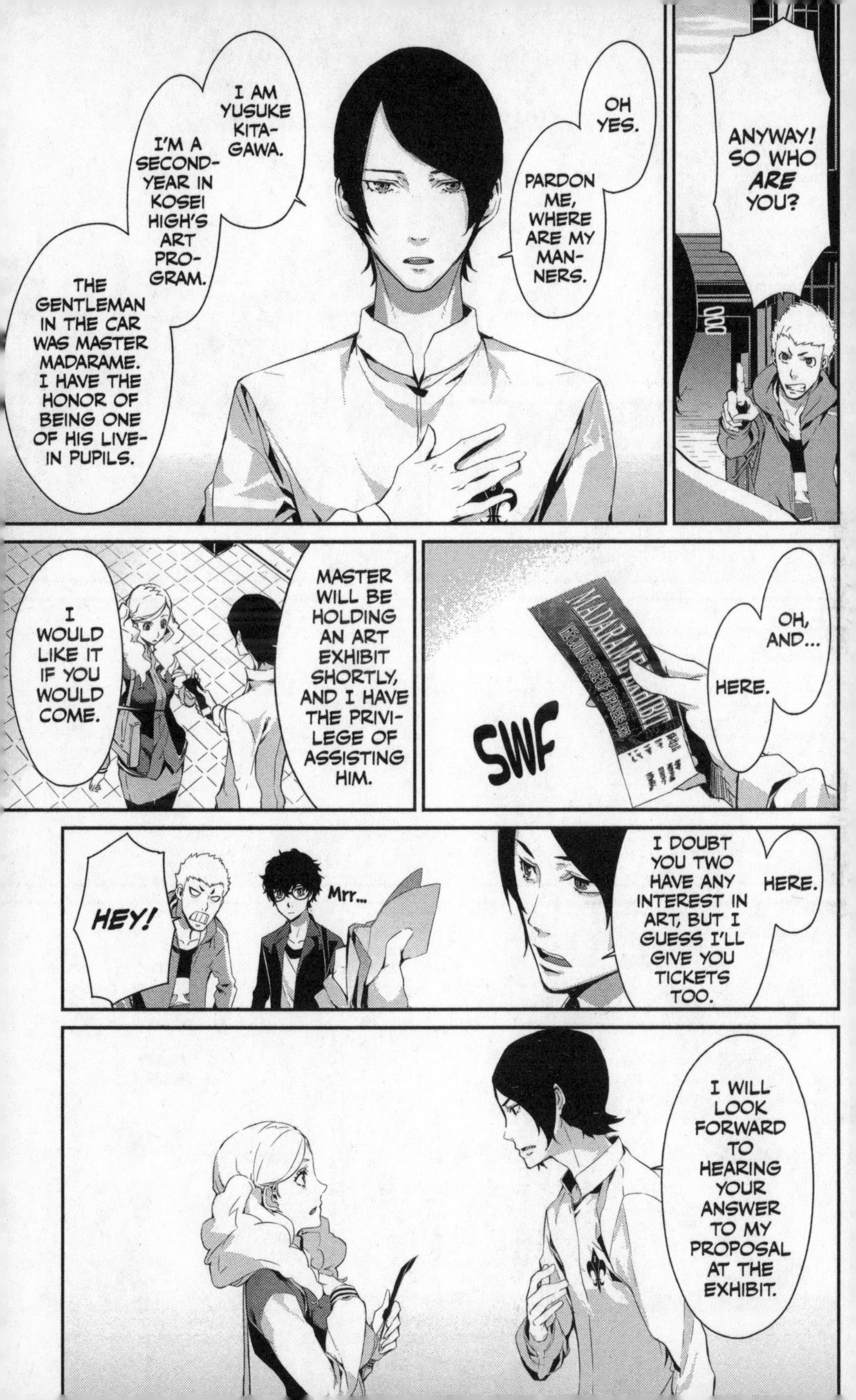

ANYWAY! SO WHO *ARE* YOU?
OH YES.
PARDON ME, WHERE ARE MY MANNERS.
I AM YUSUKE KITAGAWA.
I'M A SECOND-YEAR IN KOSEI HIGH'S ART PROGRAM.
THE GENTLEMAN IN THE CAR WAS MASTER MADARAME. I HAVE THE HONOR OF BEING ONE OF HIS LIVE-IN PUPILS.
OH, AND...
HERE.
MADARAME EXHIBIT
SWF
MASTER WILL BE HOLDING AN ART EXHIBIT SHORTLY, AND I HAVE THE PRIVILEGE OF ASSISTING HIM.
I WOULD LIKE IT IF YOU WOULD COME.
HERE.
I DOUBT YOU TWO HAVE ANY INTEREST IN ART, BUT I GUESS I'LL GIVE YOU TICKETS TOO.
Mrr...
HEY!
I WILL LOOK FORWARD TO HEARING YOUR ANSWER TO MY PROPOSAL AT THE EXHIBIT.

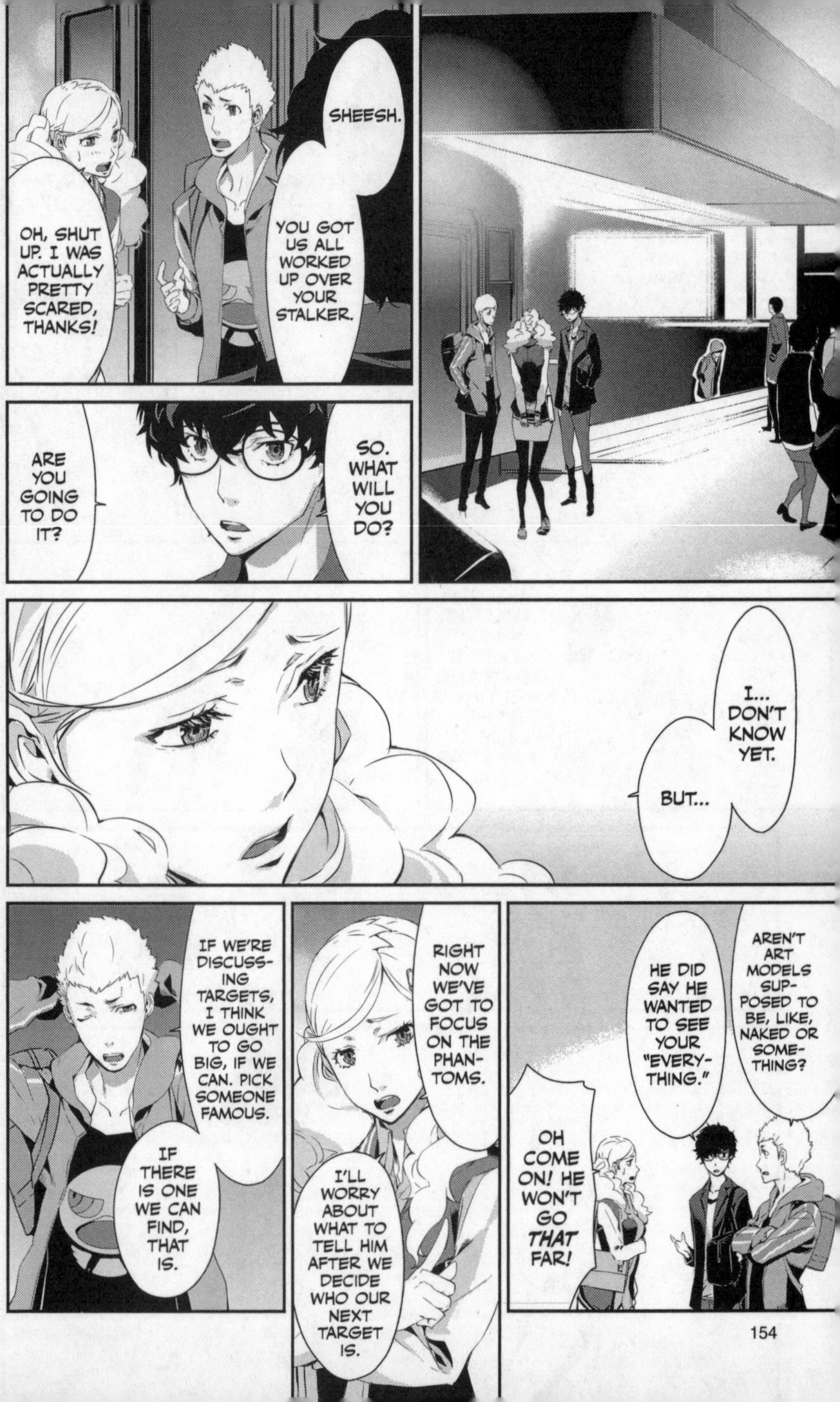
SHEESH.
YOU GOT US ALL WORKED UP OVER YOUR STALKER.
OH, SHUT UP. I WAS ACTUALLY PRETTY SCARED, THANKS!
SO. WHAT WILL YOU DO?
ARE YOU GOING TO DO IT?
I... DON'T KNOW YET.
BUT...
AREN'T ART MODELS SUP-POSED TO BE, LIKE, NAKED OR SOME-THING?
HE DID SAY HE WANTED TO SEE YOUR "EVERY-THING."
OH COME ON! HE WON'T GO *THAT* FAR!
RIGHT NOW WE'VE GOT TO FOCUS ON THE PHAN-TOMS.
I'LL WORRY ABOUT WHAT TO TELL HIM AFTER WE DECIDE WHO OUR NEXT TARGET IS.
IF WE'RE DISCUSS-ING TARGETS, I THINK WE OUGHT TO GO BIG, IF WE CAN. PICK SOMEONE FAMOUS.
IF THERE IS ONE WE CAN FIND, THAT IS.

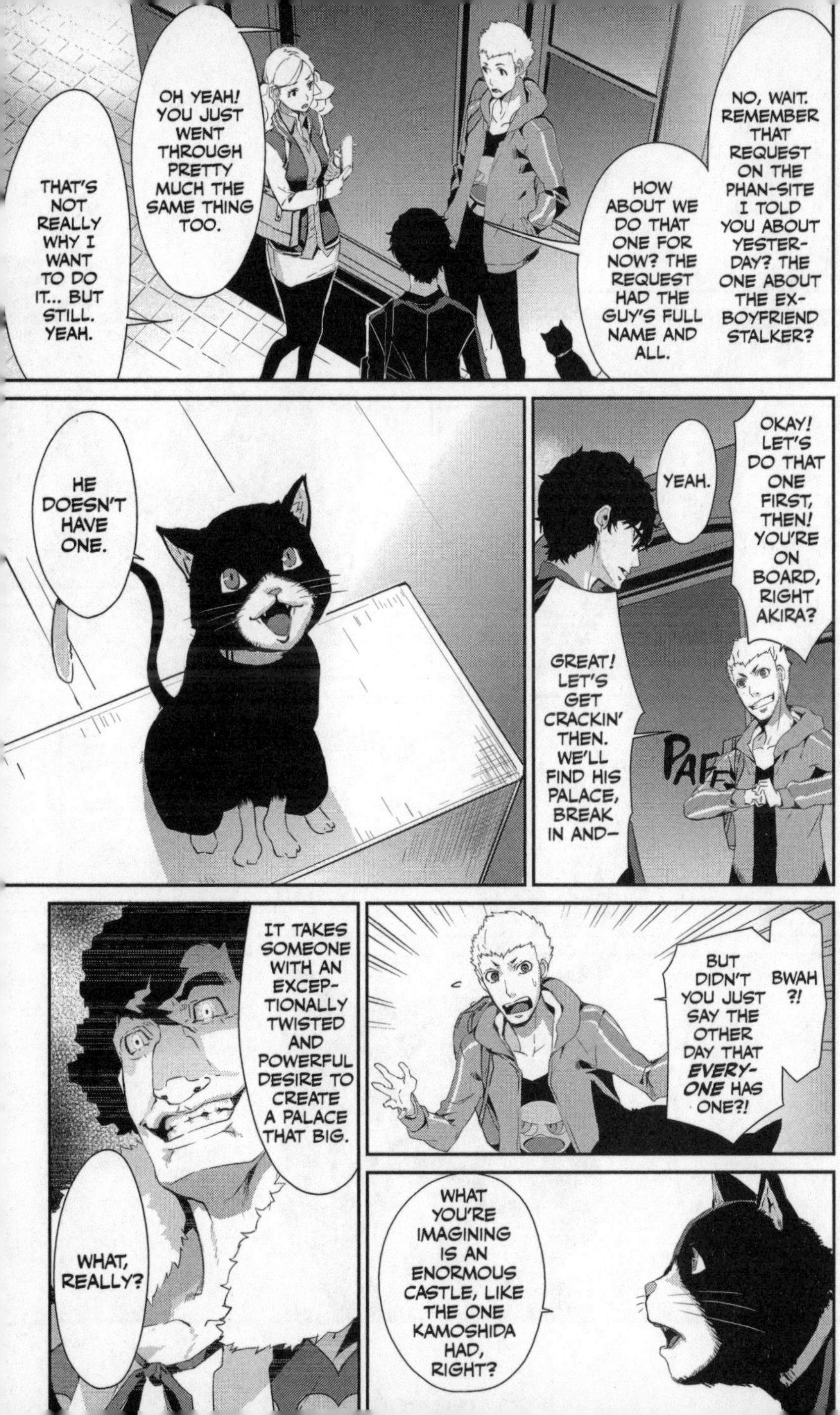
NO, WAIT. REMEMBER THAT REQUEST ON THE PHAN-SITE I TOLD YOU ABOUT YESTER-DAY? THE ONE ABOUT THE EX-BOYFRIEND STALKER?
HOW ABOUT WE DO THAT ONE FOR NOW? THE REQUEST HAD THE GUY'S FULL NAME AND ALL.
OH YEAH! YOU JUST WENT THROUGH PRETTY MUCH THE SAME THING TOO.
THAT'S NOT REALLY WHY I WANT TO DO IT... BUT STILL. YEAH.
OKAY! LET'S DO THAT ONE FIRST, THEN! YOU'RE ON BOARD, RIGHT AKIRA?
YEAH.
GREAT! LET'S GET CRACKIN' THEN. WE'LL FIND HIS PALACE, BREAK IN AND—
HE DOESN'T HAVE ONE.
BWAH?!
BUT DIDN'T YOU JUST SAY THE OTHER DAY THAT *EVERY-ONE* HAS ONE?!
WHAT YOU'RE IMAGINING IS AN ENORMOUS CASTLE, LIKE THE ONE KAMOSHIDA HAD, RIGHT?
IT TAKES SOMEONE WITH AN EXCEP-TIONALLY TWISTED AND POWERFUL DESIRE TO CREATE A PALACE THAT BIG.
WHAT, REALLY?

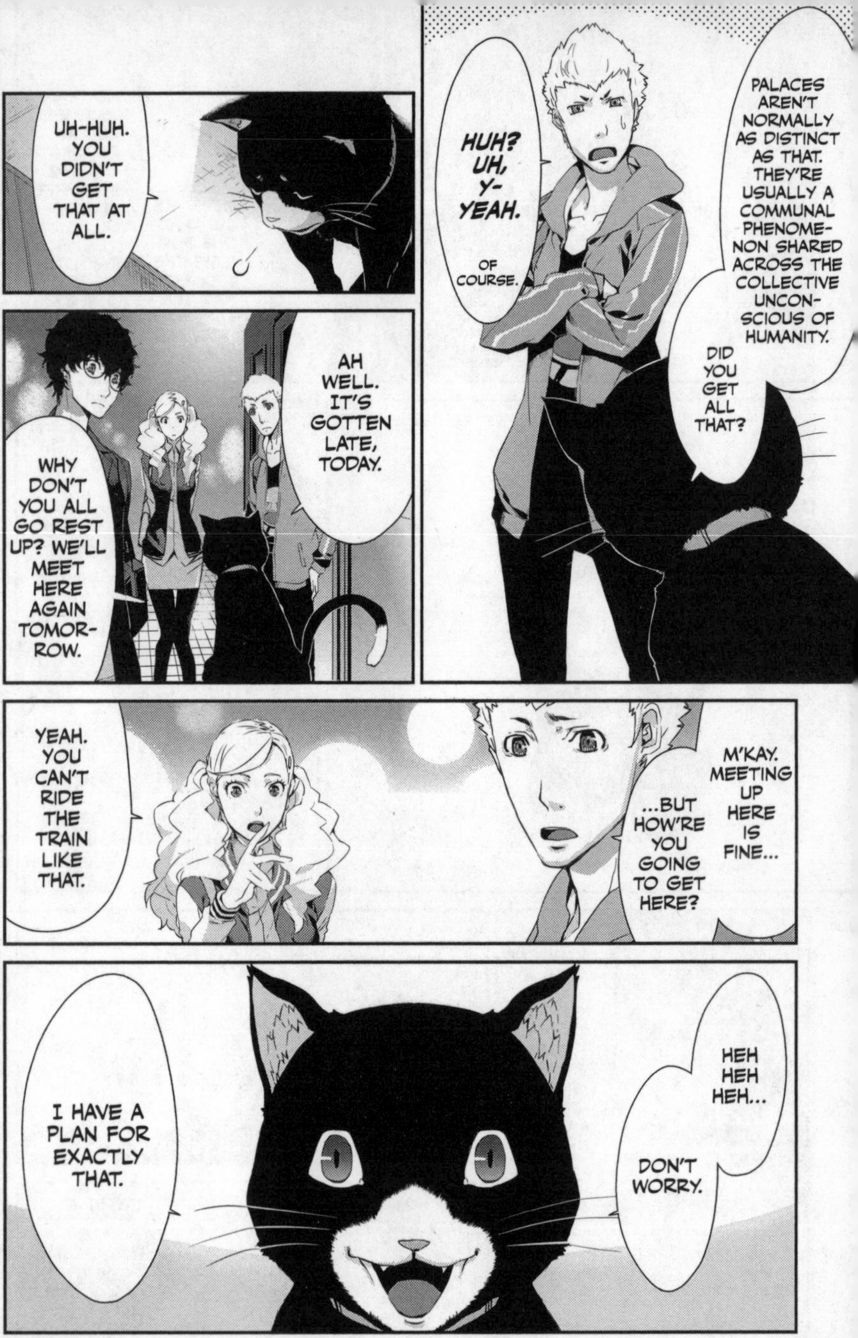
PALACES AREN'T NORMALLY AS DISTINCT AS THAT. THEY'RE USUALLY A COMMUNAL PHENOMENON SHARED ACROSS THE COLLECTIVE UNCONSCIOUS OF HUMANITY.
DID YOU GET ALL THAT?
HUH? UH, Y-YEAH.
OF COURSE.
UH-HUH. YOU DIDN'T GET THAT AT ALL.
AH WELL. IT'S GOTTEN LATE, TODAY.
WHY DON'T YOU ALL GO REST UP? WE'LL MEET HERE AGAIN TOMORROW.
M'KAY. MEETING UP HERE IS FINE...
...BUT HOW'RE YOU GOING TO GET HERE?
YEAH. YOU CAN'T RIDE THE TRAIN LIKE THAT.
HEH HEH HEH...
DON'T WORRY.
I HAVE A PLAN FOR EXACTLY THAT.

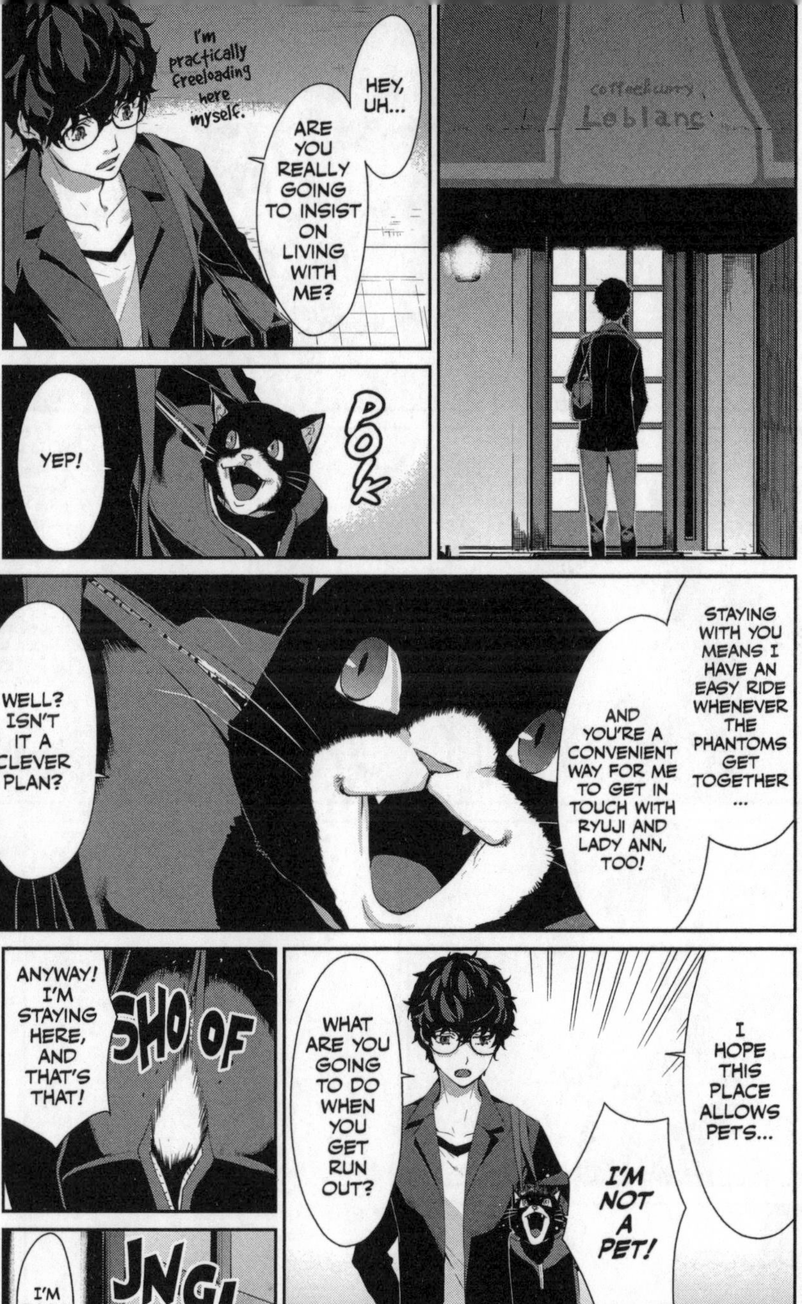
Coffee&Curry
Leblanc
HEY, UH...
ARE YOU REALLY GOING TO INSIST ON LIVING WITH ME?
I'm practically freeloading here myself.
POK
YEP!
STAYING WITH YOU MEANS I HAVE AN EASY RIDE WHENEVER THE PHANTOMS GET TOGETHER ...
AND YOU'RE A CONVENIENT WAY FOR ME TO GET IN TOUCH WITH RYUJI AND LADY ANN, TOO!
WELL? ISN'T IT A CLEVER PLAN?
I HOPE THIS PLACE ALLOWS PETS...
I'M NOT A PET!
WHAT ARE YOU GOING TO DO WHEN YOU GET RUN OUT?
ANYWAY! I'M STAYING HERE, AND THAT'S THAT!
SHO OF
JNGL
I'M BACK.

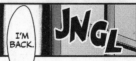

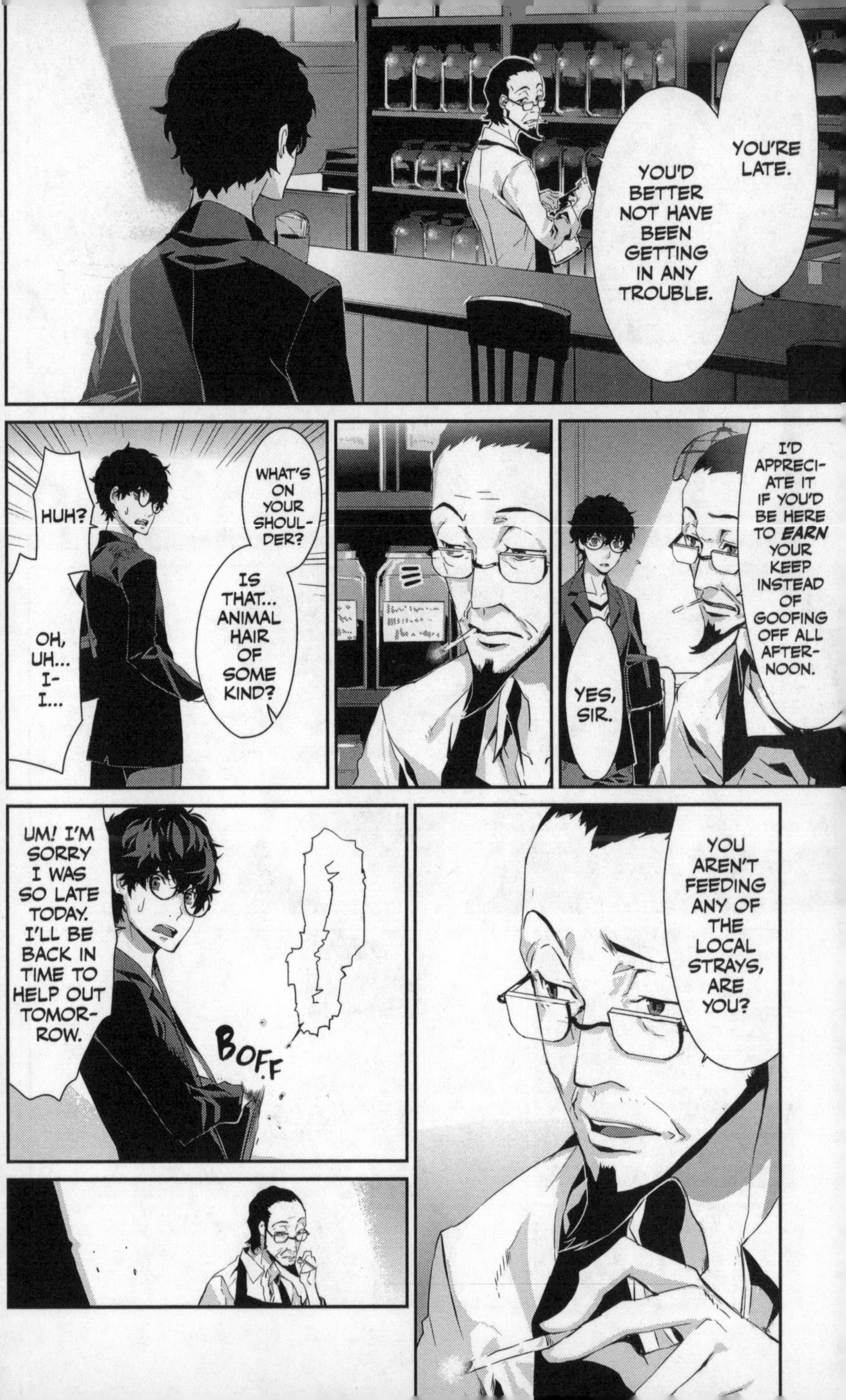
YOU'RE LATE.
YOU'D BETTER NOT HAVE BEEN GETTING IN ANY TROUBLE.
I'D APPRECI-ATE IT IF YOU'D BE HERE TO *EARN* YOUR KEEP INSTEAD OF GOOFING OFF ALL AFTER-NOON.
YES, SIR.
WHAT'S ON YOUR SHOULD-DER?
IS THAT... ANIMAL HAIR OF SOME KIND?
HUH?
OH, UH... I- I...
YOU AREN'T FEEDING ANY OF THE LOCAL STRAYS, ARE YOU?
BOFF
UM! I'M SORRY I WAS SO LATE TODAY. I'LL BE BACK IN TIME TO HELP OUT TOMOR-ROW.

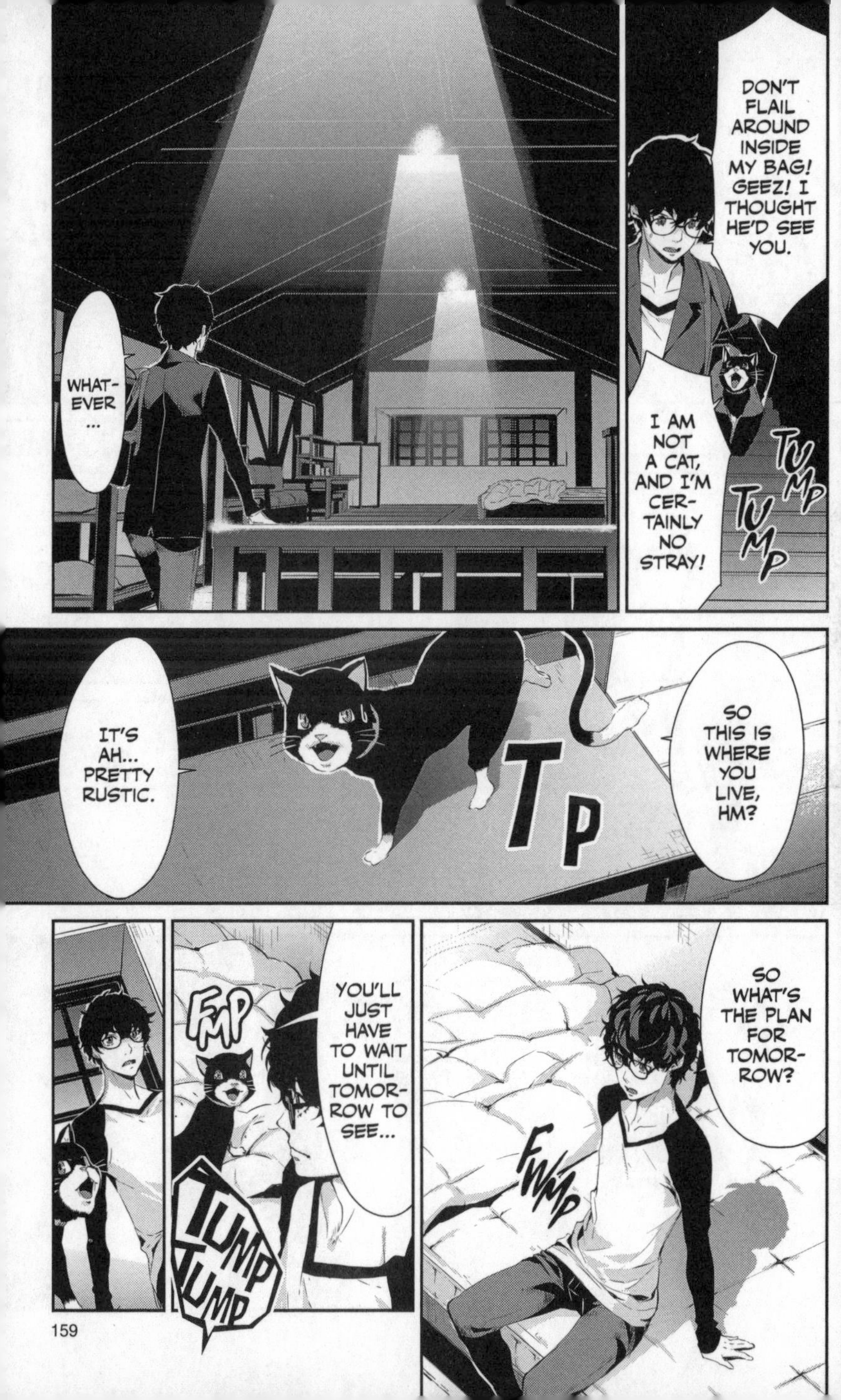
DON'T FLAIL AROUND INSIDE MY BAG! GEEZ! I THOUGHT HE'D SEE YOU.
I AM NOT A CAT, AND I'M CERTAINLY NO STRAY!
TUMP TUMP
WHATEVER...
SO THIS IS WHERE YOU LIVE, HM?
IT'S AH... PRETTY RUSTIC.
TP
SO WHAT'S THE PLAN FOR TOMORROW?
FWMP
YOU'LL JUST HAVE TO WAIT UNTIL TOMORROW TO SEE...
FMP
TUMP TUMP

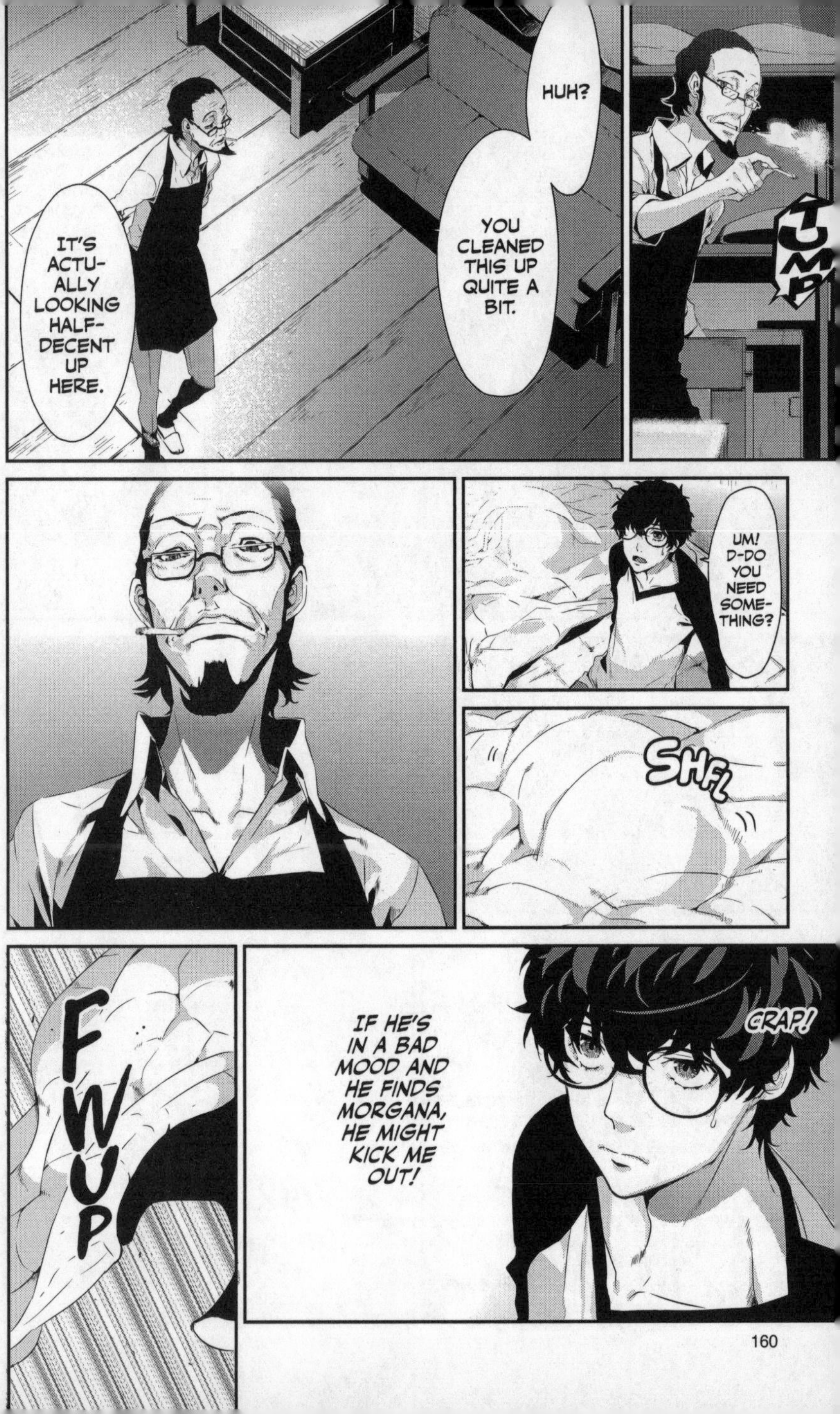
JUMP
HUH?
YOU CLEANED THIS UP QUITE A BIT.
IT'S ACTUALLY LOOKING HALF-DECENT UP HERE.
UM! D-DO YOU NEED SOMETHING?
SHFL
CRAP!
IF HE'S IN A BAD MOOD AND HE FINDS MORGANA, HE MIGHT KICK ME OUT!
FWUP

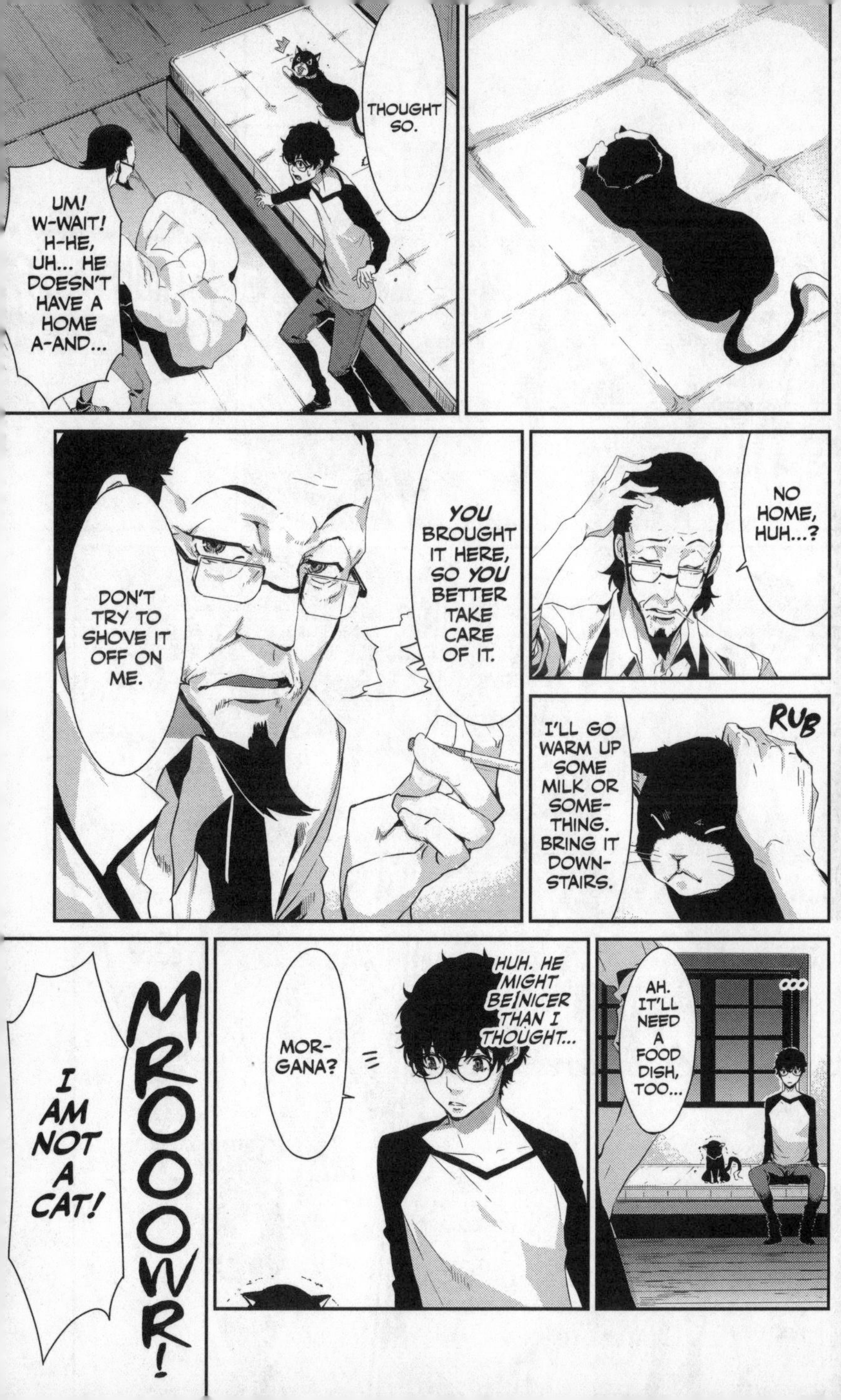
THOUGHT SO.
UM! W-WAIT! H-HE, UH... HE DOESN'T HAVE A HOME A-AND...
NO HOME, HUH...?
RUB
I'LL GO WARM UP SOME MILK OR SOMETHING. BRING IT DOWNSTAIRS.
YOU BROUGHT IT HERE, SO YOU BETTER TAKE CARE OF IT.
DON'T TRY TO SHOVE IT OFF ON ME.
AH. IT'LL NEED A FOOD DISH, TOO...
...
HUH. HE MIGHT BE NICER THAN I THOUGHT...
MOR-GANA?
MROOOOWR!
I AM NOT A CAT!

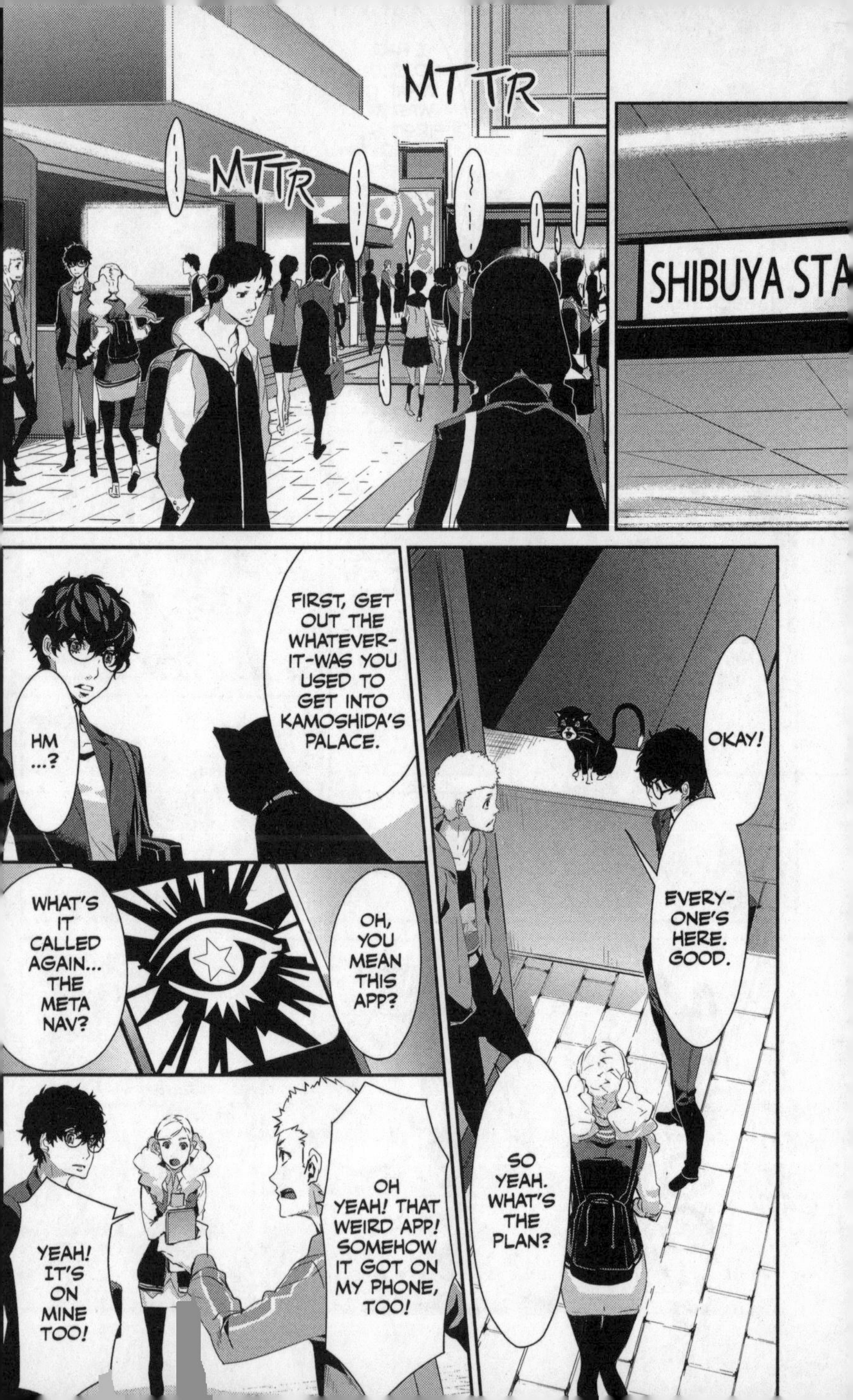
SHIBUYA STA
MTTR
MTTR
OKAY!
EVERY-ONE'S HERE. GOOD.
SO YEAH. WHAT'S THE PLAN?
FIRST, GET OUT THE WHATEVER-IT-WAS YOU USED TO GET INTO KAMOSHIDA'S PALACE.
HM ...?
OH, YOU MEAN THIS APP?
WHAT'S IT CALLED AGAIN... THE META NAV?
OH YEAH! THAT WEIRD APP! SOMEHOW IT GOT ON MY PHONE, TOO!
YEAH! IT'S ON MINE TOO!

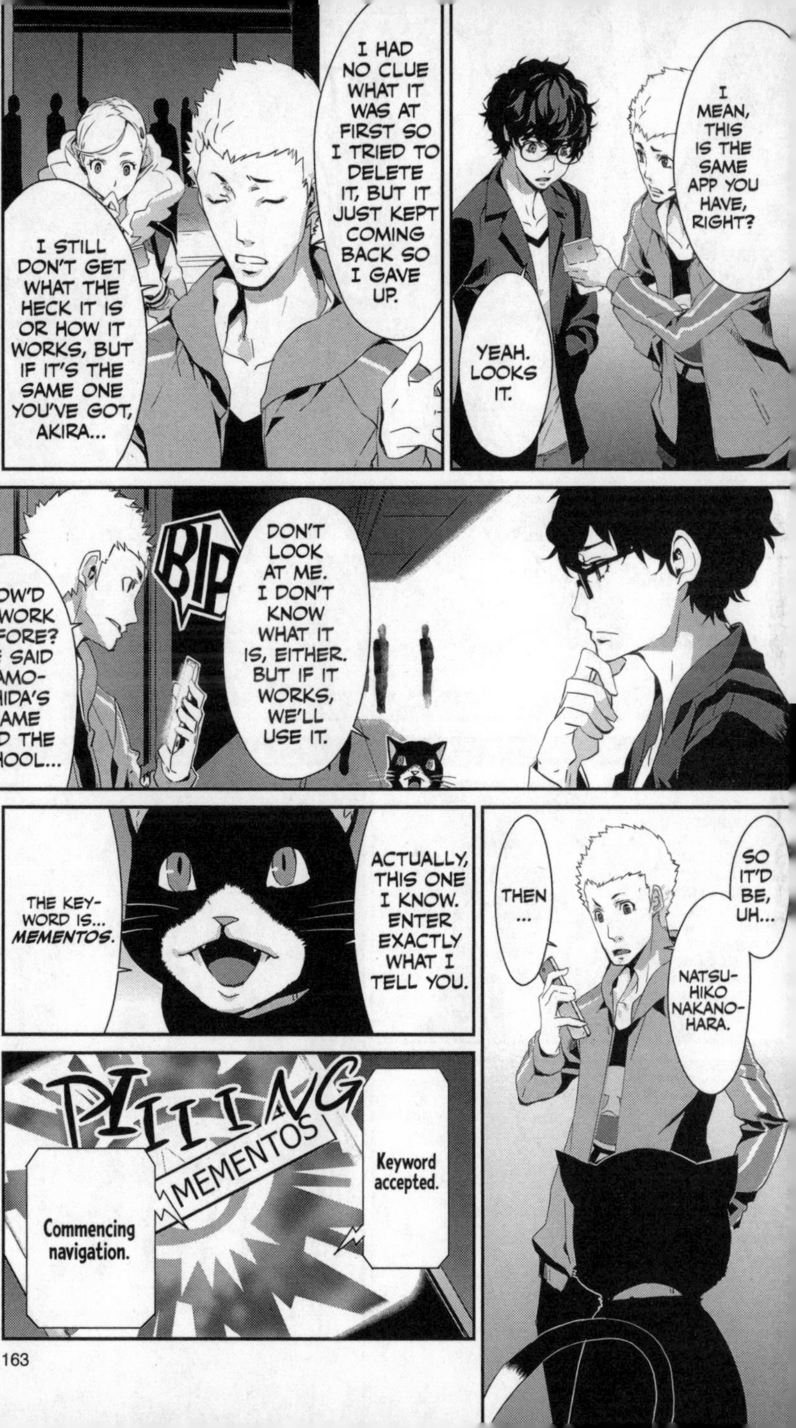
I MEAN, THIS IS THE SAME APP YOU HAVE, RIGHT?
YEAH. LOOKS IT.
I HAD NO CLUE WHAT IT WAS AT FIRST SO I TRIED TO DELETE IT, BUT IT JUST KEPT COMING BACK SO I GAVE UP.
I STILL DON'T GET WHAT THE HECK IT IS OR HOW IT WORKS, BUT IF IT'S THE SAME ONE YOU'VE GOT, AKIRA...
BIP
HOW'D IT WORK BEFORE? WE SAID KAMOSHIDA'S NAME AND THE SCHOOL...
DON'T LOOK AT ME. I DON'T KNOW WHAT IT IS, EITHER. BUT IF IT WORKS, WE'LL USE IT.
SO IT'D BE, UH...
NATSUHIKO NAKANOHARA.
THEN...
ACTUALLY, THIS ONE I KNOW. ENTER EXACTLY WHAT I TELL YOU.
THE KEYWORD IS... *MEMENTOS*.
PIIING
MEMENTOS
Keyword accepted.
Commencing navigation.

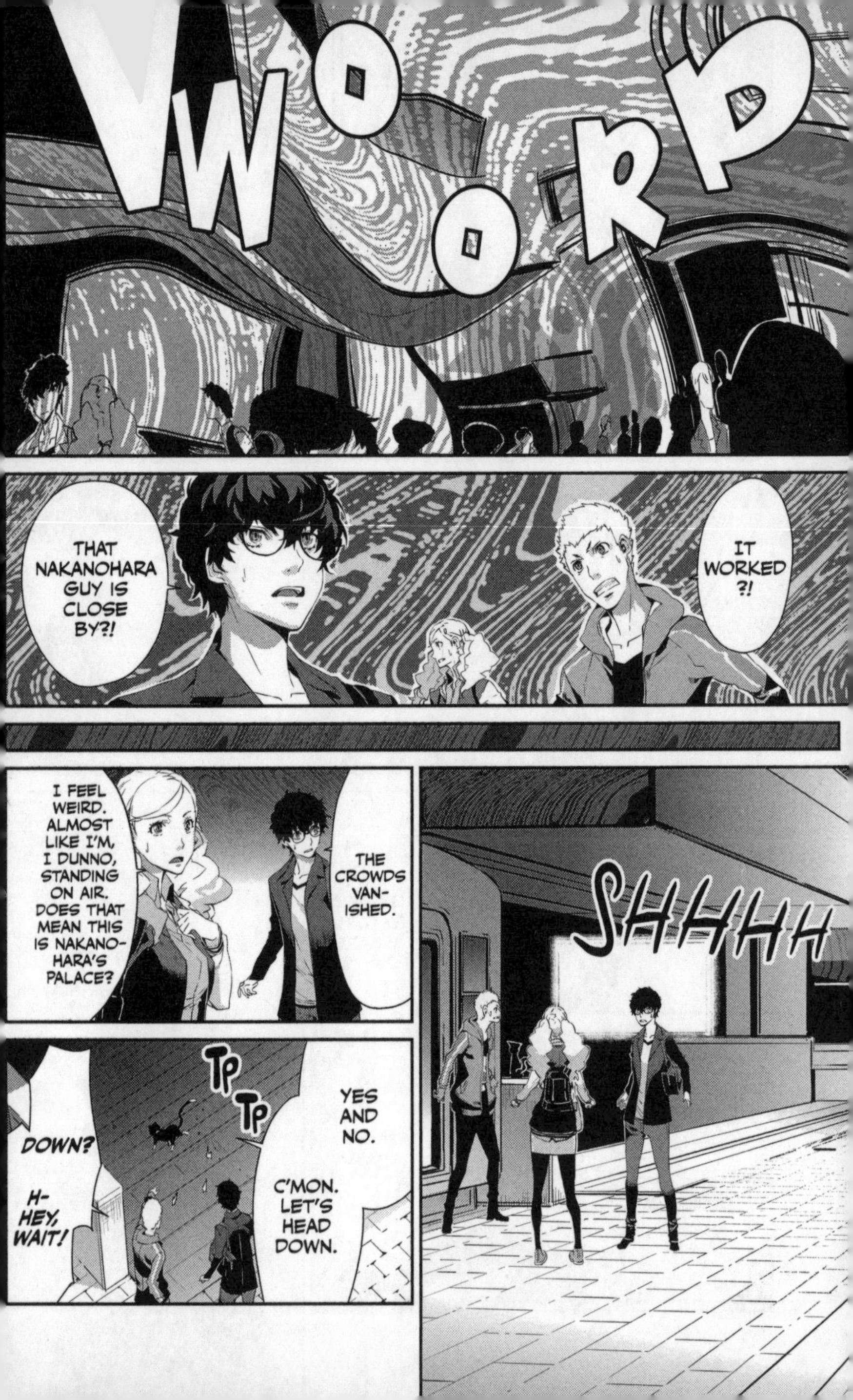
VWOORP
IT WORKED?!
THAT NAKANOHARA GUY IS CLOSE BY?!
SHHHH
THE CROWDS VANISHED.
I FEEL WEIRD. ALMOST LIKE I'M, I DUNNO, STANDING ON AIR. DOES THAT MEAN THIS IS NAKANOHARA'S PALACE?
YES AND NO.
Tp Tp
C'MON. LET'S HEAD DOWN.
DOWN?
H-HEY, WAIT!

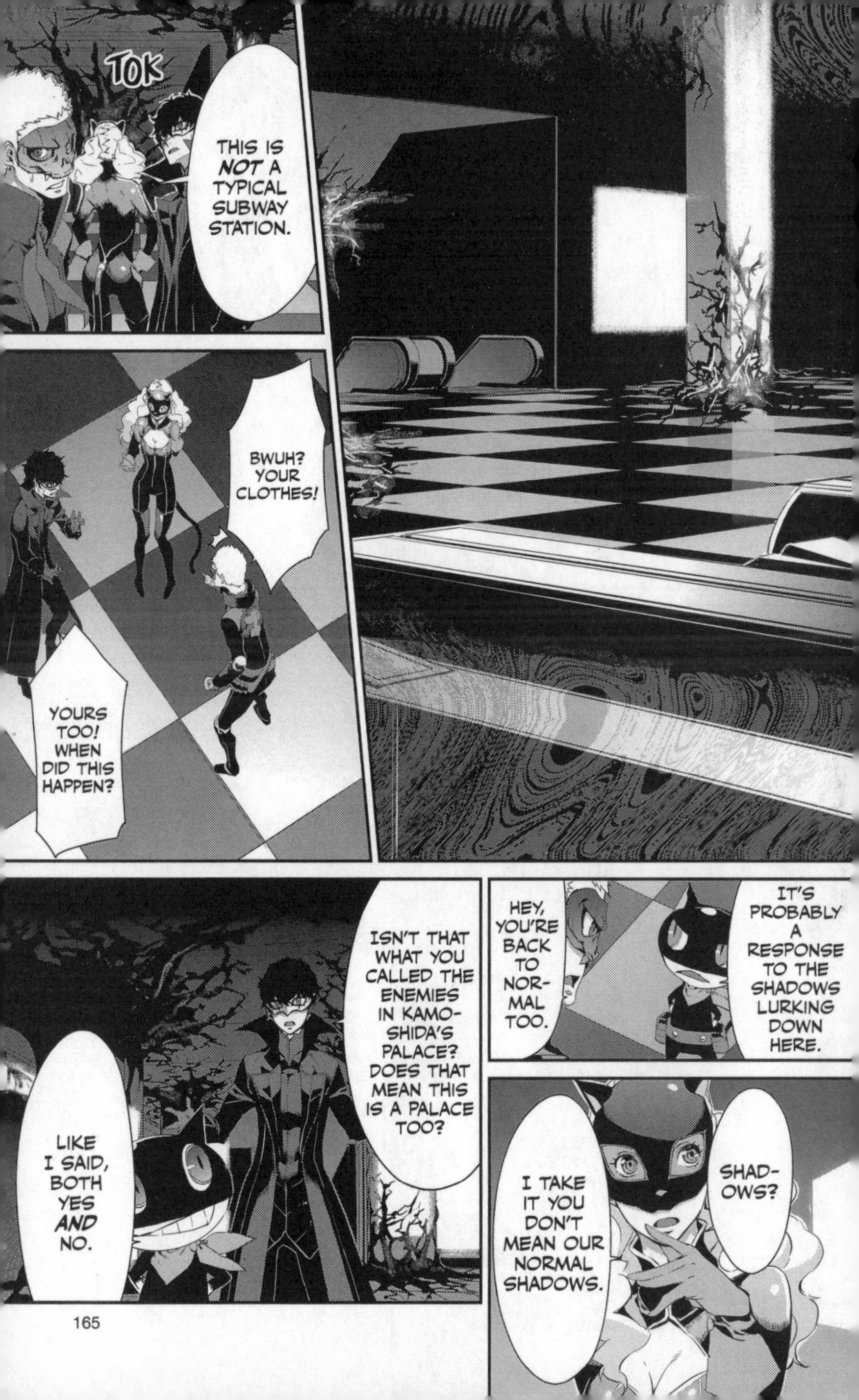
TOK
THIS IS *NOT* A TYPICAL SUBWAY STATION.
BWUH? YOUR CLOTHES!
YOURS TOO! WHEN DID THIS HAPPEN?
IT'S PROBABLY A RESPONSE TO THE SHADOWS LURKING DOWN HERE.
HEY, YOU'RE BACK TO NOR-MAL TOO.
SHAD-OWS?
I TAKE IT YOU DON'T MEAN OUR NORMAL SHADOWS.
ISN'T THAT WHAT YOU CALLED THE ENEMIES IN KAMO-SHIDA'S PALACE? DOES THAT MEAN THIS IS A PALACE TOO?
LIKE I SAID, BOTH YES *AND* NO.

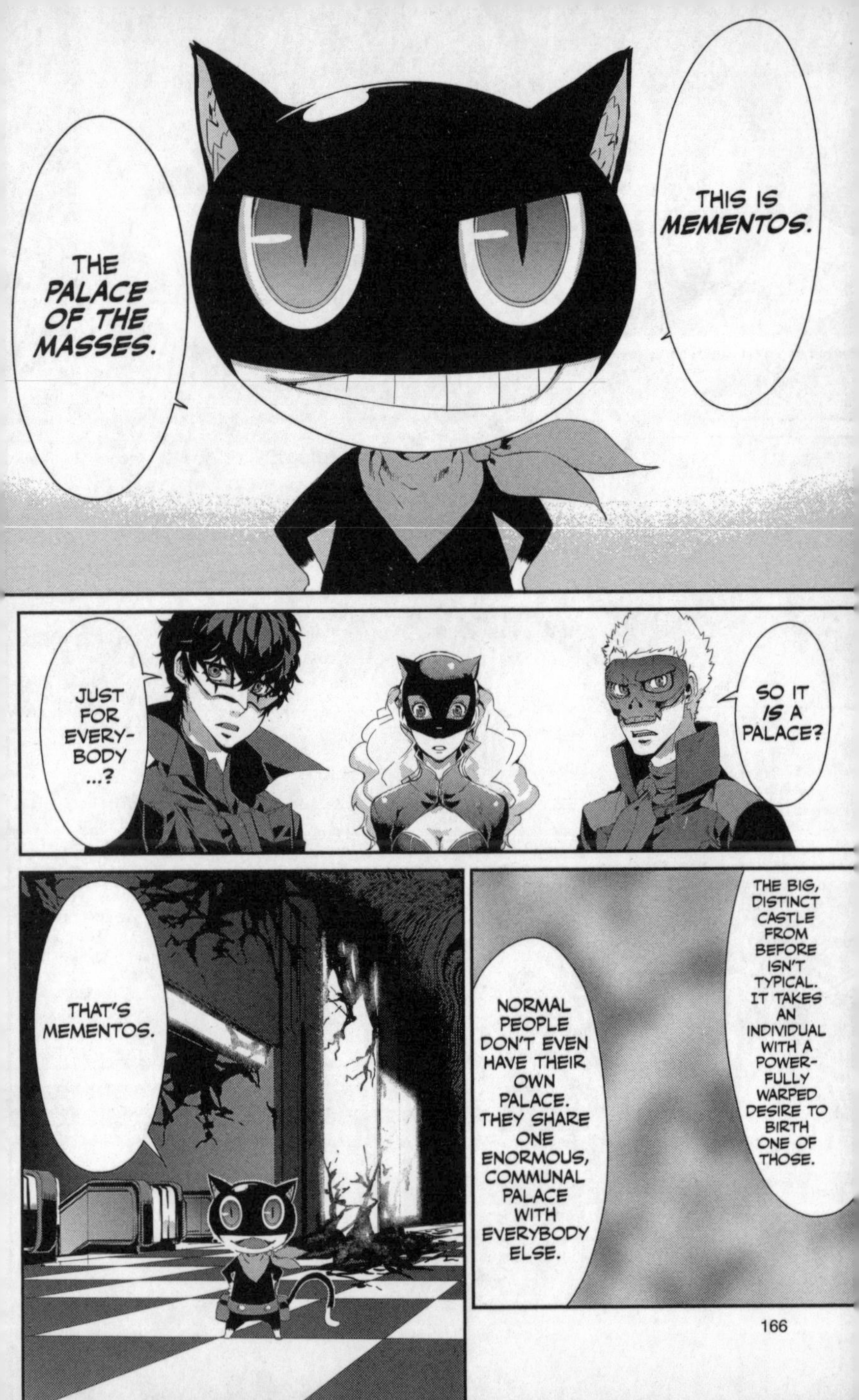
THIS IS MEMENTOS.
THE PALACE OF THE MASSES.
SO IT IS A PALACE?
JUST FOR EVERYBODY...?
THE BIG, DISTINCT CASTLE FROM BEFORE ISN'T TYPICAL. IT TAKES AN INDIVIDUAL WITH A POWERFULLY WARPED DESIRE TO BIRTH ONE OF THOSE.
NORMAL PEOPLE DON'T EVEN HAVE THEIR OWN PALACE. THEY SHARE ONE ENORMOUS, COMMUNAL PALACE WITH EVERYBODY ELSE.
THAT'S MEMENTOS.

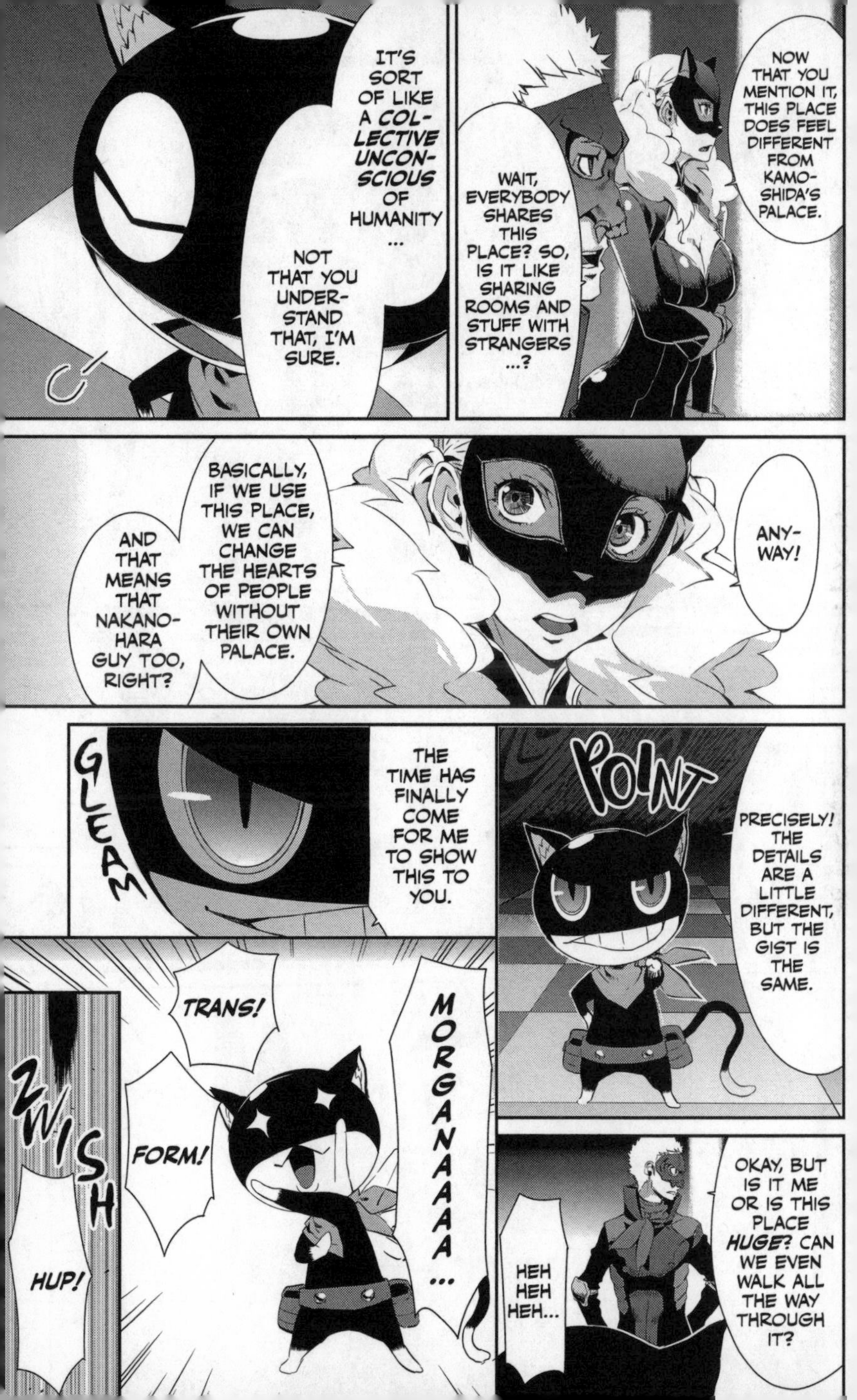
NOW THAT YOU MENTION IT, THIS PLACE DOES FEEL DIFFERENT FROM KAMO-SHIDA'S PALACE.
WAIT, EVERYBODY SHARES THIS PLACE? SO, IS IT LIKE SHARING ROOMS AND STUFF WITH STRANGERS ...?
IT'S SORT OF LIKE A *COL-LECTIVE UNCON-SCIOUS* OF HUMANITY ...
NOT THAT YOU UNDER-STAND THAT, I'M SURE.
ANY-WAY!
BASICALLY, IF WE USE THIS PLACE, WE CAN CHANGE THE HEARTS OF PEOPLE WITHOUT THEIR OWN PALACE.
AND THAT MEANS THAT NAKANO-HARA GUY TOO, RIGHT?
POINT
PRECISELY! THE DETAILS ARE A LITTLE DIFFERENT, BUT THE GIST IS THE SAME.
THE TIME HAS FINALLY COME FOR ME TO SHOW THIS TO YOU.
GLEAM
OKAY, BUT IS IT ME OR IS THIS PLACE *HUGE?* CAN WE EVEN WALK ALL THE WAY THROUGH IT?
HEH HEH HEH...
MORGANAAAAAA ...
TRANS!
FORM!
ZWISH
HUP!

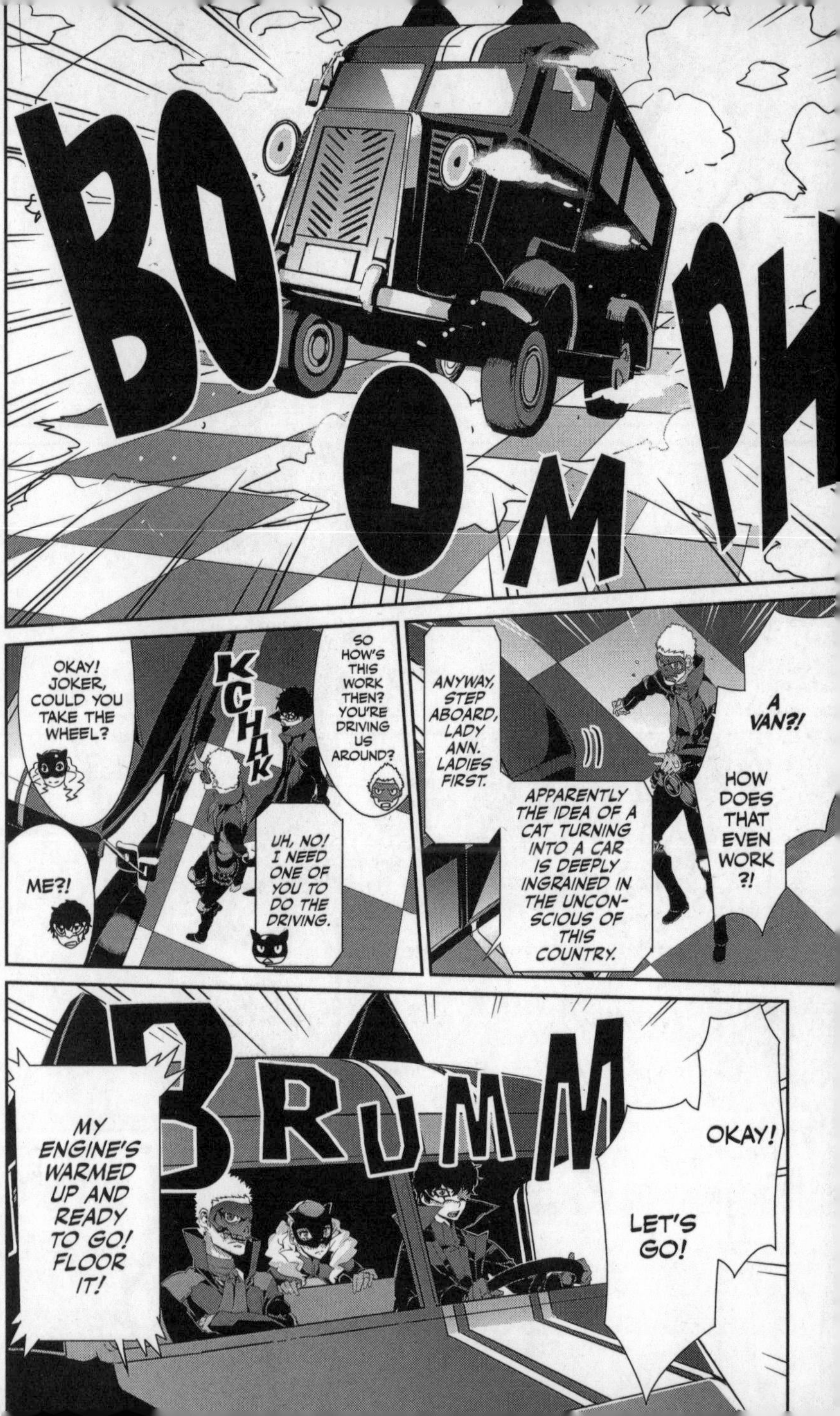
BOOMPH
A VAN?!
HOW DOES THAT EVEN WORK?!
APPARENTLY THE IDEA OF A CAT TURNING INTO A CAR IS DEEPLY INGRAINED IN THE UNCONSCIOUS OF THIS COUNTRY.
ANYWAY, STEP ABOARD, LADY ANN. LADIES FIRST.
SO HOW'S THIS WORK THEN? YOU'RE DRIVING US AROUND?
KCHAK
UH, NO! I NEED ONE OF YOU TO DO THE DRIVING.
OKAY! JOKER, COULD YOU TAKE THE WHEEL?
ME?!
OKAY!
LET'S GO!
BRUMM
MY ENGINE'S WARMED UP AND READY TO GO! FLOOR IT!

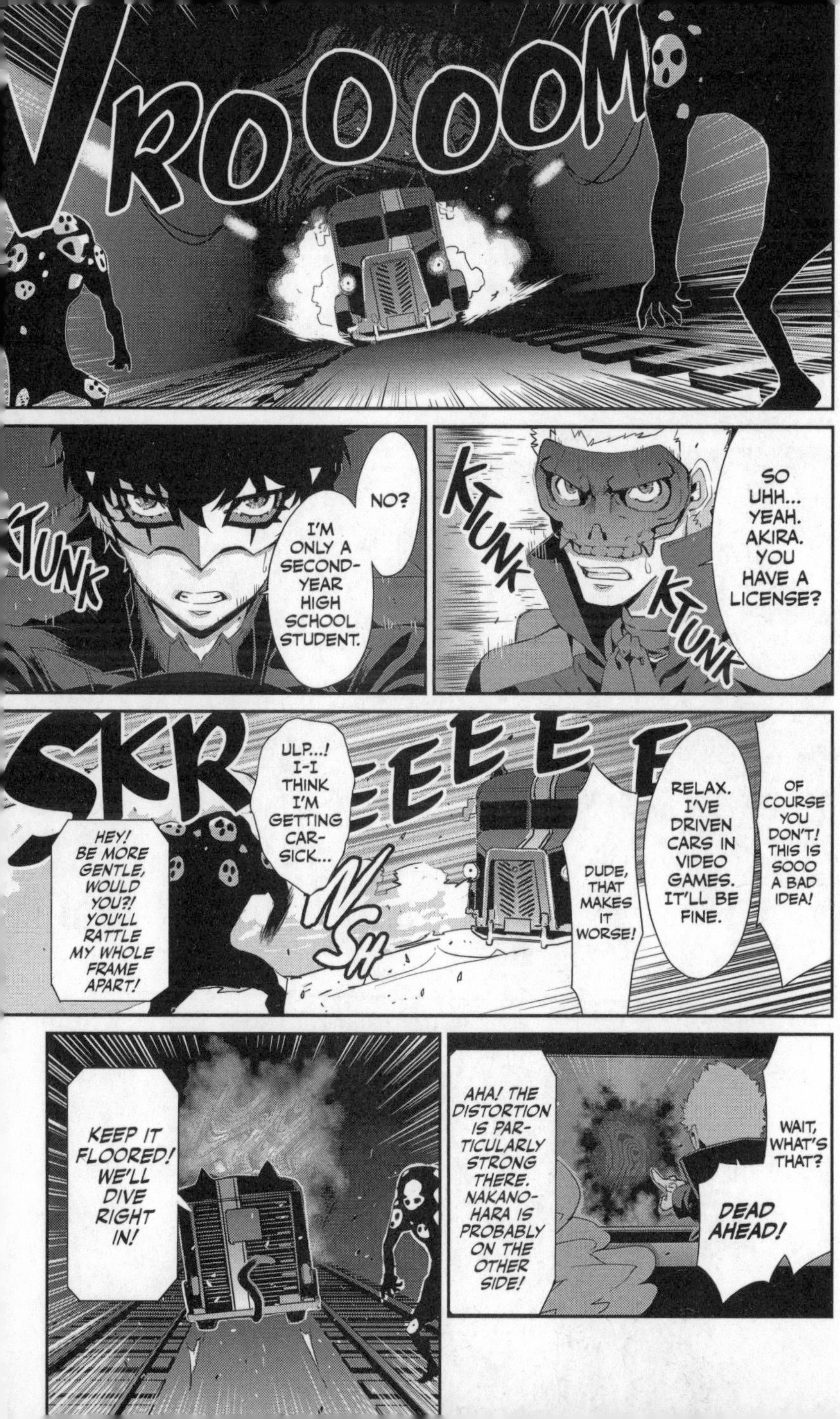
VROOOOM
SO UHH... YEAH. AKIRA. YOU HAVE A LICENSE?
KTUNK KTUNK
NO?
I'M ONLY A SECOND-YEAR HIGH SCHOOL STUDENT.
KTUNK
OF COURSE YOU DON'T! THIS IS SOOO A BAD IDEA!
RELAX. I'VE DRIVEN CARS IN VIDEO GAMES. IT'LL BE FINE.
DUDE, THAT MAKES IT WORSE!
SKREEEEE
ULP...! I-I THINK I'M GETTING CAR-SICK...
HEY! BE MORE GENTLE, WOULD YOU?! YOU'LL RATTLE MY WHOLE FRAME APART!
WAIT, WHAT'S THAT?
DEAD AHEAD!
AHA! THE DISTORTION IS PARTICULARLY STRONG THERE. NAKANOHARA IS PROBABLY ON THE OTHER SIDE!
KEEP IT FLOORED! WE'LL DIVE RIGHT IN!

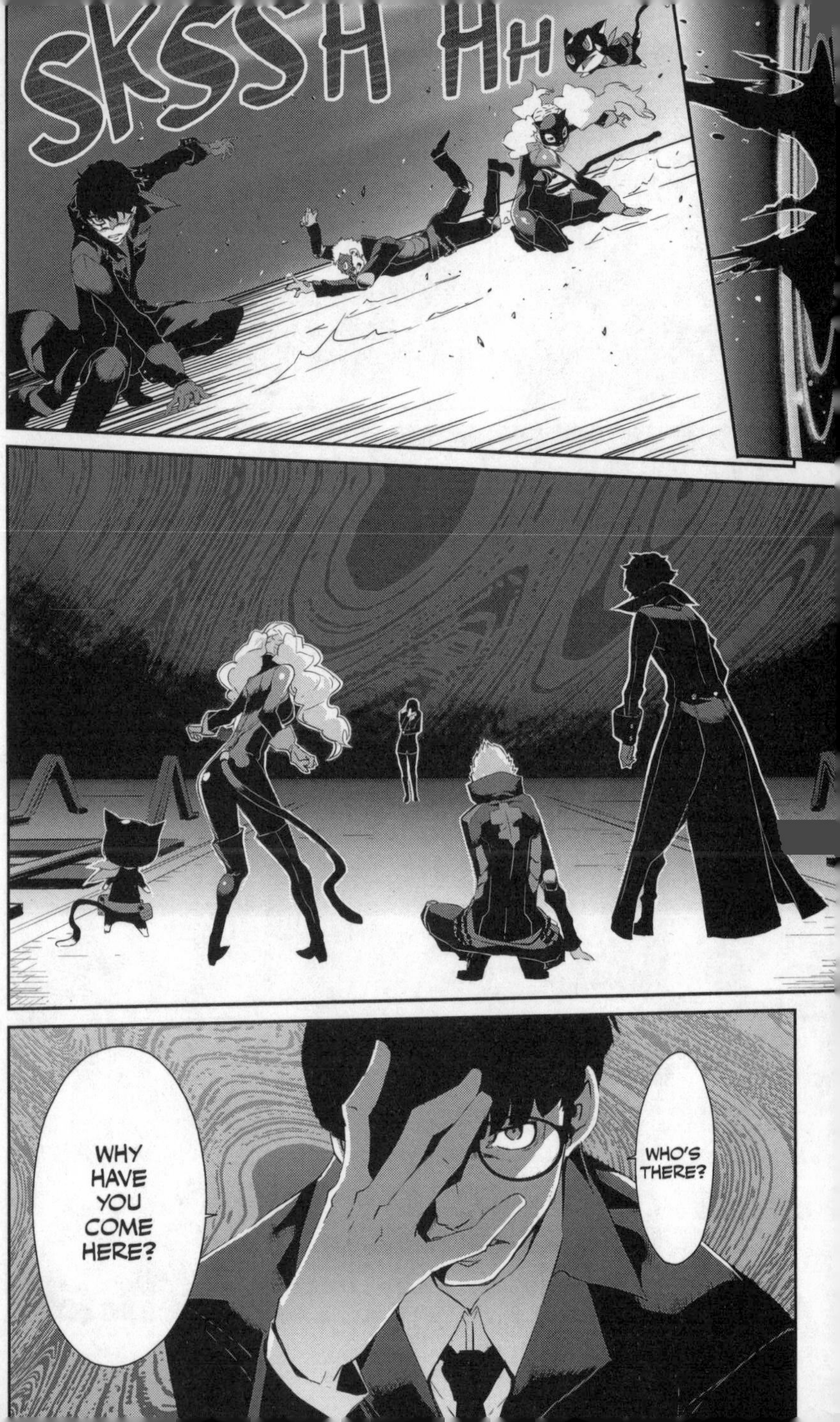
SKSSH HH
WHO'S THERE?
WHY HAVE YOU COME HERE?

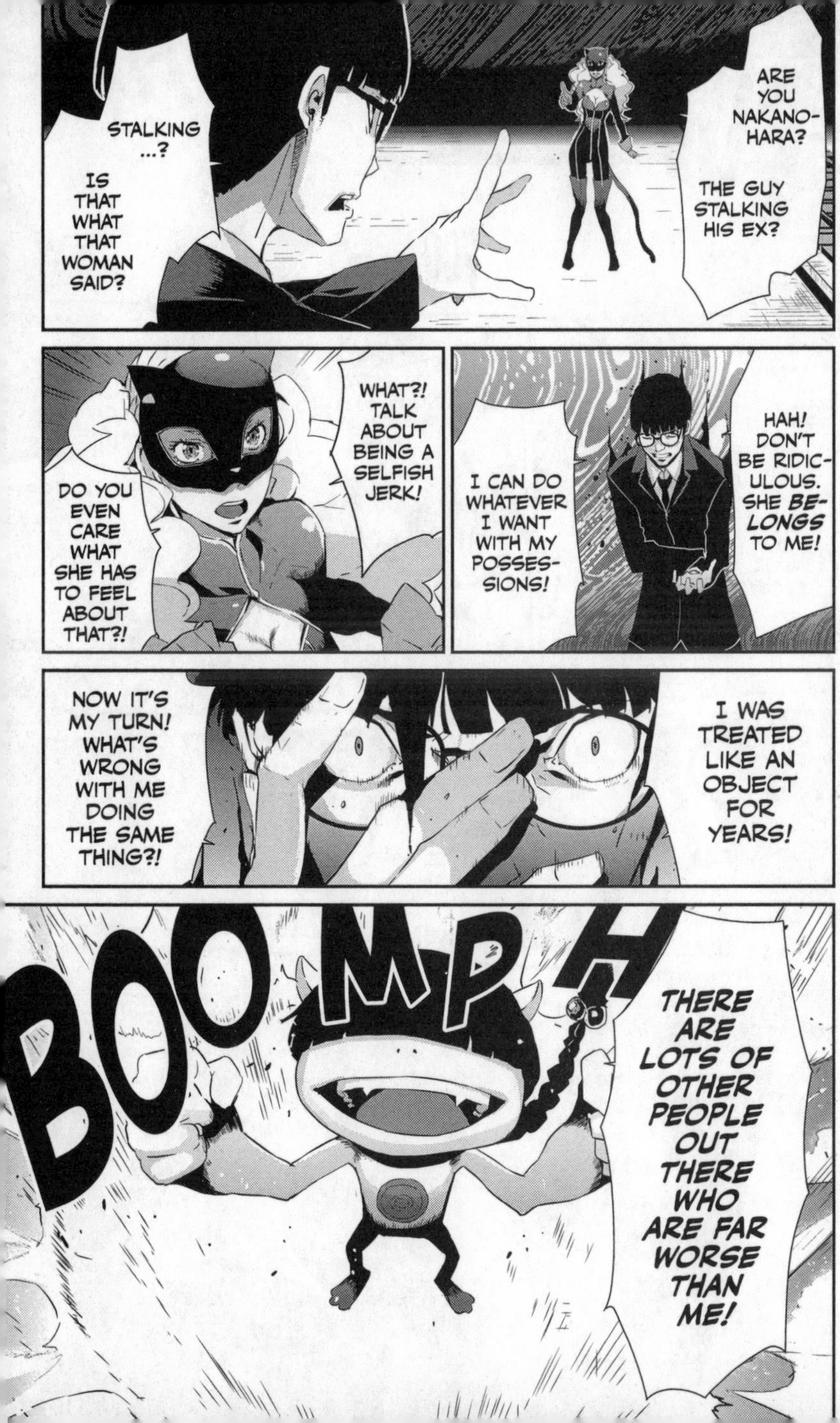
ARE YOU NAKANO-HARA?
THE GUY STALKING HIS EX?
STALKING ...?
IS THAT WHAT THAT WOMAN SAID?
HAH! DON'T BE RIDIC-ULOUS. SHE *BE-LONGS* TO ME!
I CAN DO WHATEVER I WANT WITH MY POSSES-SIONS!
WHAT?! TALK ABOUT BEING A SELFISH JERK!
DO YOU EVEN CARE WHAT SHE HAS TO FEEL ABOUT THAT?!
I WAS TREATED LIKE AN OBJECT FOR YEARS!
NOW IT'S MY TURN! WHAT'S WRONG WITH ME DOING THE SAME THING?!
BOOMPH
THERE ARE LOTS OF OTHER PEOPLE OUT THERE WHO ARE FAR WORSE THAN ME!

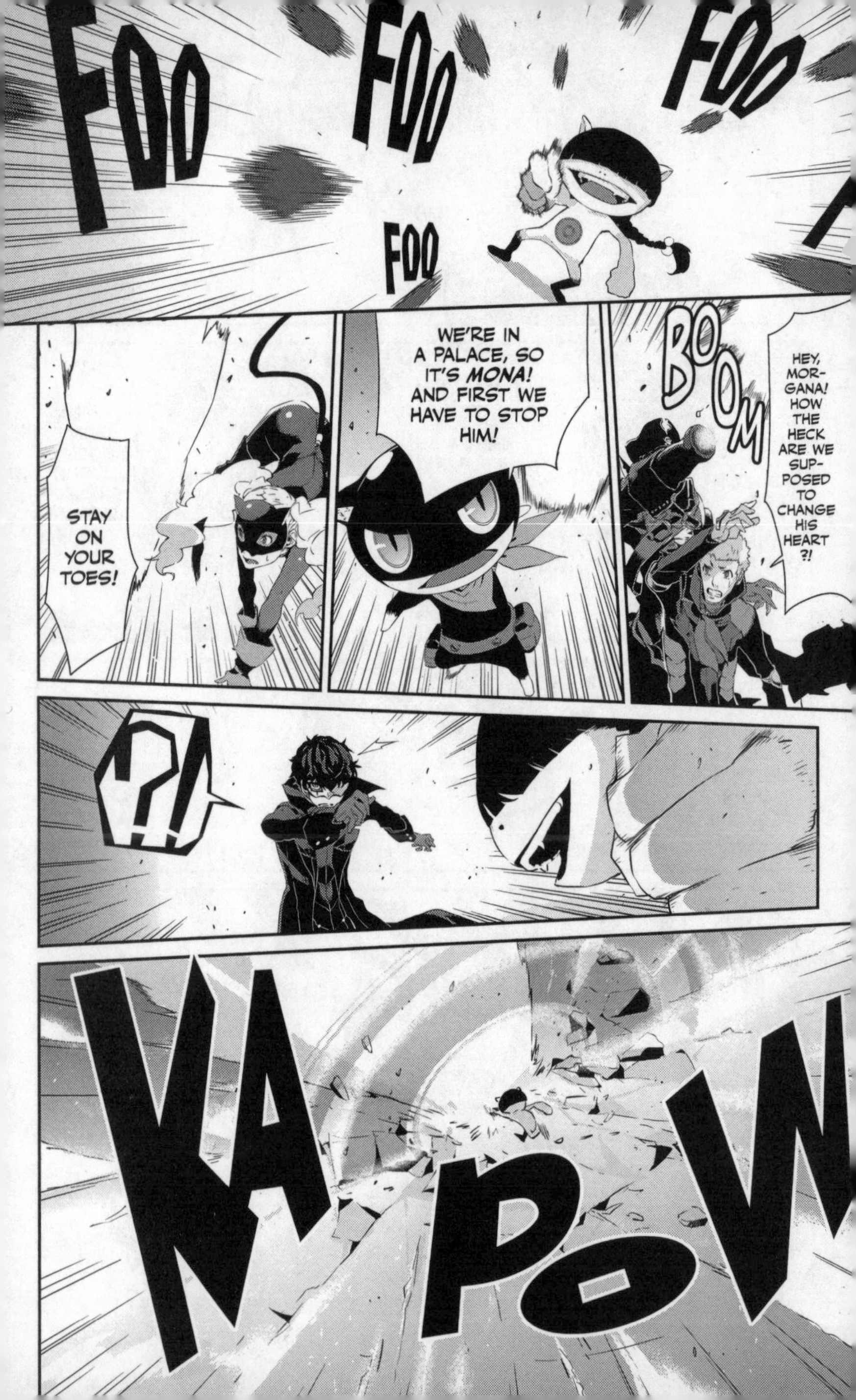
FOO
FOO
FOO
FOO
BOOM
HEY, MORGANA! HOW THE HECK ARE WE SUPPOSED TO CHANGE HIS HEART?!
WE'RE IN A PALACE, SO IT'S *MONA!* AND FIRST WE HAVE TO STOP HIM!
STAY ON YOUR TOES!
?!
KA-POW

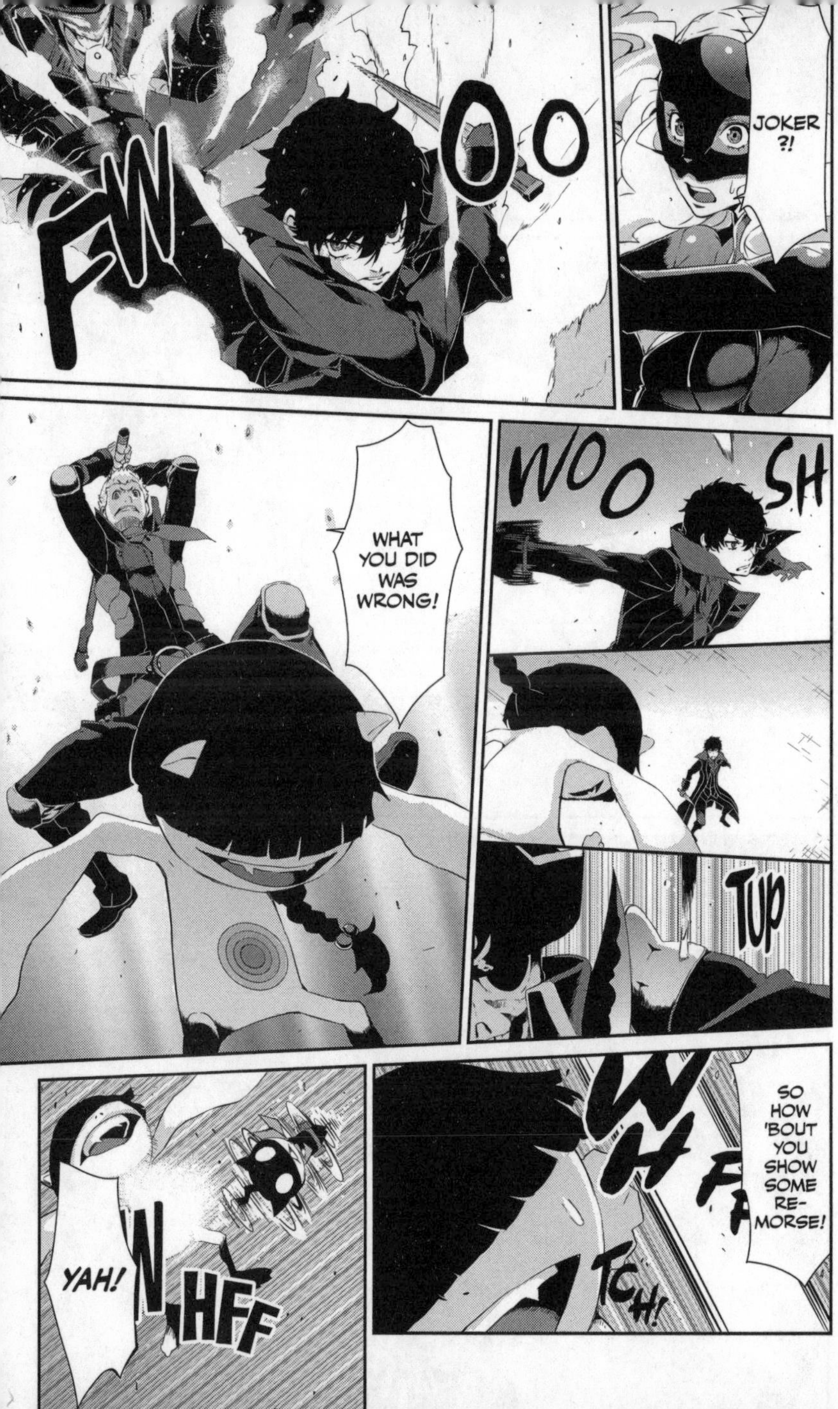
JOKER ?!
FWOOO
WOOSH
TUP
WHAT YOU DID WAS WRONG!
SO HOW 'BOUT YOU SHOW SOME RE-MORSE!
TCH!
YAH!
HFF

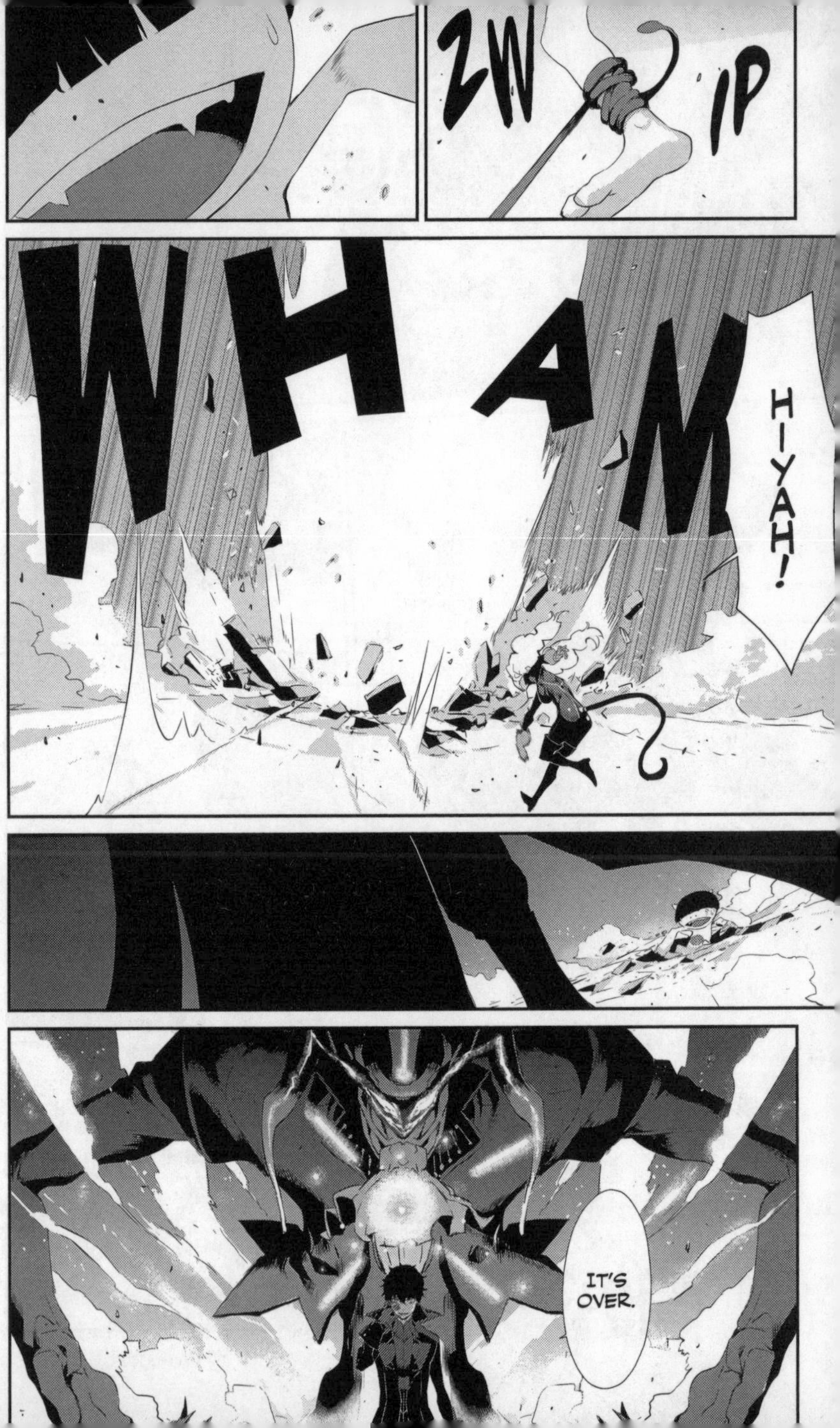
ZW IP
WHAM
HIYAH!
IT'S OVER.

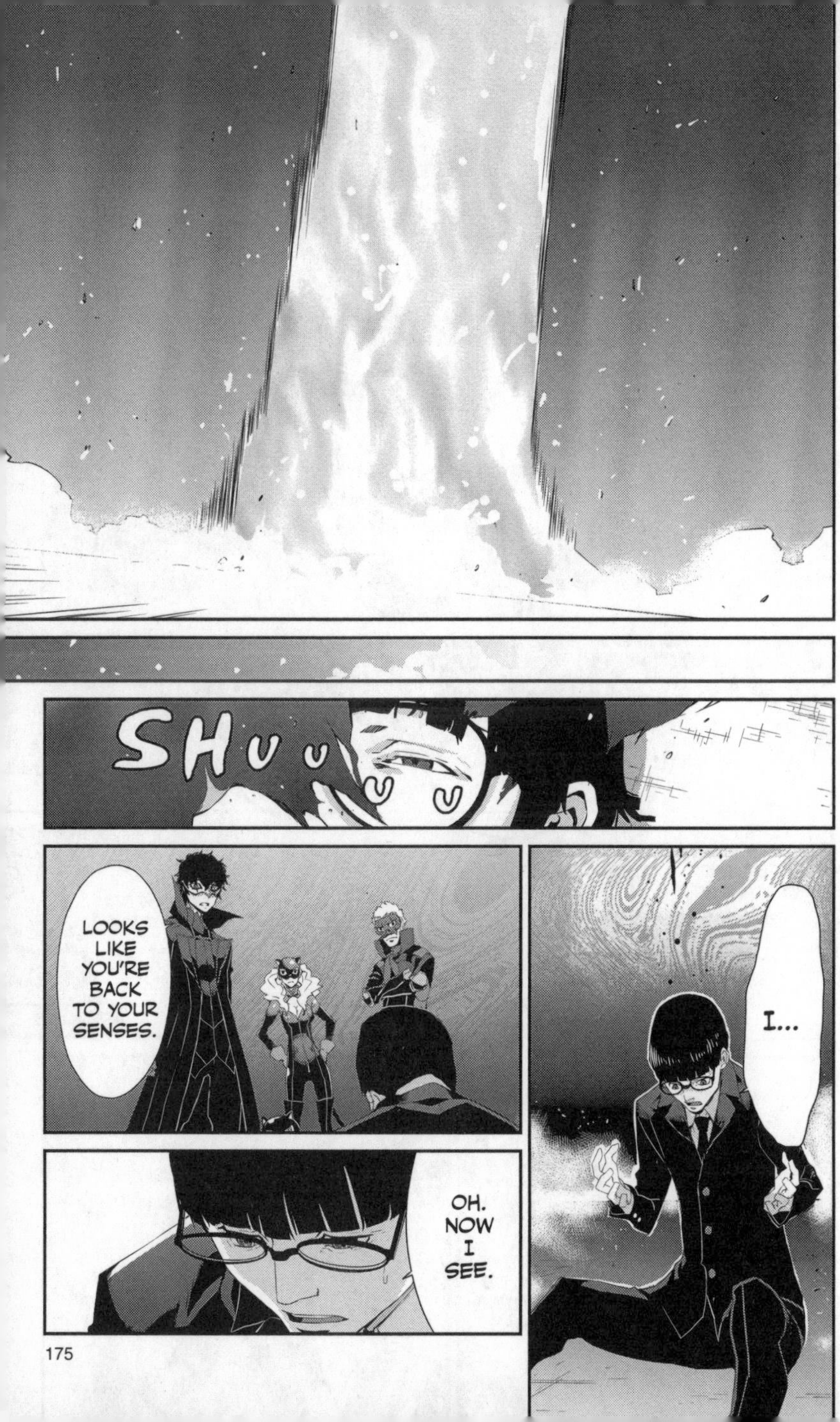
SHUUUUU
I...
LOOKS LIKE YOU'RE BACK TO YOUR SENSES.
OH. NOW I SEE.

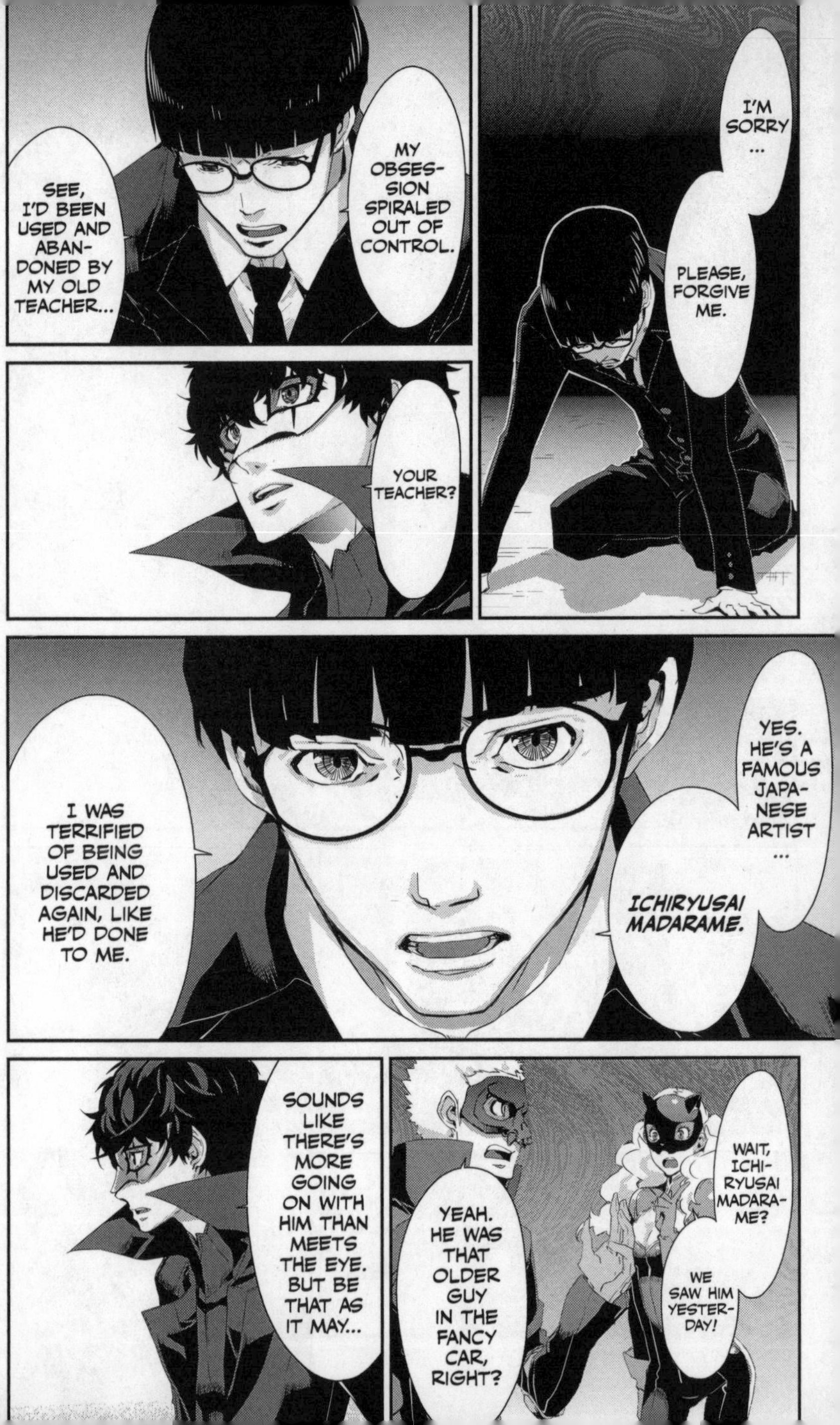
I'M SORRY...
PLEASE, FORGIVE ME.
MY OBSESSION SPIRALED OUT OF CONTROL.
SEE, I'D BEEN USED AND ABANDONED BY MY OLD TEACHER...
YOUR TEACHER?
YES. HE'S A FAMOUS JAPANESE ARTIST...
ICHIRYUSAI MADARAME.
I WAS TERRIFIED OF BEING USED AND DISCARDED AGAIN, LIKE HE'D DONE TO ME.
WAIT, ICHIRYUSAI MADARAME?
WE SAW HIM YESTERDAY!
YEAH. HE WAS THAT OLDER GUY IN THE FANCY CAR, RIGHT?
SOUNDS LIKE THERE'S MORE GOING ON WITH HIM THAN MEETS THE EYE. BUT BE THAT AS IT MAY...

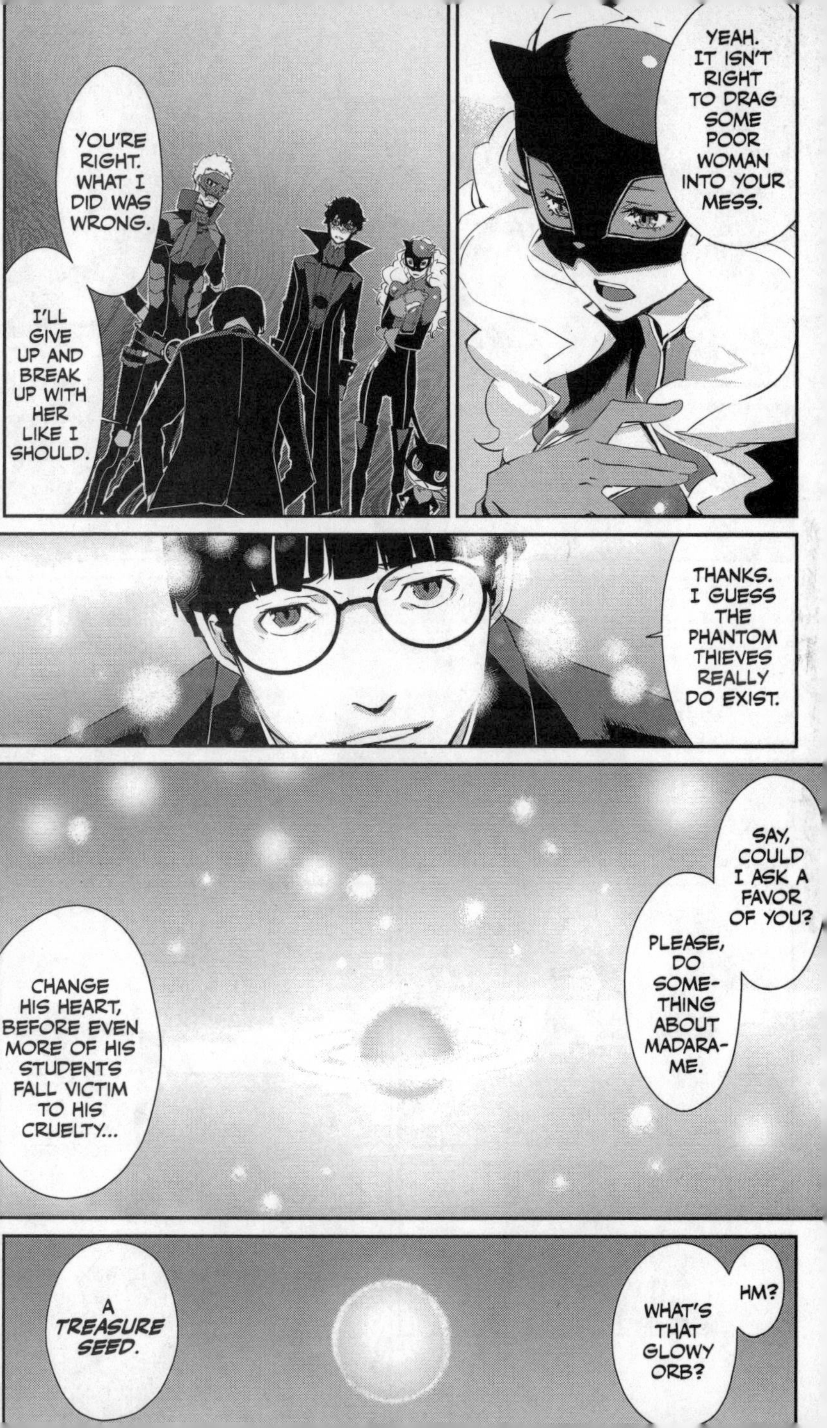
YEAH. IT ISN'T RIGHT TO DRAG SOME POOR WOMAN INTO YOUR MESS.
YOU'RE RIGHT. WHAT I DID WAS WRONG.
I'LL GIVE UP AND BREAK UP WITH HER LIKE I SHOULD.
THANKS. I GUESS THE PHANTOM THIEVES REALLY DO EXIST.
SAY, COULD I ASK A FAVOR OF YOU?
PLEASE, DO SOME-THING ABOUT MADARA-ME.
CHANGE HIS HEART, BEFORE EVEN MORE OF HIS STUDENTS FALL VICTIM TO HIS CRUELTY...
HM?
WHAT'S THAT GLOWY ORB?
A *TREASURE SEED*.

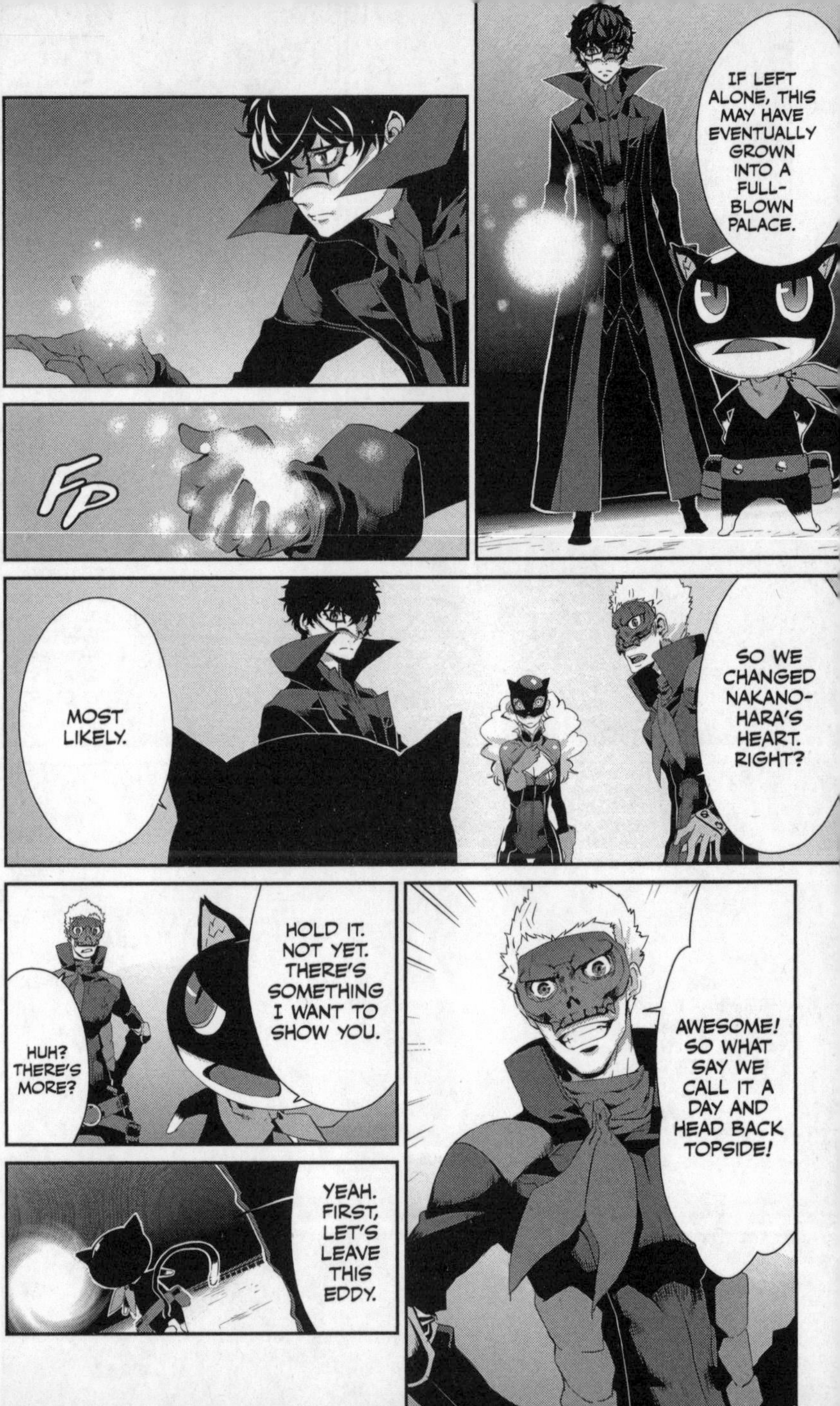
IF LEFT ALONE, THIS MAY HAVE EVENTUALLY GROWN INTO A FULL-BLOWN PALACE.
FP
SO WE CHANGED NAKANO-HARA'S HEART. RIGHT?
MOST LIKELY.
AWESOME! SO WHAT SAY WE CALL IT A DAY AND HEAD BACK TOPSIDE!
HOLD IT. NOT YET. THERE'S SOMETHING I WANT TO SHOW YOU.
HUH? THERE'S MORE?
YEAH. FIRST, LET'S LEAVE THIS EDDY.

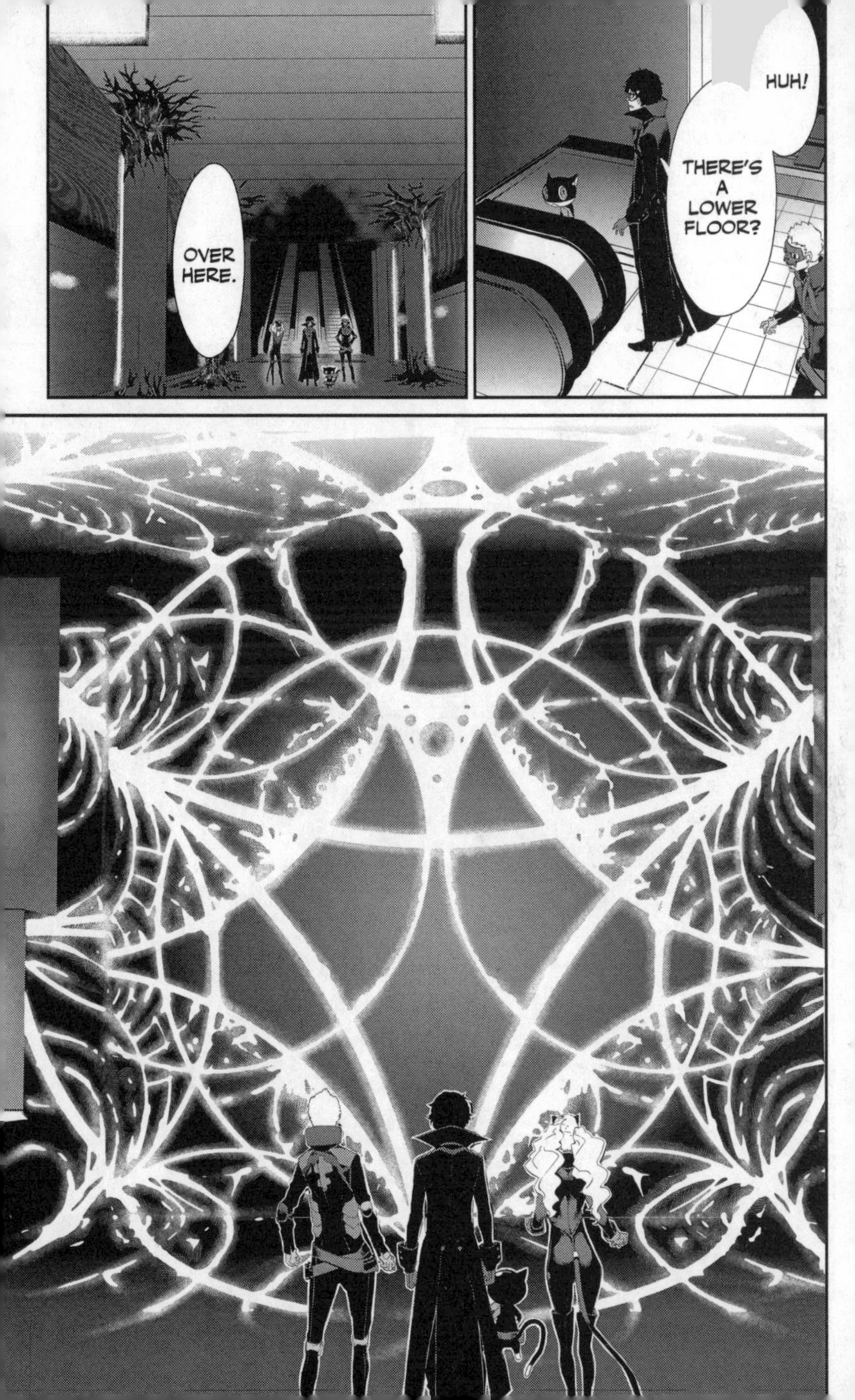
HUH!
THERE'S A LOWER FLOOR?
OVER HERE.

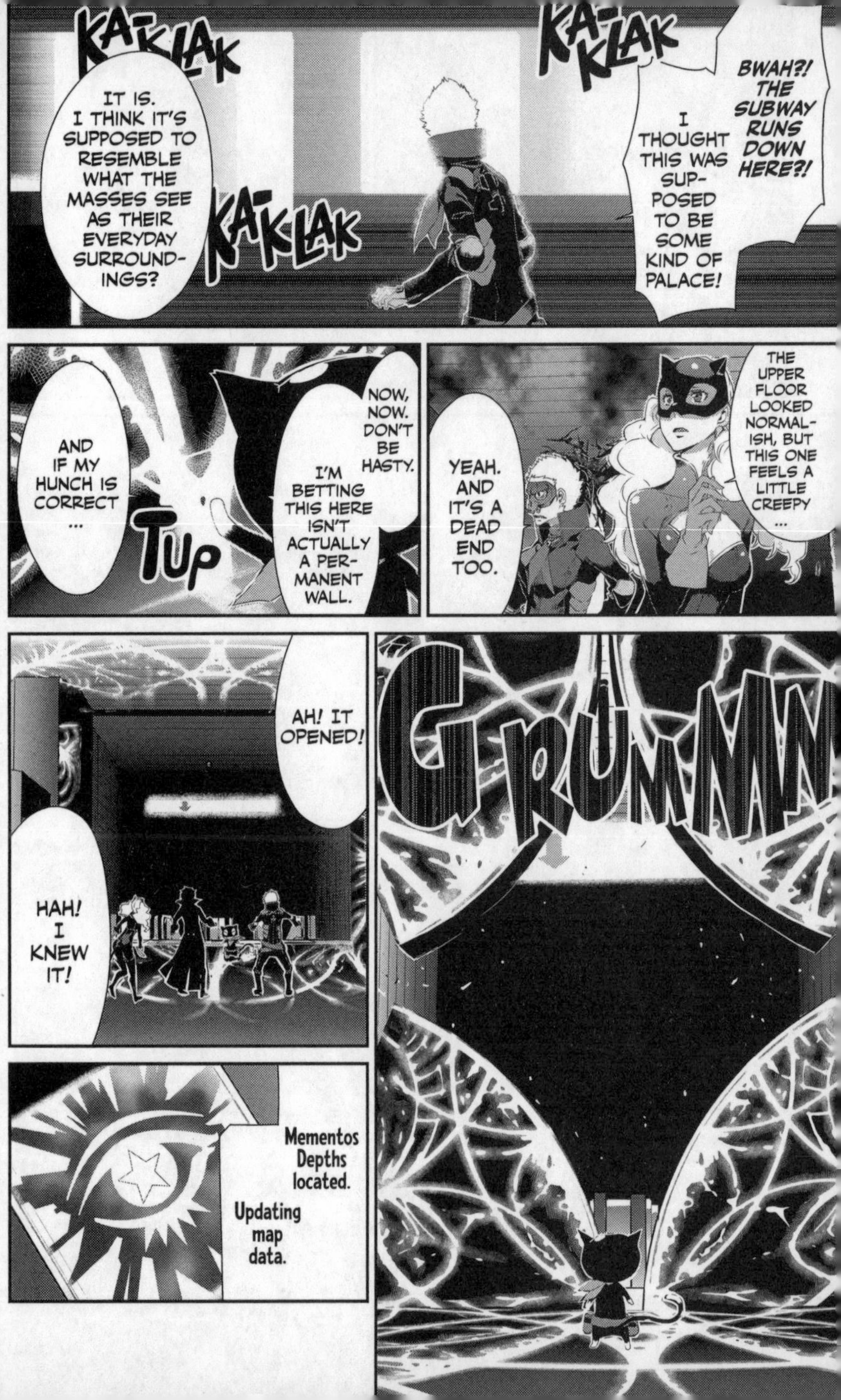
KA-KLAK
BWAH?! THE SUBWAY RUNS DOWN HERE?!
I THOUGHT THIS WAS SUP-POSED TO BE SOME KIND OF PALACE!
KA-KLAK
IT IS. I THINK IT'S SUPPOSED TO RESEMBLE WHAT THE MASSES SEE AS THEIR EVERYDAY SURROUND-INGS?
KA-KLAK
THE UPPER FLOOR LOOKED NORMAL-ISH, BUT THIS ONE FEELS A LITTLE CREEPY ...
YEAH. AND IT'S A DEAD END TOO.
NOW, NOW. DON'T BE HASTY.
I'M BETTING THIS HERE ISN'T ACTUALLY A PER-MANENT WALL.
AND IF MY HUNCH IS CORRECT ...
TUP
GRUMMMN
AH! IT OPENED!
HAH! I KNEW IT!
Mementos Depths located.
Updating map data.

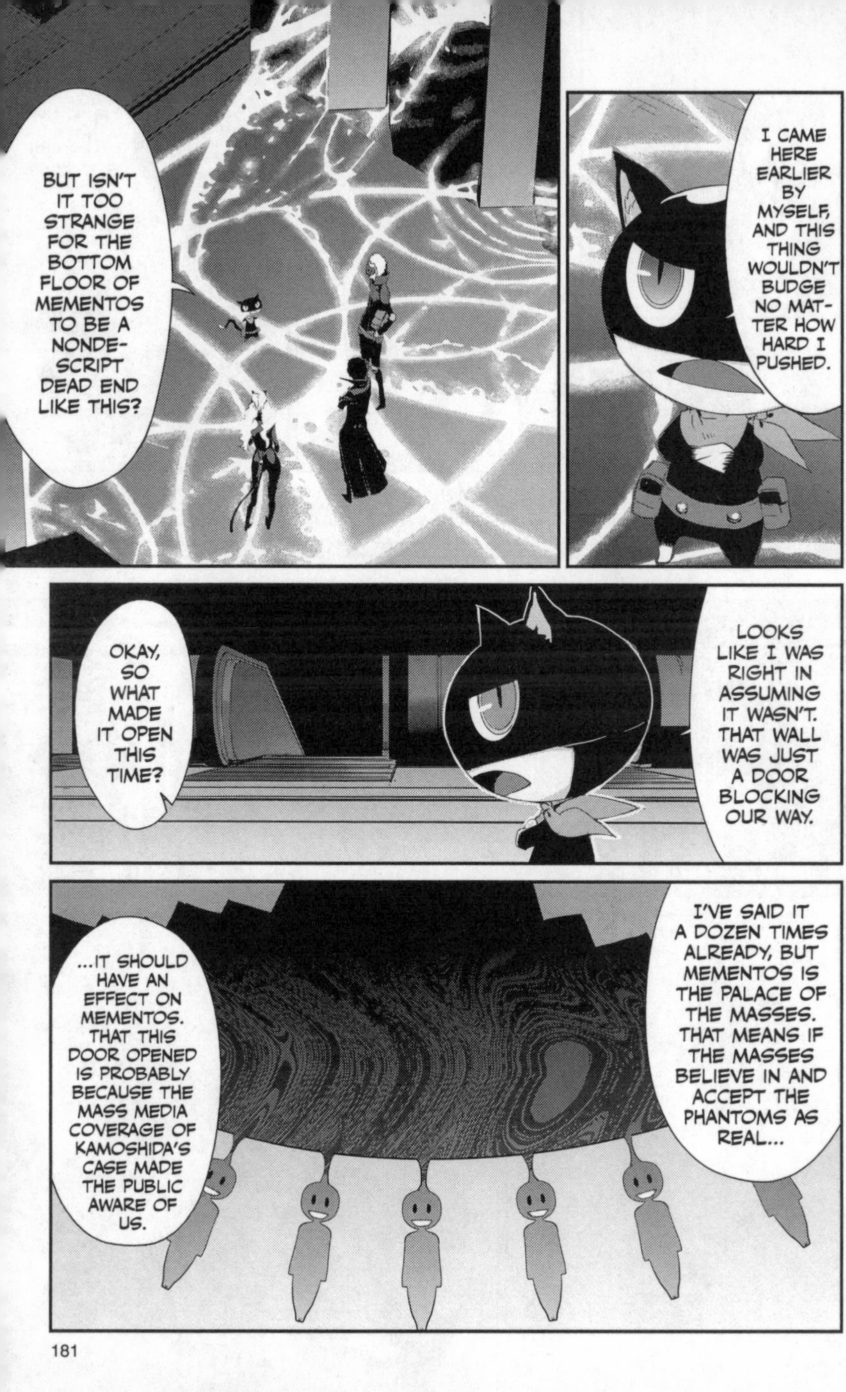
I CAME HERE EARLIER BY MYSELF, AND THIS THING WOULDN'T BUDGE NO MATTER HOW HARD I PUSHED.
BUT ISN'T IT TOO STRANGE FOR THE BOTTOM FLOOR OF MEMENTOS TO BE A NONDESCRIPT DEAD END LIKE THIS?
LOOKS LIKE I WAS RIGHT IN ASSUMING IT WASN'T. THAT WALL WAS JUST A DOOR BLOCKING OUR WAY.
OKAY, SO WHAT MADE IT OPEN THIS TIME?
I'VE SAID IT A DOZEN TIMES ALREADY, BUT MEMENTOS IS THE PALACE OF THE MASSES. THAT MEANS IF THE MASSES BELIEVE IN AND ACCEPT THE PHANTOMS AS REAL...
...IT SHOULD HAVE AN EFFECT ON MEMENTOS. THAT THIS DOOR OPENED IS PROBABLY BECAUSE THE MASS MEDIA COVERAGE OF KAMOSHIDA'S CASE MADE THE PUBLIC AWARE OF US.

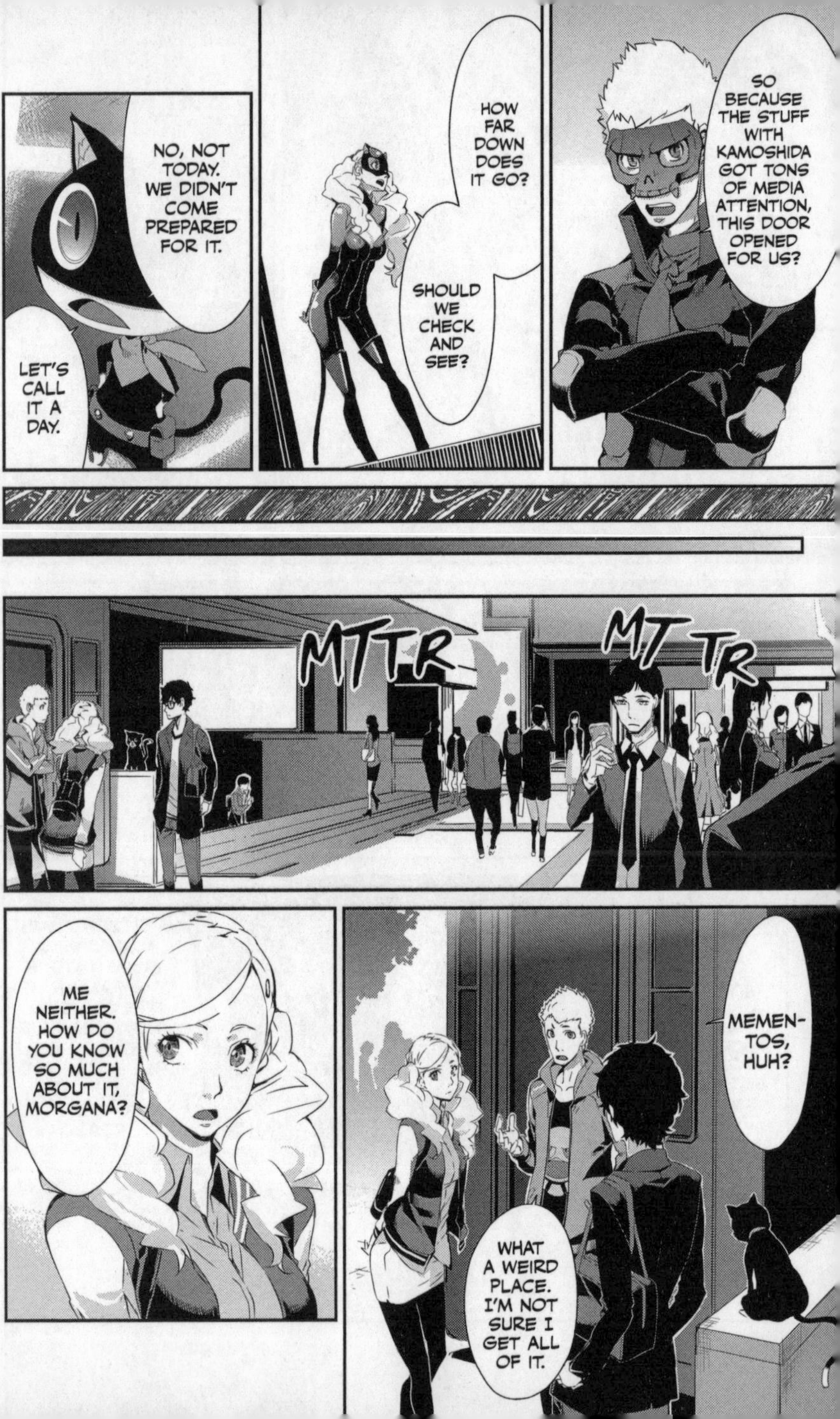
SO BECAUSE THE STUFF WITH KAMOSHIDA GOT TONS OF MEDIA ATTENTION, THIS DOOR OPENED FOR US?
HOW FAR DOWN DOES IT GO?
SHOULD WE CHECK AND SEE?
NO, NOT TODAY. WE DIDN'T COME PREPARED FOR IT.
LET'S CALL IT A DAY.
MT TR
MTTR
MEMEN-TOS, HUH?
WHAT A WEIRD PLACE. I'M NOT SURE I GET ALL OF IT.
ME NEITHER. HOW DO YOU KNOW SO MUCH ABOUT IT, MORGANA?

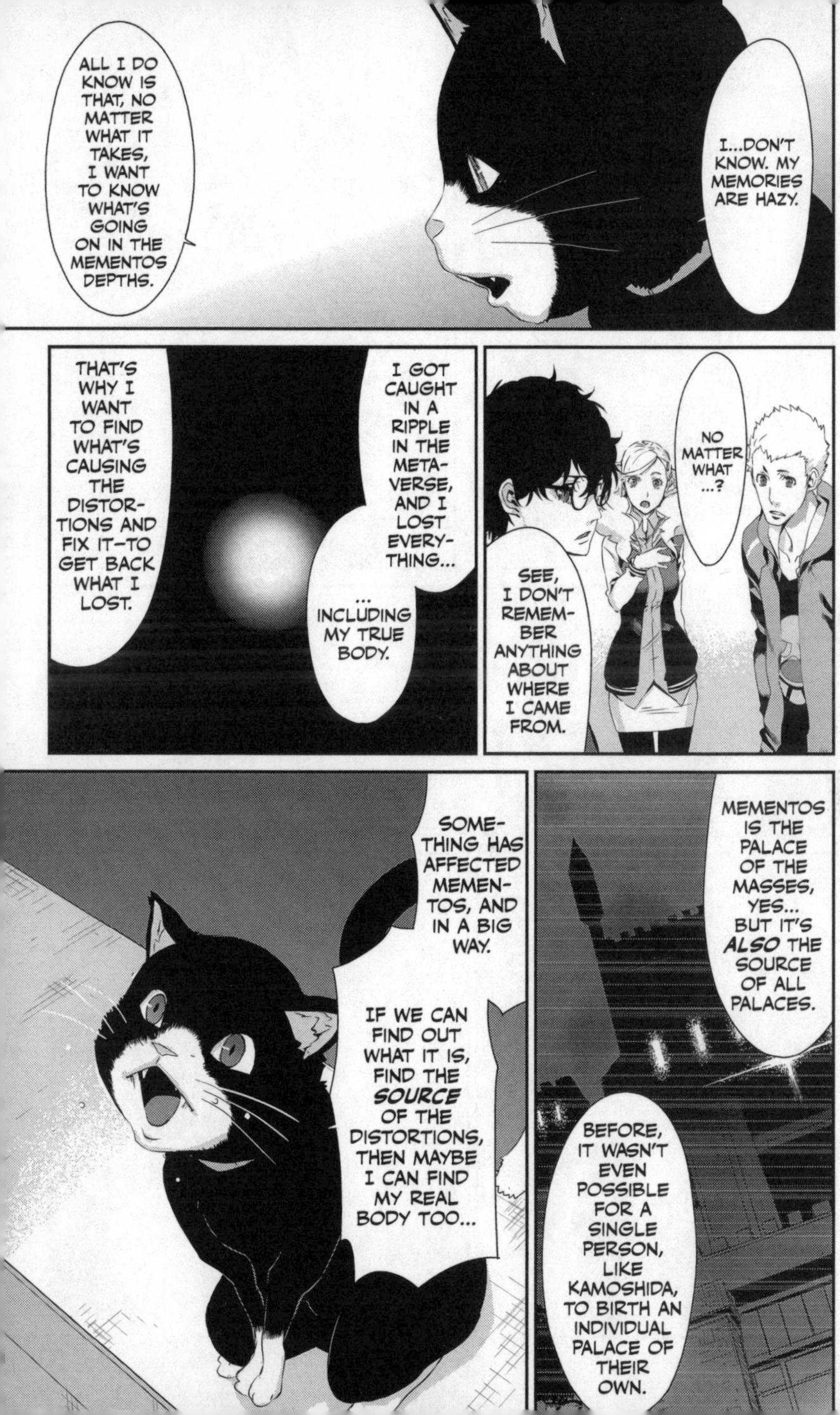
I...DON'T KNOW. MY MEMORIES ARE HAZY.
ALL I DO KNOW IS THAT, NO MATTER WHAT IT TAKES, I WANT TO KNOW WHAT'S GOING ON IN THE MEMENTOS DEPTHS.
NO MATTER WHAT ...?
SEE, I DON'T REMEM-BER ANYTHING ABOUT WHERE I CAME FROM.
I GOT CAUGHT IN A RIPPLE IN THE META-VERSE, AND I LOST EVERY-THING...
... INCLUDING MY TRUE BODY.
THAT'S WHY I WANT TO FIND WHAT'S CAUSING THE DISTOR-TIONS AND FIX IT—TO GET BACK WHAT I LOST.
MEMENTOS IS THE PALACE OF THE MASSES, YES... BUT IT'S *ALSO* THE SOURCE OF ALL PALACES.
BEFORE, IT WASN'T EVEN POSSIBLE FOR A SINGLE PERSON, LIKE KAMOSHIDA, TO BIRTH AN INDIVIDUAL PALACE OF THEIR OWN.
SOME-THING HAS AFFECTED MEMEN-TOS, AND IN A BIG WAY.
IF WE CAN FIND OUT WHAT IT IS, FIND THE *SOURCE* OF THE DISTORTIONS, THEN MAYBE I CAN FIND MY REAL BODY TOO...

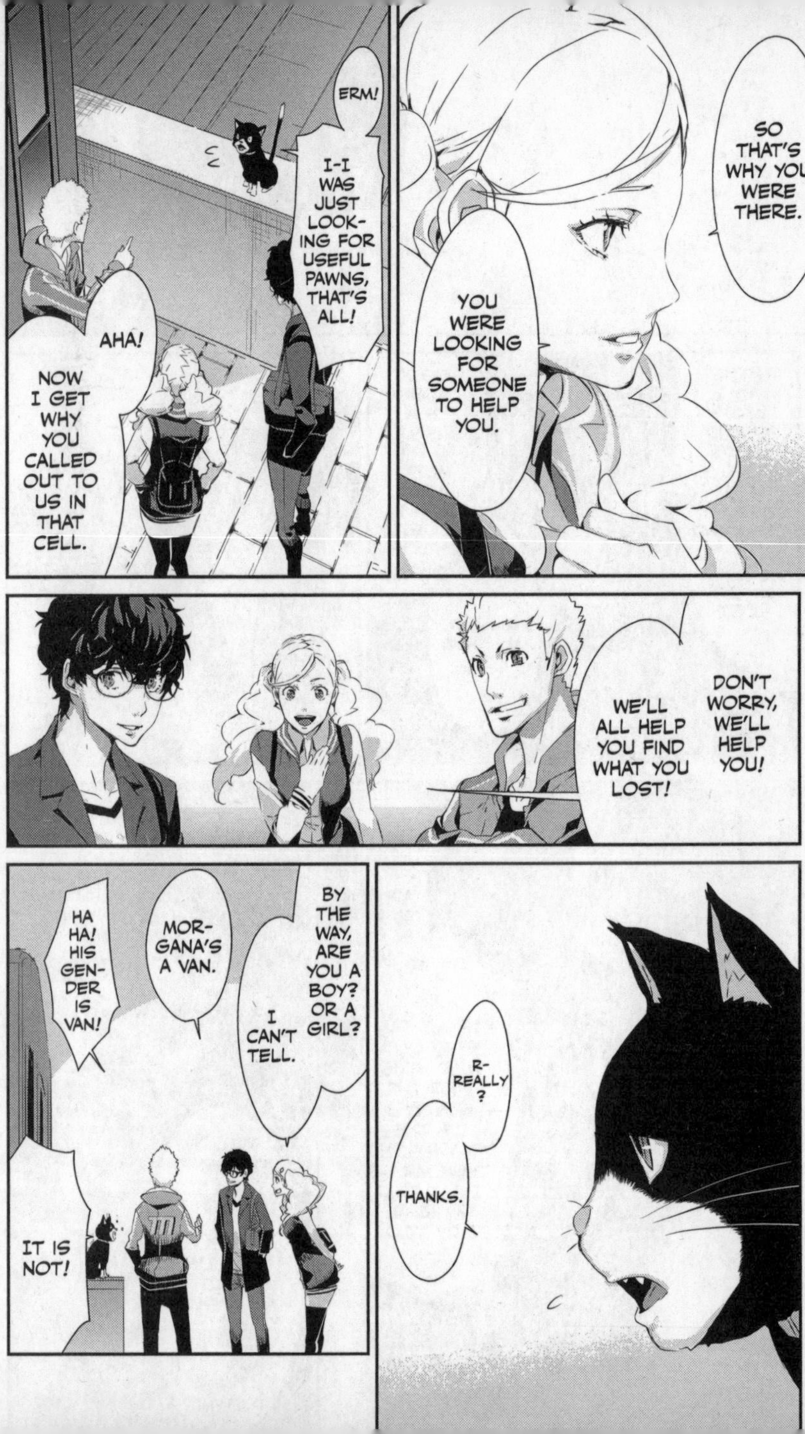
SO THAT'S WHY YOU WERE THERE.
YOU WERE LOOKING FOR SOMEONE TO HELP YOU.
ERM!
I-I WAS JUST LOOKING FOR USEFUL PAWNS, THAT'S ALL!
AHA!
NOW I GET WHY YOU CALLED OUT TO US IN THAT CELL.
DON'T WORRY, WE'LL HELP YOU!
WE'LL ALL HELP YOU FIND WHAT YOU LOST!
R-REALLY?
THANKS.
BY THE WAY, ARE YOU A BOY? OR A GIRL?
I CAN'T TELL.
MORGANA'S A VAN.
HA HA! HIS GENDER IS VAN!
IT IS NOT!

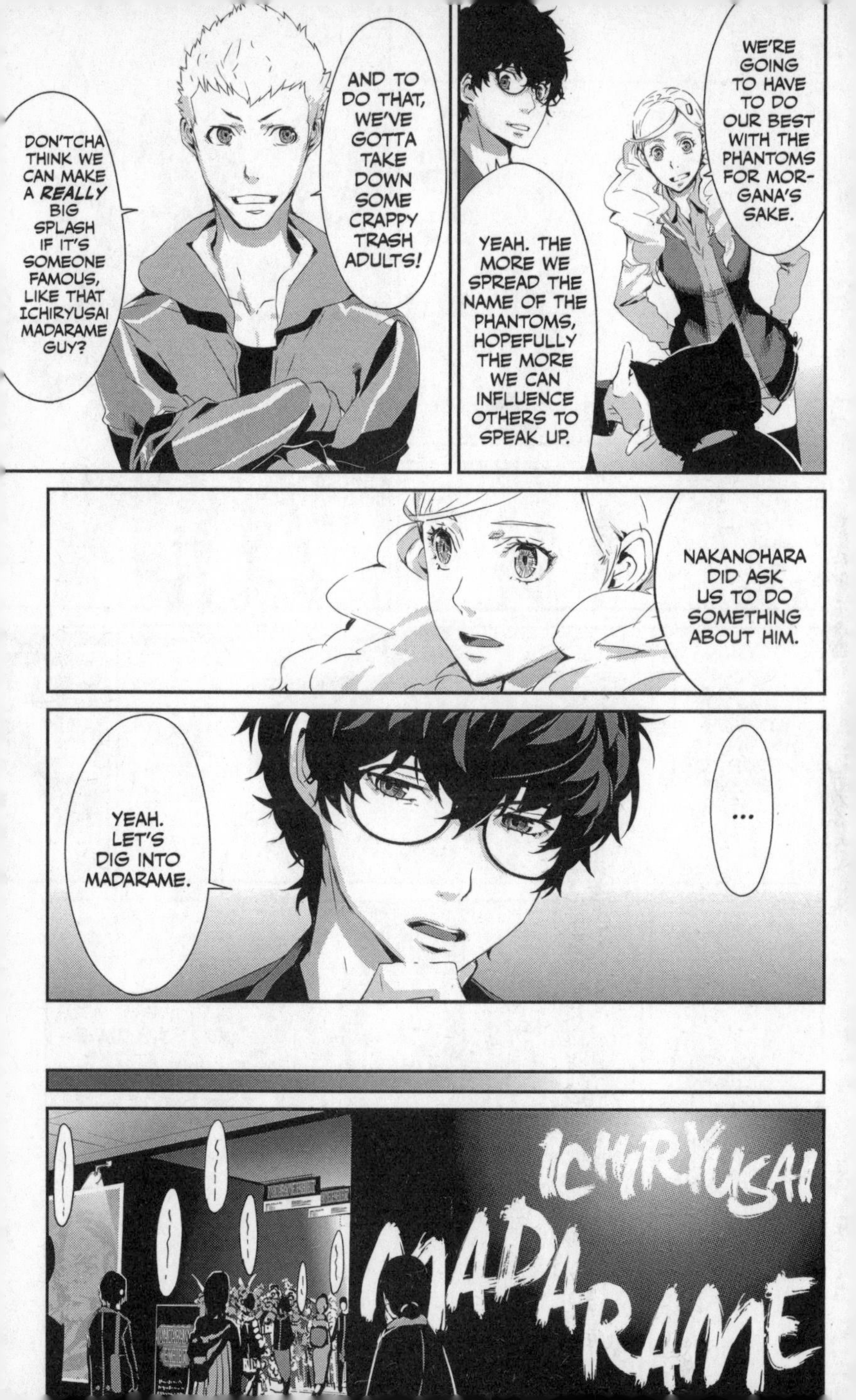
WE'RE GOING TO HAVE TO DO OUR BEST WITH THE PHANTOMS FOR MORGANA'S SAKE.
YEAH. THE MORE WE SPREAD THE NAME OF THE PHANTOMS, HOPEFULLY THE MORE WE CAN INFLUENCE OTHERS TO SPEAK UP.
AND TO DO THAT, WE'VE GOTTA TAKE DOWN SOME CRAPPY TRASH ADULTS!
DON'TCHA THINK WE CAN MAKE A *REALLY* BIG SPLASH IF IT'S SOMEONE FAMOUS, LIKE THAT ICHIRYUSAI MADARAME GUY?
NAKANOHARA DID ASK US TO DO SOMETHING ABOUT HIM.
...
YEAH. LET'S DIG INTO MADARAME.
ICHIRYUSAI MADARAME

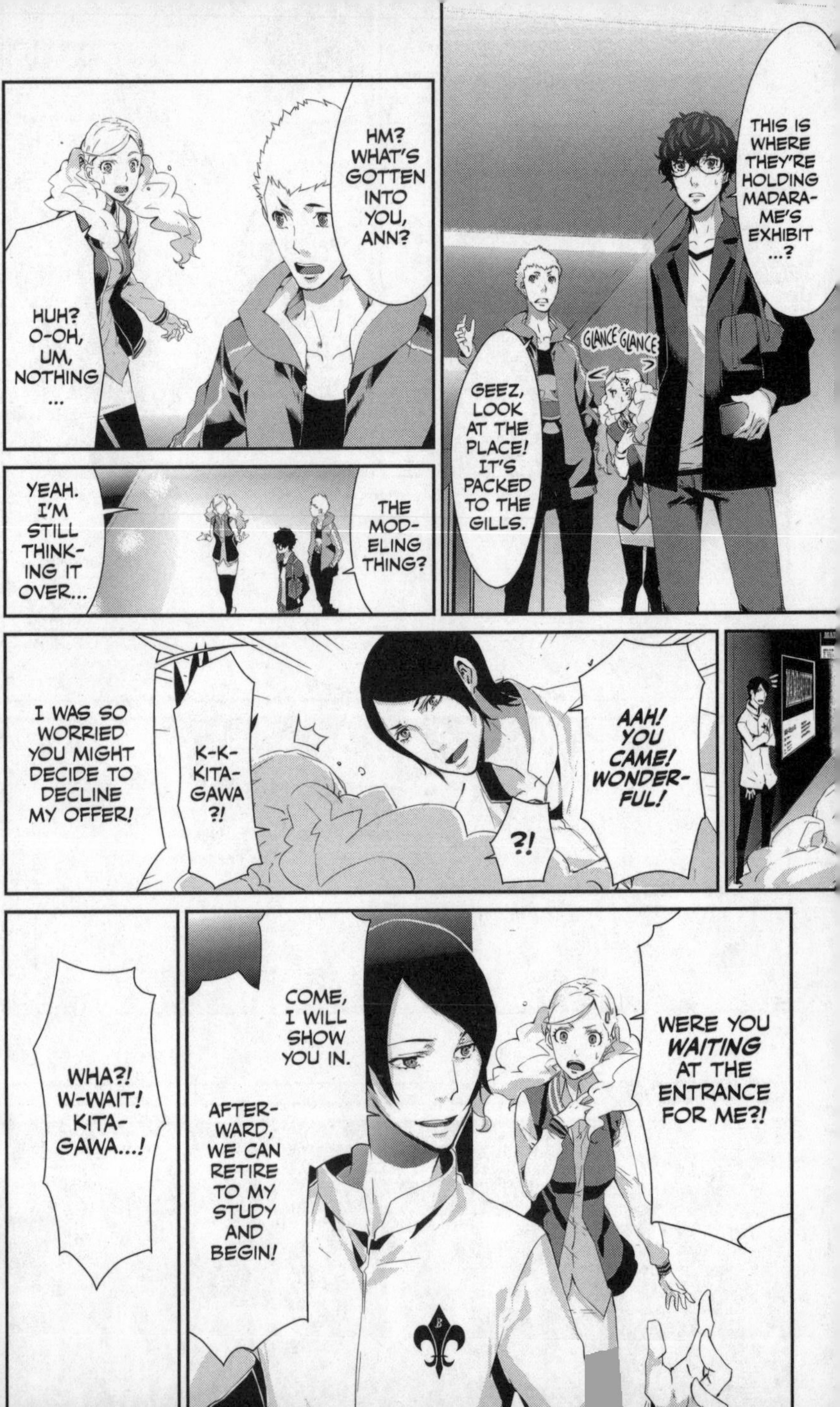
THIS IS WHERE THEY'RE HOLDING MADARAME'S EXHIBIT ...?
GLANCE GLANCE
GEEZ, LOOK AT THE PLACE! IT'S PACKED TO THE GILLS.
HM? WHAT'S GOTTEN INTO YOU, ANN?
HUH? O-OH, UM, NOTHING ...
THE MODELING THING?
YEAH. I'M STILL THINKING IT OVER...
AAH! YOU CAME! WONDERFUL!
?!
K-K-KITAGAWA?!
I WAS SO WORRIED YOU MIGHT DECIDE TO DECLINE MY OFFER!
WERE YOU WAITING AT THE ENTRANCE FOR ME?!
COME, I WILL SHOW YOU IN.
AFTERWARD, WE CAN RETIRE TO MY STUDY AND BEGIN!
WHA?! W-WAIT! KITAGAWA...!

TO BE CONTINUED!

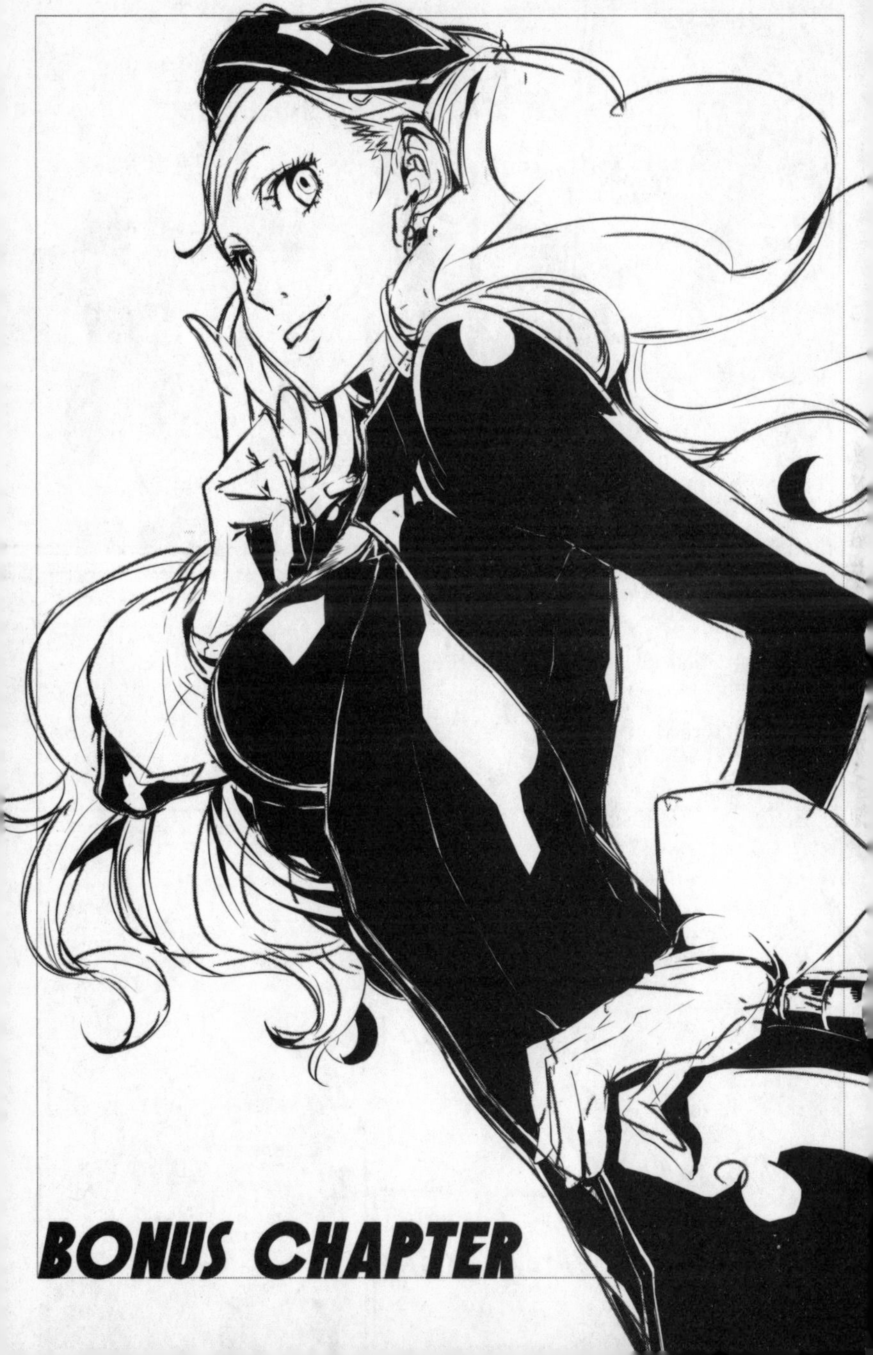

BONUS CHAPTER

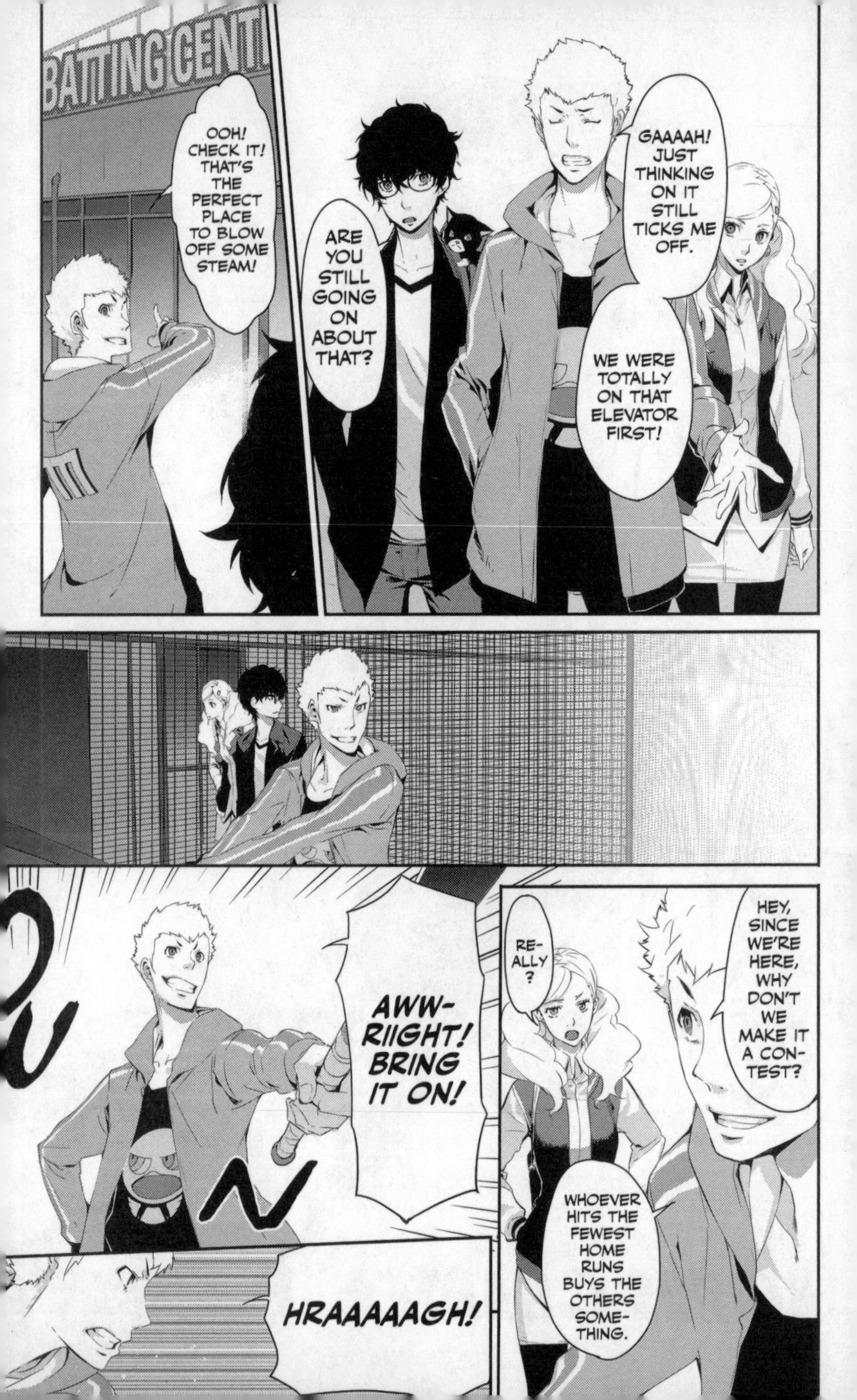
GAAAAH! JUST THINKING ON IT STILL TICKS ME OFF.
WE WERE TOTALLY ON THAT ELEVATOR FIRST!
ARE YOU STILL GOING ON ABOUT THAT?
BATTING CENT
OOH! CHECK IT! THAT'S THE PERFECT PLACE TO BLOW OFF SOME STEAM!
HEY, SINCE WE'RE HERE, WHY DON'T WE MAKE IT A CON-TEST?
RE-ALLY?
WHOEVER HITS THE FEWEST HOME RUNS BUYS THE OTHERS SOME-THING.
AWW-RIIGHT! BRING IT ON!
HRAAAAAGH!

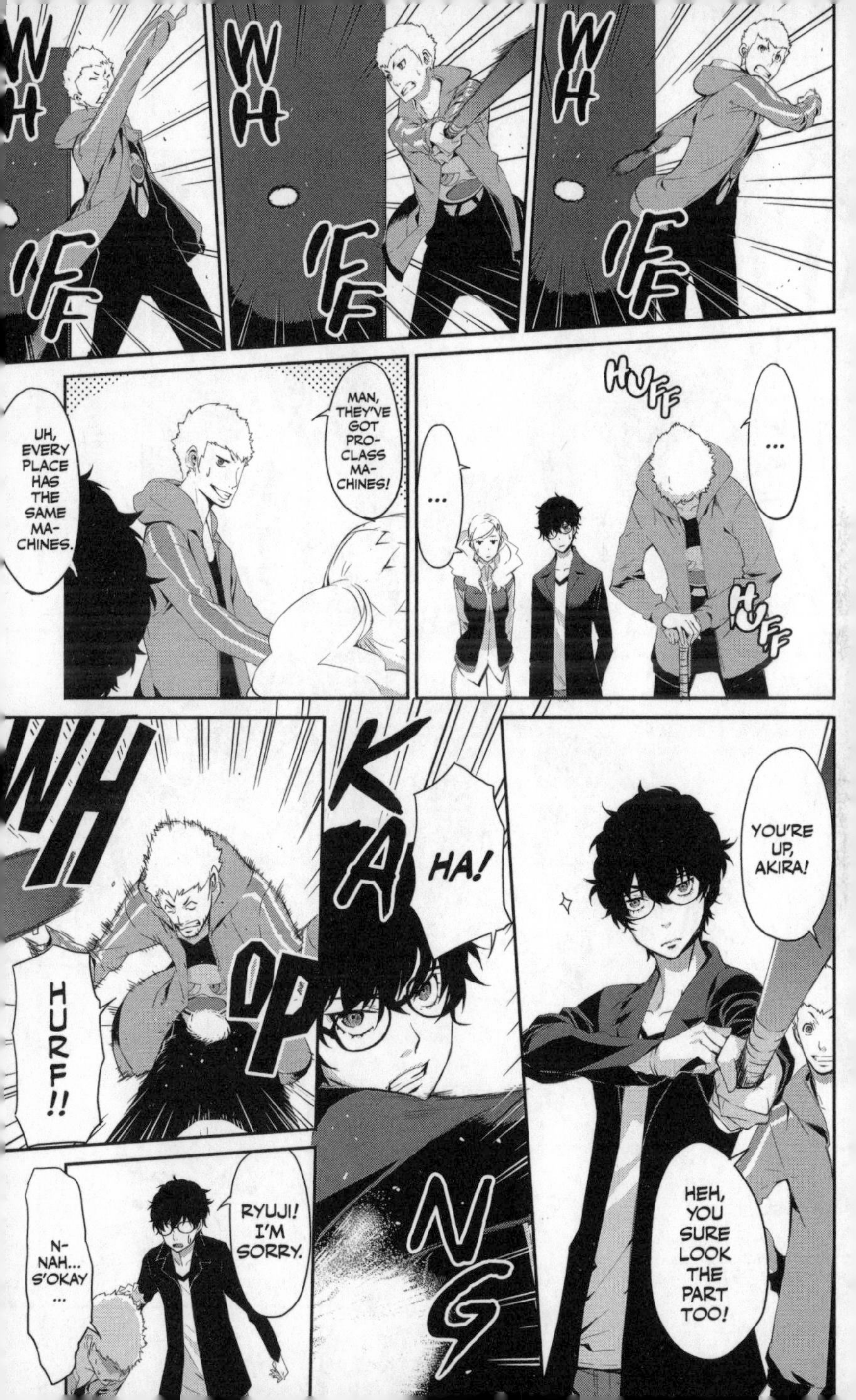
WH
'FF
WH
'FF
WH
'FF
HUFF
...
...
HUFF
MAN, THEY'VE GOT PRO-CLASS MA-CHINES!
UH, EVERY PLACE HAS THE SAME MA-CHINES.
YOU'RE UP, AKIRA!
HEH, YOU SURE LOOK THE PART TOO!
KA
HA!
NG
WH
OP
HURF!!
RYUJI! I'M SORRY.
N-NAH... S'OKAY ...

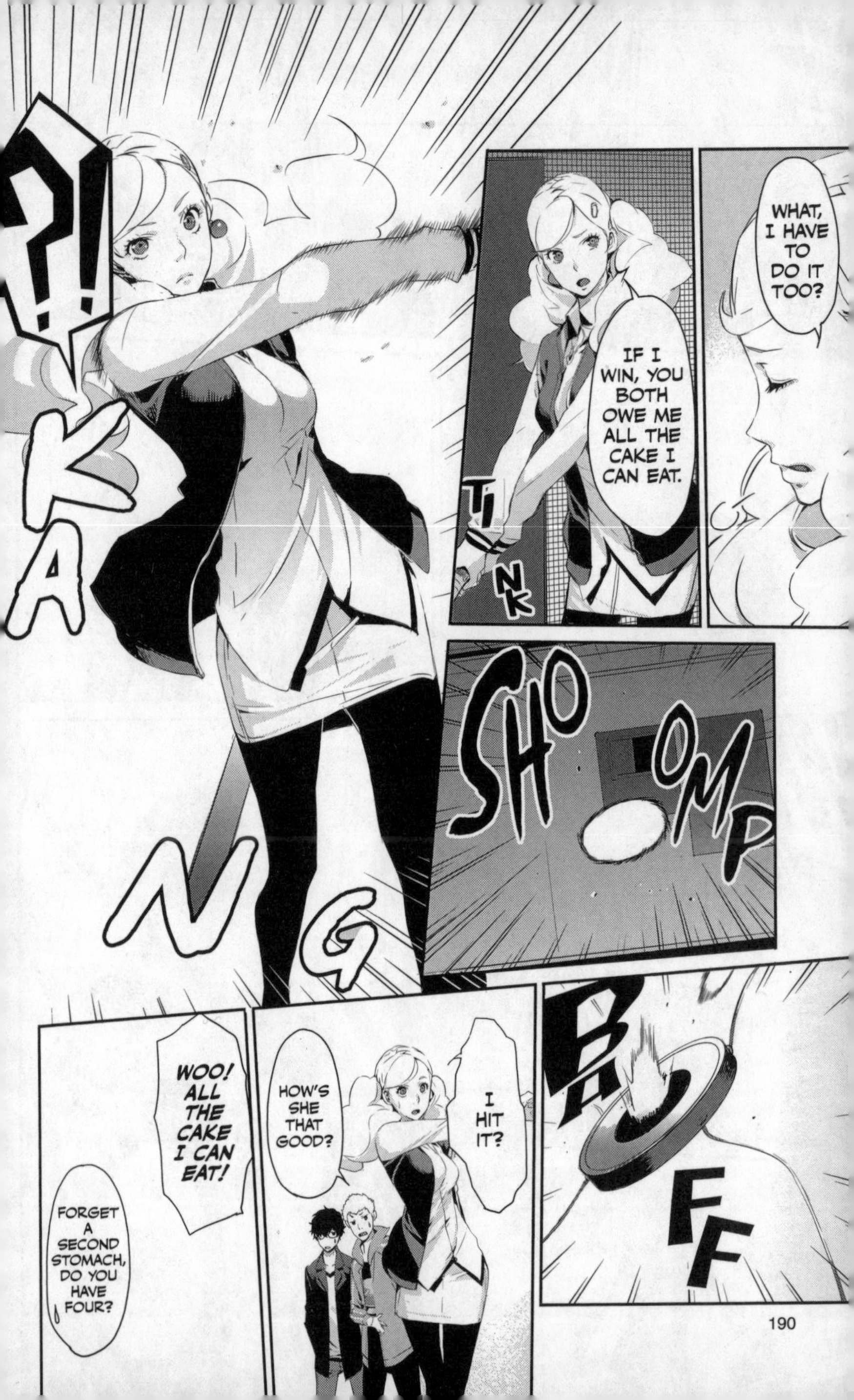
WHAT, I HAVE TO DO IT TOO?
IF I WIN, YOU BOTH OWE ME ALL THE CAKE I CAN EAT.
TINK
SHOOMP
?!
KANG
BOFF
I HIT IT?
HOW'S SHE THAT GOOD?
WOO! ALL THE CAKE I CAN EAT!
FORGET A SECOND STOMACH, DO YOU HAVE FOUR?

Staff

Chie Soraku

Ikuko Deluxe

And...
Atlus, and everyone else who has
assisted with the adaptation of *Persona 5*.

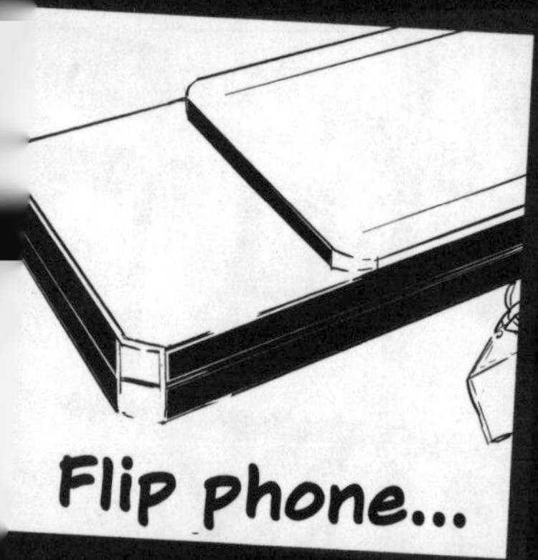
Flip phone...

ısato MuRAsAKi

of the *Persona 5* manga adaptation is on sale! Lots
ool and really cute characters are about to make
earance, so I hope you're looking forward to it! To
st, there are tons and tons more characters I wish
draw. I'm going to keep trying hard to make this a
that you can read and enjoy!

o Murasaki is a manga artist and illustrator from Japan.
as created illustrations for a number of manga and novel
s, including *Hyakume no Kishi* (*Knight of 100 Eyes*), *The
-Book of ENA*, the *D-Crackers* series, *Bravely Archive: D's
ort*. He also wrote the manga, *Boku no Mawari no Uchuujin
Alien Around Me*). He started work on *Persona 5* in 2016.

PERSONA5 5 2

ART AND STORY BY HISATO MURASAKI

ORIGINAL CONCEPT BY ATLUS

Translation/Adrienne Beck
Touch-Up Art & Lettering/Annaliese Christman
Design/Kam Li
Editor/Marlene First
Approval Cooperation/Shinji Yamamoto (ATLUS),
Miki Iwata (ATLUS)

PERSONA 5 Vol.2
by Hisato MURASAKI
Original Concept by ATLUS
© ATLUS © SEGA All rights reserved.
© 2017 Hisato MURASAKI
All rights reserved.
Original Japanese edition published by SHOGAKUKAN.
English translation rights in the United States of America, Canada, the United
Kingdom, Ireland, Australia and New Zealand arranged with SHOGAKUKAN.

Original Cover Design: Kenro YOKOYAMA (Beeworks)

The stories, characters and incidents mentioned in this publication are entirely fictional.
No portion of this book may be reproduced or transmitted in any form or by any means
without written permission from the copyright holders.

Printed in the U.S.A.

Published by VIZ Media, LLC
P.O. Box 77010
San Francisco, CA 94107

10 9 8 7 6 5 4 3 2
First printing, April 2020
Second printing, July 2020

VIZ MEDIA

viz.com

RATED **T+** OLDER TEEN
ratings.viz.com

PARENTAL ADVISORY
PERSONA 5 is rated T+ for Older Teen and
is recommended for ages 16 and up for
fantasy violence and sexual themes.

NieR:Automata™

ニーア オートマタ

NOVELS

Written by Jun Eishima and Yoko Taro

Original Story by Yoko Taro

**EXPERIENCE THE WORLD AND CHARACTERS
OF THE HIT VIDEO GAME FRANCHISE!**

When alien forces invade with an army of Machines, the remnants of
humanity must depend on Androids of their own design—the placid
2B and the excitable 9S—to survive.

©2017 Jun Eishima/SQUARE ENIX
©2017 SQUARE ENIX CO.,LTD. All Rights Reserved.

©2017 Jun Eishima, Yoko Taro/SQUARE ENIX
©2017 SQUARE ENIX CO.,LTD. All Rights Reserved.

VIZ

Kidnapped by the Demon King and imprisoned in his castle, Princess Syalis is...bored.

SLEEPY PRINCESS IN THE DEMON CASTLE

Story & Art by
KAGIJI KUMANOMATA

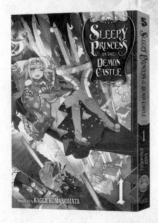

Captured princess Syalis decides to while away her hours in the Demon Castle by sleeping, but getting a good night's rest turns out to be a lot of work! She begins by fashioning a DIY pillow out of the fur of her Teddy Demon guards and an "air mattress" from the magical Shield of the Wind. Things go from bad to worse—for her captors—when some of Princess Syalis's schemes end in her untimely— if temporary—demise and she chooses the Forbidden Grimoire for her bedtime reading...

LINK MUST DEFEAT EVIL AT EVERY TURN IN HIS PERILOUS QUEST TO HELP PRINCESS ZELDA™!

THE LEGEND OF ZELDA™

·TWILIGHT PRINCESS·

Story and Art by Akira Himekawa

LONG-AWAITED ADAPTATION
of the HIT VIDEO GAME

Once upon a time, wizards tried to conquer the Sacred Realm of Hyrule. The Spirits of Light sealed the wizards' power within the Shadow Crystal and banished them to the Twilight Realm beyond the Mirror of Twilight. Now, an evil menace is trying to find Midna, Princess of the Twilight Realm, and the fragments of the Shadow Crystal to gain the power to rule over both the Twilight Realm and the World of Light.

Available now wherever manga is sold.

TM & © 2017 Nintendo.
ZELDA NO DENSETSU TWILIGHT PRINCESS © 2016 Akira HIMEKAWA/SHOGAKUKAN

viz.com

THE LEGEND OF ZELDA

LEGENDARY EDITION

STORY AND ART BY
AKIRA HIMEKAWA

The Legendary Editions of *The Legend of Zelda*™ contain
two volumes of the beloved manga series, presented in a
deluxe format featuring new covers and color art pieces.

TM & © 2016 Nintendo. ZELDA NO DENSETSU-TOKI NO OCARINA (KANZENBAN) © 2016 Akira HIMEKAWA/SHOGAKUKAN.
TM & © 2017 Nintendo. ZELDA NO DENSETSU FUSHIGI NO KINOMI DAICHI NO SHO/JIKU NO SHO (KANZENBAN) ZELDA NO DENSETSU MAJORA NO KAMEN/KAMIGAMI NO TRI-FORCE (KANZENBAN)
ZELDA NO DENSETSU FUSHIGI NO BOSHI/MUGEN NO SUNADOKEI (KANZENBAN) ZELDA NO DENSETSU 4TSU NO TSURUGI PLUS (KANZENBAN) © 2016 Akira HIMEKAWA/SHOGAKUKAN.

POKÉMON™

POCKET COMICS
Legendary Pokémon

STORY & ART BY SANTA HARUKAZE

grumph
MY FRIEND PIKACHU HASN'T BEEN SMILING RECENTLY...

THE LEGENDARY JOKE... IT'S UP TO ME TO FIND IT!
THERE MUST BE A JOKE SOMEWHERE IN THIS WORLD THAT CAN BRING BACK PIKACHU'S SMILE!

FOUR-PANEL GAGS, POKÉMON TRIVIA, AND FUN PUZZLES BASED ON THE CHARACTERS FROM THE BEST-SELLING POKÉMON BLACK AND WHITE VIDEO GAMES!

Available now!

POKÉMON
POCKET COMICS
Legendary Pokémon
STORY & ART BY SANTA HARUKAZE

**To the forest! To the sea!
To Legendary Island!**

Join our Pokémon pals on their quest through Unova—while testing your knowledge and laughing all the way!

Ask for it at your local comic book shop or bookstore!

ISBN: 978-1-4215-8128-6

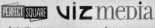

RATED A ALL AGES ratings.viz.com

PERFECT SQUARE www.PerfectSquare.com

VIZ media www.viz.com